MW01538650

HUMBER COLLEGE LIBRARY
205 HUMBER COLLEGE BLVD,
P.O. BOX 1900
REXDALE, ONTARIO, CANADA
M9W 5L7

Waiting for the End

HUMBER COLLEGE LIBRARY
205 HUMBER COLLEGE BLVD.
P.O. BOX 1900
REXDALE, ONTARIO, CANADA
M9W 5L7

Waiting for the End

Gender and Ending
in the Contemporary Novel

160101

Earl G. Ingersoll

Madison • Teaneck
Fairleigh Dickinson University Press

© 2007 by Rosemont Publishing & Printing Corp.

All rights reserved. Authorization to photocopy items for internal or personal use, or the internal or personal use of specific clients, is granted by the copyright owner, provided that a base fee of $10.00, plus eight cents per page, per copy is paid directly to the Copyright Clearance Center, 222 Rosewood Drive, Danvers, Massachusetts 01923. [0-8386-4153-9/07 $10.00 + 8¢ pp, pc.]

Associated University Presses
2010 Eastpark Boulevard
Cranbury, NJ 08512

The paper used in this publication meets the requirements of the American National Standard for Permanence of Paper for Printed Library Materials Z39.48-1984.

Library of Congress Cataloging-in-Publication Data

Ingersoll, Earl G., 1938–
    Waiting for the end : gender and ending in the contemporary novel / Earl G. Ingersoll.
        p.   cm.
    Includes bibliographical references and index.
    ISBN-13: 978-0-8386-4153-8 (alk. paper)
    ISBN-10: 0-8386-4153-9 (alk. paper)
    1. English fiction—20th century—History and criticism.   2. Closure (Rhetoric)
3. Sex role in literature.   4. Feminism and literature—History—20th century.
I. Title.
PR888.C587I54   2007
823′.91409928—dc22   2006037383

PRINTED IN THE UNITED STATES OF AMERICA

Contents

Waiting for the End

Introduction: The Beginning of the End

I BEGIN THIS INTRODUCTION WITH WHAT MAY APPEAR A SOMEWHAT unorthodox strategy. Before constructing a framework of narrative theorizing, I want to examine the plot(s) and ending(s) of a particular novel, a text well beyond the parameters of the term "contemporary." Even the choice of "I" to begin this introduction would have been unorthodox a generation or two ago. At that time our literary forebears (I am tempted to say "forefathers" because virtually "to a man" they were male) deluded themselves into believing that repressing "the personal" might lift literary criticism into a quasi-scientific realm of objectivity and truth. My strategy aims at emphasizing what is obvious yet all too obviously ignored—that is, narrative always precedes "narratology," or the study of narrative. Because the examples of narrative on which this project focuses are all "contemporary," and in some rough sense of the term "postmodern," it seems useful to start with a representative narrative—Virginia Woolf's *Mrs. Dalloway*—hardly likely to be (mis)labeled either "postmodern" or "contemporary." As a classic modernist novel, *Mrs. Dalloway* offers a provocative starting point for an exploration of ending in narrative. Through what has become a hallmark of modernist fiction, the "open ending," *Mrs. Dalloway* negotiates with its suppressed other, the "closed ending," to provide an openness in closure or even a closure in openness, if such a balance can ever be genuinely achieved.

In its title *Mrs. Dalloway* makes a suggestive gesture toward the traditional novel in specifying the central figure in the narrative by naming her. Woolf does not entitle the novel "Clarissa Dalloway," or even "Clarissa," but, as readers have frequently noted, *"Mrs. Dalloway."* In thus specifying its subject—in more than one sense of the term—the narrative foregrounds her lack of subject status as a woman, certifying her identity merely as Richard Dalloway's wife. In its own way the narrative asserts: This is a novel because it has the name of its central figure in its title; at the same time, it will not be concerned with identity in the traditional sense, because in the novel "female subjects," or women possessed of any identity, could never be anything but an oxymoron. *Bleak House* may offer a Tom Jones construct for Esther Summerson.

9

However, the disclosure of *her* parentage—that is, the revelation that she is the daughter of Lady Dedlock—cannot lift Esther to the aristocracy or to subject status in the same patriarchal context in which a Tom Jones could achieve such status in that novel's ending, with *its* revelations. Even though Charlotte Brontë may entitle her novel *Jane Eyre*—as Woolf herself as a writer *about* narrative might point out—it is not until the obstacles are removed and Jane is on the brink of becoming Mrs. Rochester that she has any being at all, given that education cruelly lifted her above her station at birth without offering her the resources to compensate for the insufficiencies of her birth, or "identity." Through her disarmingly provocative title, Woolf may be calling into question the potential of the traditional novel to be energized by a "female plot,"[1] as an alternative to the "male plot," or "The History of . . ." type in its revelation of "true" identity through its ending. If plot in the novel has its origins in the impulse to "find out," to learn the "truth" toward which plot has been driving, it seems legitimate to ask if plot in a novel invested in such "knowing" of the central male figure's parentage can extricate itself from patriarchy in which women have no "plots."

    Mrs. Dalloway, then, may be reacting against the novel as fictionalized biography in which female subjectivity is "unspeakable" and "female plots" are inconceivable. If Brontë had risked a reaction by her readers against her "giving away the ending," she might have entitled *Jane Eyre* "Mrs. Rochester," since it would appear that her title character from birth has been studying for that role. At the end of Brontë's novel, Jane duplicates—with a difference, of course—Tom's prospects of a marriage in the closing pages of his novel. In both cases, however, these are marriages typical of the traditional novel, as is manifested by the very "modern" alternative at the beginning of D. H. Lawrence's *Women in Love* in which Gudrun asks her older sister, Ursula, "You don't think one needs the *experience* of having been married?" to which Ursula quips, "More likely to be the end of experience" (1987, 7; italics in original). By framing her novel as an expression of "The History of . . ." paradigm, Brontë, from Woolf's point of view, may be doing some narrative cross-dressing in *Jane Eyre*, whose eponymous figure masquerades as a subject in a culture reserving such status for a "Tom" but not a "Jane." Thus, in determining that her novel *Mrs. Dalloway* will be organized on the model of "A Day in the Life of . . ." Woolf may be parodying female self-deprecation in a male-dominated culture, as she does in this novel with the "feminine" chimes of St. Margaret's Church, over which the "masculine" strokes of Big Ben continue to be privileged in the "modern" patriarchal world.[2]

The limited time frame reminds this novel's readers that traditionally women have been forced to operate in a world that reserves only for men the province of "events" and eventfulness commensurate with the power of becoming, as well as an ending at which their *becoming* is revealed as *being*. If men have traditionally had "lives," women have had "days," days in which they are sheltered/excluded from "events" to concern themselves with "women's work," or looking after the details of domesticity. Clarissa's day is centered in the details of preparing for the party with which her day will end—offering readers what amounts to one day in an adult lifetime of preparing for parties. What a "plot"! Indeed, this "female plot" seems to entail a single question: Will the party at day's end "succeed" or "fail"? In the narrow room such a plot constructs, the narrative sets itself the challenging task of building the sense of magnitude on which the traditional novel has had to depend for its sense of eventfulness and duration.

One way, of course, in which the narrative pushes against its narrow confinement is the power of memory to transgress boundaries, moving its central figures "back to Bourton," where the lives of Clarissa as well as Sally Seton, Peter Walsh, and Richard Dalloway perhaps have had the "endings"—not in the sense of finality but in the form of choices, if there were indeed *choices*—that have shaped their being. It is as though Woolf were writing this novel as the epilogue to *Tom Jones*, depicting the lives of middle-aged people whose marriages have been, à la Lawrence's Ursula, very much the "end of experience." That certainly describes Clarissa's adult life, whose future is troped as a narrow single bed on which the sheets will be stretched tighter and tighter with each passing year.

In the liberating agency of memory to offer escape from the "small room" of the present, the narrative is also positing telepathy, or intuition, as an occasional means of gaining freedom from the solitary confinement of separate being. As often noted, this gesture toward telepathy, here and in *To the Lighthouse*, may have been a calculated risk for Woolf, who must have sensed the potential for telepathy to be sex-stereotyped as "women's intuition." Through telepathy, however, the narrative can establish a double-plotting to allow Clarissa at the climax to penetrate the being of the dead Septimus Warren Smith and come to an understanding of why *he* ended his life in order to forestall the possible ending of *hers*.[3] The narrative can accordingly construct two parallel plots in which a woman and a man seek an answer to a central existential question: Can faith in the future be recuperated, and, if not, is there any alternative to suicide?[4]

The Septimus Warren Smith strand of the narrative seems a conventional "male plot." Although we might be tempted to call it a "subplot," many readers have agreed that Septimus and Clarissa in the end ought to be read, not as two disparate characters, but as halves, or at least *parts* of a single "character." Septimus becomes the dark heart of "madness," or debilitating paranoia, in this narrative. Having "survived" all four years of the Great War—surely an incredibly rare feat in that bloody conflict—Septimus is one of those "shell-shocked" survivors who served as a stimulus to Freud's radically new thinking in *Beyond the Pleasure Principle.*[5] Woolf's Dr. Holmes, after recognizing the limits of his ability to treat Septimus, has referred his patient to the Harley Street specialist William Bradshaw, one of the first modern psychoanalysts to appear in fiction. To Holmes, Septimus represents a failure of masculinity; accordingly, Holmes prescribes a rather confusing "cure": Septimus must "get hold of himself" because he has "lost control," and thus lost his "manhood," and Rezia, his wife, is to make him "take an interest in things outside himself," producing a double bind in "curing" Septimus. In this context interiority has been gendered by Holmes as "feminine," and yet in the larger cultural context its binary opposite, a concern for things, or "details," has traditionally been gendered feminine. What neither Holmes nor Bradshaw can see is that their patient suffers from a kind of "survivor guilt," for Septimus not only survived the death of the officer he loved but could even congratulate himself on feeling nothing at the news of that death. A modern "hollow man," Septimus is challenged with surviving the "death of the heart." Not so coincidentally, when Peter Walsh awakens from a dream of his former lover Clarissa his unconscious speaks of "The death of the soul" (Woolf 1953, 88).

With the insistent announcement of "the hours" by Big Ben and St. Margaret's Church, this male plot moves relentlessly toward the inevitability of Septimus's death. Because that death sentence hangs over his last hours, readers are impelled to pay special attention to the framing of the issues implicated in the death scene to come. Central is his struggle to recover/preserve what Clarissa terms "the privacy of the soul" against those like Holmes and Bradshaw who in their functions as "therapists" are bent on violating his spiritual integrity. (As countless feminists have pointed out, there is an ominous "message" in the term "therapist," a word threatening to self-detach as "the rapist.") And Clarissa's given name may be a gesture toward Richardson's Clarissa, struggling through hundreds of letters to stave off the inevitability of her sexual violation. The pat "phallic symbols" of the bread knife Septimus dismisses as an instrument of escape and the sharp iron railings he chooses instead suggest a willed, physical alternative to the psychic "rape" he thereby forestalls. His death becomes the secularized self-dramatization of a traditional religious construct: that man who would save his life must lose it. In the act to which Septimus is forced to resort, he tenders his life as a sacrificial offering to a quintessentially Woolfian notion of identity: to be human is to preserve at all costs the sanctity of one's soul.

That is, of course, the meaning Clarissa intuits in his dying as she ponders its text in her small room at the end of her day. Jolted by the news of Septimus's death—brought to her party by Bradshaw as his "small-talk" justification for being late, a "feminine" fault this pillar of "masculinity" ironically feels obliged to justify—Clarissa re-creates the scene through intuition or telepathy. This telepathy is justified by the text's proposal that "the unseen part of us . . . might survive, be recovered somehow attached to this person or that, or even haunting certain places after death" (232). Thus, Septimus's surviving spirit may not yet have departed from Bloomsbury. With uncanny accuracy she (re)constructs the narrative of his death scene, already dramatized in the narrative, providing a frisson of eeriness that she could be so "clairvoyant."

In demonstrating how Clarissa performs this text's tentative faith in telepathy, this scene deserves further attention as the climax of the "female plot." Clarissa thinks: "He had killed himself—but how?" As in similar past performances when "her body went through it first," she imaginatively re-creates the scene earlier dramatized, down to the penetration of his body by the spikes of Mrs. Filmer's iron fence, even though Bradshaw reported only that his patient had killed himself. "But why had he done it?" (280). *That* is the question. He had thrown "it" away, "one's parents giving it into one's hands, this life, to be lived to the end . . ." (281). He had done so to escape Bradshaw, whom she sums up as "a great doctor yet to her obscurely evil . . . capable of some indescribable outrage—forcing your soul, that was it" (281), and Septimus, this "he," has thrown "it" away to save himself from the doctors who would violate, or penetrate, the "privacy of the soul." In the context of traditional female sexuality, Septimus has thrown his life away to avoid a "fate worse than death," allowing the iron spikes of Mrs. Filmer's railings to penetrate his body to forestall Bradshaw's violation of his soul.

This scene draws together, then, something approximating a female plot for Clarissa. The narrative has stressed her joy on this June day in having survived the plague of influenza in the last year of the Great War. Additionally, she can go about in the London she loves, even though she has a clear-eyed awareness that the city is a stage on which she will one day no longer make an entrance. In the opening pages, as she recalls once having "thrown a shilling into the Serpentine . . ." (12), she ponders, "[D]id it matter that she must inevitably cease completely; all this must go on without her . . .?" (12). She comes round to a hesitant belief in an impersonal survival in what has mattered to her, such as this scene on Bond Street; she might even go on as a "part of people she had never met" (12). For example, just across the street from her small room, Clarissa can see the old woman going to bed each night alone, braving the darkness from which she might never awaken. And rounding out this segment, the narrative offers a revelation of Clarissa's central value of seeing herself mirrored in the eyes of others: "How much she wanted it—that people should look pleased as she came in" (13). In the context of the "it" of life that Septimus will choose to throw away to save his soul, this "it" Clarissa still wants—the ability to read in the eyes of others their pleasure in seeing her enter a room—seems nothing less than "life" itself for her, no matter how trivial such a "life" might seem to Woolf's reader, and perhaps even Woolf herself. This "it" is one that the narrative indulgently allows Clarissa to value and enlists its readers to accept, once they have entered the small room of her being.

This seemingly insignificant bit of knowledge of Clarissa's need to see pleasure in the eyes of those who behold her entering a room grounds the other "climax" of this narrative's "female plot."[6] At the end of the first "climax," the narrative records Clarissa's sense of gratification that Bradshaw's patient had thrown "it" away, and she is sufficiently reassured during this retreat into the small room of the self to return to the party scene. After tracing the recurrence of the phrase "there she was" through Peter's consciousness, in the hours following his visit to Clarissa at midday, the narrative offers a dozen pages of party scene in a conventional double time scheme to parallel her few moments of solitude. As the blank space on the last page begins to signal "the end" is coming, Peter's uncomprehending anxiety—"What is this terror? what is this ecstasy?"—is followed with a sudden answer: "It is Clarissa, he said. For there she was" (296). This may seem to be Peter's "climax," for it is the recuperation of his earlier love for Clarissa; it is, however, more importantly hers, since it validates her reading in the eyes of others the stigma of their desire for her, despite the "ravages of time."[7]

~

This brief discussion of a double ending to the "female plot" provides an introduction to the questions with which this book will be concerned. The first is the foregrounding of gender issues in this discussion of "female plots," and by implication "male plots" as well. In what ways, we might ask, does "gender," in the various and diverse understandings of that term, play a role in the structure of narrative, especially in the various ways in which plot may be said to "end"? And, since it is impossible to be engaged with questions of endings—whether traditional "closed" endings, multiple endings, modernist "open endings," or postmodern subversions of endings—without a renewed interest in "plot," how are we to revisit that element of critical discourse so often disdained in formalist readings? This is the second question. One way of beginning to confront these questions is by turning to a text now almost universally acknowledged as the beginning of "contemporary" concern with ending: Frank Kermode's *The Sense of an Ending*.

Kermode is among the first to theorize how ending constructs meaning in narrative. Indeed, Kermode offers my exploration of ending in the contemporary novel a powerful impetus, because he argues that it is only through the sense of an ending that readers are enabled to make sense of a narrative. At the center of narrative for the traditionalist Kermode is the agency of time, or the inevitability of linearity—the sonorous clanging of Big Ben, if not the perennially tardy chimes of St. Margaret's. Narrative in the context of Kermode's conservative theorizing is ruled by the clock; as he reminds us, clocks always "tick-tock," *not* "tock-tick," and certainly not "tick-tick," for a world or a narrative of "tick-tick" would be by implication utterly meaningless. Much as *Mrs. Dalloway* might strive to decenter such traditional—and, we might add, *simplistic*—notions of time, plot, and ending, Kermode and others who have commented on ending have consistently defended the notion that in storytelling a "tock" must appear only after a "tick," and this rhythm of sequentiality is indispensable to narrative.

What intervenes between "tick" and "tock" for Kermode is a middle with the potential for meaning, only as it provides the necessary duration for narrative. Perhaps even more importantly this middle by implication functions only as a means to an end by offering material for the "tock" of ending so that this ending may transform the specifics of the middle, as a magnet powerfully lines up iron filings into a pattern. Ending must contrive to empty the interval, or middle, of its mere "chronic-ity," to borrow Kermode's term, replacing it with a structure of significance. For Kermode, substituting the "tick-tock" of narrative for the "tick-tick" of experience "humanizes" sequentiality. Ending is all. It is a "tock" defining itself as immensely different from and more impor-tant than the "tick" setting plot in motion. Kermode goes on to analo-gize narrative's tick-tock with the psychoanalytic session in which the analyst aspires to lead the analysand out of an immersion in time-bound experience and toward a recognition of meaning made possible by the transformation of that experience in the psychoanalytic stage Freud terms the "transference." By implication, the analysand works through that "middle" in anticipation perhaps of the analyst's promise of a "tock," much as narrative carries readers toward an "end of time" at which the past can be expected to end in the transformation of experi-ence into meaning.

The question becomes, What would Kermode make of Woolf's novel in light of his concern with ending? What are *we* to make of a narrative that allows readers access to more than one consciousness, not merely the two headliners in this performance—Septimus Warren Smith and even more obviously Clarissa—but the Peter Walshes as well, and even the Maisie Johnsons? In response to the question, Whose story is this anyway? most readers would look to the novel's title. What then is the Septimus story doing in relation to Clarissa's, and how is the ending of his story related to the ending of hers? What "tock" for Clarissa can balance the thunderous boom of Septimus's ending—not so much his death per se as its power to transform the middle leading up to his sui-cide? What or when *is* the ending of *Mrs. Dalloway?*

Much as *Mrs. Dalloway* may be constructing a monument to modern-ism, Woolf's novel also leans forward to the postmodern in its use of *mise en abîme.* The Septimus story presents itself as though it were an alternative to the Clarissa story. Her story and his story might be read as the sexual binary of narrative. Indeed, as earlier noted, many readers have concluded that this narrative's headliners may be the female and male segments of a single "androgynous" being. Additionally much has been made of Woolf's revelation that she originally planned the novel to end with Clarissa's suicide, not Septimus's. This line of inquiry, how-ever, diminishes the reader's sense that Septimus, like all the other fig-ures in this narrative, has any real import, except in Clarissa's development. Unlike the other figures, however, Septimus is important primarily as the germ of a story, rather than as a figure in the web of *Mrs. Dalloway.*

In this way, Septimus may have no real value to Clarissa or to this novel beyond his function of providing the raw material for Clarissa as a reader or even a constructor of narrative. The death of Septimus is *not* an ending in this modernist context. It is not an act representing the tock of narrative but rather the stigma of narrativity, the mark of "material" for a transformative reading by the storyteller—in this case, Clarissa as the artist of the telepathic. Not simply her consciousness but even her body replicates the last minutes of Septimus's desperate effort to save his soul by offering up his body to the penetrating spears of Mrs. Filmer's iron fence. Through her mastery of the power to project herself into another's being, Clarissa reexperiences another's dying, true, but only to stamp it with the imprint of her own transformative understanding. In her mind, at birth life proffers an "it"—were she religious, Clarissa might call it a "soul"—with the understanding that the integrity of this "it" must be defended at all costs against the efforts of others to colonize it. Having lost "it," no one can hope to remain human.

In her own way, Woolf begins to problematize Kermode's sense of an ending, especially as he implies its kinship to the idea of apocalypse, the immense upheaval or mighty event—a kind of big bang ushering in a wholly new dispensation. Septimus's embracing of death may seem a conventional "ending"—tragedy, not comedy, a death instead of a wedding—but it is *not*, Woolf indicates, an ending. It is no more than life, and it remains for a Clarissa to offer this narrative its ending, not in the form of an act but through the imaginative (re)construction of that act. As a maker of narrative Clarissa provides an ending with the power to operate outside the clockwork of plot—that is, outside Kermode's structure of "tick-tock" with its aspiration to an apocalypse that in the end fails to encompass Woolf's own "sense of an ending."

❧

Woolf's problematizing of Kermode's theorizing about plot and ending should point out the complexity of the issues of gender in narrative. The strategy of my project will be to explore a couple of dozen novels from the past half-century, organized as three clusters of related approaches to the gendering of plot and therefore ending. I choose the term "cluster," rather than "part," because the latter term connotes a logic of absolute separation implicit in categorizing, a logic subverted by the novels themselves.

The first cluster is entitled "Tales of the Masculine Narrative Paradigm." The novels in this cluster resemble each other in that sense of narrative theorized by Kermode and supported by structuralists such as the early Roland Barthes and his American followers, such as Robert Scholes. The focus of this cluster's theoretical framework is the writing of Peter Brooks, who serves my project as the provocative proponent of what I have chosen to term "the masculine narrative paradigm." The novels to be explored in this cluster increasingly strain the validity of that paradigm by offering endings seemingly at odds with conventional expectations. The term "masculine" displaces the more expected term "male," because my project is intent on unmooring gender (feminine and masculine) from sex (male and female) on the assumption that characteristics of gender continue to be sex-linked, while the gender *continuum* offers a more useful model than structuralist categories of mutually exclusive elements. This principle provides the justification for including more than one novel by the same author, to be explored in different clusters. In a similar vein, this approach allows for the more obvious inclusion of novels with plots and endings in the masculine mode but written by a female novelist, as well as novels written by a male novelist in a feminine mode.

The second cluster will include novels demonstrating fairly self-conscious attempts to depart from or even subvert the conventional masculine paradigm. The operative term may well be "demonstrating," since as it should soon become evident, the very effort to deny the efficacy of the traditional model for narrative might be read as the narrative's implicit subscribing to that model. Among its novels, this cluster has a number that reveal how the women's movement has raised our consciousness of how patriarchy assumes that what the male represents is the norm. It is scarcely a coincidence that until a decade or two ago virtually all the "narratologists" were men. And as feminists would be quick to remind us, the work of women was validated two generations ago only when they thought as men did. A case in point is the first book of Barbara Herrnstein Smith on closure in the modernist poem, a project firmly rooted in traditional (male) notions of ending, and in this way subscribing to a "masculinist" criticism, even though Smith later became an eminent feminist.

The third cluster includes perhaps the least homogeneous or coherent collection of narratives. As a group these novels may be more successfully working outside the traditional model for narrative. Unlike at least some of the texts in the second cluster, which implicitly subscribe to a model by denying it, the narratives in the third cluster seem to be working in a space where the older model no longer has a presence, even in the guise of its denial. This cluster, like the other two and like the proj-

ect as a whole, struggles valiantly to free itself from restrictions of sequentiality. How may we reduce the inevitability of value judgments in
a "tock" accruing greater validity and meaning by virtue of its following
a "tick"?

One potential means of subverting this sequentiality may be the flex-
ibility inherent in these "clusters." This project invites its readers to
question and perhaps even deny the inclusion of any single novel in a
particular cluster. At the risk of undermining the reader's confidence in
my authority as a reader, I have to admit that this study of ending took
longer than anticipated to reach its own sense of an ending in part because each return to the manuscript seemed to entail a reconsideration
of the legitimacy of a particular novel's positioning in a particular cluster. Using the analogy of pedagogy, I envision this project less as a lecture and more interactively as a dialogue with its prospective readers,
who might well make a more persuasive case for the position of a narrative in a difficult cluster. To forestall the disappointment of those who
set out here in anticipation of an "ending," or a conclusion to "sum it
up," like Bernard's chapter in *The Waves*, there is no ending in this text,
in large part because it aspires to continue resonating in its reader's consciousness, like *Mrs. Dalloway*, with its complicating of simplistic notions
of what constitutes an ending.

A word concerning the method by which the novels were selected.
Because of my own investment in the contemporary English novel,
most of the selections fit into that category. At the same time, it was my
interest to get out of the box to explore other cultural contexts, not out
of some simplistic aspiration to make gestures toward diversity so much
as an effort at testing whether these concerns with plot and ending are
transnational and transcultural as well as perhaps transsexual.

Another word, or more, might be added concerning the theoretical
framework for this discussion of contemporary narrative. In an era of
what it has become chic to term "posttheory," the reader is more likely
to question extensive theoretical grounding of a book such as this one.
As even the dialogue of Woolf's narrative with Kermode's theorizing
ought to make clear, it is still valuable to consider issues of ending in
the context of narrative theory. Rather than front-loading all that theorizing into this introduction, I have included relevant discussions of theoretical background in the introductions to each of the clusters to
follow. The intent is not to fit the novels into the theorizing so much as
to explore ways in which narrative itself seems both to subscribe to and
to subvert, or even to ignore, theory. Basically it is my goal to celebrate
the supremacy of narrative itself over any theorizing to be done in rela-

tion to it. I am mindful of Margaret Atwood's anecdote about an academic, presumably an "Atwood specialist," who cautioned her that she need not write any more to keep her scholarly audience productive for some time. I would like to express my own hope at the outset that narrative has value beyond its potential to provide work for those who write about it.

Cluster 1: Tales of the Masculine Narrative Paradigm

It is a short step from Frank Kermode's *THE SENSE OF AN ENDING* to the theorizing of Peter Brooks whose 1977 essay "Freud's Master-plot," along with its amplification in *Reading for the Plot,* has offered one of the most stimulating explorations of the dynamics of narrative in the past quarter-century. Although the title "Freud's Masterplot" acknowl-edges his debt to the founder of modern psychoanalysis, Brooks clearly establishes at the outset that he is a "psychoanalytic critic" of a very different kind from the simplistic "Oedipus complex" and "phallic sym-bol" hunters of the early twentieth century. He announces his commit-ment to a new psychoanalytic criticism thus: "It is not that I am interested in the psychoanalytic study of authors, or readers, or fictional characters, which have been the usual objects of attention for psychoan-alytically informed literary criticism. Rather, I want to see the text itself as a system of internal energies and tensions, compulsions, resistances, and desires" (1984, xiv). Accordingly Brooks is interested in bringing texts of Freud as author, rather than as scientist, to bear on an investi-gation of the vector of desire in narrative, especially in the conflict be-tween a desire for the end of the plot and a desire to postpone its end, that "little death" of narrative.

The "Freud"[1] in which Brooks grounds his theorizing is *Beyond the Pleasure Principle* (1920). This watershed study has been especially use-ful, because it represents Freud's focus on the "death wish," one of his many popularized and therefore oversimplified concepts. In *Beyond the Pleasure Principle,* Freud's theorizing is centered in the reading of at least two categories of "texts." One category comprises the nightmares of World War I veterans who night after night found themselves compul-sively screening narratives of battlefield horrors, in clear violation of Freud's earlier explication of dreams as the opportunity for the uncon-scious to gratify repressed desires. The other category of text involves one of those rare occasions of Freud's reporting his observation of an actual child, in this case his grandson at play in the famous *"fort/da"* episode in which the toddler threw and retrieved a spool tied to a string.

In a brilliant leap of imaginative reasoning, Freud connected the two radically disparate phenomena as expressions of the repetition compulsion. Because the episode with his grandson operates in the arena of the "normal," the *"fort/da"* game is the more helpful of the two narratives in reading for Freud's insight. Freud hypothesizes that the child is attracted to this repetitive ritual as a means of confronting the prospect of the greatest "unpleasure" in his life—the periodic and unpredictable absence of the mother, for whom the spool is clearly a "symbol." The infant aspires to the pleasure of control over even the worst of horrors through a repetition that allows him to "master" the withdrawal of the agent of pleasure whose absence has undermined any easy gratification of desire. The compulsion to repeat represents an effort toward mastery, and the promise of a return to the state of quiescence before the arousal of desire. Death as quiescence is pursued, then, as a circling back to where the subject began, in a movement marked by ambivalence and interdependence. That is, death is no horror entirely to be feared; it is instead the quietude before the onset of desire. Desire is ruled by the pleasure principle, but desiring must always generate a state of unrest so that the initial quietude becomes inevitably attractive. In this way the pleasure principle and the death wish in Freud's "beyond" serve each other's purposes, and neither is clearly the more attractive.

Although the title of Brooks's seminal essay "Freud's Masterplot" clearly offers the palm to the "father" of modern psychoanalysis, Brooks probably found Jacques Lacan's reading of the *Beyond* more useful to his earliest thinking about plot and ending, as he would rewrite his thinking in *Reading for the Plot*.[2] Lacan acknowledges Freud's brilliant reading of the child's symbolizing of the spool in the game to represent the mother's coming and going, but he rereads the *"fort/da"* game within the context of his interest in language. In what Lacan terms "a flash of genius," Freud points the way to an understanding of these "repetitive games in which subjectivity brings mastery of dereliction and the birth of the symbol" (Lacan 1977, 103). For Lacan, however—and therefore for those with an investment in reading texts, narrative texts as well as others—the story of the child's throwing and retrieving of the spool is less significant for its content than for its function as a metanarrative, or what might be classified as an "allegorical" reading, similar to Lacan's famous allegorical interpretation of Poe's story "The Purloined Letter."[3] Lacan focuses attention on how the vowel sounds "o" and "a"—perhaps misread by Freud the symbol maker as the German words *fort* and *∂a*, or "gone" and "here"—can be understood as the child's ascension to the Symbolic register for which he has acquired the key[4] to language as a mode of representation. Central to language as representation, as Lacan points out, is the dichotomy of absence and presence. Presence, or signification, generates itself within the context of absence, or death. As Jacques Derrida will argue, any being or presence the signifier might have will always be deferred because of its grounding in absence, in its difference from any other signifier. Thus the "mastery" of the child is ultimately an illusion, dependent on what Lacan calls the "murder" of the signified through the construction of the signifier representing but also *replacing* the signified. Lacan writes:

> Thus the symbol manifests itself first of all as the murder of the thing, and this death constitutes in the subject the eternalization of his desire.
>
>   The first symbol in which we recognize humanity in its vestigial traces is the sepulchre, and the intermediary of death can be recognized in every relation in which man comes to the life of his history. (1977, 104)

Within the repetition of the *"fort/∂a"* in what Lacan calls these "games of occultation,"[5] he constructs the allegory of the child's transformation, as the child grasps for the first time the power of representation, a transformation Lacan saw as the movement of the subject to the register of the Symbolic.[6]

In Lacan's reading of *Beyond the Pleasure Principle*, Brooks discovered a model for narrative in which repetition plays a central role. Narrative is for Brooks the repetition of an action completed before the narrating begins; indeed, the impulse to repeat is what initiates narration. He writes: "Narrative always makes the implicit claim to be in a state of repetition, as a going over again of the ground already covered . . . as the detective retraces the tracks of the criminal" (1984, 97). Following Freud's lead, Brooks argues that "repetition is mastery, movement from the passive to the active" (98), and what the storyteller wants to control is what he has no choice but to submit to: an end already imposed, an end awaiting the storyteller and his audience. As a result, plot, or the "middle" of narrative, is a familiar territory through which the storyteller is leading the listener/reader.[7]

Repetition in narration is not only apparent in the repeating of an action presumably already completed before the beginning of the plot; repetition also functions within narrative as "a *return* in the text, a dou-

bling back" (100; italics in original). Here Brooks perceives an "ambi-
guity," since repetition is both a "return *to*" an earlier part of the text as
well as a "return *of*" the repressed. In the psychoanalytic context repetition is an antecedent to the pleasure principle, an attempt to reach the
end, paradoxically through compulsive and seemingly endless returns,
and a turning away from the immediate gratification of pleasure, consti-
tuting a "premature death," or "short-circuit." In this way the impulse
toward pleasure cannot begin to be fulfilled until the repressed can
make its return via a "working-through" of these repetitions.

Although it will be necessary eventually to submit Brooks's theorizing to a critique by testing its applicability to a variety of narratives, it
should already be apparent that Brooks's model for narrative has its
problems and limitations. A case in point is this slippery term *repetition*.
The notion of the narrative as a text repeating an action that has completed itself is open to question, because it merges oral and written
forms of storytelling. Readers know that they are beginning a narrative
with a completed action because they hold its presumably complete text
in their hands; listeners, on the other hand, participate in the excitement—even if the story has been told before—of hearing a narrative
whose ending may change in the present telling, thus giving it the openness of the improvisational. There is a suggestion of tautology or circular reasoning in Brooks's compulsion to trace the pattern of Freud's
Beyond onto the complexity of narrative, as though all narrative were
detective fiction. In the process Brooks may be moving toward the bed
of Procrustes with which traditional psychoanalytic readings have been
associated to their disadvantage.

Having granted its limitations does not, of course, eliminate the usefulness of what might tentatively be called the Brooksian paradigm, as
it applies to the "plot" of certain kinds of narrative. (And "Brooks" here
is standing in for many theorists of narrative who have found attractive
the conventional "climax" organization of plot, with its "male" ending.)
If we follow Brooks's argument that the "beginning" is merely whatever
arouses plot from "the unnarratable" and that the ending through its
transformative function is almost external to plot, it may be the long
"middle" of narrative that allows for the fullest exploration of the dynamic of plot. This middle is the arena of the "working-through" of the
plot, particularly in the contest between discordant desires. Once
aroused from quiescence by the stimulus of "the narratable," plot is impelled toward an ending that has the sole power to restore quiescence.
Before this desire for the end can be fulfilled, there must be sufficient
repetitions to provide a readiness for the end. Here Brooks's "master-

plot" of narrative may be departing from Freud's analysis of the repetition compulsion. In Freud's analysis the repetition compulsion is at best a neurosis in which sufferers are entrapped until they eventually free themselves through the agency of the analyst. The repetition compulsion is inevitably a "sickness" for Freud and may even be implicated in "criminality" in Lacan's reading of the "*fort/da*," where the achievement of the power to represent symbolically is troped as the "murder of the thing" by the symbol.[8]

Brooks would sanitize the associations of Freud's analysis with sickness to explain the conflicting desires of the text and therefore of the reader. Death, in the sense of an ending that reveals meaning through a metaphorizing of the plot's ordinariness, is a consummation devoutly to be wished. As Brooks argues by referring to Walter Benjamin and Jean-Paul Sartre, ending or the death of narrative is eminently desirable, for it offers in an imaginative framework what humans cannot otherwise know—the truth made possible at the moment of death, or perhaps the moment *after* death. "Death," writes Benjamin, "is the sanction of everything that the storyteller can tell" (qtd. in Brooks 1984, 22), the "flame" at which readers "warm" themselves because their lives lack such ultimate knowledge. In a similar vein, Sartre explains that as a young man he had no idea of how to live his life until he envisioned his obituary and used that "death notice" as the road map to chart his life.

If it is the ending that draws readers forward to the liberating power of its transformation in an explosion of metaphoricity, it is the associations of ending with death that impel readers to resist the desire for the end by means of the repetitions, or "bindings," representing Eros and the life impulses. As metaphor represents both the metaphoricity of ending and the bindings that delay the end, metonymy also has a dual function. For Lacan desire must always be a metonym for the Desire in the unconscious from which the toddler is evicted with accession to the register of the Symbolic. Thus desire is also a "return of the repressed," or that primal Desire we know only through its traces—the details of narrative, or the parts standing for the whole of the Real, outside the Imaginary and the Symbolic. Plot also is metonymic in its organization of those repetitions or returns, in an associative manner. This metonymic pattern is evident in the connections of plot elements in a series of "and-then" constructions whose causal relations will become even more manifest at the ending toward which readers lean "in anticipation of retrospection." In his reading of Jakobson's and Lacan's more structuralist notions of metonymy and metaphor, Brooks finds a pattern for

narrative that is more poststructuralist in its perceptions of the interdependence and interpenetration of the two tropes when he writes: "We
read the incidents of narrative as 'promises and annunciations' of final
coherence, that metaphor that may be reached through the chain of me-
tonymies: across the bulk of the yet unread middle pages, the end calls
to the beginning" (1984, 93–94).

The usefulness finally of the paradigm Brooks advances may lie in its
exploration of narrative desire, the notion of a "textual erotics" through
which readers are drawn toward the end of narrative, yet also are impelled to postpone that end. Like Roland Barthes, and unlike numerous
structuralist narratologists, Brooks is drawn to the notion of the desire
of the text as it implicates the desire of the reader. As we shall see in a
later chapter, feminists with an interest in narratology would understandably dissent from a "plot" tracing the trajectory of male sexuality
as though it represented *human* sexuality. Rather than (mis)construe
Brooks's model of plot as a *male* narrative paradigm, we might replace
"male" with "masculine," since virtually from the beginning of the
genre women have also been writing novels following the same paradigm. To avoid the notion of a narrational "cross-dressing," a "*masculine*
narrative paradigm" seems useful for writers of any sex and any sexual
orientation.

One especially useful entry to an examination of the gendering of the
traditional narrative paradigm as "masculine" is offered by Jerry Aline
Flieger's brilliant theorizing of the joke structure. In her essay "The
Purloined Punch Line: Joke as Textual Paradigm," Flieger follows Jacques Lacan's provocative lead when he cryptically cites a relatively underread text by Freud: "For, however neglected by our interest—and
for good reason—*Jokes and Their Relation to the Unconscious* remains the
most unchallengeable of Freud's works because it is the most transparent, in which the effect of the Unconscious is revealed to us in its most
subtle confines" (qtd. by Flieger 1983, 942). Because Freud focuses on
the way in which sexual desire is represented through language in the
joke, Flieger suspects Lacan may be marking for his readers a "portal
of discovery"—his recognition of just how much his perception that everything is textual may be a "punch line" he "purloined from Freud"
(1983, 942). Flieger is particularly interested in Freud's discussion of
jokes because it opens a space within which it becomes possible to read
the gendering of narrative through the positioning of the figures in the
joking narrative.

These three figures in Freud's rendition of the joke narrative are the
joke teller, the listener, and the subject, who is the butt of the joke.

Freud reads this "subject" as the object of the joke's "hostile or sexual aggressiveness" (qtd. in Flieger, 1983, 943). Since sexual desire is implicated in the joking narrative and the joke teller has traditionally been male, it comes as little surprise that the "butt," or object, of the joke is frequently female. The "hostile or sexual aggressiveness" generating the joke may be read as a displacement from the easy gratification of sexual—that is, *male*,—desire. If men were successful in all their sexual aspirations, Freud implies, it might be unnecessary for them to tell jokes. The joke, it would seem, offers the frustrated desirer a textual substitute for sexual gratification in a context where Lacan would argue that all desire comprises a series of metonyms—or more accurately, *synecdoches*—to represent Desire, left behind in the register of the Imaginary when the infant moves into the register of the Symbolic, the order of representation.

Flieger simplifies the joke story by using conventional gender designations. Boy desires Girl, but Boy loses Girl to another Boy, who might be seen as representing all the taboos serving as obstacles to the easy fulfilment of desire. Frustrated, Boy humiliates Girl through smutty language as well as through the Joke in which Girl is the butt. In this way Boy confirms the vulnerability of Girl by exposing her to the voyeuristic Boy rival who functions as listener to the Joke. Thus, the Joker "gets" the Girl by bonding with his rival as an accomplice in a kind of locker-room humor at the expense of the vulnerable Girl. At the same time, Boy "gets" the other Boy whom he has positioned as listener to the Joke, waiting for the "punch line," or "climax," of the Joker's story.

It is the engineering of the "punch line," the deft timing of the "climax," that draws Boy Joker and Boy Listener into positions of vulnerability reminiscent of the Girl's exposure as the butt of the Joke. If the Joker is off in his timing and the punch line comes too soon, the Joke fails. If the punch line takes too long and desire wanes in the waiting for the end, it also fails. In addition, the punch line must neither totally surprise the listener nor bore him by being too easily foreseen. If the Joker brings it off with master-y, he confirms his "masculinity." The Listener, on the other hand, reflects the Girl's exposure, or vulnerability, in his positioning as the passive receiver of the Joke. That "femininity" may be covered by two representations of mastery: the Listener can master his otherwise feminine role by "getting" the Girl in "getting" the Joke; more importantly, he can anticipate an opportunity to tell the Joke in the future, foretasting the pleasure of duplicating the Joker's mastery in performing the Joke. Thus, the joking chain becomes a triangle with a shadowy potential for becoming a quadrangle of Joker, Butt, Listener, and Listener-as-Prospective Joker.

Behind Flieger's theorizing about the replication of the joking triangle lies Lacan's seminal reading of the Poe story "The Purloined Letter," with its central triangle of changing figures. In Poe's story the Queen has power, represented by the phallic "letter," until she is "feminized" by the Minister, who can purloin the letter because he knows she dare not protest, lest she draw the King's attention to the letter. M. Dupin, in turn, "feminizes" the purloining Minister by repeating the purloining. In reading the implications of gender in these power positions, Barbara Johnson has provocatively argued that the letter through which the Minister achieves mastery over the Queen and through which Dupin achieves mastery over the Minister bears a "stigma," or "symptom signifying a vulnerability or privation" (Flieger 1991, 109). The letter functions as what Flieger calls a "hot potato," rendering "feminine" those who delude themselves into believing in their own mastery. In this way Flieger follows Johnson in her effort to unmoor "gender," or the constructs of femininity and masculinity, from "sex," or the categories of female and male, in order to assert that gender is not equivalent to sex. Femininity becomes "a position or locus: anyone may be on the spot, the butt of the joke" (Flieger 1983, 957), while masculinity becomes a position of mastery, or at least the *illusion* of mastery. Like Poe's purloining Minister, we need to be prepared for a mastery that "goeth before a fall," the Trumper always having the potential to be trumped himself, or in Lacan's words, "à trompeur, trompeur et demie" (qtd. in Flieger 1983, 956). For Flieger, as for Johnson, this reading of gender as positionality may be central to Lacan's poststructuralist reading of Freud. Flieger writes: "[T]he supposedly distinct and gender-identified roles of the joking triangle are not only interchangeable but are actually coincidental or superimposed: each play is active *and* passive, desiring *and* desired, giver *and* receiver, not only successively but simultaneously. Since one only receives the punch line (like the purloined letter) in order to give it away, the notions of 'active' and 'passive' lose their specificity, as do the corollary notions of 'male' and 'female' gender" (1983, 958; italics in original).

❧

The novels to be explored in this cluster demonstrate the range of what might be considered narrative in service to the masculine narrative paradigm. At one end of the spectrum it includes narratives reminiscent of the "joke" structure outlined by Flieger; at the other end, it

engages narratives moving toward subversion of the traditional paradigm. Across that spectrum are contemporary novels clearly marked by
their desire for the end.

It should come as no surprise that the novels to be explored are all
varieties of at least two plot-oriented models. The first is the joke in
which the entire text appears organized to deliver its punch line. Such
narrative seems doomed to failure if its plot is not skillfully engineered
to prepare for an ending in which timing is everything. The narrative
must be of appropriate length and offer an ending the listener/reader
can accept as a logical outcome of what precedes the punch line. A useful example is provided by Ian McEwan's Booker Prize-winning novel
Amsterdam, a narrative that may have offended its readers by drawing
them into a joke, only to discover in the end that they have joined the
novel's central characters in becoming the butt of that joke. The other
textual model for the masculine narrative paradigm is the detective
novel, opening with a mystery to be solved or a question to be answered
at the end. Kazuo Ishiguro's novel *When We Were Orphans* represents
this model in part because its narrator is a professional detective, chosen by his profession at the age of eight when his parents mysteriously
disappeared in 1930s China.

In addition to the McEwan and Ishiguro novels that seem to have
been written for this cluster, there are several narratives that begin to
strain the conventional notions implicit in the masculine narrative paradigm. This group includes four very different and dramatic expressions
of the climax variety of ending. These novels range from the powerful
but elusive revelation at the end of Steven Millhauser's "little" novel
Edwin Mullhouse and the disclosures at the end of Margaret Atwood's
"big" novel *The Blind Assassin* to two novels whose endings represent
the energy of transformation, personal and national: Colum McCann's
This Side of Brightness and Salman Rushdie's *Midnight's Children.* The
cluster "ends" with two novels already problematizing the sense of an
ending. Graham Swift's *Waterland* seems the more modernist in its investment in more than a single ending, reminiscent of Woolf's structure
in *Mrs. Dalloway.* D. M. Thomas's *The White Hotel* is in many ways a
"natural" for this exploration of the masculine narrative paradigm. It
offers a central character based on the historical Freud who operates as
a detective tracking down the roots of a patient's "hysteric" symptoms.
In one of its endings, the narrative reveals the joke has been on Freud,
who totally misdiagnosed his fictional patient, "Anna G.," as suffering
from "hysteria." The Thomas novel also has a key place here, because
it offers a segue to the next cluster, focusing on the unraveling of the

masculine narrative paradigm. These narratives reveal that Brooks's notion of ending as the consummation of the reader's desire for meaning is being displaced by more sophisticated notions of ending, or closure, having little to do with plot or action.

CITY OF ENDINGS: IAN MCEWAN'S *AMSTERDAM*

In a context of jokes and endings, Ian McEwan's Booker Prize-winning[9] novel *Amsterdam* (1998) offers a brilliant starting point. The novel begins dramatically with an ending: the cremation of Molly Lane's remains. Although her husband George has deliberately chosen not to mourn her passing with a memorial service—at least not at *this* point— Molly's friends and former lovers have come together to mark the end of her tormented latter days. Molly's ending brings a heightened awareness of their own possible ends to at least two of her lovers/mourners, Clive Linley and Vernon Halliday,[10] and precipitates a complex structure of endings, or deaths, ranging from physical demise through the trajectory of sexuality to issues of narrative closure. In the end, that construction of endings becomes most fully represented by "Amsterdam," McEwan's city of endings.

Walter Benjamin asserts that "[d]eath is the sanction of everything that the storyteller can tell,"[11] and McEwan ends his story with two deaths that are the logical outcomes of the death having taken place before this novel begins. Clive, who ultimately gains the lion's share of the narrative's "focalization,"[12] sets the plot in motion with the decision he makes after recognizing that Molly's painful end could also be his, especially since he lives very much to himself. He faults her doting husband, George, for a love so possessive it became impossible for George to rescue Molly from the agonies of terminal cancer. The horror of Molly's incredibly rapid mental and physical deterioration at only forty-six offers first Clive and then Vernon the object lesson of the need to prepare for one's end, not as a traditional soul might prepare to escape the hell of an afterlife but as a psyche might ready itself for a future inability to save the body from the torments of hell in this life. Thus, the plot is set in motion by the two friends' pact for each to ease the other's passing, in case terminal illness denies him the ability to find his own means of escape from pain.

In this way, the two friends write a "suicide pact." It is a suicide pact with a very large difference, however, for the two have no intention of taking their own lives at the same time, of course, but of serving as each

other's "true friend," to whose helpless suffering the merciful survivor
is no longer able to bear witness. As Vernon indicates, the arrangement
involves a strange sense of "intimacy," as each assumes responsibility
for the other's death. An analogy might be found in our culture's mythologizing of a permanent bond between a pair after one has *saved* the
life of the other, and clearly the two friends see the task as one of "saving" the other's life by ending it. The relationship between Clive and
Vernon is complicated, however, by the knowledge of each friend that
the other has also been Molly's lover, just as each knows that the husband, George, is also aware of his dead wife's former lovers. At the risk
of oversimplifying Eve Kosofsky Sedgwick's seminal theorizing about
our culture's grounding of homosociality in the repression of same-sex
relationships, it cannot be easily dismissed that the friendship-unto-
death of these two men is generated out of the horrible demise of a
woman with whom both were sexually intimate. (Indeed, they seem an
"odd couple" from the outset, since Clive composes music and Vernon
edits a newspaper.) The dark humor of the opening scene at the crema-
torium is played out like conventional sex farce[13] with the complaisant
husband contending with the presence of at least three of his dead
wife's lovers. For this reason he has ruled out a memorial service, hoping to forestall overhearing the lovers "comparing notes" and "exchang-
ing glances" during his eulogy (McEwan 1998, 9).

As it will become brilliantly clear at the end, this widower's management of his wife's end provides the narrative its "framing"—its beginning and its end, creating a symphony of interrelated endings. The
opening notes of that "symphony" are apparent in a segue readers
might easily pass over without noting its subtle brilliance. In this early
passage the narrative indicates the husband's grimly farcical situation
and then enters Clive's consciousness: "[George] could do nothing
about [Molly's] affairs, but in the *end* she was entirely his. . . . The *end*.
All [Clive] wanted now was the warmth, the silence of his studio, the
piano, the *unfinished score*, and to reach the *end*" (6–7; emphasis added).
The passage offers a little masterpiece of ironic discourse, because, as it
will become unmistakably clear, this is not "the end" at all, but the beginning of the end, just as it is literally the beginning of the narrative.
Furthermore, this term "score" is deeply ironic. Even more telling,
however, is the last statement denoting the end of Clive's symphony in
progress; like a Freudian slip, it also suggests that the unconscious has
spoken Clive's longing for the end of his being as well.

As the narrative oscillates between the two friends as objects of its
focalization, Clive's longing for the end overrides the attention the nar-

rative focuses on Vernon. The latter is energized by the effort to "save" his newspaper, the *Judge*, by stopping its hemorrhaging of readers. Even more grandly, Vernon constructs himself as a liberal warrior, bent on a preemptive strike against the potential ascension of Adrian Garmony, the right-wing foreign secretary, to 10 Downing Street. These professional and political "good reasons" increasingly appear to mask the editor's aspiration to glory, a grander version of the "Pategate" Vernon precipitated by exposing an American president's misuse of public funds to buy himself a toupee. Clive's parallel obsession/compulsion is more likely, however, to draw the reader's sympathy, because Clive is an artist. As a composer he is presumably consumed by the desire to bring to completion a major work of art he has been composing on commission, a work already dubbed by the media the "Millennial Symphony." In this way the narrative draws upon yet another ending—the ending of the millennium to inflate the importance of Clive's efforts to complete "the unfinished score, and to reach the end," if only he can overcome a composer's equivalent of writer's block.

Through its privileging of Clive as the object of its focalization, the narrative allows such extensive access to his consciousness that the recognition of his entrapment in the isolate's hell of solipsism may come as a major shock to readers in the later chapters. Unlike Vernon, whose deepest motives are rather quickly exposed as grounded in shabby self-aggrandizement, Clive has the luxury of longer reader sympathy,[14] one suspects, because his obsessive aspirations are culturally legitimated through his art. In addition, his effort to finish the "Millennial Symphony" provides something of a *mise en abîme* effect for the narrative as a whole as it works toward its own ending. In this way the narrative seduces its readers by performing sympathy[15] for Clive in the attempt to create the sense of an ending for the work as a whole.

This longing for the end draws on both romantic and modernist constructs of the artist's herculean struggle with paint, or notes, or words, to find a means of ordering his material to make meaning. After attending Molly's cremation, Clive returns to the piano and he composes on it in the "exhausted afternoon light" (20). He is impelled to shape the notes into a pattern he seems unembarrassed to identify as "the truth." Furthermore, Clive has conventionally modernist aspirations to see his "work" in a quasi-religious context, as "'a secular communion' . . . grasping a 'fundamental truth'" (24). Alternately, Clive sees this monumental opus as a mighty construction with its own energy to move toward closure: "[H]e had brought this massive engine of sound to a point where the real work of the finale could begin . . ." (26). The *mise en abîme* effect of having a composer working on a musical text within the story provides a postmodern gesture toward self-reflexivity as the narrative problematizes the facile confidence of another kind of writer that his composition can attain truth-value in this rather conventional humanist supplanting of religion by art. At the same time, this composer's pursuit of "truth" in his text provides the grounding for the reader's eventual recognition of Clive's entrapment in self-delusion.

And to make matters worse, in attempting to complete his Ninth Symphony, so to speak, Clive raises the stakes by arrogantly melodramatizing this final, major composition as the final chapter of his entire life's work. Looking back over his earlier musical production, he convinces himself that his oeuvre embodies his life itself, so that "what would remain of Clive Linley would be his music. Work—quiet, determined, triumphant work . . ." (149). Once again, Clive is unembarrassed in making such a romantic gesture, reminiscent of Shakespeare's assertion in Sonnet 18: "So long as men can breathe, or eyes can see, / So long lives this, and this gives life to thee"—and presumably "me," the artist, as well. Accordingly, when he loses the overblown confidence that his symphony will serve as the end-piece to give his entire oeuvre meaning, Clive thinks he has lost "his masterpiece, the summit of his lifetime's work," something that might have "taught his audience how to listen to, how to *hear*, everything he had ever written" (152–53; italics in original).

Clive's obsession with the "finale" of his symphony, but even more his obsession with the notion that this symphony is the sole agency by which his life's work can achieve meaning, moves him toward a massive "fall," appropriate to a tragic context, and to "the end" of his life as well. The implication of death in his longing for the end of his work has been clear from the outset with his desire to complete the "unfinished score, and to reach the end" (6). Indeed Clive seems to be fashioning himself on the paradigm of the tragic artist—more specifically, of Beethoven, the epitome of the composer who was able to transmute the suffering of his personal life into the magnificence of his art. Early on, Clive applauds Molly in retrospect for rejecting his marriage proposal, because it gave him the time to write his *Three Autumn Songs* in less than a month" (8). The erotic dimensions of his desire for the "finale," or "climax," of his symphony reveal themselves most fully, however, in the episode in the Lake District, where he has sought refuge to work on the closing movement.

It could hardly be more appropriate that the narrative arranges a rape scene to intrude upon Clive's scene of inspired composition. (Indeed, one could provide a short list of alternative crimes that might have served just as well as intrusions upon his moment of "inspiration.") Hardly has he discovered the "gift" of his desperately pursued "theme," when he witnesses what he tellingly misrecognizes as a rural "assigna- tion." The desire for "the end" here could not be more blatantly sexual. Distracted by the woman's pleas for help, Clive "flounders" briefly, "and then he had it [his theme] again . . . so elusive the moment his attention relaxed" (92). This orgasmic "it" eludes him in the end, how- ever: "Something precious, a little jewel [his theme], was rolling away from him" (94). In an artistic equivalent of coitus interruptus[16] he al- most grasps the end of his desire, as he laments: "[W]hat he had been doing, until interrupted, was *creating* [his theme], forging it out of the call of a bird" . . . (94; italics in original). This last phrase is likely to recall the beach scene in Joyce's ironic "portrait of an artist," with the youthful Stephen Dedalus involved in his own hyperbolic "forging" of art. When the narrator offers the assertion that Clive "found that not only this passage but the whole movement had died on him" (151), it becomes difficult not to suspect that this narrative is punning on orgasm as the "little death" Clive has been denied. The composer may struggle on, even deluding himself that he has reached his "finale";[17] however, as the grim ending of the novel makes clear, the desire for the end of his work is left in a permanent state of the interruptus.

The hapless victim of the Lake District rapist's attack functions for Clive as "a spoiler," just as Garmony's wife does for Vernon when she publicly lies about having known for years that her husband shared J. Edgar Hoover's alleged penchant for cross-dressing. Clive chooses to entrap himself in both an older as well as a more modern version of the myth of the "inspired," and often somewhat demonic, romantic artist. The older version draws upon Coleridge's mythologizing of interrupted composition when the spirit, or demon, of "inspiration" allegedly de- serted him during the hour he entertained the visitor from Porlock, a suspect "explanation" for the "lack" of an ending to "Kubla Khan."[18] The other, more modern rendition of the myth is Faulkner's notion of the "demon-driven" artist, willing to sacrifice anything or anyone to his art. Faulkner notoriously responded to the *Paris Review* interviewer's question, "Do you mean the writer should be completely ruthless?"[19] by saying: "The writer's only responsibility is to his art. . . . Everything goes by the board: honor, pride, decency, security, happiness, all to get the book written. If a writer has to rob his mother, he will not hesitate; the *Ode on a Grecian Urn* is worth any number of old ladies" (Faulkner 1956, 30). Faulkner's use of "he" is tellingly appropriate here, and one suspects that male readers may be more sympathetic than female readers to Clive's anguished dilemma: either to commit a sin of omission and accept complicity in rape in order to maintain his focus on his work, or to risk the artist's version of coitus interruptus.

The sexist, if not misogynistic, implications of this myth of the demon-driven artist could not be more appropriate to a traditional notion of the sexual overtones of artistic creation, both in its production and in its product.[20] If a sexual undercurrent is apparent in Clive's, and to a lesser degree Vernon's, desire for the end of his "work," it is an undercurrent of which McEwan cannot have been unaware, for the implication of erotic impulses in creating texts and therefore in creative texts has had a long history. As recently as a generation ago, Robert Scholes could still assert without discernible embarrassment: "The archetype of all fiction is the sexual act. . . . For what connects fiction — and *music*—is the fundamental orgastic rhythm of tumescence and detumescence, of tension and resolution, of intensification to the point of climax and consummation" (Scholes 1967, 26; emphasis added). In any case, *Amsterdam* may be read as a pastiche of the masculine narrative paradigm, perhaps even turning that paradigm into a postmodern joke. Once again the *mise en abîme* effect of positioning a composer/ writer within the text provides an element of self-reflexivity to the larger narrative.

Having escaped to the Lake District to eliminate London's distractions, Clive has felt confident that he could grasp the "theme" for his final movement. He has "done the background work in his studio," but more importantly he is "working backward really, sensing that the theme lay in fragments and hints in what he had already written." This seems crucial to him, for "[i]n the finished piece the melody would sound to the innocent ear as though it had been anticipated or developed elsewhere in the score" (McEwan 1998, 81–82). If readers have not already been paying attention to the "fragments and hints in what [McEwan] had already written," they are likely to start doing so from this point forward, especially since the crucial scene of Clive's moral dilemma will follow immediately upon this foregrounding of the writer's beginning to make preparations for the end.

In its fashion, this narrative leads its readers toward one possible ending—possible, virtually from the beginning—while it is also engineering what increasingly seems the "punch line" of the actual ending. Once again the pairing of Clive and Vernon functions well by turning each into the cruel analyst of the other's moral depravity. Adding to the acid public criticism of Vernon, begun by Garmony's wife in her press conference when she pillories him for having the "mentality of a black-mailer, and the moral stature of a *flea*" (135; italics in original), Clive sends his nasty postcard. Vernon responds by reporting Clive to the police as a material witness in the Lake District rapes, at the very time his former friend needs to concentrate his energies on finishing the great symphony he believes "almost done" (146). Ironically, both members of this "odd couple" seem to be approaching a psychological/spiritual form of the hopeless state each foresaw as the result of terminal illness, and thus each becomes ready to start the journey to "Amsterdam."

Amsterdam as the city of endings undergoes a radical transmogrification as the potential nobility of a Roman (or Japanese) suicide to preserve honor devolves into a murderous vengefulness. It is as though the tragedy of a Brutus had been supplanted by the ruthless vengeance of a Macbeth, intent on destroying others in an effort to save himself, as Clive and Vernon seem impelled to bring down those who appear to have conspired with calamity to frustrate their aspirations to complete the mighty monuments to their desires. Accordingly, Clive and Vernon separately arrange an appointment with a Dutch "Dr. Death" to "ease" the other's passing from an existence of painful and irrecoverable mental illness. Earlier Clive may have been convinced that "[w]ork—quiet, determined, triumphant work, then—would be a kind of revenge" (149). Now that "work" is no longer possible, he seems prepared to settle for merely "revenge." In describing the deranged candidate he is putting forward for euthanasia, Clive unwittingly describes himself: "the symptoms: unpredictable, bizarre, and extremely antisocial behavior, a complete loss of reason. Destructive tendencies, delusions of omnipotence" (169). Thus Clive has degenerated into a variety of the mad artist,[21] on the model of the mad scientist, and such madness is demonstrated by his total lack of compunction about his moral dereliction in the Lake District. Indeed, he thinks of "the 'Nessun dorma' of the century's end, the melody . . . for which he had been prepared to sacrifice an anonymous rambler. And rightly" (170–71). Like his former friend whom he is about to murder in the guise of a "mercy-killing," Clive has the "moral stature" of a *"flea."*

With the sudden movement of the narrative to Amsterdam, readers are prepared for the springing of the mousetrap, or, for the punch line of a narrative that has moved toward "gallows humor." The accelerating speed of the reader's withdrawal of sympathy from these two "characters," especially Clive, is astonishing, but crucial to this city of endings.[22] Because Clive is a composer, and an aging one at that, his plight may have a certain resonance for readers who have thought of themselves as "writers"—along a range from the gifted and celebrated to the ordinary sort who work with words. Clive's self-delusion that his "Millennial Symphony" will be acknowledged as his masterpiece is ultimately belied by the response of music critics, to whom this *"chef d'oeuvre"* seems schlock, an embarrassingly transparent pastiche of Beethoven's truly great defining masterpiece, his Ninth Symphony. To those who work alone and for whom creating of any sort is impossible without preserving confidence in the value of its result, what we might term "Clive's syndrome" may be a painful nightmare of recognition.

The narrative, however, is intent on "sailing to Amsterdam" with dramatic urgency. Ironically, this "city of reason" has become a haven for irrationality, since its "reasonable laws" legalizing prostitution, drug use, and so forth, have attracted those whose "destructive [and self-destructive] tendencies" abuse its liberal philosophy. Clive and Vernon, who have moved in the inner circles of power and culture, have reduced themselves to ridiculous buffoons in a farce, trying to remember which glass of champagne contains the sedative and to devise some means of ensuring that its intended target drinks it. In the end both of these characters who had been desperately attempting to "bring off" a life's work to grasp a place for himself in history, on the model of the young John Keats striving to write the great odes that might elevate him to the pantheon of English poets, become ludicrously obsessed with plotting the end of the other's life and ironically his own.

"It wasn't a double suicide at all," Garmony tells George; "It was mutual murder" (191). This is not the ending toward which the narrative has been leading its readers, however. The punch line is hinted at by George's backhanded compliment to Garmony: "You know, I think you came out of it bloody well. . . . Most men would have hanged themselves for far less" (190). The punch line toward which this "joke" has been moving approaches with the assertion of George's pleasant thoughts of his former rivals for Molly's affection, what with "Garmony beaten down . . . and now Vernon out of the way, *and* Clive. All in all, things hadn't turned out so badly on the former-lovers front. This surely would be a good time to start thinking about a memorial service for Molly" (192–93; italics in original). George as the deadly jokester, it would appear, has reached the end of *his* plot.[23] By offering Vernon the photographs Molly took of Garmony in drag, George apparently was certain of their being printed, causing Garmony enough embarrassment perhaps to hang himself and leading to Vernon's condemnation as Garmony's murderer. (How like explaining a joke this becomes!) The jokester's plot did not work out quite as planned, however, since not even George could have foreseen that Mrs. Garmony would save her husband in the gesture by which Vernon sees himself foiled: "It's a spoiler" (134).[24] After all, she was not playing her bedroom-farce role of the betrayed wife! George appears to be "philosophical" about not precipitating Garmony's suicide as well, for he managed to eliminate Clive, apparently without intending to. If "Amsterdam" for this narrative has become a "city of endings," it is a deeply ironic and complicated trope the narrative has constructed.

Once again, as Jerry Flieger reminds us, the joke has traditionally been an expression of sexual aggression—against a woman, or against a man who is "feminized" through his position as the butt of the joke. The joke framework in *Amsterdam* offers a reminder of how the "feminine" in its more conventional sense is positioned as vulnerable and therefore powerless in this power structure of desire. In this context Molly is the center of "femininity," the butt of the locker-room joke of the "fast" woman who deludes herself into believing that she can be just as sexually liberated as the traditional male. Once the narrative exposes George as a perverse, perhaps even monstrous, jokester, attempting to settle old "scores" on the "former-lovers front," it becomes difficult not to suspect him of incredibly more perverse "joking" in refusing to ease the ending of Molly's life. Throughout the narrative women are constructed as vulnerable and therefore powerless—whether it is the dyslexic subeditor at the *Judge* or the latest victim of the Lake District rapist. Even the former lovers—Garmony, Clive, and Vernon—are positioned as feminine when they become the butts of George's sick joke. Only Mrs. Garmony seems to have the power to turn the tables by becoming a variety of jokester herself with the "spoiler" strategy of stealing Vernon's thunder. She offers an excellent example of the construction of gender defined as positioning in the power play of the joke. Like Poe's detective M. Dupin, the clever plotter who gets the better of the Minister by replicating the purloining of the Queen's letter, Mrs. Garmony outplots the hapless Vernon, just as George outplots his wife's former lovers.

More importantly, however, the joke functions as an analogue for the male narrative paradigm itself. Like the genre of the detective novel Brooks considers the epitome of narrative, the joke offers a complicated engineering of anticipations, postponed gratification, and sexual aggression toward the "feminine," but preeminently a longing for the end. The self-conscious management of timing, the positioning of the listener as vulnerable in relation to the power position of the mastering jokester, the anticipating of the punch line with its undercurrent of erotic desire and aggressive violence: all these are evident enough not to require extensive rehearsal here—at the end. In this way the pursuit of an ending draws together the conventional trajectory of male sexuality, the masculine narrative paradigm, and a desire for the end of life, if that ending promises a sense of meaning not earlier attained. The last pages of this "Sailing to Amsterdam" brilliantly underscore the generation of desire and its end.

The return to Poe and "The Purloined Letter," one of his contributions to the invention of the detective story, offers an opportunity to bring together the joke and detective fiction as related expressions of the masculine narrative paradigm. Although it may be subtly suppressed, the detective story functions in *Amsterdam* on a moral level. That is, Clive and Vernon have, like Garmony and perhaps others, felt themselves the masters of the situation, erotically speaking, in their "borrowing" of George's wife and their assumption that George is willing to play out the farce role of complaisant husband. As "victim," George patiently bides his time until he can draw Garmony and Vernon into a plot to discredit each other, a plot in which he succeeds beyond his wildest dreams. George ends up as that rare bird of detective fiction, the criminal who "gets away with it" by committing the "perfect crime." And as in much detective fiction, the joke is on those readers who failed to figure out this looming "punch line" before it was revealed.

THE LURE OF THE DETECTIVE STORY: KAZUO ISHIGURO'S *WHEN WE WERE ORPHANS*

Kazuo Ishiguro's novel *When We Were Orphans* is in several senses a "detective novel."[25] At the same time, it is also turning detective fiction inside out, certifying itself as "postmodern" in at least the narrow sense that like a Möbius strip its inside and outside are interchangeable. It is a detective novel in part because its central figure and narrator, Christopher Banks, is a detective by profession. Indeed, he claims an international reputation as a famous private detective, a profession that seems to have chosen him when both his parents disappeared in Shanghai in the 1930s. The power of having been "called" by his profession as a child is so great that even though Banks thought he was concealing his ambition from his school chums in England, where he was sent after the disappearance of his parents, he did not succeed, because his friends gave him a magnifying glass as a birthday present. Furthermore, he still uses this banal emblem of his trade in his professional work as a detective.

If *When We Were Orphans* were a traditional modernist narrative, this birthday present of a magnifying glass would be foregrounding itself as a "symbol" of the centrality of seeing to the narrator's function as a detective. In his role as the novel's narrator, Christopher is a "private eye," and accordingly he is constructed as "masculine" by virtue of his position as the subject-who-looks, since obviously enough it is through his eyes that readers "see" the narrative. Through the agency of the narrative gaze, Christopher benefits from a power dramatically in excess of the impotence readers are likely to perceive in this affectless, solitary, and socially inept figure. In the opening scene, for example, Christopher as a young adult has invited a former school chum to be the first guest in his London apartment; he admits surprise when Osbourne remembers him as "an odd bird at school" (Ishiguro 2000, 5), since his own recollection is that he "blended perfectly into English school life" (7). Similarly, he excuses his lack of a social life—"detectives tend not to participate in society gatherings" (12)—and when Sarah Hemmings brushes him off at the Waldorf where he arrives, flush with confidence from having solved the Mannering case, he explains that her rejection was "providential," because it reminded him that he must not allow himself to be "distracted" by socializing. After all, he has dedicated himself to "cherished goals," the first and foremost of which is "to combat evil—in particular, evil of the insidious, furtive kind" (22).

As a result of his exposing a limited ability to "see," Christopher's "masculinity" may seem "open to question," for he appears to be blinding himself to actualities readers are likely to see more clearly than he allows himself to. At the same time, however, Christopher's position as narrator/looker is likely to give readers pause, because he has been author-ized to shape the narrative as he needs to see it. Ironically, he would see his mission as a comic-book hero "combat[ting] evil," when in actuality he devotes his energies to tidying up the messes of the rich and powerful whose servant he is.

Christopher is complexly gendered in his functions as narrator/looker and as detective. In the former function he is "masculine" in being positioned as one with power; in the latter, there is a touch of the "feminine" in his preoccupation with "details," traditionally associated with "women's work." About a third of the way through the novel, Christopher discloses his awareness that he may have failed miserably to be observant of the smallest matters of daily experience. He indicates that he has returned again and again to the day of his father's disappearance, and struggles to organize the specifics of the scene as he recalls them. For a budding detective, he fails to remember anything out of the ordinary. Indeed, he asserts that his memory cannot produce a single aspect of his departure for work that would distinguish it from every other morning's setting forth (106). It is worth noting that Christopher the detective has recalled this scene many times before he finally begins to acknowledge failure in *not* having been more observant. Not far beneath the surface here seems to be a professional and personal guilt for failing to be more attentive, for a detective is constructed essentially as one with an eye for details—like a housekeeper, or a butler such as Stevens in Ishiguro's best-known novel, *The Remains of the Day*.

Christopher's English education and his success as a young professional seem little more than a preparation for the day when he would return to Shanghai to solve the mystery of his missing parents. It is tempting to say, "the mystery of his parentage," since he has a kinship to the first detective in Western literature, Oedipus, seeking the truth of who, or *what*, his parents were. The analogy to the Oedipus of the first play in the Sophocles trilogy is apt. Christopher reveals at the outset that he deludes himself about his power to see the truth and to use that vision to "combat evil." Like Oedipus, he has a boyish confidence in the black-and-white world of mutually exclusive notions of good and evil. Perhaps their shared function as detectives impels both Oedipus and Christopher to believe that the truth can be both knowable and beneficial. The connection of Christopher to Oedipus may go some way toward preparing readers for a revelation that ought to cause Christopher's whole world to collapse, when he is finally forced to confront a complex of truths that exceed his powers to accommodate. Because of Christopher's movement within the Oedipus paradigm of truth as something knowable and ultimately "good," it would seem that he fits the construction of narrative with its "masculine" pursuit of a transforming truth.

As a "detective novel" *When We Were Orphans* both is and is *not* following the masculine narrative paradigm, however. The narrative certainly establishes the mystery of the parents' disappearance—actually, disappearances, since Mrs. Banks disappears even more mysteriously several days after her husband leaves for work one morning and never returns. Christopher himself is implicated in his mother's disappearance when he is taken by "Uncle Philip," a friend of the family, to another part of the city and left to find his way home, slowly enough for Mrs. Banks to be "disappeared" while he is away. Thus, it comes as no surprise that "Uncle Philip," who was clearly implicated in at least the second disappearance, will be a "material witness," if not an "accessory to the crime." Brooks would approve of the timing here, as the narrative suggests that the "truth" will be revealed "in good time." Clearly Christopher as narrator/storyteller is postponing the end, in part for the pleasure of anticipating the gratification of his desire to know the truth.

In addition, it is appropriate that Christopher was nine when this foundational detective case of his career was generated, almost as though its real purpose was to justify his adult life. Still a child, he had only recently reached the beginning of the traditional age of reasoning. Childhood itself is all about the detective work of trying to figure out what being an adult means, listening to adults talk when they may not be aware the child is listening, or when they are speaking in codes or elliptically.[26] The desire to penetrate the efforts of adults to police the boundaries of their knowledge implicates the child, the detective, and the reader of narrative in a common desire to know—what Brooks terms "epistemophilia," or the *pleasure* of knowing. Epistemophilia names this desire for the end, that death of narrative, or ending, where readers as detectives find out what "really" happened. The detective story is useful, because it both arouses the desire to know and problematizes what is meant by "knowing." It also generates the counterdesire of that desire to know, because any knowing is a dying of innocence, the little death of "childhood," in knowing whatever it is that transforms us.

This may explain why Christopher Banks obsesses over gaining entry to the house where he naively believes his parents are still being held prisoner after several decades. The word "obsesses" is appropriate, because Banks strives to impress into his service a unit of the Chinese army, defending Shanghai against the invading Japanese. Incredibly, like a naive and stubborn child, Christopher attempts to persuade the Chinese officer that freeing Mr. and Mrs. Banks is really more important than stopping the Japanese, who are after all merely adult versions of his boyhood chum Akira. Why, the reader has to wonder, hasn't this great detective turned immediately to the most likely lead, the man whom he still calls "Uncle Philip" and who still addresses Christopher by his family nickname of "Puffin"?

The implication of "Uncle Philip" in at least the mother's disappearance is something Christopher seems to "forget," just as Oedipus "forgets" that he would be wise not to kill a man or marry a woman old enough to be his parent. He admits that he hardly missed his father after he disappeared because he still had "Uncle Philip," no *blood* relationship. The narrative lures readers into some amateur psychologizing by impressing "Uncle Philip" and Mr. Banks into service as the Good

Father and the at-best Good-Enough Father, respectively. As this protracted story of Christopher's life as a basically dysfunctional overaged child finally gets around to the long-delayed conversation of Puffin and Uncle Philip, the end is obviously near and along with it whatever it was Christopher could have revealed at the outset. That assertion needs qualification, however, because the novel is narrated by Christopher as a "journal" through whose logic the illusion is maintained that events "happen" and he simply records them without yet knowing how the whole story will end. This narrative strategy violates Brooks's assumption that plot can begin *only after* all the action is complete. Christopher's narrative posits an indeterminacy concerning a future within which "life" has not finished the story, or *fabula,* so that the plot, or *sjužet,* can complete its function of narration.

Before this revelation scene the narrative seems loose and rambling, as though bumbling its way toward a truth that may be uncannily already known. As the narrative organizes itself for this scene, it reveals that the story has always been within Christopher's control, and his postponement of the revelation is rather like a cruel attempt to fuel the imagination's anticipation of the desired ending. By delaying his interrogation of the prime suspect, Christopher as narrator acts as the agent for that powerful desire in narrative to avoid a quick and expeditious movement toward the revelations in its ending. Such desire to defer the ending slips dangerously close to the perverse, as this desire implicates readers in something like sadism. Laura Mulvey asserts that "sadism demands a story," and Teresa de Lauretis may be right on the money when she transposes Mulvey's assertion to make her own point that a "story demands sadism," not only in its subject matter but in its power plays vis-à-vis the reader, whose desire for the end must wait upon the narrative's working toward completion—in its own good time.

The Christopher[27] who returns to Shanghai to solve the mystery of his parents' disappearance differs only superficially from the boy who was shipped out of harm's way at nine. As his "Uncle Philip" tells him at the outset of his revelations, Christopher was the victim of a well-intentioned conspiracy of kindness to maintain his innocence. Once again the parallels here with Oedipus are striking: How can one escape from the horrors of the "truth" when the comfortable blindness of innocence persists into adulthood? And for Christopher, can the "Reality Instructors" resist the perverse pleasure of destroying the innocence they have contributed to by preserving it long enough for the truth to have its maximum devastation?

The revelation scene begins with assertions of "recognition." Christopher says, "Had I not been expecting to see him, it is perfectly possible I would have failed to recognise Uncle Philip," hinting at an awareness that this recognition scene has been anticipated, perhaps from the very day of his mother's disappearance. Perhaps even more to the point, "Uncle Philip" embodies exactly what Christopher will not or cannot "recognise." Uncle Philip tells him: "You haven't changed so much, you know, Puffin. Easy to see the boy in you, even now" (304), an ironic assertion for one who has been so responsible for encasing "Puffin" in that boyhood! To preserve that innocence, Mrs. Banks and Uncle Philip did not inform Christopher that his father arranged his own disappearance to be with his mistress, and died of typhoid two years later in Singapore. In contrast, Mrs. Banks is still paying an exorbitant price for her idealism in working to eradicate the opium trade introduced into China by her countrymen. Philip, perhaps to help justify his own crimes, explains that she may have pushed her husband into another woman's arms by condemning him for profiting indirectly from the opium trade. Later Christopher's mother offended a Chinese drug lord, Wang Ku, who exacted the revenge of forcing her to become his concubine. Philip conspired in her kidnapping to "save" Puffin, whose upscale lifestyle continues to be supported by his mother's captor, who enjoys whipping Mrs. Banks in front of his dinner guests to demonstrate how he has "tamed" this Englishwoman. Had Philip not so exquisitely preserved Christopher's innocence into early middle age, the narrative might have ended here with the imposition of an unbearable guilt in discovering he has lived well off the sexual colonization of his mother's body by a "foreign devil."

This scene continues, however, as though cruelty released as "revelation" must replicate itself with its own demonic energy. To Puffin's question, "Why torture me like this?" Philip's reply is a surprising accusation of Christopher for thinking he is a "despicable creature." He says, "You've despised me all these years, Puffin, the closest thing I ever had to a son . . ." (314). The real "devil" is not Wang but Philip, who completes this tale with the obscene consequences of his complicity in Diana Banks's tragedy. This "uncle" has been a Claudius who lusted for his brother's wife and saw his opportunity to have her when Mr. Banks decamped with his mistress. Once again her idealism undid Diana Banks, who condemned Philip for his involvement with Wang, who took over the opium trade when the British were forced out. Philip's revenge against Mrs. Banks for her contemptuous rejection of his "love" turns him into Wang's even more perverse "brother." Uncle Philip sadistically revels in revealing to Puffin the countless nights he gratified his lust for Diana Banks to the accompaniment of fantasies in which Wang is raping her as his sexual slave.

And his revelation scene forecasts future horrors. Philip's revelations threaten to force Christopher to confront the evil he was unwittingly a party to, just as Oedipus was crushed by the burden of the Shepherd's well-intentioned but horrible revelations that he "saved" the child so that it could grow up to commit murder and incest. The narrative might pose the question, How does a Puffin live with the knowledge that such obscene evil is still supporting his posh lifestyle? Christopher has had his Conradian encounter with "the horror, the horror," embodied in Philip as a Kurtzian idealist, once a benefactor of humanity, now a moral monster. Paradoxically, Christopher Banks is "saved" by never having been anybody but Puffin. Unlike Oedipus, who can punish himself mercilessly for what he did in ignorance of his parentage, Puffin remains impervious to the guilt from which his "innocence" insulates him.[28] As Marlow lies to protect the "innocence" of Kurtz's intended, Christopher shares none of the truth with his ward, Jennifer, and by extension protects his own innocence of any implication in "the horror, the horror."

Thus, in the scene of his reunion with his mother in Hong Kong, when she is elderly and he himself is approaching old age, Puffin can find "atonement" in a mother's unconditional love. In a sense, her senility has returned her to a period when she "mothered" him from afar by submitting to sexual slavery so her boy could survive. When he asks her to forgive her Puffin, she appears not to recognize him: "Whatever for?" she says, and "beaming" with happiness adds: "That boy. They say he's doing well. You can never be sure with that one. Oh, he's such a worry to me" (328). On his return to England, he reports to his ward, Jennifer, on what may be his delusion of atonement: "I realised she'd never ceased to love me, not through any of it. All she'd ever wanted was for me to have a good life. And all the rest of it, all my trying to find her, trying to save the world from ruin, that wouldn't have made any difference either way. Her feelings for me, they were always just *there*, they didn't depend on anything" (328; italics in original).[29] Like Ishiguro's butler, Stevens, Christopher seems radically disabled from absorbing the "truth." Had he been Oedipus, Puffin might have easily dismissed the Shepherd's revelations with some banal response, such as "Accidents *will* happen!"

Appropriately, the revelation of Uncle Philip's sadism provides the climax to this ersatz detective story. If, as Brooks (like Todorov) theorizes, the detective story offers the quintessential pattern for narrative, it becomes increasingly apparent that the effort of narrative to control the working out of a story as plot—luring the reader toward the revelation at its ending, but also protracting the moment of that revelation to maximize desire for the postponed ending—can resemble the impulses of sadism and its "vicissitude" of masochism. The disengagement of the storyteller from the materials of that story—especially in the detective narrative, in which the investigator and controller of the plot must preserve an "aesthetic distance," lest his "reason" become contaminated by the pathos of the crime's victims—can have a chilling effect on the aficionados of narrative art.

As noted earlier, if the ending comes too quickly, the climax will be flat. For someone else this recognition scene might have generated a later life of "torture." For Ishiguro's detective the recognition scene can do little more than lock him into an impenetrable innocence in which obscene evil can be countered by a mother's love. The narrative reveals Puffin's discovery of whodunit, but however "logical" the revelation may be it seems wildly out of keeping with the detective's world with its delusion of an "evil" easily cordoned off like a cancer to be surgically removed, leaving the dangerous impression that all's well that ends well. It is a world that takes perverse cruelty as a given, perhaps like the power the storyteller arrogates to *him*self to control his material and to force the plot to take its course in a manner advertising that power. The Christophers may believe that a mother's love is enough to counter sadism. Others will have their doubts.

Ishiguro seems to both affirm and subvert the masculine narrative paradigm by offering a dramatic climax and recognition scene along with an ending out of keeping with its middle. Like the springing of the mousetrap in McEwan's *Amsterdam,* Philip's revelation of how evil replicates itself may overwhelm the reader, just as that evil appears unable to penetrate Christopher's schoolboy mentality. The ending eerily recalls the endings of Sherlock Holmes tales, such as "The Speckled Band," arousing the reader's desire for the end. Once the desire is gratified, the knowledge contained in the "solution" to the mystery can prove strangely easy to forget, so that some readers can read the tale over again without being absolutely certain of the "answer." Accordingly, *When We Were Orphans* clearly offers an ending, at the same time it withholds a "sense of the ending." It is not so much that the ending seems a surprise as that this ending crushes the narrative with a perception of "the horror, the horror" so devastating as to be incommensurate with the narrative it completes.

Writing Like a Boy: Steven
Millhauser's *Edwin Mullhouse*

Exploring *When We Were Orphans* offers a useful segue to Steven Millhauser's *Edwin Mullhouse,* a novel that seems yet another classic example
of the masculine narrative paradigm. Like Ishiguro's novel, *Edwin Mullhouse* relies heavily on a "climax" that first-time readers may find difficult to grasp. Just as the "eventfulness" of the ending with its
anagnorisis has been deferred so long that when it comes neither Christopher nor the reader seems able to easily assimilate its import, so too
the ending of Steven Millhauser's "little" novel *Edwin Mullhouse,* with its
heart-pounding climax, seems too large for a narrative, parts of which
many readers will find so exquisitely tedious as to risk exhausting the
resources for narrative, not to mention the reader's patience.

On the face of it, Millhauser's novel may appear "little" because its
subjects are children. More importantly, *Edwin Mullhouse* might be considered "little" because it offers a pastiche of the novel as fictional "biography," making a gesture toward the beginnings of the novel in *Moll
Flanders, Tom Jones, Humphrey Clinker,* and an almost endless list of others.[30] Most importantly, this novel extends that postmodern gesture of
foregrounding itself as a narrative through its trompe d'oeil subtitle, for
this novel is: *Edwin Mullhouse: The Life and Death of an American Writer,
1943–1954 By Jeffrey Cartwright.* Readers may be drawn in by Millhauser's joke in attempting to pass off his novel as a biography written by
an unknown novelist, named Jeffrey Cartwright, a writer who is only
a half-year older than his main character, Edwin Mullhouse, who we
are asked to believe ascended to the pantheon of the "American Writer"
at the tender age of eleven. The English may cherish the memory of a
minor writer such as Thomas Chatterton who died at seventeen, or
John Keats, who had to labor to write the odes he hoped would earn
him admission to the company of Chaucer, Shakespeare, and Milton
before his death at twenty-five. Edwin, however, managed to become
an author as a preadolescent.

The narrative centers then on "littleness" of various kinds. The subject of this ersatz biography is a "little" writer whose "little" biographer/
novelist is a "little" friend whose self-assigned mission is to give a sense
of the magnitude of a life cut "tragically" short by an early death. Because Edwin was a child "author," poor Jeffrey confronts a seemingly
insurmountable task: how to construct a full-length narrative with
barely enough material to fill a paragraph. Like contemporary biogra-

phers, "Jeffrey" has decided that length can be achieved by maximizing the import of the smallest *details* of his friend's experience. In the context of all those gargantuan biographies our age has witnessed, Jeffrey becomes obsessed with the metonyms, or synecdoches, of "Mullhouse." As a biographical narrative *Edwin Mullhouse* resembles, for example, the ponderous first volume (of three) of D. H. Lawrence's life, whose 600+ pages include details such as these: his sister "knitted well" and Lawrence recalled that he "used to pull her hair till she cried" (Worthen 1991, 51).[31] This compulsion to include every "little detail"—suggesting Freud's Hausfrau's complex in its concern for minutiae—implicates this narrative in a lunacy anticipating Cartwright's bizarre revelation in the end.

Jeffrey's obsession with details begins at Edwin's birth, August 9, 1943, an event Jeffrey claims to remember, even though he was only a few days over six months. What is more, when Jeffrey talks to Edwin at ten about becoming his friend's biographer, Edwin claims to remember that meeting. This first section, "The Early Years," includes a list of Edwin's "utterances" at three months, beginning with "*aaaaa* (crying) *nnnnn* (complaining)," followed by "more elaborate combinations" at six months, such as "*chfff* (an early version of Jeffrey?)" and "*keeee* (accompanied by a grin and flapping)" (Millhauser 1972, 17). Then Jeffrey offers the following text, Edwin's "song":

> *keeeeeeeeeee aaaaaaaaaa*
> *keeeeeeeeeee aaaaaaaaaa*
> *keeeeeeeeeeeeeeeeeeeeeeeeeeeeee*
> *koooooooooooo aaaaaaaaaa*
> *koooooooooooo aaaaaaaaaa*
> *koooooooooooooooooooooooooooooo*

This leads the biographer to conclude that the "song" is actually Edwin's "first poem" (20). By extravagantly pointing to Edwin's first "poem" at six months in this "portrait of the artist" as an infant, Jeffrey attempts to one-up Joyce's *Portrait*, to which Millhauser is making unmistakable gestures, recalling the much older (perhaps two-year-old) Stephen Dedalus's lisping "O, the green wothe botheth" (7), often cited as *his* first poem.

Joyce's presence is clear also in Jeffrey's listomania, on display when he names every last book in Edwin's library when he was a toddler. This list runs on for over a half-page (41–42). More than a page and a half is devoted to the citing of the sentence per page of a picture book,

The Lonely Island, for a time Edwin's favorite. In his "middle years" Edwin himself makes a list of the more than two hundred cartoons he has watched, and the narrative cites the entire list, justified by their "influence" on Edwin's "masterpiece," *Cartoons*. This preoccupation with details foregrounds itself in Jeffrey's begging pity for the novelist who "must contrive to drop bits of important information into the swift current of his allpowerful plot" (54). This assertion provides an ironic commentary, since this so-called plot is almost as far from being "allpowerful" as Christopher Banks's "plot" in *When We Were Orphans*.

In these "middle years" Edwin begins to evince the awareness that his "biographer" provides him of his end. Obviously this bizarre narrative partakes of the detective novel in the announcement in its subtitle of Edwin's death at eleven. As the last section, "The Late Years (Aug. 2, 1952—Aug. 1, 1954)," draws near, suspense builds concerning the circumstances of Edwin's early death, and its occurrence on his eleventh birthday, to boot! One clue is provided when Edwin shows Jeffrey the Colt automatic he got from the boyish desperado Arnold Hasselstrom, for a time Jeffrey's serious rival for Edwin's friendship. Edwin's tenth birthday party, the narrative indicates, was his last. Similarly, another chapter begins with the reminder that for Edwin fifth grade was his last. If Walter Benjamin was in fact accurate in his assertion that death is the flame at which narrative warms itself, then this story—immersed for over two hundred pages in a "feminine" obsession with details, deferring its climax—is beginning to rouse itself through its desire for the end. As a preadolescent, Jeffrey has an intellectual knowledge that desire impels narrative toward its ending, but he is presumably not yet old enough to imagine his narrative as the map of desire. Like his boyish brother-in-narrating, Christopher Banks, Jeffrey is signally inept in getting to the endgame expeditiously.

Increasingly this narrative reveals itself as metanarrative, foregrounding its awareness of itself as a story and rehearsing its preoccupations with the traditional model of narrative theorized by Kermode, Scholes, Barthes, Brooks, and Co. A half-year before Edwin dies, Jeffrey stuns him with the announcement that he intends to become his friend's biographer. Tellingly, Edwin asks Jeffrey if he has considered the difficulty of writing the biography of someone who is not dead. The chapter ends ominously with Jeffrey's rejoinder: "'You don't have to be dead,' I sneered, though as it turned out I was mistaken" (270). Unlike the youthful Sartre imagining his distant obituary, Edwin resists at first the construct of biography because it bears the smell of death. Jeffrey must assure Edwin that his subject need not die to prepare for his biography, and yet the seed has been planted. Conventional wisdom still contends that the subjects of biography can oblige their biographers by being deceased to remove the anxiety that further "life" after the biography is published might radically change its meaning.

Edwin and his biographer soon become immersed in the game of manipulating life as the raw material for art. Or, to be more accurate, Edwin plays the game: "'Life is useful,' he would say, twirling an imaginary mustache, 'for the purposes of fiction. Jot that down, Jeffrey'" (276). Jeffrey, however, is *deadly* serious about this game of choosing one's death to give meaning to one's art—in this case, Edwin's "masterpiece," *Cartoons*. After announcing his intention to become his chum's biographer, Jeffrey begins to fetishize the debut of his own art. His description of going to his room the night after his conversation with Edwin about writing his biography is full of the details that seem to be riveting this experience in his consciousness. He focuses on the "brand new three-ring notebook in blue cloth" and the "brand new perfectly sharpened No. 2 yellow hexagonal pencil" with which he drafts the title, "EDWIN MULLHOUSE: THE LIFE OF AN AMERICAN WRITER" (276). He may stare at the blank page for three hours without writing a single word; however, when he turns out the light, Jeffrey ominously records "how bright that blackness was, how lively that silence" (276). The power to construct the "life" of his friend Edwin, to turn life into art, overwhelms this fledgling writer. With the benefit of hindsight, the reader is left to wonder how much that "blackness" and that "silence" represent Jeffrey's epiphany of an even greater power to shape his subject's life by generating its ending, a silent explosion of black light.

Edwin, however, is ambivalent about this game of being the subject of a biography right from the start. He may assure his friend that Jeffrey has "'saved' his 'soul' by making him think of his life as a biography—that is, a design with a beginning, middle, and end"—and yet Edwin pains his friend by relegating this game to other children's games (277). Part of this subject's ambivalence toward the biography game may well be apprehension about the "endgame," that sense of ending luring him to desire knowledge of the end, but with the corollary uneasiness about the end. This uneasiness may be assuaged through the "aesthetic" game of suicide, that is, playing with the knowledge that the end will come at a predetermined time. At one point Edwin asks Jeffrey to consider the "'design'" one's life would have after learning the precise day on which he would die (278). Edwin glosses that concern with "design" in the context of writing, where knowledge of the end has a tremendous impact on what leads up to it. With surprising speed Edwin has established that "time": 1:06 a.m., August 1, 1954, his eleventh birthday.

Jeffrey's stress on Edwin's "aesthetic" preoccupation with "design" is of course a projection of his own. It is Jeffrey, the mad artist, who "jokingly" offers his friend the line, "'I aspire to the condition of fiction'" (279). Later in his performance of a decadent's privileging of art over life, Edwin will end his suicide note with the postscript, "Goodbye, life. I aspire to the condition of fiction" (296), moving *Edwin Mullhouse* toward a pastiche of Sartre's notion of becoming one's obituary. And yet it is Jeffrey who is compelled as biographer to shape his friend's life as art. Short though Edwin's life may be, it is divided for Jeffrey into three parts, and he can already see his subject approaching his "tragic end": having finished his book, Edwin has nothing left to do but "bow and depart" (281). This "book" presumably is *Cartoons*; however, this "book" we are reading becomes Edwin's biography, whose subject dies at the prearranged moment of the highest aesthetic appeal.

Moving into the endgame, "mere pages" from the ending, desire for knowledge of Edwin's death draws the narrative forward without check. This "climax" promises to offer the metaphorical transformation of metonymic details into transcendent meaning: how Edwin dies will move this narrative to a new level on which its readers will be repaid in a moment of recognition for the tedium of moving through its "middle," all those pages of exhausting detail with which the narrator/author has been obsessed. Jeffrey, however, has not completed his hausfrau's function of providing the plethora of details deferring the narrative's desire for its end. Accordingly, he itemizes the contents of his "small overnight bag" right down to a description of the wrapping paper on his birthday gift to Edwin (289). This pastiche of the storyteller's strategy of a seemingly endless deferral of the end is duplicated in the list of the contents of Edwin's closet, a list too long to cite here, as we too lean forward expectantly to the end.

These details give way to the countdown to 1:06 a.m. When Jeffrey handles the "suicide weapon," Edwin cautions him to wipe off his fingerprints. Drawn into the game of art, Jeffrey remarks: "Carefully I wiped the clip and gun and then reloaded without touching metal. For indeed I had no desire that his suicide should be mistaken for murder" (298–99), a powerfully ambiguous assertion in its dedication to "truth." "You're so serious, Jeffrey," Edwin giggles naively, and when 1:06 finally arrives he *says*, "Bang, I'm dead" (301), falling to his bed with the "silent gun." Signification rapidly becomes slippery here, as this modifier "silent" denotes both "fired" and "unfired." The chapter's ending provides its readers impatiently waiting for the end a real bang for their buck: "In a split second I was leaning over him, gripping the gun-gripping hand; and I remember thinking, quite lucidly in the midst of a dreamy numbness, that the entry under "I Am Born" in MY STORY: A BABY RECORD allowed a certain leeway in the matter of seconds" (301).

In this way the narrative performs the reader's desire for the end through the author—Jeffrey—who has shown just how far he will go to transform the "messiness of life" into "meaning."

The "climax" represented by the single sentence in which Jeffrey implicates himself in Edwin's death provides an ending that is both melodramatic in its extensive buildup and yet curiously undramatic, because it fails to square itself with the rest of the narrative.[31] In conventional detective-story fashion, the narrative certainly offers enough clues to this ending; Edwin and Jeffrey *are*, however, still children, or what our culture has constructed as the child. What's disturbing, of course, is Jeffrey's absolute lack of remorse. Indeed, he describes how three hours after murdering its subject he is hard at work beginning the "biography" of his friend, carefully supplying a caret and the words "AND DEATH" to its subtitle. This provides the very retrospection readers may have anticipated in the earlier scene when Jeffrey stared for three hours at the blank notebook in which he intended to write his friend's biography, but presumably could not begin because Edwin was still very much alive. Once again, he fetishistically offers the details in a kind of autoerotic gesture, focusing on the "three-ring notebook and a sharp No. 2 yellow hexagonal pencil" (303), the latter for all the world like the instrument with which he will nail his subject to that blank page. The apparent absence of remorse for his crime is belied by Jeffrey's mad compulsion to write, well aware that stopping might cause him to "brood . . ." (303). In retrospect it is clear that the tedious drawing out of the story to 300 pages represents its narrator's defense against the guilt and more conventional evidences of madness such "brooding" might produce: "I forced myself to go more slowly, to reflect more deeply, to write more carefully, to revise elaborately all my earlier pages" (304).

In the end Jeffrey even allows himself the fantasy of Edwin's having one-upped him, because his death forced on his "biographer" this compulsion to write. Jeffrey makes a play for his reader's sympathy as "the foul devil lashed to a relentless hell" to which he has been consigned through the "usual cunning" of his "innocent and sainted" subject (305). Millhauser offers here yet another facet of the mad artist in Jeffrey's self-serving delusion that he has been "feminized" by Edwin, the male with the power to compel his friend to murder him in order to finalize his short life's meaning in this *Kunstlersroman,* or "portrait of the artist." This sense of Jeffrey as the laboring storyteller whose subject he has killed off to make his art is one we need to bookmark for the discussion of Ian McEwan's *Atonement.*

Steven Millhauser offers a bizarre "detective story" acknowledging its debt to Poe, its inventor. This tediously long "little" novel buries its readers with details to test their persistence in making it all the way to end, but even more to maintain their vigilance in processing those details. Incredible though it might be to imagine in this pastiche of the detective story, a less than ideal reader might read the death scene so carelessly as to miss Jeffrey's telltale admission of guilt in the passage cited above, where it seems evident that Jeffrey turned "assisted suicide" into murder. The prototype for Jeffrey as mad storyteller is Poe's narrator in "The Tell-Tale Heart" whose madness inheres in his semblance of rationality. After sending up a "silent prayer to the guardian spirit of Biography for having impelled me to make a copy of *Cartoons,*" Jeffrey indicates his plan to send copies of *Cartoons* and his biography to professors at a nearby college, who will help him find a publisher (303). This aspiration offers a joke within a joke. Self-deluded writer that he is, Jeffrey fails to anticipate that sharing this manuscript with anyone who knows how to read carefully could lead to severe consequences, such as, his facing criminal charges for Edwin's death. Within the logic of this text however, that is exactly what did not happen, for the text exists within its readers' hands.

These issues take us back in the text to its "introduction." Like epilogues and afterwords, introductions are indeterminate texts, part inside and part outside the text. This one is clearly part of the narrative because it supports the joke of this novel's being written, not by Steven Millhauser but by Jeffrey Cartwright. The ersatz introduction, ascribed to the fictional Walter Logan White, frames the narrative with another joke. "White" claims to have met Jeffrey in sixth grade, presumably the year after Edwin's demise. He recalls Jeffrey as a nerdy "brain" who carried his books in his arms as a girl might. Perhaps because they never spoke and White left within a year, he forgot Jeffrey until ten years later, when he "discovered" *Edwin Mullhouse* in a used bookstore near Columbia. White turns out to be a "professor" who cites his own critical article in the ersatz scholarly *Journal of American Letters* 22 (1966): 22–43, in which he proclaims Cartwright's novel "a modern classic." Not surprisingly, Jeffrey Cartwright cannot be found, and White expresses hope that he never will be. Despite his assertion that his article "takes issue with a number of lively misreadings of Jeffrey's pellucid work" (viii), the joke seems to be on White as well for having missed the point in commending a murderous biographer and misread the ending.

WRITING "LIKE A MAN": MARGARET ATWOOD'S *THE BLIND ASSASSIN*

Margaret Atwood's *The Blind Assassin* also offers a detective story of a kind. As her given name suggests, Iris Chase Griffen, the narrator, is an "eye" as well as an "I." Her function as master of the narrative gaze resembles Christopher's in the Ishiguro novel, even though obviously Iris is a female narrator, constructed by a female author. The narrative gaze in Iris, moreover, exceeds the power of Christopher's, because from the very outset it is clear that Iris is more deeply implicated in the story she is telling than the boyish "Puffin" was with his. Even more than in Ishiguro's pastiche of the detective novel, *The Blind Assassin* begins with a strong sense of a possible crime that may have been committed, making the novel a clearer expression of the whodunit than *When We Were Orphans*, with its ironically inept narrator/detective. As noted earlier, the premise of Christopher's "writing" the novel as a "journal," recording events as they occur, undermines the reader's confidence that this narrator is telling a story whose ending he knows.

Iris's narration begins with a parody of the conventional dramatic opening sentence: "Ten days after the war ended, my sister Laura drove a car off a bridge." This blunt assertion with its ambiguous "drove" raises immediate questions: Was Laura's death the result of an ordinary automobile accident or did she commit suicide? In either case, what led up to her death? Was anybody responsible for Laura's "precipitous" death? Iris makes it clear that she, if anyone, should know the circumstances of her sister's death, and that she will *in good time* reveal the "truth" toward which this narrative has been set in motion with its first sentence, almost as though Iris had read some of the late twentieth-century theorizing about the arousal of desire for the end with its accompanying desire to know. As in *When We Were Orphans*, the power to reveal the truth at the end of narrative and to control, even to manipulate, the reader's desire for the end genders Iris as "masculine" in a complex of power positions within which she has finally gained ascendancy. Like Elaine Risley in *Cat's Eye* and Grace Marks in *Alias Grace*, among other female leads in Atwood's earlier fiction, Iris has prevailed over the losses of a past in which her powerlessness has "feminized" her, and she has now become empowered as a survivor of potential victimhood, in part through the agency of her writing.

Iris's mastery of the truth and thus her mastery of the narrative revealing this truth have been enhanced by her advanced age and this narrative's confessional mode. Iris's heart has put her on notice it could fail her at any time. While she is writing, Iris is made dramatically aware of her narrating as a race with time;[32] at the same time, the possible nearness of death is also liberating. Too little life remains to be concerned with "consequences," her advanced age freeing her to speak her mind, like Lear at the end of his life. Iris's narrating raises those issues of timing, theorized by Brooks in the conflict between the desire for the knowledge promised at the end and the counterdesire to postpone the end. As Hamlet remarks of his possibly imminent death, "The readiness is all." Given that its narrator might not survive to finish her job, *The Blind Assassin* generates anxiety; there is comfort, however, in the first "law" of first-person narration, namely, that the narrator *must* survive until the plot is complete.

The Blind Assassin cues its readers that a major revelation will come as the "climax" of this long narrative by engaging them in a race with Iris to guess the truth before she reveals it. Part of that "truth" is the identity of the woman in the novel-within-a-novel. That mystery pales, however, before the whodunit theme for which readers become "detectives" on the model of Iris herself, the detective who may, like Oedipus, turn out to be the criminal as well. The dealing out of clues must be meticulously managed, since obviously readers enjoy having their suspicions confirmed at the end, but not too soon, lest they lose interest in the story. In contrast, even though Grace (in the Atwood novel that immediately preceded *The Blind Assassin*) is the object of the focalization—to borrow Gérard Genette's useful term—her complicity in the murders of her master, Thomas Kinnear, and his mistress, Nancy Montgomery, cannot be so easily established, since many years have elapsed and Grace herself cannot "confess" to having been a free and willing accomplice in any psychologically credible manner. Laura Chase's suicide is far different, since from the beginning Iris subtly communicates the knowability of the suicide's causes and indeed even who is responsible for it.[33] The very length of *The Blind Assassin* suggests that knowing the truth will be possible, in the fullness of time, but only by establishing its background.

Furthermore, it must be remembered that Iris is not only a "character"/narrator in this text but also an "author," albeit an unacknowledged one. Because Iris, *not* her sister Laura, is the author of the novel-within-a-novel, this text entitled *The Blind Assassin* that she is also supposedly "writing" becomes ever the more deeply implicated in textuality. It might even be argued that Atwood's novel is in its own way a narratological text, *representing* narrative as an example of a story but also raising some fascinating issues *about* narrativity itself.

In this way, the narrative becomes metafictional in the *mise en abîme* effect of its novel-within-a-novel construction but also in its masquerading as a novel being generated before the reader's eyes.[34] Periodically the novel focuses on an Iris who is preoccupied with the act of writing. The effect is not only to enhance the self-reflexive, metafictional status of the text but also to increase the anxiety that its narrator might not reach The End. In part this strategy makes the not entirely positive character Iris more sympathetic by emphasizing the humor of her "whistling past the graveyard." Iris is not morbidly preoccupied with death, but she savors the irony of her state, recalling a youth in which she occasionally expressed a desire for the very death that will soon become a reality, even though she may no longer have that desire (Atwood 2000, 42). Through Iris the narrative focuses on the writing scene, likening her fingers to inefficient and unreliable writing instruments, as she writes, "hunched over as if sewing[35] by moonlight" (Atwood 2000, 43). Later she comments on how pens "no longer scratch" but allow the words she writes to "roll smoothly and soundlessly . . . ; it's getting them to flow down the arm, it's squeezing them out through the fingers, that is so difficult" (66). Iris's whole body has become the writing instrument, recording this narrative.[36]

This trope of the writing body has other implications, as the narrative explores provocative issues of the audience for texts and the impact of a sense of audience on the writer's function as a constructor of "truth." At first Iris claims she has no reader or audience in mind because she has no aspiration to write for a "stranger," and she herself may be a long shot as a prospective reader of her own text, since she may not have enough time left to write it, much less read it: "Perhaps I write for no one" (43). As it becomes less possible to "write for no one" and she identifies Myra, her nanny's daughter, and then more importantly her granddaughter Sabrina as her prospective reader, Iris's troping of the writing act gathers implications. She notes that writing with no audience in mind may be the only way to represent the truth, because any sense of audience, even the writer herself as a prospective reader in the future, undermines the potential truth as the writer begins to excuse herself. Impossible though it may be to imagine such a writing practice, the writer, according to Iris,[37] must be prepared to erase with the left hand what the right hand has just written. The passage ends with Iris almost crooning, as though the words were casting a spell on what she is writing, the following invocation: "I pay out my line, I pay out my line, this black thread I'm spinning across the page" (283). In this way Iris appears to be admitting her own unreliability as a narrator.[38] Quite simply, it may not be possible to avoid "excusing yourself" as a writer when there is an identified reader in mind. In addition, her repeated troping of the flow of the words from her body as a "line" can suggest two equally important (and less than positive) implications: either Iris is "feeding a line" to her readers with the bait of a revelation to come when they are "hooked," or she is spinning out the thread of a web in which unwary readers will eventually find themselves ensnared.[39]

Through this seemingly unintentional troping of her writing as a "line," Iris contributes to the textuality of this narrative, making it more similar to *Alias Grace* than might at first seem apparent. It ought not to be missed that much of the life Grace is textualizing for the benefit of her doctor/analyst was troped in the context of sewing, especially patchwork quilting. Grace stresses that she is very deliberately choosing what to tell Dr. Jordan. She could well be dangling the baited hook of her dead friend Mary's demonic spirit as acting through her (Grace), thus supporting the novel's title, *Alias Grace*. Alternately, the line or thread with which Grace sews may well suggest a web of textuality in which she hopes to trap the intelligent but naive Dr. Jordan, whose desire for Grace is implicated in his desire to exculpate her of guilt in the deaths of Kinnear and Montgomery. Like Iris, Grace becomes increasingly concerned with the audience for her narrative, for if she is to be set free before the completion of her sentence she must persuade Jordan of her "innocence."

Brian McHale's distinction between modernist and postmodern narrative is useful here. McHale argues that modernist narrative is energized by the "epistemological dominant," the desire to know. A novel like William Faulkner's *Absalom, Absalom!* is set in motion for McHale by Quentin Compson and his Canadian roommate Shreve's pursuit of the truth of Quentin's family as well as his cultural heritage. On the other hand, postmodern narrative is grounded in the "ontological dominant," the exploration of a world in which issues of truth and knowability are destined to remain indeterminate. Unlike *Alias Grace*, whose readers grow less confident the truth of Grace's culpability can ever be determined, *The Blind Assassin* offers a narrative in which the truth will ultimately be revealed. Accordingly, Iris's reliability as a narrator be-

comes crucial to *The Blind Assassin*, whose ending promises to reveal
long-awaited and unambiguous truths. In *The Blind Assassin* Atwood is
constructing a modernist narrative much closer to the whodunit she
was deconstructing in *Alias Grace*, with its metafictional patchwork quilt
of received and "fabricated" texts that end up problematizing the conventional boundaries between textuality and reality.

Despite some similarity in the functioning of Grace and Iris as perso-
nae, *The Blind Assassin* is moving toward a different kind of ending. This
is a story that must end in tragedy, because Iris alone knows who is
guilty of precipitating Laura's death. In "The Blind Assassin," the
novel-within-the-novel, the man tells the woman that he can only tell
sad stories "because at the end [of life] everyone dies" (Atwood 2000,
349). Iris recalls a motel whose name, "Journeys End," must have
sounded "too sinister, a building all entrances but no exits" because it
was eventually changed to "Journeys. . . . So much better to travel than
to arrive" (290). Iris is well aware that she is nearing the end of her
own "crabwise"[40] journey across the sheet of paper on which she is
writing: "It's a slow race now, between me and my heart, but I intend
to get there first. Where is there? The end, *The End*. One or the other.
Both are destinations, of a sort" (222–23; italics in original).

Eventually Iris subverts her earlier commitment to writing "the
truth"—erasing with the left hand what was written with the right—
when she admits that she is writing "to" Sabrina and also that she is
reading what she has been writing. It is not a matter of inaccuracy that
she is concerned with so much as the omissions. Reading what she has
written, she condemns it on the grounds of "frivolity" (417), the details
making up the daily lives of the characters as they await the tragedy
waiting in the wings for them. These "details" are also the metonyms of
desire for this *middle* of life readers may understandably want to prolong
against its counterpart, the desire for the end. Iris makes much of those
seemingly trivial details preceding the moment in which tragedy strikes.
Metonymic details representing the desire to connect us with experience in time function here as a temporary counterbalance to the desire
for a metaphoric ending that will allow meaning to show itself forth, but
at a terrible price. Indeed, as Iris's revelations begin to approach in her
narrating, she frustrates readers with a maddening array of details—
metonyms of desire for everyday life—impediments now to the head-
long rush of the desire to end this narrative and to *know*.

That epiphany toward which Iris is leading her readers is in part the
revelation of what Yeats called the "fury and mire of human veins."
Looking back to the fatal encounter of the sisters a half-century earlier,

Iris alone can reveal that it was probably *she* who pushed Laura toward suicide by telling her why she, and not Laura, received the telegram announcing Alex's death. Furthermore, she appears to have the need to emphasize that she *had* a choice: "I could have said, *There must have been a mistake, it must have been meant for you.* . . . Instead I said, '. . . we'd been lovers, you see'" (488; italics in original). Clearly this is "the end," or climax, toward which Iris has been leading her detective-readers, who should have already figured out this "truth" by the point of its revelation. And yet the ending Iris cares about most involves her function as "writer" and perhaps as "blind assassin."

Here again Atwood's choice of title seems a gesture toward modernism. The *mise en abîme* effect of the novel-within-a-novel has less to do with moving the narrative toward a metafictional position in which readers suspect that everything is text than with teasing them to pursue the identity of this "Blind Assassin." Barbara Mujica speculates that Time itself is the Blind Assassin. In contributing to Laura's death by sharing the "truth" of being Alex's lover, Iris certainly qualifies for that title. As so often happens with these long-postponed and mighty revelations at the ends of novels, there is too little time to examine fully the implications of Iris's apparent "slip of the tongue" in revealing what she herself later indicates she had no need to disclose, almost as though she is marveling at the power of the unconscious to "speak" through her as though she were the Delphic oracle dispensing a knowledge that will prove deadly. It is ironic that when readers move to this "recognition scene" in which Iris reveals her complicity in Laura's death, they are encouraged to focus on all of these players as moving in a tragedy for which Iris appears to be the stage manager and recorder.

Iris reveals herself to be less concerned with the *fact* of her complicity in Laura's death than with the need to lift the story of Laura, Alex, and herself out of the trivia, or "frivolity," of life into the stability and stasis of tragedy, or art. Iris as the self-styled tragic artist offers two alternatives to tragedy within her text; not surprisingly, both are varieties of Garden stories. The first is the narrative made up by the man in the novel-within-a-novel when the woman wants a story with a happy ending. The Alex figure offers her the story "Peach Women of Aa'A." In it Will and Boyd discover an Eden of instant gratification, but Will decides that this cannot be anything like paradise, because "anything you can't get out of is Hell" (355). The other paradise is the photograph with which the story begins and to which Iris returns at the end. Iris stares into the picture of Alex, acknowledging that this is the paradise lost to which she has sought to build a memorial. It is a world in which "[s]he's never been this happy before. Everything is fresh again, still to be enacted" (11).

The story Iris is attempting to craft is diametrically opposed to the photograph's world she desperately wants to memorialize. In contrast to the photograph representing happiness, this (or any) story can never represent happiness: "Happiness is a garden walled with glass; there's no way in or out. In Paradise there are no stories, because there are no journeys. It's loss and regret and misery and yearning that drive the story forward, along its twisted road" (518). As a storyteller Iris seeks to fit the narrative as "journey" into the glass-walled garden of happiness. Because this novel is more modernist than postmodern, the text inevitably generates the question of who or what the Blind Assassin of its title might be. By returning to this photograph as though it were a work of art—a painting of the Garden of Eternal Delights, a glimpse of new love that can never grow old—the narrative fashions a site of *ekphrasis*, a looking into a work of art with echoes of the ambivalence at the center of Keats's *Ode on a Grecian Urn*. Art impels the creator to lift material from its immersion in time, where love and beauty are born only to die, and to transform experience by distilling its essence for art. The price of that transformation, as Keats was tragically aware, is life itself. As an "artist," Iris must be cruel only to be kind to the essence of experience. If Iris and Alex's love for each other is to have its "memorial," first Laura's and then Iris's lives have to be sacrificed to this impulse to freeze time before the Blind Assassin can steal what is most precious to them—and to all of us. Yeats, who accounted himself one of the "last romantics," memorialized the evanescence of what humans value in the haunting lines: "Man is in love and loves what vanishes, / What more is there to say?"[41]

If, as Iris "confesses," *The Blind Assassin* was a memorial for herself as well as for Alex (512), the novel in which it is nested as a Chinese box or Russian doll is more importantly a memorial to the modernist concept of transformation. The novel's last scene celebrates the modernist (perhaps Yeatsian) artist struggling in one last effort to bring the narrative to its conclusion, with an interesting metafictional twist. Iris has been anxious about the survival of the manuscript representing most of the novel—with the notable exception of the newspaper clippings, positing a "real" world outside this memoir of Iris—against the vagaries of a world in which handwritten manuscripts have a romantic vulnerability.[42] Iris's demise is announced in the newspaper report, preceding the last segment of the novel. She was found sitting in her garden where she was writing, a site Yeats would identify as "no country" for the old.[43] It's spring and "almost dusk," Iris writes, and the "wild phlox is in bloom." She continues: "The scent of moist dirt and fresh growth washes over me. . . . It smells like youth; it smells like heart-break" (Atwood 2000, 520). The images here of "moist dirt and fresh growth" (especially the almost painfully lush colors of wild phlox) echo the tropes of the older Yeats, exiled from this "country" of the young. The "moist dirt" recalls the "shit" Reenie once advised Iris in a rare moment of self-abandonment that people have to put up with in order to get the flowers. It is also Yeats's "mire of human veins," without which there is no art.

Iris ends by questioning whether her manuscript will ever be found. She intends to stow it in the steamer trunk that now contains her trous-seau for the afterlife. Since the newspaper report indicates her corpse was discovered in the garden, the narrative offers an existential frisson, as we read Iris's last words, knowing the manuscript obviously *was* found because it became this novel, *The Blind Assassin*, we hold in our hands. Thus, the end of Iris's narrating eerily coincides with the end of her life and a moment of confidence and resignation in putting herself in the reader's hands, literally and metaphorically: "By the time you read this last page, that—if anywhere—is the only place I will be" (521).

As these lines suggest, the text on which Iris had been working in her last days has been completed and "found"—by Myra or perhaps even Sabrina. Its existence as a text in hand raises provocative questions. In a Brooksian context, where is the ending here? Is the ending Iris's revelation that she uncovered her relationship with Alex just before Laura took her own life? That certainly *seems* to be the kind of ending Brooks could accept as a climax, one allowing the narrative to move metaphorically onto another plane by undergoing a transformation to provide the sensation of knowing/feeling what this long narrative has been meaning to mean. Clearly, it offers that anagnorisis at which "an-ticipation of retrospection" finds its end, along with the details of the long middle that now line up like iron filings near a magnet. Still, there are alternative "endings."

One plot that is ending involves Iris's life after the deaths of Laura and Richard. The narrative sketchily offers some motivation for her so-cial suicide in her inconsolable grief at losing Alex. In addition, the plot demands that Iris must become socially and morally vulnerable, so that her wicked sister-in-law can gain custody of the daughter who bore the name of Iris's husband, even though the child was probably, but only *probably*, not his. Iris as narrator makes a very *large* point of Aimee, the "love child," having dark hair, while Iris and her husband's family are all fair. How much is Aimee's paternity "history," and how much is it the "fiction" in which this narrative implicates itself? Iris constructs her memoir as the tragedy of a woman sold into a loveless marriage by her bankrupt father to preserve the family's social and economic standing, only to lose the only man she ever loved, along with her reputation, and even the love of her lost daughter, a kind of Perdita. The further loss of her granddaughter, Sabrina, recalls Greek tragedy, with the curse on this house of Chase being visited unto the last generation, reminiscent of Faulkner's doomed aristocratic families running out in a "watering of the blood" in the final generations. Iris even adds a "Gothic" or Harlequin Romance[44] element to generate speculation about Myra's paternity. With little support for the speculation, Iris slyly hints that she and Myra may have had the same father (Atwood 2000, 388). This passage is fascinating also for the narrator's impulse toward cruelty in playing cat and mouse with the feelings of Myra, on whom she has depended in her last days, and taunting her for curiosity in reading this book.[45] Approaching death, Iris may become a more sympathetic figure, and yet her narration is painfully implicated in a sadism such as this gratuitous cruelty to yet another potential "sister."

And there is Iris's life as an artist that also qualifies as an alternative "plot" coming to its ending. In the end, so much in the other plots of this novel comprises what Iris sees as "trivia." This "memoir" she has been composing implicates the narrative in several issues of "ending" and "closure." Because in the context of her own trope, Iris has *not* erased with the left hand what she wrote with the right, she has been implicated—as are we all—in establishing her own private and idiosyncratic version of the past, just as Port Ticonderoga's war memorial has frozen into art the community's ravenous desire to believe in the efficacy of "sacrifice." In the context of Time as the Blind Assassin of everything that humans value, one means of contesting time, of beating the Blind Assassin to one's own throat, is through art. One strategy of the artist is to offer up sacrifices of experience to the Blind Assassin as artifacts, a strategy mitigated by the awareness that this cruel divinity demands what we are all required to pay to time anyway, but with the promise of "memorials" by which the detritus of experience may be saved for the future.

There is also the very large issue of closure in Iris's emotional life. As the newspaper report indicates, her corpse was discovered in her garden chair, presumably with the manuscript she meant to stow in her steamer trunk. Was it Myra who found her? Or has this narrative of Iris's heart veered into the territory of Shakespeare's "problem plays," those "mouldy tales" in which the lost child Perdita may be found or the dead wife Hermione recuperated when her statue comes to life? Could Sabrina have arrived as her grandmother was dying, after penning the last words of her "memoir"? Was it Sabrina who saw the manuscript through its publication as a gesture of reconciliation, like those similar gestures the aging Shakespeare became so fond of in his late plays? Is there enough to ground such a satisfying sense of closure—the circle of the family closed once more with Sabrina finally coming to understand and thereby transcend animosities to love her grandmother at last and publish this memoir as a "memorial" to Iris, despite the unpleasant matters it reveals about her forebears? Even here this novel performs its own title by representing the way in which the human impulse to make sacrifices for art, or "memorials," may be overriding the understandably human instincts in a Myra or a Sabrina to destroy this sorry history of the family, just as the Blind Assassin—time—seems to have destroyed the desires for love in the family. If we grant that suffering and loss are inevitable anyway, is it better to bear witness passively to the stealthy assassinations of time, or to construct "war memorials" celebrating the victory of one Blind Assassin only by replicating its depredations in the name of sacrifices to art? This narrative that begins by performing the stimulation of desire to know, as the "beginning" of plot, ends by problematizing the quasi ending it rehearses, offering a "truth" more indeterminate than readers might desire.

The conclusion of *The Blind Assassin* raises provocative questions about ending, because like many other contemporary novels—for example, *This Side of Brightness* and *Waterland*, to be examined soon—the plot of the "present" is coming to its end as the story of the "past" is concluding. These two plotlines are not simply running on parallel rails, and yet the two stories have an impact on each other so that the past is recounted in a manner that illuminates the present, just as the "present" of the narrative controls what is being remembered of the past. Iris's revelation of how she spoke Laura's doom by indicating Alex was her lover may seem at first the ending readers have leaned forward in anticipation of eventually knowing. It is, however, the consequences of that "ending" that ultimately have greater moment for the reader.

THE METAPHORICITY OF ENDING: COLUM McCANN'S *THIS SIDE OF BRIGHTNESS*

This Side of Brightness offers a classic example of the masculine narrative paradigm. It provides a particularly useful example by affirming the very deep implication of the paradigm in not only realist narrative, but especially in modernist fiction, whose endings often credit the potential for transformation. Such narrative finds its analogy in detective fiction, also centered in ending as a metaphor for transformation. Just as the reader of a Sherlock Holmes story is drawn toward the ending because the detective's revelations will transform ignorance and confusion into the "solution," so too the reader of the modernist novel leans forward to its ending because modernism is grounded in the persistent faith that the daily bread of life can be transformed into something lasting and transcendent. The troping of modernism's transformative powers as religious, particularly Roman Catholic, makes a gesture toward arguably the greatest modernist, James Joyce, who appropriated the symbol of the Eucharist to represent the priestly artist celebrating the ascension of bread into Body. This Eucharist trope offers a useful entry to an understanding of the monumental stature of the "work of art" and the sense that each modernist was unique. Proust, Joyce, Woolf, and Faulkner might all be working within a similar mode, conventionally classified as "stream of consciousness," and yet few readers would confuse the work of one with the work of any other of these modernists.

The postmodern text, on the other hand, appears toward the end of modernism, and other literary "periods" when the writer gives the appearance of having read too much. Roland Barthes's notion of the *déjà lu* is useful as a reminder of the complex intertextuality within which a text comes into being as an inevitable reading of the "already read." The weight of that *déjà lu* can strain modernist faith and trouble the assurance of any narrative that the intersection of the evanescent and the eternal in an epiphany is possible. It loosens the substantiality of the ending so that the climax may seem routine, pat, even a violation of the integrity of the middle. Modernism and postmodernism interpenetrate within the moment as two binary "opposites" being simultaneously present—like the optical illusion of the white vase and the black silhouettes of two faces. This conjunction of modernism and the postmodern is crucial to the construction of an ending with the power to give the illusion of difference and yet preserve the past, that long middle for which the ending opens a door into the light, while standing in the good darkness it will not wholly relinquish. *This Side of Brightness* is just such a crossing of modernist and postmodern impulses.

This Side of Brightness plays with these binaries of light and darkness, present and past, death and rebirth, ending and middle, on a complex scale of narrative possibilities. The novel alternates between two time frames, one beginning in 1991, the other in 1916. The time frame of the past, or "History," beginning in 1916 engages in a leapfrogging to catch up with a present in which time seems immobilized. In the present, day merely repeats day in a variety of repetition compulsion. Time is being filled, or killed, or served within the "nest" of Treefrog, the viewpoint character, who has receded into a monastic cell of faithless, compulsive, animal existence. The narrative is impelled toward satisfying—in its own good time—the desire to know why a man of Treefrog's gifts has gone "underground," in service to a metaphor stretching back through Ellison to Dostoevsky to create the sense of the "already read" within the context of *Invisible Man* and *Notes from Underground*. The locus of anomie and despair in the central consciousness of the 1991 plot generates a corollary desire to "know" experientially that the world above of light and space has not been forever foreclosed. The narrative rehearses a working through of the past and specifically Treefrog's past, to find the door into the future and to risk crossing its threshold. As the history that includes Nathan Walker barrels along on its rails toward the present, Treefrog's past looms increasingly larger on the narrative's scene, as if to meet this seemingly unrelated past. Desire to know what kind of past produced this future of Treefrog grows more intense as the number of pages dwindles. It is enhanced by that other desire to credit the possibility of clambering up out of the dark prison/nest of compulsion that has forced, not only Treefrog but also the Walker Family, America, humanity, and finally narrative itself, to rehearse endlessly all their stories in pursuit of an ending that promises release from the compulsion to repeat the history of injustice and suffering.

That is the ending(s) we are impelled to begin with, and it is tempting at this point to explore the complex and powerful dimensions of its metamorphosis, as all the binaries the narrative has been oscillating between are reconciled in a moment of imaginative and spiritual ascension, suggesting a Eucharistic transfiguration. In Joycean terms, however, we would give in to impatience here by attempting to consume the bread and wine of artistic transformation without reverencing their long history in the grain and the grape that made such an end possible. It is that middle to which we must return, because just as the beginning of narrative represents a return to a past completed before the first word is spoken/written, so too it is the long "middle" of narrative that focusing on narrative's climax can often obscure.

That middle of *This Side of Brightness* begins in 1916 with Nathan Walker, a "Negro" "sandhog" three years older than his century. Although it begins in 1991 with the devastated "homelessness" of Treefrog, the narrative follows its own logic in launching backward to the year before the United States entered World War I. It quickly lays down material to contextualize the 1916 event that actually begins the plot within a story of sandhogging, or tunneling, beneath New York's East River. The focus is a team of sandhogs including Con O'Leary and his fellow Irishman (perhaps a Protestant one) Sean Power; "Rhubarb" Vannucci, the Italian, or "Mediterranean Irish"; and Nathan Walker, the black "Irish" of the racist culture of the "New World." It offers a sepia-tinted view of an era in which mutual esteem for hard work, talent, and immense courage create for a time the possibility of not only "tolerating" but *relishing* ethnic diversity, even if mainly "underground" among socially "invisible men." Although he is black and the youngest, Walker "leads" the team in the "art" with which he performs his job, as his shovel becomes part of his body, moving with "the quiet mastery of his burrowing" (McCann 1998, 12). When Power puns that his black fellow worker is "the king of spades," Walker does not read the remark as a racial slur: "He knows there is a democracy beneath the river. In the darkness every man's blood runs the same color—a dago the same as a nigger the same as a Polack the same as a mick . . ." (9). There is also a bit of "democracy" above in the world of light in a saloon whose barman, Brickbat Jones, is the only bartender around who will serve Walker; he does so because Walker once saved the barman's life. This "blood-brotherhood" repeats another episode in the darkness of racism in the world above, in which Con O'Leary runs naked from the communal showers to save Walker from being beaten to death by four white welders who resent this uppity "nigger" in their midst. Walker's world is grounded in the good darkness below, where his connectedness to his world beneath the river in the "belly of darkness" is underlined by his taking off his shirt to smear the "river's muck" on his body, the same muck that he knows could be filling his lungs at any moment.

With little warning, the plot erupts into existence with the calamity of a blowout in which Walker and two of his fellow workers are propelled up through the river, under which they have been tunneling, in a scene of death and rebirth of classic proportions. Walker, Vannucci, and Power are saved, while their fellow sandhog Con O'Leary is buried forever in the riverbed. The sacrifice of the Roman Catholic Irishman O'Leary is worth pausing over, for it echoes Yeats's poignant lines, "Romantic Ireland's dead and gone, / It's with O'Leary in the grave," but also foregrounds the Easter Rising of 1916, another rite of sacrifice, and McCann has made it known he deliberately moved the date of the "blow-out" in which his O'Leary died to 1916.[46] This calamity shakes the narrative out of its quiescence to launch the plot into the future.

The quartet of sandhogs is reduced to a trio. The sacrifice of O'Leary consecrates erotic connections within the ethnically diverse community, as the bond among Walker, Power, and Vannucci is strengthened through mourning for their lost comrade. This surfacing of desire will eventually bring down suffering and destruction on the Walker family. In the end, love for O'Leary impels the noble gesture by Walker that puts at risk the continuance of the Walker line.

That metaphor of a "line" is appropriate to a narrative strung together in a web of metaphors preparing for the ending by suggesting the continuing potential of the real to erupt into the metaphoric. The pressure for love, both erotic and brotherly, to find and to found a line into the future through progeny is foregrounded in Walker's scrupulously restrained Sunday visits to O'Leary's widow, where his future becomes interwoven with the life of O'Leary's infant daughter, for whose adulthood Walker will patiently wait to affirm his love. Long before that line begins, Walker generates his own being through a set of compulsive gestures. He wears a red hat with a string tied under his chin, for example, and the same shabby overalls as a signature of his personality. The red hat is even troped as Walker's "autograph" (McCann 1998, 22). The impulse to repeat is most evident in the long years Walker ritualistically visits O'Leary's widow, choosing the bright daylight of Sunday afternoons, because he knows the consequences of a black man visiting a white woman after dark. Through these visits he comes to know and love Con's last child, Eleanor, born days after the calamity that launches Walker's line. The sense of ritual is enhanced by his powerful impulse to repeat, as we see in the indication that each Sunday Walker leaves a silver dollar on the mantelpiece for Maura to put away for Eleanor (45). Walker's need to repeat is reflected in Con O'Leary's "trick" of holding a bullet in a fold of his bare belly all day to entertain his fellow workers with his self-discipline.

The sense of ritual is also clear in the ceremony to mark the opening of the tunnel Con O'Leary lost his life to build. The sandhogs add to the ritual quality by *not* wearing their best clothes but rather their work clothes, and of course Walker wears his signature red hat. Children are present, and two of them participate in a little bit of history by playing catch with a baseball, a story Walker will mythologize as "the first subaqua pitch in the history of the world" (49). Sean Power corrects his nephew's slur against Walker: "He ain't a nigger, son, he's a sandhog" (51). The ceremonial situation impels Walker to ask those assembled to join him in a moment of silent remembrance of those who died constructing the tunnel. His priestly function is further enhanced by his private ceremony with Power and Vannucci, after the others have drifted off. He takes out Maura O'Leary's wedding ring and following her instructions tosses it by the train tracks for Con's spirit to find so "he can buy his land from God" (53) in the world beyond.

Nathan Walker establishes and maintains the "line" of his family through the repetition of gestures and rituals that are nothing short of imagining a mythology for his family. Walker's impulse to repeat is further reinforced through ritual with the birth of his and Eleanor's children. When each is born, Walker holds the infant close to him while he whispers a variant of what he has said about himself, "You are so goddamn handsome, Nathan Walker!" (91), as though he aspires to ground the child's psyche in the preciousness it represents to Walker and the family. In addition, Walker functions as a griot, passing on the family's history, especially the power of love he read in his mother's stern lecture on the reverence for all living creatures after she discovered he had killed a snake just to use its skin for a wallet. Walker's stories include his memory of seeing sandhill cranes dancing in Georgia, a sight he was never able to share with his children. And he has the stories about Eleanor's father she repeatedly asks him to tell her. After they marry and Eleanor introduces him to the ritual of afternoon tea, he is bemused by the tea cozy, something as alien to him as a samurai's hat. In his later years, when he is so crippled by arthritis he can no longer do the work he loves, he replaces his signature red hat with this tea cozy to amuse his children, as a house husband, while Eleanor works in the paintbrush factory.

Their interracial marriage and the births of their children confront the utopian underworld of sandhog brothers-in-love with an Old World of fear, hatred, and cruelty straining the impulse to connect and eventually decimating the Walker family. The insidiousness of that old heart, not fully renewed in the American dream of genuine equality, surfaces in the "traumatic" moment of (mis)recognition of Clarence by his mother, to whom he proudly carries his report card with the A in science because he cannot wait until she returns from the sweatshop. In a moment of racist panic to which many white liberals can easily relate, Eleanor denies that Clarence is her son. Although she does not ask forgiveness but only understanding, Clarence will send his forgiveness years later from the other side of the world while fighting for his racist motherland in Korea.

Clarence survives in part because America has begun again to dream its dream. Jackie Robinson has broken the color barrier in American sport, probably a more important milestone than *Brown v. the Board of*

Education. The President who sends Clarence to Korea as part of that United Nations "police action" is the same Harry Truman who braved the wrath of the Pentagon by integrating the armed forces. Clarence survives, however, in large part because he is his father's son, who has learned that whites suffer from a repetition compulsion to be racists. Walker has learned to risk the expression of his anger only "in-house," and even at the risk to Eleanor's love of him. When she complains, for example, that a shopkeeper refused to sell her a hat because he disapproved of her marriage to an African American, he commits sacrilege in saying that eventually she will recognize how routine racial oppression is: "It gets so you think God is just shittin' on down every minute of the day. Like He's gone and got Himself a bad case of diarrhea. Like it's raining on down from His ass" (101). Despite this offense to her religion, Eleanor can be brought around by Walker's singing the Bill Broonzy song, "Lord, I'm so lowdown, baby, I declare I'm looking up at down" (101). Appropriately, the next episode is the birth of their son. When Eleanor objects to Walker's placing his red hat on the baby's head, Walker takes Clarence out shopping for flowers for the new mother, and when the shopkeeper says he would prefer not to serve the "Colored," Walker throws the change on the counter to pay for a block of ice to cool the shopkeeper down. It is then that he begins the ritual: "Clarence Walker, you are so goddamn handsome!" (103).

Clarence Walker will survive Korea to return "half-blind," or biracial, to a culture that entraps itself in compartments, those "nests" of illusory safety from a world too full of complications for it to understand. The Old World almost triumphs through the death of Eleanor Walker at the front end of the drunken Hoofer McAuliffe's car, running a red light. This is the same Irishman Walker almost killed for lewd advances toward his daughters. Clarence's beating of his mother's killer to death, along with the policeman who tries to apprehend him, is turned against him when he seeks refuge in his father's Georgia home and is bludgeoned virtually beyond recognition by some "good ol' boys" who can read biracial only as the signifier of the miscegenation their ancestors taught them to abhor but practice as white men with black women. These events require rehearsal here, because this is the "plot" of history in the "New World," as each generation compulsively repeats this death wish until it can work its way to the beyond of desire, even when desire must console itself with only the impulse to survive as a family with some simple but fundamental legacy to pass to the next generation, a hope perhaps for the renewal of America's dream of the power of transformation.

That intergenerational impulse to connect through legacy offers a response to the negative implications of the repetition compulsion. In
Freud's *Beyond the Pleasure Principle*, read by Peter Brooks as a masterplot for narrative as well as for life, the repetitions are grounded in a
desire to master an external world continuously threatening to demonstrate our "femininity," or vulnerability, as agents of desire. To desire,
as Lacan taught, is always to be reminded of metonymy, lack, the part
for the whole, the "whole" being that Desire forever foreclosed through
accession to the register of symbolic representation. And yet repetitions
are not entirely negative, for they produce the mastery of our talents in
a continuing pursuit of the transformations that represent the narrative
of our becomings. Thus, these repetitions in the service of the death
wish and its desire for a return to quiescence, once the energy of desire
is dissipated, are also the bindings of metaphor in the service of and the
preparation for that final ending in transformation.

The ending of the plot, or what might be termed the "end of history,"
offers a brilliant example of the tragic resonances inherent in the masculine narrative paradigm, as the past finally catches up with the present
in a moment of recognition and transformation. In chapter 11, "the way
God supposed," the narrative positions a segment of one plot directly
after a segment from the other plot for the first time in the same chapter.
The recounting of the past is about to overtake the stasis of the present.
Walker's grandson Clarence Nathan has become a high-altitude construction worker, implicating his identity in Treefrog's building his underground nest, high above the train tracks where he knows few would
dare follow him. In chapter 12, "split open with sunlight," Treefrog's
former wife, Dancesca, becomes Clarence Nathan's wife as the plot accelerates toward its revelation of why a prince of a fellow like Clarence
Nathan has been transmogrified into a Treefrog.

Much of that accelerated pace is the product of Treefrog's recovery
of desire in his brief rescue of the homeless Angela from his underground neighbor Elijah, who beats her. Making love for the first time
in years allows Treefrog to recuperate the Clarence Nathan who made
love with his prospective wife, Dancesca, a choice approved of by
Walker, who tells his adolescent grandson, "Hold on to her" (211).
Clarence Nathan is so embarrassed by his grandfather's certification of
his manhood that he nicks his grandfather during his ritual shaving of
Walker, who tells his reflection in the glass, "Nathan Walker, you are
still so goddamn handsome!" (211), suggesting some small recuperation
of his own youth through his grandson. The stirring of Eros propels
Clarence Nathan out of the quiescence of his paralysis in "homeless-

ness," and he corrects Angela when she calls him "Treefy" by telling her his given name, a name that joins his father and his grandfather. One of the initial questions this narrative posed was, What is the connection between its two plots? The accelerated pace of its resolution excites desire for an answer to the more complicated question of what transformed Clarence Nathan into Treefrog and whether that spell can be lifted so that history can move Walker's family past this Slough of Despond representing Treefrog's "homelessness." Clarence Nathan appropriates the narrative, as he tells Angela the story of how he became a Treefrog. He has already exposed his sense of being on the brink of self-transformation by cutting off his beard and hair to mark his readiness for rebirth.

Chapter 14, "now that we're happy," represents the culmination of Walker's rituals and comes close to naming them as the bindings of the long middle of life and narrative's "middle" in preparation for the return to quiescence offered by death. All the repetitions of Walker's having been forced to stomach racism and the suffering that racism has visited on his family seem to have readied him now for the reign of the pleasure principle. Clarence Nathan and Walker risk something like hubris when they sing, "Lord, I'm so high up I believe I'm looking down at up" (254), yet another movement up the scale from tunneling under rivers to constructing the steel frames of skyscrapers. Clarence Nathan recalls his grandfather's virtually manic state, in which he said, "I heard sometimes if you know you're gonna die then you get energy" (256), as one expression of an ironic lack of awareness that a tragic fall inheres in his grandfather's suggestion that they go for a walk through the tunnel to "say hello to my old friend Con" (256). The two complete Walker's sentimental journey by reaching the platform on the other side of the river, but in a scene right out of the classic nightmare, Clarence Nathan thinks, "Man, we're home free, we are home free" (258), just as the train looms toward them, and Walker, who has reached down to retrieve his tea cozy, slips from his grandson's grasp.[47]

The melodrama of the scene is enhanced, of course, by Clarence Nathan's telling this story to the battered Angela, whom he has temporarily rescued from the brutal Elijah. His excitement in the narrating becomes powerfully evocative, as he repeats the litany of how he loved his grandfather, in whose face he read the poignant question: "What do we do now, son, now that we're happy?" (260). Whether Clarence Nathan's rendition of the scene grasps the "truth" of Walker's dying is probably less important than the effects of its telling on the teller. Clearly, this is the endlessly screened nightmare from which Treefrog has been trying to awaken to recuperate at least the chance of becoming Walker's grandson again. This, and its subsequent nightmare of chopping off the hands that could not grasp the patriarch who more than anyone was responsible for his having survived to young adulthood.

The telling of this tale is foundational to Treefrog's eventual transfiguration as an escapee from the darkness of the underworld. In relating the tale to Angela, through whom he has begun to lift himself from the hell of inertia and despair, Treefrog takes responsibility for the Clarence Nathan who failed, just as he has taken at least short-term responsibility for her. It can be only "short-term," because he has no illusions that he can stop her return to Elijah, who supplies her with "candy." Perhaps for the first time in screening this dream in support of the *un*-pleasure principle, Clarence Nathan has begun to read more perceptively the gesture of Walker's seemingly compulsive reaching down into peril to recover his signature tea cozy. Walker has labored long in service to the compulsion to repeat in a history of repetitions that one is reluctant to call totally positive or negative. Walker reaches out to embrace the end toward which he has labored nearly a century. This story will have its last ending only when Clarence Nathan can not only bear this transfiguration of his grandfather but find his own potential for self-transformation.

The climax of the family history, however, is still some years to come, after Clarence Nathan and Dancesca's daughter has moved to the brink of young womanhood. The sense of chronicle persists in Clarence Nathan's recalling how his grandfather "baptized" Lenora, as he had her father, whispering in her ear that she is beautiful. And years later when Clarence Nathan prospers from his art as a steel-beam walker, Walker accompanies the family to South Dakota to pay respects to his grandson's mother, the doomed Louisa Turiver, an American Indian, who destroyed herself through drug addiction. There Walker teaches Lenora the dancing of the sandhill cranes, as he remembers it from his own childhood.[48]

The end of the family history comes in Clarence Nathan's retreat into paralysis when he cannot shed the guilt of failing to save Walker's life, even though what Walker wanted perhaps was to save his soul by setting it free, like the homing pigeons from his youthful hours with Vannucci and Powers. Because one of his hands slipped while trying to grasp the Walker who wanted to slip away, Clarence Nathan has become a compulsive repeater of actions, so that the second hand must always touch what the first hand has. Eventually this compulsion will turn him into a Treefrog when he touches his pubescent daughter with a second hand after accidentally touching her with the first. The first episode is repeated with his touching Lenora "just around the armpits," where, of course, his hands had failed to grasp Walker. Readers understand his repetition compulsion, but his wife and daughter flee the apparent menace of incest. This is the "answer" postponed from the beginning until its full resonance could be felt, and especially within the context of Treefrog's reaching out to Angela, who he knows will also slip away from him once she hears this story.

The last chapter is entitled "our resurrections aren't what they used to be." "History" in this narrative has come to an end by arriving at the present, only to pose again the crucial question at the outset, Can Treefrog "go home"? Readers are drawn forward with heightened desire for the end, as the remaining pages dwindle. The narrative makes gestures toward "resurrection" in Treefrog's touching a dead tree and recalling a tree in Harlem, called the "Tree of Hope." Clarence Nathan moves into a fantasy journey underground, recognizing and saying good-bye to Treefrog, and more importantly reprising Walker's life, ending with the questioning look of "what do we do now, son, now that we're happy?" (283). Clarence Nathan may finally be confronting what tragically destroyed his well-being by allowing his grandfather's impulse toward ritual to become something like a perverse rendition of the repetition compulsion. If, as African Americans have reminded us, slavery and racism have been their Holocaust, Clarence Nathan may be staring into the face of his own kind of survivor guilt: How can one be happy in the present, knowing the suffering of one's forebears who made such happiness possible? How to bear the transfiguration of the grandfather who resorted to ritual in order to confront the daily assaults of a racist society determined to deny him full personhood? How to live in a state of being "up" when it can only serve as a reminder of the long, long history of being "down"? How to suffer the light without the guilt of abandoning entirely one's family history in the darkness underground?

Clarence Nathan makes an effort to diminish the scale of the coming "resurrection" by thinking that there is not "a burning bush or a pillar of light," and yet the narrative has its way with him by constructing him as a phoenix setting his nest afire in preparation for rebirth. The narrative is bent on the fulfilment of its desire for the end, with its powerful transformation of the whole long middle of "history." Returning to the last paragraphs, readers may be disappointed that the desire seems somewhat diminished, because of course no subsequent reading can recuperate the first. In that first reading narrative desire for transformation wrings the reader's aching heart with its longing for even the *possibility* of shedding all the painful repetitions of the past we call "history," in order to become American dreamers once more, drawn forward by the frail promise of recovery as we allow ourselves to desire what the Old World decided millennia ago was a mere pipe dream. Clarence Nathan dreams of setting straight his clumsy gestures to Lenora, as he has with Angela, even though he senses he may fail. The promise is all: "And at the gate he smiles, hefting the weight of the word upon his tongue, all its possibility, all its beauty, all its hope, a single word: resurrection" (289). Risky as the gesture may seem, the narrative reaches out to the promise of spiritual transformation, the willingness to risk desiring the recovery of hope. In doing so, this narrative brilliantly demonstrates that the power of narrative to implicate its readers in the desire for the end has not been diminished, even though the masculine narrative paradigm may have fallen into some disrepute. The power of the transformation inherent in Clarence Nathan's recovery of spirit recuperates that Hegelian sense of *Aufhebung*, or uplift, cited by Lacan as a reminder of the agency of metaphoricity, lifting without ever abandoning recognition of the lower depths from which it lifts up the spirit.

ENDING IN A PICKLE: SALMAN RUSHDIE'S *MIDNIGHT'S CHILDREN*

Midnight's Children raises the fundamental question in any discussion of endings where "reading for the plot" is a focus: Whose story is this anyway? In the final two chapters the narrator, Saleem Sinai, struggles with the seemingly impossible task of finding the means to end *Midnight's Children*. At this point Rushdie's novel is just under 600 pages from where it began with the return of Saleem's grandfather to South Asia as a young man. Saleem asserts: "I reach the end of my long-winded autobiography" (1981, 585), and in one sense it actually *is* his "autobiography." Saleem is not just any South Asian who was born at midcentury. He is one of the metaphoric "midnight's children," born in the early minutes of the first day of India's and Pakistan's independence, as was Rushdie himself.[49] Saleem and the other 420 or so "midnight's children" who survived to adulthood make up the first generation of postcolonial South Asians. Saleem may be the most important of these postcolonial pioneers, but because he remains only *one* of them, his "autobiography" must also be theirs.

As a fictional autobiography or multiple biographies, *Midnight's Children* faces the challenge of quasi-biographical narrative that ends before the central figure's death. In the context of Sartre's youthful dilemma of how to lead his life before he happened on the strategy of envisioning his obituary, Rushdie's novel is guaranteed to face its share of difficulties coming to a close without even the "open ending" with which readers have become familiar in modernist classics such as *Ulysses* and *Mrs. Dalloway*. Saleem has survived to young adulthood—no mean feat, given the violent birthing of the nations that once constituted the colony of "India" under the Raj: not only India, and Pakistan, but also Bangladesh, originally East Pakistan, separated from its larger Western sector by the broad expanse of present-day India. Because *Midnight's Children* also comprises the stories of other "children," it inevitably develops a looseness in "plot," if there *is* one, making the task of ending the novel a near impossibility.[50] Saleem's attempt to find an ending is a reminder that large, "epic" novels seldom offer the kinds of memorable endings of novels such as *Amsterdam*.[51]

Added to the difficulties of this gargantuan "story" is, of course, the issue of identity, virtually a tradition in the novel. The nursemaid Mary Pereira, we discover, switched babies on the momentous day of independence so that the child of the establishment family has been raised as Shiva, the beggar's child, while Vanita's child, probably sired by a departing Englishman, William Methwold, has been raised as Saleem Sinai—a cuckoo in another's nest until his parentage is revealed as an adult. Saleem represents the amalgam at the center of the postcolonial: its "post" points toward its being *after* colonialism; however, the presence of the signifier *colonial* reveals the stigma of a past from which the postcolonial has not fully "posted" itself. This doubleness of colonialism/postcolonialism is central to Saleem, who is both the child with opportunities for advancement and the spawn of the British man who rapes the beggar "India" one last time before departing.

This problematizing of identity in Saleem/Shiva plays itself out in a narrative calling on the strategies of magic realism to move its "plot" forward. As the narrative moves into the endgame, the elements of magic realism proliferate. The fight in the jungle and the disappearing/reappearing market comment on a world in which the solidity of the real continually gives way to magic, or illusionism. Rushdie's world, not so unlike ours, is a world in which things are usually not what they appear, and as a result the "mouse-trap" ending of an *Amsterdam* whose plot sets the trap at the outset seems a world apart—although we need to beware of "orientalizing" Rushdie's South Asia as a projection of Western notions that "the East" is more "mysterious," indeterminate, and ultimately "unknowable" than Euro-North America with its concepts of rationality, stability, and solidity.

   In the closing pages, Saleem foregrounds his awareness that his narrative must soon end. He even prompts himself to find some means to make an end, saying, for example, "Quickly now, because we have come to the end of incidents . . ." (Rushdie 1981, 580). But how to end a narrative with such a sense of plotlessness? Perhaps it is appropriate that Saleem should end at the pickle factory run by Mary Pereira, whose "social engineering" brought a beggar's child into the privileged house of the Sinai family. This "pickle" is no kosher dill or sweet gherkin, of course, but South Asian chutney. In the restaurant where Saleem has taken his son Aadam to eat, he remarks on the wonderful chutney, perhaps recalling the special recipes of his nanny, Mary. When the waitress brings him a jar of Braganza Pickle, Saleem sets off with his son for Braganza Pickles (Private) Ltd. In a moment of revelation, Saleem sees how this discovery of Braganza Pickles, like his life from its first minutes, is a throw of the dice: "Once again an abracadabra, an open-sesame: words printed on a chutney-jar, opening the last door of my life . . . I was seized by an irresistible determination to track down the maker of that impossible chutney of memory . . ." (580). This "chutney of memory" is ambivalently suggestive both of a remembered chutney from his childhood and of memory itself as a variety of "chutney," a pickled mix of apparently disparate bits and pieces that may also be the result of a maker's "recipe." This metaphor of the "chutney of memory" becomes in the end a metaphor, too, for metaphoricity itself, another means of troping the transformation traditionally associated with ending in narrative.

   The growing sense of unruliness and instability in the narrative as well as in its subject matter is supported here by Saleem's encounter with a "champion defecator," who offers a kind of revelation, or "epiphany," in the fifteen-inch "turd" he manages to "extrude." This revelation generates an even more bizarre revelation on Saleem's part—"the longest turd I have ever seen" (582). Readers are likely to be surprised that Saleem, or anyone else for that matter, would care to observe and record this Guinness Book of World Records variety of "champion" performance. In something like a surreal or dreamlike encounter, the champion asks the narrator how many inches he can manage, and Saleem responds, "Seven on a good day" (582). This "champion" seems to have stepped right out of myth or folktale, as either might be read through the lens of Freudian theorizing about artistic production as compensation for being shamed as a child for playing with one's feces or compensation for embarrassment that one's "member" is too short to function sexually.

Saleem may well be doing more than simply revealing some "dirty little secret" from the back of his psychic closet—"Seven on a good day"—or merely papering over with whatever words come to mind his concern that he must end this narrative before *he* ends and the narrative merely stops in midsentence. He rues his lack of energy to tell this man's story (582); however, this "champion defecator" will have to settle for just a shorthand sketch, because Saleem has begun to notice the "cracks" forming on the surface of his being. Foregrounding himself as narrator, Saleem writes into the text this sense of decomposition, or nearing his own end, since as storyteller he cannot survive the telling of his story, whose end he assumes will be on his thirty-first birthday. Shades of Edwin Mullhouse! Thus, the opportunity to offer the "life-story" of the "champion defecator" is one he must forgo, because, as he indicates, all that is left for him to write are "epitaphs" (582). These "epitaphs" (reminiscent perhaps of Sartre's obituaries) offer yet another ambivalent term, for they are of course additions to texts as well as the texts written about a dead person.

Saleem turns his attention back to his son Aadam—actually, Aadam was fathered by another man—for yet another revelation. This revelation seems a miraculous one, appropriate to the ending of a long and large narrative such as *Midnight's Children*. Without warning, Aadam begins to speak for the very first time. "Ab . . ." he begins, making Saleem expect he will say, "'Abba . . .' Father," but instead Aadam begins "Abracadabra," the conventionally dismissive term for incomprehensible language. As Saleem's story is about to end, Aadam's story begins in a variety of revelation—in what was for Jacques Lacan the toddler's accession to the register of the Symbolic with his first speaking, in which signifier and signified finally lined up in the "miracle" of representation (dramatically troped in *The Miracle Worker* when the young Helen Keller finally connected "wah-wah" and the American sign language representation for the *thing* water).

From this point the narrative moves further into a self-reflexivity, prepared for by the trope of making chutney and by Saleem's sense of his body cracking open. He speaks first of his "special blends," the chutneys representing the individual chapters of *Midnight's Children*. Now we are finally in the pickle factory with the master pickler, working on the blend to go into the very chapter we are reading, a jar called "*Special Formula No. 30: Abracadabra.*" And for those who may not have been counting chapters, Saleem indicates that this is the thirtieth chapter. Storytelling itself is a "chutnification" whose results he can point to in the thirty jars of life pickled by memory and imagination and now assembled on the shelf as art. Should there be any doubt concerning this metaphor, Saleem works back through the jars, or chapters, to comment on what he can see as the "distortions" in the contents of each.

Saleem now becomes the critic of his own "chutnification." He admits that the early-morning baby switching could have been a means of easing the guilt of the incest taboo by making "Jamila Singer" not his sister but "actually" Shiva's. Similarly, he wonders if the "Accident in the Washing-chest" was necessary to achieve his powers of telepathy when the other midnight's children already had their special talents at birth. And given his telepathy, he wonders why he would have been surprised by Mary Pereira's revelation that she switched Saleem and Shiva. He ends by acknowledging that he ought to revise what came before, but he has wound down (586). The Saleem who speaks here is less the storyteller than the subject of the telling, now fixed and not to be altered.

The trope of chutnification allows the narrative to wax expansive[52] on life and art, but always in the "tropical" realm of domestic cookery to hold it back from aesthetic inflation. "In the spice bases, I reconcile myself [he says] to the inevitable distortions of the pickling process. To pickle is to give immortality, after all: fish, vegetables, fruit hang embalmed in spice-and-vinegar; a certain alteration, a slight intensification of taste, is a small matter, surely? The art is to change the flavour in degree, but not in kind; and above all (in my thirty jars and a jar) to give it shape and form—that is to say, meaning" (586–87). It is the single, unfilled jar that tropes the need for ending: "One empty jar . . . how to end?" (587). Aadam's speaking at last could provide a "happy ending," or the lost ones from this narrative could lend it a melancholy ending. Perhaps it could even provide an "end in the tragedy of the disintegrating effects of drainage," for Saleem is drying out, vulnerable to a "lifetime's battering. And now there is rip tear crunch, and a stench issuing from the fissures, which must be the smell of death" (587). He is too dry to bleed. "Am I already so emptied desiccated pickled? Am I already the mummy of myself?" (587). Or, since he has begun to dream of out-of-the-body experiences, is his body merely the husk of a chrysalis from which he is due to break out, metaphoricity giving way to metamorphosis? Certainly the mummy trope is pertinent to transformation, since this is not merely embalming the body to keep it from rotting while the survivors are having their way with it, but the Egyptian gesture toward assuring an afterlife in which the spirit will recover the body it once animated.

What will go into this thirty-first jar but the future? It is a future he can prophesy, but a future that obviously cannot be contained in a pickle jar as easily as the other chapters of the midnight's children's lives. Saleem cannot "see" what he or some other chutney maker might one day fill the this jar with. This life not yet ready to be pickled or embalmed is "merely" life with its promise of the power of metaphoricity, of transformation in endings that are only beginnings elsewhere. The cracking of his husk gets troped one last time through the metaphor of explosion. Saleem calls himself the "bomb in Bombay . . . a broken creature . . . because I have been so-many too-many persons, life unlike syntax allows one more than three . . . , release" (589). This is a peace that passes understanding, the peace of an ending that is also a beginning, a death that allows the radiance of meaning to show itself forth.

Saleem's final vision is one of disintegration as an individual in order to become part of humanity marching with him in time,[53] but also treading on his body as the spirit moves toward an at-one-ment with others. He indicates: "I am alone in the vastness of the numbers . . . , buffeted right and left while rip tear crunch reaches its climax, and my body is screaming . . ." (589). In the closing lines Saleem looks farther into a future in which Aadam and future generations will share his fate as they also find themselves beneath the feet of these numbers. Rushdie provides his seemingly plotless narrative—plotless because it is the eternally recurring story of a life—with a "climax" worthy of a "big" modernist novel such as D. H. Lawrence's *The Rainbow*, which has a similarly massive vision of the viewpoint character being swept up by the mighty forces of being as the individual dies to this life in order to access the mystical entrance into the very heart of things.

A Proliferation of Endings: Graham Swift's *Waterland*

The double time scheme of *This Side of Brightness* is echoed in Graham Swift's *Waterland*, whose present of 1980 bears haunting parallels to the past of 1943 when the curse on the House of Atkinson set in motion the tragedy of Mary and Tom Crick, whose ending was a denouement of madness for one and alcoholism for the other.[54] Like Kazuo Ishiguro's *When We Were Orphans*, *Waterland* pays homage to the detective novel by drawing readers in with the promise of fulfilling their desire for an ending at which they will know "whodunit."[55] As a teacher of history, Tom Crick self-consciously immerses himself in what he knows is probably the self-delusion that explanations can be found, seeing himself as an intellectual detective trying to resolve the issues of guilt and responsibility in which this narrative is grounded. As in the Ishiguro novel, *Water-land* enlists its readers in the ranks of detectives, studying the clues supplied by its narrator, Tom Crick, a detective who, like Western literature's first detective, Oedipus,[56] seeks a criminal who turns out to be himself.

The narrative of the past is logically set in motion by the momentous narrative of the present, the present reflecting the ambiguities or indeterminacies of the past. At fifty-two, after apparently having been fulfilled by working with the elderly, Mary Crick "retires" and begins an affair with God, who promises her, she says, the child she has been unable to bear. Tom's difficulty in dealing with his wife's delusions makes him an increasingly eccentric instructor, rejecting the curriculum of European history to begin teaching what he had announced as a writing project for his retirement—a history of the fens, or waterland, of eastern England. This history (d)evolves into the history of both sides of his family and eventually his and Mary's story—more specifically, the trauma of their sixteenth year in 1943. The logic of cause and effect on which historiography depends will become as indistinct as "waterland" itself, as readers struggle to determine the connections among Tom's confrontations with enforced retirement, the social stigma of Mary's insanity, and an increasingly eccentric pedagogy. Lewis, who edged out Tom to become headmaster, may be only rationalizing Tom's termination as a policy of reducing instruction in history. Students apparently are coming to see less value in studying the past as the future threatens the "end of history" in a nuclear Armageddon.

When the investigating police officer asks Tom to "go back to the beginning" in explaining what led Mary to kidnap the baby she thinks God has given her, Tom ponders: "The beginning? But where's that? How far back is that?" (Swift 1983, 314). The task assigned Tom by the policeman poses challenges, because this narrative cannot meaningfully start at any particular point. The "beginning" for Tom as storyteller is the phrase "Once upon a time . . ." with which his father began stories: for example, the night in 1937 when Henry Crick took Dick and Tom (aged fourteen and ten, respectively) out to set traps for eels and told them the stars were "the silver dust of God's blessing" (1). That night stands in idyllic contrast to the night of July 25, 1943, when Tom and his father discovered the body of Freddie Parr, Tom's classmate, floating in the River Leem. The contrast measures Tom's expulsion from the haven of childhood, as he begins to read the body of Freddie as a signifier of a deeper implication in adulthood than even his erotic explorations of Mary Metcalf's body appear to have initiated, for as it becomes clear, Freddie's death was probably neither an accident nor suicide. This "beginning," if narrative must have one, prompts the "Once upon a time . . ." that will become the signal for Tom's class to close the assigned textbook with its accounts of the bloody deeds during the French Revolution so that they can attend to the fable of how Mary received the child God promised her. As it will later be revealed, Tom has already begun to replicate his father's very last words: "Once upon a time . . ." (343). Thus, Tom begins a "whodunit" with the pursuit of the criminal(s) who caused that body of Freddie to float in the Leem and of other "crimes" with which the death of Freddie is implicated. The desire for an answer to the question of "whodunit" will persist until the novel's final chapters, even though the criminal(s) may seem to be identified earlier. Only the ending promises the fullest understanding of responsibility, not merely the "who" of a simpler notion of plot, but also the "how" and "why" of a deeper understanding of human culpability. This desire for the end, with its metaphoric transformation of meaning, must be deferred through the metonyms of details and events, included in part to perform the "arabesque" of a very long middle in order to forestall "short-circuiting," or too quickly gratifying, the desire for the end. This continual supplying of "middle" to forestall the "end" can occasionally impress readers as something like the perverse holding back of climax—in the male, of course, since as feminist narratologists have reminded us women are not similarly "privileged" to control their playing with the end. Accordingly, just after it has drawn readers in with a rapid movement through the events of Dick's murder of Freddie Parr and of Mary's revelation to Tom of her pregnancy, the narrative offers a long history of the fens and a scene from the recent past—Tom's virtual firing by Lewis—to slow down its gratification of the reader's desire to know too quickly "whodunit." Only then does the narrative allow its readers to return, as it will again and again in a repetition compulsion of its own, to the point where the story broke off with the recovery of the body and Tom's observation of his father's apparently clumsy maneuvering of the boat hook to produce a wound atop a fainter wound to the corpse's right temple. (When Tom discovers the bottle that appears to be the murder weapon, a long history of the Atkinson family, encompassing several dozen pages, holds back the narrative desire to move toward the next "end" of a further revelation.) The narrative then flashes forward to Tom's encounter with Mary later that evening when she tells him: "I told him it was Freddie. Dick killed Freddie because he thought it was him. Which means we're to blame too" (35).

In this way the narrative appears to be short-circuiting the whodunit by revealing too early that Mary and Tom are implicated, from *her* standpoint at least, in Dick's murdering of Freddie Parr. The narrative provides more short-circuiting by revealing that in the coroner's report Freddie's death is classified as an accident—a reasonable conclusion, since his heavy drinking and inability to swim are well known. Tom asserts, "End of story," then like a ventriloquist he feeds lines to his class: "But sir! Sir! That can't be all. What about that double bump on the head? What about that freaky brother? And this thing with you and Mary what's-her-name? (Hey, we never knew you—) What about our detective spirit? Don't stop, keep telling. That can't be the end" (109). And obviously it is not the end, because the book in the reader's hand contains over 200 more pages.

The appearance of short-circuiting acts as a lure to draw readers forward to the "real" ending. It also problematizes the sense of an ending by offering a red-herring ending, only to accentuate that larger and deeper desire to know the fullest ramifications of this "ending" seemingly "given away" at the very beginning. Thus, the apparent short-circuiting of the desire to know "whodunit" leads only to the larger issues to be later unpacked, such as Mary's assertions of "blame." The complications are increased by Tom's unexplained assertion that "something else [that] floated down the Leem, was seen and fished out only by me" (36), an instructive use of the passive voice to record Tom's revelation that he becomes an "accessory after the fact" to murder by concealing what probably was the murder weapon, repeating his father's complicity in concealing the stigma of foul play with his "accidental" maiming of the corpse. The assertion also records Tom's recognition that if he had not found the empty beer bottle, this story might have had a different outcome. And beyond that, these early revelations support the growing anticipation that the telling of this tale represents an attempt to unpack "history" in order to confront and work through guilt resulting from participation in a chain of cause and effect that has produced suffering and destruction the actors never intended.

The mystery of Mary's assertions on the evening Freddie Parr's corpse is discovered begins to be resolved the next afternoon when the two meet in the abandoned windmill where they have been making love for almost a year. Curiously, Mary has already informed Dick of her condition as part of her apparent ploy to save Tom from Dick's wrath by offering Freddie Parr as the alleged father of her child. When Tom is understandably uncertain about the paternity of Mary's child, she adds that Dick could not be the father "because it was too big" (58). Confusion abounds concerning the paternity of this child with which its mother seems to be playing a variety of shell game. "Explanations" again and again produce only more mysteries, for even if the adolescent Tom is too overwrought by the news of his "precipitate paternity," readers are likely to wonder how Mary *knows* this "it" of Dick's was too big, without some effort to ensure that it was *not* "too big," an effort that might have provided sufficient physical contact for conception to occur, given the narrative biologists have constructed of how "determined" the spermatozoon is to complete its mission.

This whole matter of the "it" tempts readers into a Lacanian explication of the Phallus, especially since the narrative, or its primary narrator Tom Crick, returns compulsively to Dick's . . . well, penis. As Lacan's writing reveals, the Phallus is and is not the penis: it represents the paradise lost of Desire before the fall into the register of the Symbolic with separation from the (M)Other and with accession to language as a means of symbolic representation. The Phallus may be symbolized by the penis, even though Lacan denies its equation with either female or male genitalia, but the Phallus itself is representative of a lost preserve of Desire, for which lowercase "desire" is always a metonym. Most importantly, Lacan asserts that the Phallus has power only as it is concealed, for were it to be revealed as the penis its symbolic agency would dissipate into the literal.

Accordingly, "Dick's dick"[57] provides the agency of the Phallus for Mary in this narrative, and perhaps even more for Tom. The agency of the Phallus as signifier of desire is contextualized for the other young adolescents whom Mary draws into a rather belated expression of earlier childhood games of "I'll show you mine, if you'll show me yours." The scene in which Mary discloses her pregnancy to Tom is prepared for through background indicating that although Tom lost his mother at the tender age of nine, Mary never knew her mother at all, since, like Mary Shelley's birth, Mary's brought about her mother's death. The preparatory material also includes this curious assertion: "Dick Crick, it was generally rumoured—even his own brother was unable to refute it—possessed a penis of fabulous dimensions" (Swift 1983, 50). (Readers can only wonder how and why Tom might be called upon to "refute it!") The statement is peculiar, because the narrative seems to have its own compulsion to register Dick's claim to the "fabulous" before it dramatizes the belated children's game Mary initiates. In the "real time" of the novel's "story," Mary, Tom, and the other boys already *know* of Dick's "fabulous dimensions," so there should be no need to speak in terms of what is "generally rumoured."

This "revelation scene," or "showing-forth" (a pastiche of the

Joycean epiphany?) occurs halfway through the novel. Because narrative film resists the novel's disjunctive plot, the makers of the film adaptation of *Waterland* positioned this revelation scene at the outset to arouse the spectator's desire for the end. In the novel, the scene is set against the background of "history," as Hitler meets with Goering in July 1940 to discuss strategy for the air war against Britain. The disclosure scene in which Mary offers to bare her genitalia if the boys will first bare theirs foregrounds the range in age of its participants, for the term "boys" is appropriate, their average age being, according to Tom, thirteen and a half, while Dick is seventeen. Rather than embarrassment over baring the stigmata[58] of their desire, it is embarrassment over the meager showing of their "manhood" that overwhelms the boys, or at least Tom, and then Mary changes the rules. Both Mary and Tom, unlike the others, have become aware of Dick's observation of the game from a distance, but not such a great distance as to conceal the outline of Dick's own showing forth in this revelation scene. Mary offers to expose herself to the boy who can swim farthest underwater, and it is difficult not to suspect that she can also predict the victor, since Dick is in the fullest possession of young manhood, whether he is a "potato head" or not. Dick competes, Tom thinks, less to win the privilege of Mary's showing forth than to conceal his arousal, and perhaps Tom is right, since Dick fails to claim his prize, and it is the hapless Freddie who demystifies desire by dropping a live eel into Mary's knickers.

This scene contributes strongly to the narrative's contamination with erotic desire. Epistemophilia, or the desire to know, reads as a desire to pursue the truth in the way a "private" detective might, but such an impulse is also deeply implicated in the desire to see the "privates" of not only the other sex but one's own as well. The narrative arouses the impulse to psychologize Tom's repetition of the crime of Cain, impelled by resentment against Dick's "fabulous dimensions," especially after the narrative offers the underplayed but wrenching appearance of the nine-year-old Tom dismissed by his dying mother in favor of Dick, to whom she passes the phallic key of Desire. Twenty chapters pass before the ultimate desire to dispel mystery is confirmed, as Tom is confronted by the arresting police officer, who wants him to go back to the "beginning" of how and why Mary stole the baby. It is at this point that Tom offers the "confession"—internally, at least—of being responsible for three deaths (314). As readers are swept forward to the ending of the novel in chapter 50—Dick's apparent suicide—they breathlessly await the revelation of exactly how Tom brought about his brother's death.

The narrative justifies its long middle through the metaphor of water, with its strong sense of eternal recurrence. The prime example is the clearly symbolic bottle of Coronation Ale Dick used to intoxicate Freddie Parr and then to strike him on the temple, perhaps hard enough to knock him into the river so that the water could drown Freddie, who could not swim. The bottle "returns" for Tom to recover it and plant this symbol of the "return of the repressed" in Dick's room to announce Tom's awareness of what Dick may have expected to be washed out to sea, like Freddie's body. That flow into the Great (M)Other from which life advanced upon the land and to which Dick himself will return in the end must be expected to continually return its detritus as reminders that in a tragic context nothing can ever be erased. To use Freud's own trope, the unconscious is like the child's Magic Slate upon which we write and lift the cover sheet to "magically" remove our writing, but the surface below bears the ghostly residue of that writing and makes its return inevitable.

This "return of the repressed" is, of course, the essence of the tragic construct. Laius and Jocasta delude themselves into believing they have erased the son who would murder his father and then father his mother's children. Oedipus naively assumes he can escape "the horror" simply by fleeing his "parents." His mother's recognition, followed by Oedipus's, represents less a sense of having done wrong by attempting to do right or even a sense of having foolishly defied the gods than an acknowledgment that the repressed *must* return, for the present is written in the past. Similarly, Tom as the center of tragedy has learned from the example of his mentally challenged brother that the evidence of crime cannot be repressed, since bodies and beer bottles represent the flotsam and jetsam of the life of the unconscious. Of course, by the time Tom narrates this episode of youthful nightmares, he has already come to the end so that the narrating is contaminated with the knowledge of how impossible it was to avoid acknowledging the return of the repressed.

The narrative generates greater tension as it moves toward its end for the very reason that its detective-readers are increasingly challenged to anticipate what its ending will be, given that at least one ending has already been supplied in the "present" of 1980. Despite the desire for the knowledge implicit in the ending, the narrative must work through its middle to ready itself for that end. As it moves through its "plot," in contrast to the "story" that this plot is referencing in its disjointed fashion, the narrative confirms the connections of "past" and "present," the history of the fens and the family history, to cue readers that the end is near. "Past" and "present" merit "scare quotes" because the terms are

problematical, the "present" of the narrative being an already past
when the novel appeared in 1983. Nothing however affirms the tragic
nature of the narrative, or the power of trauma, more convincingly than
knowing that the "past" is the "present" for Tom and Mary, who "died"
at sixteen. The term "died" is used advisedly, because the Tom, who is
falling apart in the classroom, enjoins his students to "be curious," for
"Curiosity begets love. It weds us to the world. . . . People die when
curiosity goes" (Swift 1983, 206). The aging process for Mary and Tom
announces their right to discard the mask of life they donned to "survive." More relevantly, the "curiosity" that this narrative has revealed
as the implication of Eros in the desire to know will also "die" for its
readers when the ending produces the anticipated transformation.

That end cannot come, however, before the narrative has worked
through a past that also represents its present. The second-to-the-last
generation of the family's connection with the past, or the history of the
Atkinson family, is developed in the nightmare of the so-called Great
War that haunts Tom, the last Atkinson to bear the name, as well as his
father, Henry Crick, one of those shell-shocked survivors whose name
was legion. Ernest Richard Atkinson carries the plague of the nineteenth century into the twentieth with his given names. Born an heir to
the Atkinson fortune, Ernest embraces Victorian earnestness by becoming a Fabian socialist, only to have his views rejected by the dispossessed whom he wants to benefit; that rejection in turn pushes him to
become his mad grandmother Sarah's heir by adopting the role of a
Cassandra prophesying the Armageddon to come. The Coronation Ale
Ernest brews for the ascension of George V in 1911 will offer a preview
in microcosm of the madness in the killing fields to come. Maddened by
the utopian impulse of the nineteenth century, Ernest scatters the seeds
of his lunacy in the succeeding century through the child he coerces his
daughter Helen to bear: a Richard, who will be "the Saviour of the
World." Working back and forth between Eros and narrative desire in
"Freud's Masterplot," Peter Brooks identifies incest as the erotic counterpart to the short-circuiting of narrative desire in a death, or a climax,
that comes too soon. How appropriate that this narrative offers its revelations of Ernest Atkinson's legacy of incestuous lunacy, over two hundred pages into the novel—a point at which other novels might
end—and just as readers may be looking for the end of this long, disjointed novel. This painful longing for the end is exacerbated because
the end has already been revealed, that is, Mary has been confined to an
insane asylum and Tom appears to face death by drowning in alcohol.

The earlier mention of Freud is a reminder that at the very time the

fictional Henry Crick was recuperating from shell shock at Kessling
Hall Home, Sigmund Freud was working on the very analysis—*Beyond
the Pleasure Principle*—Peter Brooks would later read as the "masterplot"
of narrative, making for another conjunction of psychoanalytic practices and insights to this novel.[59] As Brooks argues in *Psychoanalysis and
Storytelling*, a successful series of analytic sessions might be plotted as
an analysand/narrator's constructing the past as a movement toward
transference, a Latinate form of the Greek *metaphorein* and an analog for
the German *Übertragung*, a "carrying-across." In the climactic session,
the analysand should have established the pastness of the past to unmoor the present for its journey forward—for Lacan an uplifting, a
movement not only "across" but "up."

Waterland cues its readers that they are nearing the end, not simply
because the narrative has run through most of what is generally considered history—the history of the fens, of the Atkinson family, and so
forth—but also because the revelations homing in on Tom's tragic guilt
begin to cost more to produce. Tom's earlier "confession" of responsibility for "the death of three people" sets up the expectation of further
revelations. Virtually from the beginning, Tom has followed Mary in
assuming responsibility for Freddie Parr's death. The last chapters will
have to "explain"—in a text where "explanation," Tom asserts, is a
strategy of evading the facts—these other two deaths, the abortion and
the carelessness leading to Dick's suicide. When the ending of the story
is offered to Tom's students they press him for further explanation. Tom
is all too willing, as he also was in reporting the coroner's conclusion
that Freddie Parr's death was due to accidental drowning, to "close the
books" by relaying the information that the stolen baby was restored to
its mother and its kidnapper warehoused in an insane asylum, "jetti-
soned," if you will, by a narrative unwilling to offer her any hope of
redemption—a Cordelia caught up in the tragic sweep of events. Tom
allows his students to criticize him for professing to be a "classroom
sleuth" but refusing to provide an "explanation," even though he ought
to know that they, like all of us, "can't do without stories" (Swift 1983,
314–15). What follows offers itself as that "explanation," the ending to
complete the tragedy confirmed in the present by Mary's "crime" and
the return of the repressed.

It is hardly a coincidence that Tom reveals at this point his disobedi-
ence of the injunction not to look back at the fetus as he jettisons it into
the water. Martha Clay, the local abortionist, warns him it is "[n]othin'
but bad luck if you looks," but Tom *must* look at the stigma of his complicity in Mary's crime, and Dick's. The return of that repressed mem-

ory unlocks the series of events ending in Dick's death, or disappearance. Tom in the present of Mary's loss to lunacy is the plotter of this narrative who must position these events at the end because more than anything this is *his* story and in *that* there can only be "more," as he warns his father when he tells him, "I'm afraid there's more" (318). This "more" can only be what Tom cannot "explain" to anyone, including himself: Why did he lead his brother up into the attic to open the chest containing Dick's "legacy" and reveal to his brother the contents that Tom as reader constructs from the texts he finds in the chest?

Because the number of the book's pages is rapidly diminishing, the journey to the attic with its resolution of the mystery of why their dying mother dismissed Tom to pass on the "key" to Dick indicates that this narrative is surely moving toward its end. These last chapters may be problematizing traditional notions of "the end," since the ending for Mary and for Tom in the present of 1980 has been fixed by their acts in 1943. The narrative insists that these events be viewed with what the Irish philosopher William Desmond has termed "the posthumous mind," suggesting that they interest us as the shadows cast on tragic consequences we already know about. Furthermore, the narrative has already indicated just exactly what Tom does not yet know as he climbs the stairs to the attic—namely, that Dick is his uncle as well as his brother. It is crucial that the narrative reveals the outcome of the abortion in Tom's being "tasked" to dispose of the fetus he presumably helped to create, without "looking back" at it, as a prelude to what is shaping up to be the ultimate "looking back" for Dick and Tom in the 1943 plot sequence and now for Tom alone in 1980 at the other end of his life. And yet in the end it may be less *what* Tom tells Dick than *how* he relates it that devastates Dick and leaves Tom bearing the mark of Cain.

As he remembers the scene decades later, Tom first reads and then summarizes their grandfather's letter. Even Tom the explainer acts mystified by his own behavior: "And the second thing I say—it spills out almost before I have decided to say it—is: 'Dick, I'm sorry. I lied to you. It wasn't your baby. It was my baby'" (321). This "spilling out" is at least doubly curious: it suggests Lacan's sense of how the unconscious "speaks" us, as though the unconscious were an Other that will not be repressed, but must communicate even obliquely in slips of the tongue and through ellipses when the tongue mutely speaks volumes; and this "spilling out" seems an ejaculation that short-circuits the timely gratification of desire by coming too soon. If Tom earlier "lied" to Dick to get the key, the impulse behind this spilling out of the truth may be less a matter of epistemophilia, so strong that its fulfilment can no longer be contained, than "the horror" of darker desires lifting a brother's hand against his brother. This *Brudermörder* clearly repeats the impulse behind the RAF's nightly raids on Hamburg, Dresden, and Berlin to make their German brothers-in-murder pay for the incendiary bombings of Coventry, Manchester, and London two years earlier.[60]

Tom as reader of their grandfather's mad text is not finished, however. Ernest's letter to Helen's firstborn is a "purloined letter," since the narrative does not cite the letter verbatim, supplying instead Tom's unreliable reading of its contents to his brother. Tom continues with the (mis?)information that Ernest Atkinson has cautioned Dick against having children because his father was also his mother's father. Because the plot is rushing toward its ending, as is customary in "thrillers," no time or space is provided to question how a "potato head" will grasp the complexities of heredity. Indeed, if Dick learned Henry Crick's lesson that babies come from love, anyone who loves can father a child, without physical contact. Tom goes on to spell out what must be even more painful to Dick: "My father isn't your father" (Swift 1983, 322), never mentioning, of course, that they are still brothers because they share a mother. Although the sixteen-year-old Tom has devastated Dick with more "truth" than he needed, the language here is that of the fifty-three-year-old Tom voicing perhaps for the first time his recognition of the consequences of his earlier "carelessness" in making these disclosures, just as Oedipus in learning of the horrible acts he may have unwittingly committed must acknowledge *his* earlier "carelessness" in killing a man old enough to be his father and marrying a woman old enough to be his mother. It is also difficult not to wonder how closely Tom's lethal revelation to his brother replicates Iris's murderous disclosure that she, not her sister, was Alex's lover. Finally, as Tom describes the year-long affair with Mary when they were sixteen, readers may begin to suspect that he could be pondering unconsciously why after presumably many episodes of unprotected sex Mary suddenly became pregnant when Dick came onto the scene, as though Tom's unconscious had read Mary's child as Dick's and turned Tom's hand against his brother.

Later, when Tom and Henry Crick rush to the dredger *Rosa II* on which Dick has become a moderately satisfied and successful member of the working community, Tom cannot reveal the causes of Dick's desperate departure. He explains, instead, "'He's gone barmy.' (Forgive me, Dick.)" (351). Given that Dick is already "gone" to some "beyond" to which Tom has hurried him, this injunction "Forgive me, Dick" must be read as the Tom of the present seeking forgiveness for much more than simply calling Tom's desperation "barmy," that is, his having devastated Dick by labeling him a genetic "monster." In retrospect, Tom recalls telling Dick "he's a bungle" and hearing Dick's response of "S-s-sorry, Tom. S-s-sorry" (323). Although supposedly only on the borderline of humanness, Dick in turn asks his brother's forgiveness for being a bungle, even though others are responsible, and even though his brother is "carelessly" adding to his "guilt" for being a bungle. Delayed almost four decades, this recognition of the need for forgiveness on the way to atonement will provide *Waterland* its ending.

The limits *Waterland* sets on the fulfillment of desire for the end are inherent in its problematizing of Brooks's overconfidence that an action will have completed itself before its narrating begins. Tom creates the "reality" of the story in the present, as he says goodnight to Mary in the asylum and offers, in one sense, a radical critique of Brooks's notion of arousal of a desire for the end with narration's beginning in quiescence: "First there is nothing; then there is happening. And after the happening, only the telling of it. But sometimes the happening won't stop and let itself be turned into memory" (329). This present "won't stop" so that the telling can end, in part because the narrative has been impelled forward by Mary's theft of the child. The theft, like the plague in Thebes, reminds those in the present that the crimes of the Past will not simply go away or stay buried. The murdered will not rest until the murderers seek atonement.

The "openness" of *Waterland*'s ending exceeds the "open ending" of modernist fiction. If traditional fiction resolves the mysteries with which it begins, and if modernist fiction often ends with a poetic sense of opening out into "possibilized" futures, *Waterland* offers as its ending a mystery more dependent on acts of faith than on rational explication. The American sailors, whom Tom and Henry Crick have enlisted in their search for Dick, shout his name, assuming he can hear it in the depths where he swims. As though through Tom's consciousness, the narrative speaks the possible miracle of Dick's survival: "He's on his way. Obeying instinct. Returning. The Ouse flows to the sea . . ." (357). The ending forces a return to the middle of course if it is to be "explained." Such an effort at explanation is overborne, however, by the image of Dick swimming submerged to the sea in a "return" drawing upon magic, if not upon some faith in a "beyond," a region outside the power of narrative to represent.

The image of Dick's death as a return foregrounds Tom Crick as a tragic figure. Mary's mad belief that she and Tom have atoned for the termination of her pregnancy by patiently bearing the pain of childless-ness and that God offers a child as the promise of forgiveness rouses Tom from the delusion of psychic success in leading a good life as a teacher of others' children. The film adaptation of *Waterland* recon-structs the story with a plot different from Tom Crick's as narrator. In-stead, it positions the abortion at the end to establish it as the crime for which Tom as well as Mary must atone. The film ending, especially with Mary's being neither arrested nor institutionalized, but allowed to re-turn to the fens for a potential "happy ending," writes a very different plot from Swift's. In the novel Mary's desperate pursuit of atonement is like Jocasta's in rushing offstage to hang herself, and only exacer-bates Tom's recognition of the need finally to confront his own crime. He was not so much Mary's accomplice as he was an autonomous agent in destroying his own brother by robbing him of a father, and even more by denying Dick a last shred of humanity by stressing that he was a "bungle," a madman's monstrous progeny, for whom the best thing would have been never to have been born. With Mary lost to him in madness, Tom may begin his own quite separate journey toward atone-ment, now that he can begin to confront a "crime" for which he could in part excuse himself as Mary's accomplice. Perhaps "in the end," if Tom is to survive, he will seek atonement for the "carelessness" through which the unconscious spoke Dick's death sentence. Like Oedipus, Tom will have to assume responsibility for not only acts deliberately committed but also for lapses in caring, in a fault that few of us escape.

THE JOKE'S ON FREUD: D. M. THOMAS'S *THE WHITE HOTEL*

In many ways, the novel with which an exploration of masculine nar-rative paradigm might have been launched is D. M. Thomas's novel *The White Hotel*. Like *The Blind Assassin* with its foregrounding of endings in the narrative itself, *The White Hotel* seems to have been written with late twentieth-century theorizing in mind. Not coincidentally, as he indi-cates in his memoir, Thomas had read *Beyond the Pleasure Principle*, along with a number of other central Freud texts, when he wrote *The White Hotel*. This novel offers a pastiche of one subgenre of the contemporary detective novel—the narrative in which psychoanalysis parallels crimi-nal detection.[61] It promises to find an answer to the question, Why is this character exhibiting such bizarre "symptoms" for which medical science has no rational explanation? These "symptoms" parallel the clues in the whodunit in which the roots of the subject's symptoms must

be traced back to childhood. In childhood may be found the phenomena
that set into motion, say, a compulsion to repeat, making it necessary
for the subject to "work through" the past in the analysis before the
pleasure principle can begin its operation. This pursuit of an answer,
offering knowledge of the "truth," generates a desire for the end of the
plot where epistemophilia will achieve its gratification. Furthermore,
The White Hotel is a likely candidate, because the psychoanalyst whom
its central character Lisa Erdman consults is none other than Freud
himself.

As readers gradually become aware, the story of *The White Hotel* comprises the efforts of Freud and the narrative to come to an understanding of Lisa Erdman's symptoms. Lisa consults Freud in 1919, following
several years of separation from her husband. They were physically
separated because he was involved in the First World War, but they
were also legally separated because she feared sexual intercourse, lest it
result in pregnancy, and resorted to coitus interruptus. When her husband manages to gain leave from his wartime duties, she has recur-
rences of an ailment whose symptoms include shortness of breath and
pains in her left breast and her left ovary. Lisa's symptoms began when
at fifteen she was attacked by a gang of sailors who abused her as a
"Jewess." Her early life had been happy until at five she learned of her
mother's death in a hotel fire; then, some months later, she learned of
the death by heart attack of a favorite uncle, the husband of her mother's sister. Because the aunt and uncle had been frequent guests, Lisa
felt further bereft by the disappearance of the aunt from her life, especially because she was her dead mother's identical twin. Soon Lisa's
father also withdrew his attention and affection, and Lisa was left essentially alone. As a young woman she fell in love, but her lover left her
because of his political activities, and a fall put an end to her aspirations
to become a dancer. This is the skeleton of Lisa's story—or the story of
Frau Anna G., since "Freud" masks Lisa's identity, changing only a few
details, such as Anna's being a cellist while Lisa is an operatic singer. It
is important to stress that this is Lisa's life as reconstructed by the novel's Freud in his case study, "Frau Anna G."

Having established these "facts" of Anna's early life in the novel's
third section, "Frau Anna G.," "Freud" poses the questions a Sherlock
Holmes might ask to amaze his partner Dr. Watson before beginning
to demonstrate his prowess as a master of ratiocination. Although this
"Freud" is not concerned so much with the whodunit as the "whatdunit," he sets out like a detective with Holmesian questions, probing
Anna's symptoms as clues to what is causing her neurosis. What follows

in this chapter is Freud's reconstruction of the major line of his investi-
gation, or analysis, of that "hidden factor" whose revelation will provide
"his" (and this novel's) readers with the sense of transformation they
have come to expect at the end of this genre—psychoanalytic case study
and detective novel. Along the way, the analyst will direct attention to
the "clues" or "symbols" provided by the analysand, the "secret" she
both knows and does not know, or "the repressed" that will inevitably
"return." "Freud" likens the hysteric's psyche to a child with a secret
through which it tantalizes everyone by leaving "clues" to what is hidden, or repressed (Thomas 1993, 99). This is the "Freud" whose affection for the "symbol" drew him into the simplistic and reductive
symbolic readings of which Thomas offers a pastiche in the "interpretation"of the room in the white hotel as the womb awaiting the entry of
Anna's father's penis to conceive her: "The drying-out umbrella in the
hall was symbolic of the discharged penis" (106). Unfortunately such
symbol hunting, particularly of "phallic symbols," persists in our own
time.[62]

The object of Freud's pursuit will be that "child" in Anna/Lisa who
is "scattering clues," encouraging him to focus on the left breast and left
ovary, "for the unconscious is a precise and even pedantic symbolist"
(Thomas 1993, 99). Many of Freud's readers today might accuse him
of projecting onto the unconscious his own tendency to be a "pedantic
symbolist"; thus, when his Anna speaks of her "white relationship" with
A., the young man who abandoned her, Freud pounces on the association with the white sails of her father's yacht in a classic expression of
his appetite for "symbols." Like a clever detective, Freud has deduced
that Anna's fumbling with her crucifix is a clue to her dissembling, and
he employs this observation as a primitive polygraph machine. This
strategy becomes clear when Freud virtually assaults Anna with an interrogation of that "white relationship" and forces her to confess she
had had relations with A., or "fallen," as part of his effort to probe her
explanation of the "fall" that ended her career as a dancer. Yes, she
admits, she deliberately fell at dance practice to abort A.'s child. When
she expresses astonishment that her analyst "had found out her secret,"
Freud almost says "Elementary, my dear Watson" as he leads her back
through the "clues" in her earlier remarks.

Before we proceed it is instructive to examine the gendering of this
narrative, the ersatz case study Freud is (re)constructing from what he
remembers of his observations of Lisa Erdman. As the "father" of modern psychoanalysis, Freud is the "master" here. He is involved in what
Jacques Lacan has called the "illusion of mastery," for this psychoana-

lytic detective will inevitably be "duped" as soon as *he* arrogates to himself the notion of mastery. As countless writers on Freud have noted, his patients, or analysands, suffering from hysteria were virtually all female. As so many feminists have noted, the ailment's very name, "hysteria" (from the Greek word for "womb"), suggests this sexist gendering of psychological dysfunctions. It is no coincidence that Freud troped the female genitalia as a "dark continent," nor that he troped himself not as a scientist but as a "bold conquistador." This Freud prides himself on his "eye" for details—the "symbols" or "clues" in the discourse of women—and sees himself as a "private eye" in pursuit of a woman's "secrets." In the guise of the scientist he becomes an author in the case study, assuming the powerful agency of narration, as an "I" who is reconstructing stories that draw their readers in through the lure of epistemophilia, with its highly erotic charge of desire for knowledge of a woman's "dark continent."

In this way, Freud's organization of his narrative of Anna G. becomes an effort to "corner" the woman, or more precisely her "psyche," in line with his boastful remark that the "psyche of the hysteric is a child with a secret." As it becomes clearer that Anna/Lisa's secrets are to be found by taking her back to explore her childhood memories of her parents, readers are likely to begin admiring the flash of imaginative brilliance in Thomas's constructing of Lisa's mother and aunt as identical twins. This strategy of twinning allows Thomas's Freud to track Lisa's "hysteria" back to her having actually witnessed a "primal scene." I say, "actually," because in the popular (mis)conception of a "primal scene" the child wittingly observes the parents having sexual intercourse, while in Freud's theorizing the primal scene occurs *nachträglich,* or belatedly, as a recovered memory of the sexually mature adult who finally recognizes that the brief glimpses or overheard sounds were underread "clues" to the parents' "secret" lovemaking.

In this case study, "Freud" examines the texts he encouraged Anna/Lisa to write during her visit to Gastein—the first two sections of this "novel," "Don Giovanni" and "The Gastein Journal." In both texts the "symbol" of the "white hotel" dominates the subject's writing. In a brilliant pastiche of Freudian theorizing, Thomas offers a symbolic interpretation of the white hotel as the mother's body in its immersion in infantile orality, evident in Lisa's obsession with "sucking, biting, eating, gorging, taking in, with all the blissful narcissism of a baby at the breast. Here [Freud continues rhapsodically] is the oceanic oneness of the child's first years, the autoerotic paradise, the map of our first country of love . . ." (116). This is, of course, the white hotel from which the child Lisa was forever foreclosed by her mother's ultimate abandonment of her in death. It goes without saying that the historical Freud's preoccupation with the repetition compulsion in his grandson's *fort/da* game is implicated in his reading of Anna's fantasies of the mother who abandoned her.

The "key" to opening the door foreclosing Anna from her past is the crucifix symbol—by the end of this novel a truly "overdetermined" symbol in its multiple, competing meanings. Anna remembers that her symptoms recurred on the day she heard the news that her old friend Madame R—clearly a surrogate mother—was pregnant. And when Anna recalls her promise to serve as godmother to her friend's child, the pains in her breast and ovary grow more intense. The increased pain seems surprising, since she had admitted to having had sexual relations with her husband, "ending" in coitus interruptus, a strategy even *she* recognized as an illusory means of forestalling pregnancy, and therefore motherhood. The puzzle is, Why does the prospect of even *surrogate* motherhood intensify the symptoms, while the threat of *actual* motherhood as a result of practicing coitus interruptus maintained those symptoms at a moderate level? The "clue" is offered through the agency of the crucifix. When Anna consults her aunt concerning a christening gift for her godson, she (re)learns that her aunt never removed the crucifix she (and her sister) received as a christening gift, while Anna's mother tore hers off because their parents objected to her marrying a Jew. This crucifix is the very one Lisa/Anna never takes off. The crucifix symbol unlocks a memory of this primal scene in a minor expression of the anagnorisis, or tragic recognition, toward which this whole narrative is moving with the inexorability of Oedipus's discovery of *his* identity.

Anna recalls herself as a small child approaching the summerhouse in which her aunt and uncle were involved in what she only later recognizes as lovemaking. As an adult she can "see" that the woman had no crucifix, suggesting that it was her mother who was making love with her uncle. "Freud" reconstructs his own excited desire for the end, indicating that in listening to her narrative he is drawn forward "with a growing assurance of its conclusion" (135), thus confirming the erotic charge of epistemophilia. Now Anna is able to flesh out the memory scene of being abused by the sailors, recalling that they taunted her with the adultery of her mother and uncle, who both died in the hotel fire (137).

After reading the poem "Don Giovanni" and "The Gastein Journal" he had encouraged her to write while away at a resort, Freud becomes convinced that Anna has not revealed the full story of sexual intercourse in her marriage. His description of his "forceful" extraction of the truth from Anna is worth noting for his vehement accusations that she is wasting his time with her lying. In a self-congratulatory extension of this rendition of his response, he notes it was through these "threats" that he could "drag" the truth out of his patient (123). In essence, the "truth" that this self-styled "conquistador" wrests from her is essentially that during intercourse she hallucinates the horrors of her poem and journal—the flood, the fire, the falling from great heights, the avalanche (in short, the catastrophic suffering taking place)—while she is supposed to be experiencing intense pleasure.

Section 3, Freud's case study, ends with his expected generalizations about his analysand. Playing out the "Electra complex" Freud belatedly constructed for women who could not fit the "Oedipus complex," Anna resented her mother as a rival for her father's love, and magically her "wish" for her mother's death was granted in the hotel fire. She was prevented by guilt from enjoying her victory however, and her later life witnessed her affection for a series of mother surrogates to whom she may well have been homosexually attracted. "Freud" trades in simplistic witticisms (he tells Anna she is "cured of everything but life") and psychoanalytic platitudes ("No analysis is ever complete," a rendering of the historical Freud's assertion that "the analysis is interminable"). In another expression of Freud as the author manqué, he announces that he is nearing the "end" of his own text with a comment on Anna's journal. In his analysis, she longs to return her mother's womb of which the white hotel is clearly a symbol (143), suggesting again the conventional wisdom that much of the historical Freud's writings were less science than autobiography.

The "novel" is barely half-finished, however. And the term "novel" here deserves scare quotes as one means of paying attention to this text, or this series of texts, as a radical departure from the conventions of the genre. In one sense, *The White Hotel* is a pastiche of the modernist notion that form and content are one and the same. At its center is the content of Freud's writing on the repetition compulsion and its grounding in the desire to work through the repetitions until the desire for the end can finally be fulfilled. This content is (re)presented in the ersatz case study "Frau Anna G." as that text is a representation of Lisa Erdman's life. This principle of nested narratives with its *mise en abîme* effect not only implicates narrative in an endless slippage from one text to another, problematizing what is "real" and what is textual; it also represents in a microcosm Peter Brooks's notion of conflicting desires impelling narrative forward and holding it back so that narrative achieves an autonomy light-years beyond the sense of a consciously contrived story being told by an author.

The central question of this "novel" is, Where does it begin? Page ix is the crux: its "contents" lists both an "author's note," beginning with page vii and a "prologue," beginning with page 1. Is this "author's note" outside the novel and the "prologue" inside? It seems reasonable that the "author's note" was written after the completion of the narrative, when the author became the reader of his text, and may well have been the result of an editor's advice that the novel really could use a framing device to establish a "real" world in which the text to follow would have a credible existence. Accordingly, the "author's note" performs the binary of "fact" versus "fiction" in the narrative proper. With its pagination as "1," the prologue is logically inside the novel, offering a fictional reconstruction of what a Freud might have written to his associates about his anonymous analysand, not yet "Lisa Erdman" nor "Frau Anna G." Given the conventional understanding that like author's notes, prologues, forewords, and introductions are written by readers (the author or another reader) after the narrative has been completed— like epilogues, postscripts, and afterwords, we might hasten to add— this prologue to *The White Hotel* causes problems for the conventional notion of narrative. In somewhat the same way, the apparent epilogue, the last chapter following Lisa's death, will prove problematical.

What are we to make of this strange prologue that seems no more than an exchange of fictional letters? Is it doing anything other than repeating within the text the extratextual notion of a real/fictional binary? Accordingly, it is a false start. As it becomes clearer in the narrative poem, "Don Giovanni," readers are expected to connect with Freud's analysand through the centrality of the white hotel and the details in his letter to Sachs in which he indicates that the woman had never met his son Martin, whom he had merely mentioned during a session. One can only wonder how Freud the scientist would have alluded to his son, the prisoner of war, in speaking with an analysand when he never indicated in *Beyond the Pleasure Principle* that the toddler playing the *fort/da* game was his own grandson, presumably to enhance scientific objectivity. In the same letter, he alludes only briefly to his dead daughter, his "Sunday child" (10).[63] In any case, the pagination of this prologue insists on its status inside the narrative, yet "Don Giovanni" seems a new start. This phenomenon proves instructive because the next section (one wants almost to say "the next text")—"The Gastein Journal"—is yet another new start. Thus, this narrative, the novel as a whole, performs the very repetition compulsion that is its content.[64] The novel performs a series of moves from text to text, oscillating between "prose" and "poetry" or "fact" and "fiction" or "reason" and its Other. This Other comprises the alternative explications of Lisa/Anna's ailments. Thus, it is appropriate that we begin with an author's note exercising the illusory truth that authors are supposed to trade in, then move to an unedited or unframed epistolary exchange, followed by a narrative poem, a journal of fantasies, and a case study. In one sense, "Frau Anna G." provides the core of this narrative's deconstruction of the fantasy/reality binary, for even as readers are finishing this text they have a sense that Freud's rationalizing of Anna's symptoms represents the illusion of mastery stigmatizing it as the masculinist pursuit of truth in what might be called the "fantasy of rationality."[65] The rest of this narrative will provide evidence to its "Freud" that the analysis is indeed never finished, for the truth is not insights to be systematized as "science," but the ongoing "talking cure," synonymous with an unending narration, since ending can never be more than the illusion of closure, an imposition by the process of narration that *will* drive on to its climax, regardless of whatever may stand in its way. "Freud" must have a conclusion for his case study, an ending to transform confusion into knowledge so that the desire for the end will be fulfilled, but even *he* knows that the narrative, like analysis, is "interminable," and it is only the masters who impose its ending.

This sense of both the analysis and the narrative as interminable is evident in the next section, "The Health Resort," in which Lisa Erdman becomes the reader/editor of Freud's manuscript for the case study "Frau Anna G." In line with the notion of the narrative itself performing a series of texts, each of which represents an expression of the repetition compulsion, this fourth section, or text, draws readers into the illusion of mastery. After an erotic—some would say pornographic—narrative poem, an equally erotic journal, and a case study, the novel seems to settle into its business of conventional narration. What could be more conventional than its opening sentence, "In the spring of 1929, Frau Elisabeth Erdman was travelling by train between Vienna and Milan" (147)? The comfortable third-person narrator lures the reader into an illusory sense that the storm of the narrative's irrational earlier stages has passed, and the author has taken charge of an unruly narrative that has been insisting on starting again and again until it finally "gets it right." Lisa is "on her way," not simply to Milan to substitute for a diva who has broken her arm but also to the promise of moderately good mental or spiritual health. Dr. Freud seems to have done his job, and Lisa is "cured of everything but life," as he quipped. This comfortable atmosphere increases as the narrative moves its readers into this modest "success story," never playing to a reader's furtive wishes that this viewpoint character can ever expect to become a "star," but simply acquit herself well as an aging, at best second-tier, performer. As she herself admits, she was a last resort for the role. Her response is surprisingly, perhaps alarmingly, positive: She considers herself "lucky" to have this one last opportunity to sing in a leading role at La Scala and to be able to recall this minor success in her later years (Thomas 1993, 150).

And soon the narrative moves on to Lisa's relationship with Vera Serebryakova, whom she "replaces," and the singer Victor Berenstein, whom Lisa is embarrassed not to have known was the husband of Vera as well as the father of her child. Although the couple cannot be much older than Lisa, they soon become surrogate parents, perhaps in part because of Lisa's earlier deprivations. The narrative moves along on this "success story" plane, generating anxiety for at least some readers, made uneasy by its apparent easy optimism. Lisa seems to be settling into her room in the white hotel, and yet the narrative begins to allow nightmare images to surface: Lisa thinks, "Of all suffering, she could least tolerate the suffering of children" (159), anticipating another image from her letter to Freud: "I have always found it difficult to enjoy myself properly, knowing there were people suffering 'just the other side of the hill'" (191). Thus, this conventionally realist segment of the narrative performs its own repetition of the "white hotel" sections, "Don Giovanni" and "The Gastein Journal." The pleasure principle seems to reign, but the dreams of comfort and ease grounded in the illusory security of rationality are increasingly troubled by bits of potential nightmare, as if the narrative, like Lisa's psyche, has repressed the dark and deadly Other that must inevitably "return" to demolish any illusion of reason's power to dispel the nightmares.

When Vera dies and Victor is left alone to raise their son, Kolya, readers are impelled to wonder, Can a woman bereft of a mother at an early age refuse to adopt this child? And not surprisingly, the deaths of Vera and of Ludmila Kedrova ("Madame R." in the case study) bring about the "return of the repressed" through the familiar symptoms, as these two motherless children call out to her to relieve their suffering through surrogate motherhood. The return of the symptoms, just when Lisa must have begun to believe herself "cured," is instructive. If, as Freud once joked, psychoanalysis is a plague,[66] Lisa may have contracted one form of it in his naive faith in the power of reason to discover the truth and to enact a "cure." Indeed, much of the latter section of this chapter is devoted to what becomes the poignant correspondence between the aged Freud (he would have been seventy-five in 1931) and the Lisa who has only *seemed* to succeed through his "cure." The recurrence of the symptoms suggests a "cure" may be tantamount to becoming like Oedipus, who began to believe that he was finally "safe," that he had outwitted fate. It is hardly a coincidence that Lisa shares with Freud the news of her recent appearance in an oratorio with the intriguing title *Oedipus Rex* (200).

This exchange of letters concerning the case study Freud seeks to publish as "Frau Anna G." and shares with Lisa for her input and approval offers further evidence that "the analysis is interminable." For Lisa the correspondence concerning the case study offers the opportunity for the "talking cure" to continue on paper as she "corrects" his errors and even supplies additional information. Lisa as storyteller is now empowered in somewhat the same manner as "Anna O." (Bertha Pappenheim) was empowered as the patient of Freud's mentor, Joseph Breuer, to conceptualize her discourse in their sessions as the "talking cure." This suggests that the discourse itself is producing the "cure," rather than the male psychoanalyst's rational conclusions drawn from that discourse. As Freud's "editor" as well as the storyteller controlling the discourse, Lisa positions herself as "masculine" in the power relationships grounded in positionality.[67] Freud seems, in contrast, strangely "feminized" by his position of vulnerability as Lisa wields the power over his writing, like a sympathetic mother who pities his naïveté in not getting her story quite right. This is no longer Freud the bold conquistador, wresting the treasure of "truth" out of the "dark continent," but a rather feeble, pathetic, broken man, recovering from surgery for cancer of the mouth and throat, and struggling with the prosthesis supplying him with a kind of mechanical mouth.

Lisa's corrections of lies and errors as well as the additions she can now supply render the case study of "Frau Anna G." extremely problematical. With her father's death, she learns from Aunt Magda, the sole survivor of that generation, more about her mother's relationship with Lisa's uncle, Magda's husband. Lisa admits that the summerhouse "primal scene" was in fact a "cover memory" for an incident of her mother, aunt, and uncle aboard her father's yacht. (She also admits to unjustly maligning her lover, A., who was never abusive.) Now Lisa seems more receptive to the probability that her so-called uncle was actually her father, having suppressed that probability during her analysis to keep Erdman, a Jew, as her official father, lest she offend Freud. Similarly, she indicates it was because she was Erdman's daughter that the sailors abused her; furthermore, she reveals that they forced her to perform fellatio on them, denigrating her as a "Jewess" who had no more worth than as a performer of sodomy.

Lisa's last letter, in which she tells Freud she has sung in *Oedipus Rex*, requires further attention, because it offers a rich text, as the narrative begins to signal readers that she is on her own way to a tragic end. This last letter is written in response to Freud's open and generous letter expressing his intention merely to add Lisa's "corrections" as an appendix while publishing the case study itself as he originally sent it to her, thus confirming his identity as an author, rather than as a scientist. He reveals to Lisa that her prophetic powers were accurate, and his grandson Heinz followed his mother, Sophie Freud Halberstadt, by dying at a tender age, adding: "With him, my affectional life came to an end" (Thomas 1993, 195), a truly rare expression of Freud's feelings. And after she communicates her sense of responsibility for these deaths because she foresaw them, he attempts to allay her guilt by confirming a willingness to subscribe to a belief in "telepathy" (not quite the same thing!), encouraging her to cherish the gift of her clairvoyance. Sensing that this exchange of letters is ending, Lisa confesses her delight in discovering from her aunt that she probably is not Jewish. In addition, she admits to Freud that years ago she wrote to her husband that she was finally prepared to "go the whole way," only to experience such "dreadful nightmares" the same night that she began to have new misgivings. Her husband, whose job it was to prosecute deserters, had just written a gloating letter about his brilliant performance in persuading the military tribunal to condemn a deserter to death. Lisa foresees the impossibility of enjoying the ecstasies of connubial bliss while another is suffering the agony of execution. As earlier noted, she has already written to Freud: "I have always found it difficult to enjoy myself properly, knowing there were people suffering 'just the other side of the hill'" (191).

Toward the end of this letter, Lisa "crave[s] more stimulating company. I would give much for one of our discussions of the old days" (200), suggesting *her* awareness that the "analysis is interminable." The allusion to her singing in *Oedipus Rex* itself is probably meant as a flattering gesture toward Freud's concern with the Oedipus complex. She does not identify her role. On second thought, however, she doesn't need to: unless the director of the production was experimenting with transgendering the parts, she must have enacted Jocasta, the grieving mother who foolishly conspired with her husband to circumvent the prophecy by killing their son and then even more foolishly took a second husband young enough to be her own son. What Lisa, and

"Freud," could not see was that the return of the repressed operates as something very much like "fate." The repressed can be understood, not so much through reasoning as through suffering again the consequences of the delusions that the repressed has been "conquered" through explication. Lisa can babble in this last letter about how much better she felt when her analyst encouraged her to "dig out" the truth of her mother's affair: "I felt excited at the way it cleared up mysteries. Clarification! Anagnorisis!" (200). This blithe rendition of tragic mysteries, however, can only unsettle readers, aware that the narrative has not run its course, aware of the advice of the chorus in the closing lines of *Oedipus Rex:*

> Let every man in mankind's frailty
> Consider his last day; and let none
> Presume on his good fortune until he find
> Life, at his death, a memory without pain.
>
> (Sophocles 1977, 81)

Lisa's patently naive confidence in the power of reason to clarify mysteries is the very center of the "plague" she has caught from Freud, who read *Oedipus Rex* to confirm his science but failed to *see* the potential for hubris in the overweening faith in the ability to gain insight without paying the horrible price of suffering and loss.

In this way the stage is set for the tragic ending of this oedipal plot. Section 5 is entitled "The Sleeping Carriage," with perhaps the same irrelevance as the title of section 4, "The Health Resort." As in the enactment of the repetition compulsion in the earlier sections, the narrative begins over again with a text in which readers must search for familiar characters. In contrast to the warmer realist style of the preceding section, this "last" major section, "The Sleeping Carriage," has moved to a cold, harsh naturalist style to tell the story, as though from a vantage point of outer space. Without preparation readers are thrust into Kiev "on the morning of Monday, 29 September 1941," where the invading Germans are rounding up Jews to transport them to "the Promised Land." Lisa and Kolya are being marched to Babi Yar, where they are stripped, beaten, and lined up for the firing squad—all with the suddenness of nightmare, in which the only hope seems to be awakening again to an apparently stable and secure world of reason.

As Lisa attempts to grasp what is happening, it becomes clear that this nightmare *is* the world of reason in which she and Freud had grounded their humanist faith. Indeed, Lisa's first response is the futile attempt to make sense of this madness: "[T]here was simply no reason to kill all these people" (244). It must be a joke, she decides; the Germans are merely firing over the heads of the naked Jews, and having had their fun they will tell the victims of this practical joke to get dressed and board the train to the promised land. "It was mad, but not so mad as the alternative" (244). The madness overwhelms Lisa because she cannot accept the starting assumption of these reasoning madmen that some groups are "vermin"; once the Nazis have made such an assumption, all this rationally engineered extermination became possible, in much the same way that *A Modest Proposal* proceeds with mad humor once Jonathan Swift's persona has accepted the notion that the Irish are animals. The conjunction of humor and madness dominates the scene of horror—from Lisa's pathetic effort to rescue herself and Kolya by claiming she is not Jewish to the sleepwalking of the doomed to their places of execution at the edge of the trench. The irony of tragedy within which we are defeated by our best intentions offers a chilling parallel to the joke mechanism, suggesting the notion of "tragic jokes."

Like Oedipus, Lisa is overwhelmed by anagnorisis while she waits with Kolya for death. Brooks seems absolutely correct in arguing that the approach of death transforms everything that comes before. Suddenly Lisa *knows*, and the readers of this narrative know, too: "Now she knew why she ought never to have had children," but that knowledge provides no escape, any more than her futile attempt to gain release by revealing her non-Jewishness can save her, once she has borne witness to this atrocity and gained the power to undermine its continuing efficacy by revealing what is on "the other side of the hill." The novel says, "And yet the thought of Kolya, her son, being here with strangers . . . was a hundred times worse than the terror of death" (245). It is as though the narrative itself begins to "remember" all the clues it unconsciously offered, pointing toward this horrible ending. The central "clues" for Lisa have been her inability to bear the suffering of children or to experience pleasure while others are suffering out of sight.

This "recognition scene" toward which this narrative has been inevitably moving gives way to yet another with even more monumental ramifications. Now that Lisa *knows*, perhaps the narrative will allow her and Kolya to escape to tell their tale. This false hope is fed by her clever jumping with Kolya into the seething trench of corpses as the hail of bullets approaches them; and, indeed, she at least survives for some time, until she draws attention to herself by calling out and the SS man sees the glint of the symbolic crucifix. Suddenly the narrative has its "real" ending. It enacts a masculine, or oedipal, ending with a powerful and overwhelming "climax." As Lisa has been transformed into a full-scale tragic hero, she recognizes in a blinding flash of insight[68] that her efforts to escape her rendezvous with Babi Yar have been foolish and that all the symptoms have been not the return of the repressed from childhood but flashes forward to the "ending" of her life, to the end of her story, to the masculine paradigm's alignment of narrative climax and sexual orgasm, enacted in the pastiche of Lisa's "rape" by the German's bayonet—where else but in the left breast and the left ovary? Lisa's demise, the death of the narrative, and the *petite mort* of sexual pleasure come together in the awful pun of this tragic reversal, with its anagnorisis. In a moment of metaphor's power of transformation, the narrative performs Lisa *knowing* why. Reenacting Oedipus, or *his* mother, Lisa has invested in the illusion of rationality, or Lacan's "illusion of mastery," encouraged by rationality.

In this way, "Freud" is overmastered by the very "telepathy" or clairvoyance he nostalgically wished to have another lifetime to study. Lisa's symptoms were not the stigmata of hysteria to be understood by tracking down the "whatdunit" in her childhood. They are the body's clairvoyance, the wisdom of the body with its own reasons, as it anticipates the horrors to come. In one sense, Freud is correct in his notion that the death wish, with its teasing of the subject into desire, impels the subject to anticipate the moment of death as a threshold to reentering that quiescence predating life. In yet another sense, Freud misread psychoanalysis as scientific conclusions and expository texts, when this narrative suggests what he must have also known: psychoanalysis is narration, talking/writing and listening/reading. At the very most, all we can do is retell. As we begin to draw conclusions, we move toward the illusion of mastery, inviting the return of the repressed.

And the final section, "The Camp," continues the undermining of faith in the rule of reason in which Freud had invested so heavily. Reason would remind the atheist Freud that the afterlife is a self-delusion; here, however, is the afterlife represented as though the scene were a camp for displaced persons, and what is more, he himself is in it! His humanist faith in the power of knowing through reason is undone at Babi Yar, and then undone again in "the camp." And Brooks's confidence that he has discovered the "masterplot" for narrative seems to come undone in the pastiche of his theorizing in the ending of this narrative, giving way to a recognition that it was not an ending after all. As Freud pronounced, yet did not entirely accept, the interminability of the analysis, so too Brooks must confront in *The White Hotel* a narrative, itself intent on deconstructing his faith in Freud's "masterplot."

In any case, *The White Hotel* offers a provocative segue to the next section of this exploration of ending in narrative. Few would question the powerful ending the narrative offers in Lisa's tragic recognition scene at Babi Yar, an anagnorisis that reads Oedipus's blinding insight of having run into the jaws of the very fate he attempted to escape. This expression of ending in the masculine paradigm for narrative is clarified, countered, subverted—depending on the reader's preference—by at least two endings, if not more. With the inclusion of "the camp"— what may be either the afterlife as purgatory or the unwillingness of the psyche to accept the quiescence Freud understood as the goal of the death wish[69]—the narrative reminds readers that the very nature of this text as a collection of interconnected yet disparate texts, masquerading as "chapters," has been undermining the logic of narrative structure from the outset. The text entitled "The Camp" seemingly has no place in the narrative "proper,"[70] because it contests the rationality on which psychoanalysis and narrative structure have been thought to rest. In contrast to the dramatic "climax" of the masculine plot at Babi Yar, "The Camp" offers a vista that shows no signs of ever ending.[71]

And as if that ending in unendingness were not enough, the literal "ending" of *The White Hotel* circles back to an earlier scene readers may not have attended to fully. Lisa recalls in the closing lines an intense image of "the scent of a pine tree. She couldn't place it. . . . It troubled her in some mysterious way, yet also made her happy" (Thomas 1993, 274). The image may trouble readers too if they cannot "place it," but it occurs at the end of Lisa's return to the Erdman summerhouse with Victor and Kolya. She has what seems a mystical experience of a "clear space opened to her childhood," and she knows the full limits of human happiness: "It was not a memory from the past but the past itself, as alive, as real; and she knew that she and the child of forty years ago were the same person" (213–14).[72] The recuperation of this pine-scented image at the end of the narrative further problematizes this apparent expression of the masculine narrative paradigm by impelling us to suspect at this moment that the narrative's genuine ending was not at Babi Yar nor in "the camp" but in this mystical experience of a state of being that ineffably transcends all else. The text seems to be positing Lacan's Real with its existence outside of the registers of both the Imaginary and the Symbolic. If this text is indeed ending in the Real, Thomas's narrative may be moving toward a most radical deconstruction of itself as a text, undermining the very register of the Symbolic within which texts operate. In this way, *The White Hotel* renders naively simplistic the traditional notion of ending as a "tock," opting instead for its sense of an ending in the unending "tick" of a Real forever outside the textuality with which the Symbolic attempts to cope with that Real.

Cluster 2:
Undoing the Paradigm — Perhaps

ONE STARTING POINT FOR THE NEXT CLUSTER OF NARRATIVES IS TO note the growing complication in issues of ending in the preceding cluster. Once *Amsterdam* has announced its mousetrap or joke structure and the narrative has set up the situation of Molly's agonizingly long nightmare of dying and the euthanasia pact of the two men, whose lack of close family ties might doom each to a living hell, the ending of the two men transforming mercy killing into mutual murder proceeds with its own frightening logic. Similarly, in *Edwin Mullhouse* the narrative is set into motion when the narrator emphasizes that this "biography" of a young writer will end at the tender age of eleven, stimulating the reader's hunger to know *how* Edwin's life ended so "prematurely." The revelation of that ending is one toward which readers are drawn with a sickening but feverish desire to know. When the narrator reveals his complicity in Edwin's death, the narrative generates a confusion strikingly similar to the reader's response to the endings of other novels in this cluster, such as *When We Were Orphans* and *The Blind Assassin*, in which the knowledge disclosed seems almost too immense to be easily incorporated into the reader's sense of the "middle" from which these revelations generated themselves. By the "end" of the first cluster, a novel such as *The White Hotel* should already have begun to leave readers with the sense that the masculine narrative paradigm was coming undone, for this narrative offers more than a single ending, although it does so less "dramatically" than does *The French Lieutenant's Woman*, the novel with which this second cluster will begin. *The White Hotel* complicates the conventional notion of "plot" and "subplots," making the multiplicity of ending in narrative inevitable.

It should come as no surprise, then, that novelists were registering their discontent with what I have termed the "masculine narrative paradigm" well before academics were beginning to theorize those discontents. Fowles published the first novel in this cluster, *The French Lieutenant's Woman*, in 1969, and Doris Lessing published the first novel

in the next, *The Golden Notebook*, in 1962. As noted earlier, "narratology"
theorizes what has already happened in narrative, and novelists obviously have no interest in writing fiction to provide examples of one the-
oretic perception or another. And it should be no surprise that it was
not *male* theorists who began to draw attention to the gender blindness
of an almost exclusively male writing in narratology and that it was
feminist narratologists who began to complicate our understanding of
narrative and ending in the late 1970s.

Among that generation, one of the most provocative was the feminist
film theorist Teresa de Lauretis. Perhaps because of her investment in
film theory, grounded in the seminal work of the Lacanian theorist
Christian Metz and the brilliant theorist Laura Mulvey, Lauretis seems
not to have been aware of Peter Brooks's essay "Freud's Masterplot."
Lauretis notes that Roland Barthes connected Eros and epistemology
by linking both narrative and language with the figure of Oedipus.
Barthes concludes: "The pleasure of the text is . . . an Oedipal pleasure
(to denude, to know, to learn the origin and the end), if it is true that
every narrative (every unveiling of the truth) is a staging of the (absent,
hidden, or hypostatized) father—which would explain the solidarity of
narrative forms, of family structures, and of prohibitions of nudity"
(qtd. by Lauretis 1984, 108). It is, however, in the writing of Barthes's
American disciple Robert Scholes that Lauretis focuses on expressions
of the even more blatant analogy between narrative and the trajectory
of (male) sexuality. Scholes writes:

> The archetype of all fiction is the sexual act. . . . [W]hat connects fiction—
> and music—with sex is the fundamental orgastic rhythm of tumescence and
> detumescence, of tension and resolution, of intensification to the point of
> climax and consummation. In the sophisticated forms of fiction, as in the
> sophisticated practice of sex, much of the art consists of delaying climax
> within the framework of desire in order to prolong the pleasurable act itself.
> When we look at fiction with respect to its form alone, we see a pattern of
> events designed to move toward climax and resolution, balanced by a
> counter-pattern of events designed to delay this very climax and resolution.
> (qtd. in Lauretis 1984, 108)

Seemingly "determined to run his metaphor into the ground," says
Lauretis, Scholes indicates that the relationship between writer and
reader, if each makes an effort to avoid "acts of mental masturbation,"
may aspire to a "marriage of true minds" in which this joint immersion
in fiction "is perfect and complete" (108). As a woman, Lauretis reminds her readers, it may not be quite so possible for her to adopt the

reading practices Scholes prescribes: "Those of us who know no art of delaying climax or, reading, feel no incipient tumescence, may well be barred from the pleasure of this 'full fictional act'; nor may we profit from the rhythm method by which it is attained" (108). In this brief discussion Lauretis brilliantly points to what male theorists writing about the "rhythm" of narrative had been missing for years, perhaps millennia—namely, that notions of narrative structure have been blind to the implications for gender in their theorizing and that female sexuality might be examined as a potential field of alternatives to the monolithic male model.

With the increased participation of feminists in the project of "narratology"—a term many feminists have resisted as "masculinist"— theorizing about narrative and especially about the ending of narrative began to direct attention to the impact of gender. Indeed, it might be argued that the most provocative and insightful work in narratology in the past two decades has been produced by feminists intent on exploring alternatives to the oedipal plot, whose ending is "ejaculatory," to borrow Joseph Boone's term. Because our culture has struggled to disentangle concepts of gender from notions of sex differences and because much of earlier feminism was entrenched in structuralist binaries separating women and men, there is a wide range of narrative theorizing about the investment of narrative in desire.

A characteristic response to the traditional notion of plot and ending as grounded in the trajectory of male sexuality may be found in the writing of Rachel Blau DuPlessis. DuPlessis turns to the fiction of a "lost," early twentieth-century novelist, Mina Loy, as an example of narrative grounded in the female or "seismic" orgasm. DuPlessis writes: "There has emerged, thanks first to Freud and then to Peter Brooks and Roland Barthes, a suggestive discussion, with universal claims, of narrative design and sexual trajectories" (1985, 187–88). Hypothesizing that this paradigm may be the product of "pressures on gender and sexuality created by feminisms" (188), DuPlessis contests the Brooksian notion that narrative depends on a male model of orgasm, and argues that female orgasm may be providing its own model for narrative, presumably narrative produced exclusively by women.

DuPlessis notes the work of Susan Winnett in her widely read *PMLA* article, "Coming Unstrung: Women, Men, Narrative, and Principles of Pleasure." Winnett memorably opens her essay with the provocative assertion, "I would like to begin with the proposition that female orgasm is unnecessary" (1990, 504). Her project is to point out the implication of the Brooksian paradigm that it pertains to *all* narrative as a first step toward exploring the possibility of a female alternative to the male paradigm. Like DuPlessis and some other feminists such as Lauretis, Winnett skates perilously close to the essentialism that has tied paradigms for narrative—female as well as male—to the biology of sexual difference. What may be more useful here is a kind of "deconstruction" of these structuralist binaries to complicate our notions of narrative as implicated in "gender," rather than sexual biology. Indeed, the movement from feminist studies in the 1980s to gender studies in the 1990s marked a greater (and salutary) subtlety in "narratology." Judith Butler, among others, has directed attention to the continuum of gender, enabling our focus on the ways in which "femininity" and "masculinity" are not mutually exclusive, but merely the ends of a gender spectrum, along which engendered narrative may also range. Thus, individual writers, male or female, may produce narratives in which gender-generating elements run the gamut from the "masculine" to the "feminine."

Another writer who has made a major contribution to the gendering of narrative is Marianne Hirsch. In framing her examination of what she terms "the mother/daughter plot," Hirsch argues for the need to move beyond the study of women who have written within traditional literary conventions, and accordingly have defined the feminine from a male viewpoint. Hirsch directs attention to "female plots" as theorized by feminists such as Patricia Yaeger. The subtitle of Yaeger's book, *Honey-Mad Women: Emancipatory Strategies in Women's Fiction,* offers us an entry to the concept of strategies employed by women to write themselves out of traditional (male) models for narrative. Those "emancipatory strategies" include, in Hirsch's words, "the revisions of endings, beginnings, patterns of progression." Hirsch continues: "This process of resistance, revision, and emancipation in the work of women writers is, as Nancy K. Miller has argued, a *feminist* act defining a *feminist* poetics and it needs to be identified as such" (Hirsch 1989, 8; italics in original). It may not be entirely coincidental that in her rendition of "emancipatory strategies," Hirsch begins her triad of "revisions" with "endings." Furthermore, it is apropos that Hirsch singles out the revision of the traditional narrative paradigm as theorized by Peter Brooks as her focus, commenting: "Peter Brooks's theory of plotting can serve as a symptom of recent theoretical preoccupation and procedure. I concentrate here on Brooks's theory because I find his dynamic model of plot construction particularly appealing, but also particularly gender-blind" (53). To Brooks's insistence on "retard, postponement" or "deferral," Hirsch would counterpose *"continued opposition, interruption, and contradiction"* (102; italics in original). In her focus on Brooks's rendition of the traditional paradigm for narrative, Hirsch joins DuPlessis, Winnett, and other feminists in helping to support my linkage of Brooks with that paradigm in this project.

In opposition to Brooks's emphasis on repetition in plot, Hirsch would stress principles of *"contradiction* and *oscillation"* (italics in original). Following a perceptive and provocative discussion of Virginia Woolf's *To the Lighthouse* in which she maps those principles in that novel's "plot," Hirsch goes on to say: "This sense of discomfort and irresolution does mark the plots I am discussing, in which the oscillation between opposites, the shifting allegiances, the duplicitous posturing are not resolved into comfortable or harmonious ordering. No clearcut [*sic*] sense of closure ensues and the narrative remains prospective and proleptic, poised at break of day, or focused on the process rather than the product of vision" (118). Hirsch goes on to concede that "contradiction" need not be seen as a denial of repetition but merely as the opposite pole of contradiction. In this way, repetition's binding through metaphor, or the same-but-different, may be counterposed with what Hirsch calls "a refusal to return, a looking forward, a bonding, which is implied in the idea of maternity and the experience of reproduction" (118).

The principles theorized by Hirsch as a "female plot" raise provocative questions about whether *"continued opposition, interruption, and contradiction"* are the exclusive province of women and a narrative construed as "female plot." Might it be possible to unmoor these principles from the "female plot" and gender them "feminine" so that narrative written by men or narrative with fictional characters who are male could embrace such "femininity," in opposition to and in conjunction with Brooks's "repetition"? That is, if Hirsch in arguing for a "female plot" is willing to risk falling into essentialism, would she be willing to accept a larger and more free-ranging, more contemporary, notion of gender by which biology gives way to cultural constructions of "gender"? Might it not be possible to conceive of a male writer focusing on the experience of male characters in his fiction and yet practicing the "emancipatory strategies" Yaeger proposes for women?

As a group the narratives in the cluster to follow seem to be troubling, if not overtly contesting, the traditional narrative paradigm. The title for this cluster, "Undoing the Paradigm—Perhaps," intimates some of the need to preserve as much openness as possible in examining these strategies of "undoing." A number of novels follow the pattern set in John Fowles's *The French Lieutenant's Woman* of *seeming* to undermine the traditional notion of a narrative having a single ending. (In saying the "traditional notion" I except, of course, the ending(s) of a novel such as *Great Expectations,* whose readers registered their disapproval of the first ending Dickens supplied and forced him to provide one closer to their liking.) The moot question will be, To what degree does the contesting or even the outright denial of a single ending paradoxically confirm the traditional notion of ending as the final determinant of a narrative's meaning?

The novels examined in the first cluster succeed in seducing readers into waiting for the end in large part because the reading of narrative has been culturally constructed to have both a "sense of the ending" and an ending to make sense of the narrative. These novels may have postmodern elements such as self-reflexivity, especially the foregrounding of storytelling by the narrator. They run the gamut from straightforward traditional narratives (such as we have seen in *Amsterdam*) with the clear sense of *an* ending to those (such as *Waterland* and *The White Hotel*) in which it might be argued the novel ends two or three times, perhaps more. The incidence of more than one ending in these novels *seems* to undermine the traditional "masculine" paradigm. However, it might also be argued that the multiplying of endings has the opposite effect, a shoring up that paradigm by focusing on how dependent meaning is on the ending(s) of narrative. Accordingly, whichever ending readers choose as *the* ending confirms the particular meaning the reader wants to see the narrative supporting; in the process, the preferred ending buttresses the traditional paradigm in which a single ending has usually established its meaning. A novel such as *Waterland,* like *This Side of Brightness* with its own two endings for a past and a present story line, ought to provide few problems for the masculine narrative paradigm. *The White Hotel* is quite a different matter, because its several endings move toward a problematizing of the paradigm, especially in the very last lines. Lisa's recollection of the smell of pine needles in the camp, when she is presumably "dead," reminds readers of that earlier argument for a variety of "oceanic" sense, outside time and chronology, and therefore partaking perhaps of a nonnarrativity, or perhaps demonstrating a "feminine" paradigm, outside the end orientation of the masculine paradigm. It is this hint of a nonnarrativity, or a narrativity working toward freedom from sequentiality, that will serve as the territory to be explored in the pages to follow.

THE SHELL GAME OF ENDING(S): JOHN FOWLES'S *THE FRENCH LIEUTENANT'S WOMAN*

The French Lieutenant's Woman offers what at first seems a conventional expression of the traditional paradigm. Charles Smithson and his fiancée, Ernestina Freeman, encounter a mysterious figure positioned dramatically at the end of a seawall on the English Channel, apparently staring toward France from which the French lieutenant of the title had come. The episode allows the narrative to construct this figure as alternately "the French lieutenant's . . . woman," or "Tragedy." Since the third-person narrator is relying for this public construction of Sarah Woodruff on Tina, a more constant visitor to Lyme Regis than Charles Smithson, the narrative encourages the reader to play detective, along with Charles, who, functioning here like the listener, is aroused from a state of quiescence. Charles is generated by this narrative as the man who desires to *know* the mystery of this "fallen woman," who apparently is self-consciously participating in the construction of herself as "Tragedy," the woman who flagrantly risked the likelihood of ill repute. The narrative immediately poses questions arousing conventional erotic energy: How did she become a fallen woman? And perhaps, even, Why? The narrative quickly moves, however, to the more complex question, Why does Sarah call attention to her outcast state by so publicly positioning herself at the sea's edge, across which she stares toward the France of her betrayer?

As the masculine narrative paradigm demands, the narrative generates itself out a desire to know the truth. This epistemophilia is centered in the male viewpoint character here and appeals to the "masculine" reader, whether male or female, stimulated by this desire for the end as a transformation of the mundane into the transcendent. Sarah's "crime" is fornication—the ellipsis marks in Tina's explanatory "the French Lieutenant's . . . Woman" suggesting the stigma of the unspeakable word *whore*—even though Sarah could perhaps have achieved pariah status just as easily as a thief or arsonist. The plot energized by Charles Smithson's desire to know, as a model for the reader, moves quickly into a conventional and perhaps appropriately nineteenth-century fictional representation of marriage as the approved but too constricting channel for the fulfillment of erotic energy. Potential endings begin to generate themselves: Charles will become involved with Sarah and be forced to forgo either the conventionally sanctioned outlet for Eros with Ernestina, on the one hand, or the more powerfully energized but fugitive pursuit of this mysterious "fallen woman," on the other. Were the setting France—according to the cultural construction of "France" by the English—and were Charles a French hero, say, a Charles de Bougainville[1] of the nineteenth century, he might simply make one woman his wife and the other his mistress. The anticipation of a more conventionally "English" ending in which a Charles Smithson will choose only *one* woman, and presumably Ernestina, is complicated by numerous factors, primarily through its multiplying of possible endings to the plot just set in motion.

The first of at least three possible "masculine" endings presents itself to Charles on the train returning him to Lyme Regis and Ernestina from his meeting with her father in London. This perhaps *most* "masculine" ending dramatizes Charles's return to make a clean breast of his foolish decision to meet with Sarah in Ware Common after Mrs. Poulteney dismissed her. Charles justifies his meeting with Sarah as an effort to assist Dr. Grogan in forestalling her suicide. He is buoyed by learning that apparently no one other than his servant Sam and Ernestina's servant Mary know about the meeting—both of whom he is confident of controlling. His efforts on this Borgesian "forking path" of the narrative seems fairly straightforward damage control.

This narrative path appears to end abruptly, barely three pages into chapter 44. Following the ellipsis marks terminating Charles's "explanation" of his last meeting with Sarah in Ware Common and a brief white space, we read: "And so ends the story" (Fowles 1969, 337). The announcement produces a narrative shock: this is not a film, the timing of whose ending the audience can less accurately predict, but a novel a quarter of whose pages remain. This is narrative short-circuiting with a vengeance, for the ending is both premature and facile. What's worse, the narrator dismisses Sarah—"What happened to Sarah, I do not know" (337)—only to proceed with a Fieldingesque pastiche of an epilogue in which readers discover "the truth" of Charles and Tina's future in "plot-summary" fashion. That the narrator is amusing his readers, like some reincarnation of P. T. Barnum, becomes clearer as the chapter ends with the "joke" of Mrs. Poulteney's death and appearance at the "Pearly Gates," from which she is summarily dismissed to "a much more tropical abode" (338). This joke ends in the "punch line" opening the next chapter: the narrator indicates that the narrative conveyed in the preceding two chapters did occur, but only in Charles's imagination (339).

The narrator continues his explanation of this "joke," making it less amusing to readers who have been trained by established reading practices to trust narrators. Granted, narrators may be "unreliable," in line with what Wayne Booth[2] has taught readers; even so, narrators have not traditionally been constructed as tricksters (barring early eccentrics such as the narrator of Laurence Sterne's *Tristram Shandy*), any more than readers are prepared for the news of a narrator's death in a novel's closing pages. The joke played on them by this narrator ought to prepare readers for further deceptions in a narrative whose objective may be to turn fiction inside out, or to reconstruct narrative as a Möbius strip whose inside and outside are one and the same. Although *The French Lieutenant's Woman* predates much of the contemporary theorizing about endings, the narrator seems to have read Brooks and "constructed" the narrative, as though he were the "Author," in the form of a web to snare the unwary reader who is self-consciously "reading for the plot."

Emboldened by his success in persuading readers to accept as fictional "truth" what he explains as a mere "flash-forward" in the overheated imagination of Charles Smithson, the increasingly prominent narrator turns this text into a web of baseless expectations and contrived revelations. The false "epilogue" he provides to the silly conventional "ending"—a marriage of convenience, followed by the hero's social adjustment to the humdrum of "reality"—is intended to set readers up for this story's "climax" in the anticipated gratification of desire. That gratification of desire—the reader's as well as Charles's—is supplied by the love scene with Sarah, followed by the "real" confrontation scene with Ernestina in which Charles confesses his infidelity and asks to be released from his betrothal vows. This alternative to the imagined scene is surely closer to the heart's desire of not only Charles but also the reader.

Chapter 55 begins, then, with Charles boarding the train to London, where he expects to find Sarah and to spend his life with her as the woman for whose love he has been willing to renounce even his claim to being a gentleman. This "world well lost for love" conclusion of the plot appears to be the "happy ending" toward which desire in the narrative has propelled Charles and the reader. In the train scene, however, the narrator begins to fuss about the boarding of a "latecomer," undeterred by the hero's "Gorgon stare," meant to ensure solitude in the compartment. This "traveling companion"—whose "cannibalistic stare" Charles succeeds in fending off until sleep exposes his vulnerability to the "male gaze," thus positioning him as "feminine"—eventually doffs the mask of a belatedly introduced character to reveal himself as the "Author," who apparently has also been masquerading as the narrator. In this way the narrative playfully makes gestures toward the naive reader's suspicion that the narrator in most stories is probably the concealed author anyway. As compensation for the trick of appearing to introduce a character this late in the narrative, readers are offered the consolation that this "Author" is merely being "honest" in unmasking himself.

The "Author" engages next in a confidential exchange with the reader, reminiscent of the playful exploitation of the narrator-reader nexus by pioneers of the novel such as Fielding or Sterne. This unmasked "I," or "eye," after directing his gaze at Charles, his creature, whom he must now decide what he will "do with," diverts his gaze to the more challenging object—the reader, whom he must also decide how to dispose of. The two projects are, of course, related, because Charles is waiting for the end, that is, Will he find Sarah and reconstruct himself as her life partner of one kind or another? Or, Will he be doomed by this "Author," as a deus ex machina, to a purgatory of agonizingly unfulfilled searching for the end of his desire? More importantly, the "Author" has ensnared himself in his own devices by fueling the desire of the reader for *any* ending—"happy," "tragic," "open," or whatever—as long as it is *an* ending. A single ending is "artificial," however, making plot into a "fight" the "Author" "fixes." Better to offer at least *two* endings; that strategy is rendered problematical, however, by the inevitable implications of linearity: whichever ending comes last is the "real" ending. Better to flip a coin and let "chance" rule the sequence. As a result the "happy ending" of reunited lovers and the acknowledgment of their single act of sexual union in the issue of a daughter, Lalage, is followed by a second ending in which Sarah does not reveal whether the child is hers and Charles leaves her sight forever to return to America. Neither of these two "endings" can satisfy readers, because the existence of even a tentative alternative undermines the substantiality of "the" ending readers might choose, and of course the trickster "Author" knows that perfectly well. The narrative moves into Barnum's world of trickery. It is one thing, however, to follow the sign pointing to the egress only to discover one has been duped into making an undesired exit; it is quite another thing to have desire unfulfilled, only to be reminded such a desire for the end is tawdry anyway.

The question arises, In what sense, if *any*, is *The French Lieutenant's Woman* providing its readers with an "undoing" of the traditional paradigm in which ending is the ultimate and crucial agency of meaning? Does this narrative's "playing around" with the notion of ending represent a demolition of the traditional paradigm, or is it a backhanded gesture of support? Does *The French Lieutenant's Woman* deny the centrality of ending to plot, or does it force its readers to rethink the concept of ending on a level other than "plot"? Can readers resist the impulse to repeat their reading of this text immediately, even in a cursory fashion, to explore how "plot" entails *more* than the inexorable movement of the action toward an ending? In a strangely ironic way, this novel may be teasing its readers into a "return" in this narrative to explore this "more," with an eye to discovering what has been energizing desire in *The French Lieutenant's Woman*, a desire operating "beyond" the "pleasure principle" of Charles's apparent erotic attraction to Sarah Woodruff.

As in the surprise ending of a whodunit, *The French Lieutenant's Woman* may be forcing its readers into a repetition compulsion, into retracing their footsteps through the narrative to discover how the ending (or lack of an ending) has been anticipated. In its theatricalizing of the narrative's beginning, the opening scene itself ought to provide the first clue to this narrative's intentions. The cinematic treatment of the scene, almost a pastiche of the opening scene from the film adaptation of *The French Lieutenant's Woman*, establishes the principle of distancing as a narrative strategy. Another theorist on narrative whom this novel seems to have read is the Laura Mulvey, whose seminal essay on the male gaze in film (1975) has provided provocative insights for readers of fiction. The narrator's eye becomes a camera whose "gaze" at Sarah Woodruff is aligned with the staring of the male lead Charles Smithson and the imaginary "looking" of the reader as spectator. The desire to know almost immediately generates its counterpart in the desire to possess, or to appropriate, the object of the gaze, whose vulnerability in that object-position genders "her" feminine.

This scene offers the first clue to a pattern of reversals of expectation through dramatic reversals in the construction of gaze positions. If, as Mulvey theorizes, the gaze is "male" (or perhaps more accurately "masculine," once gender is unmoored from biology), the figure first identified as the French lieutenant's woman will be gendered "feminine" as the object of the gaze—Charles's, the narrator's, and the reader's. The figure of Sarah, however, first appears ungendered, as an "it," in a long coat that could just as easily conceal a man's physique. When the narrative specifies Sarah's sex as female, it almost immediately begins to gender her "masculine," as the one empowered by looking. While Charles merely looks at her as an object of desire(s), Sarah displays a superior power, because she looks into the void, a look that will be her signature. After Charles has spoken to alert her of his presence, "she did not turn." As he moves to look at her face, the narrative indicates that Sarah's gaze is "aimed like a rifle at the farthest horizon" (Fowles 1969, 9). Once he has gained her attention, "She turned to look at him—or as it seemed to Charles, through him." Further establishing her phallic gaze, the narrative adds: "Again and again, afterwards, Charles thought of that look as a lance. . . . He felt . . . both pierced and deservedly diminished" (10). Charles is expeditiously constructed as the one who looks at the woman with the desire to know, yet is gendered "feminine" by the power of the woman who looks at *him* with a phallic gaze, anticipating future reversals of expectation. It is clearly Sarah's power as the Other, the outcast or the stranger, that most attracts a Charles who has concealed his own intimations of otherness through the trappings of power and position.

This opening scene must also be read in the context of the French existentialism dominating Fowles's early thought.[3] Beneath its pastiche of the Victorian "love story," this novel supports its narrator's point that there are no "historical novels" but merely contemporary stories in period costumes and sets. The narrative grants the figure of Sarah Woodruff the existential perceptions of a reader in 1967, not a Charles Smithson of 1867. As the narrative eventually reveals, Sarah's powerful looking represents an elaborately metaphorical construction of attitudes and positions.[4] Playing to an audience of Mrs. Poulteneys, whose moralistic repression of sexuality stigmatizes them as obsessed with sexuality, Sarah constructs herself as the fallen woman, even though the narrative eventually reveals that she never "fell." Similarly her gazing into the void is (mis)read by the sexually obsessed as a longing for the return of her betrayer, despite Sarah's revelation she knew he was married. Furthermore, in the "climax" of the novel in Exeter, Charles's bloody shirt front discloses the crux of that construction: her fall was postponed to implicate Charles in its consequences.

If *The French Lieutenant's Woman* has *an* ending that might satisfy the traditional expectations of ending and closure, it is probably not so much "plot" that is moving the development of the narrative toward its end. As the narrator points out more insistently in the last chapters, this narrative has been proceeding on at least two levels. First, as we have seen, it offers a pastiche of the nineteenth-century realist novel with its two key themes: channeling erotic desire into the institution of marriage, and working out the financing of marriage and the family. On that level, whether Charles inherits the family title and fortune or faces the relative poverty of about $120,000 a year has some importance, just as whether he maintains his snobbish disdain for "trade" or becomes his father-in-law's managerial successor may also project how "good" the marriage to Ernestina Freeman can be. Whether Charles commits social suicide by involving himself with a fallen woman determines how that "plot" will end. On this level, the narrative offers readers the later nineteenth-century novel its narrator has been announcing all along. On another level, however, the narrative offers a contemporary "plot" in line with its enunciation of more existentialist concerns.

Here the title — *The French Lieutenant's Woman* — offers the most reli-

able clue to its purposes. The appearance of Sarah Woodruff's centrality to the narrative is just that—an appearance—and it is Charles
Smithson who represents the narrative's center. Because they have
been lured into the desire to penetrate the "mystery" of Sarah—in fact,
right to the very end—readers may lose sight of the fact that her only
function is as the agent of Charles's fall into freedom. Within the existentialist context of its conception, *The French Lieutenant's Woman* must
in the end deny the desire of Charles, and the reader, to *know* Sarah.
The attempt to "penetrate" the mystery of Sarah must fail, because her
Otherness represents the inner otherness of those who would attempt
to penetrate her as some externalized other. Sarah has no being, or essence; indeed, the narrative can only play out the choices by which she
constructs whatever being she has. And the author's existentialist lean-
ings are anticipating a poststructuralist context within which meaning
and being are far less clear and stable.

Sarah's final role is as the agent of Charles's liberation. As the opening scene testifies, Charles has been attracted to Sarah as his other, "a
stranger in a strange land," as he will also construct himself. Once
Charles has returned to his rooms after the fateful encounter with
Sarah, the first thing he is described as doing is "star[ing] at his face in
the mirror" (11), suggesting Lacan's mirror stage. Like the infant looking in the mirror, Charles affirms a (mis)recognition of unity in the mirror image, so different from the sense of an inner "self" in pieces. This
image is merely that: an image belied by the first sense of an inner void
where "being" has been assumed. Unlike Sarah who has been forced to
acknowledge her irrevocable otherness, first by her father's educating
her beyond her prospects for personal fulfilment, and then by her construction of herself as a social pariah, Charles appears to have an embarrassment of riches in his freedom to make choices of what he will
"do with himself." He has chosen to construct himself as an amateur
paleontologist, a more advanced form of the "naturalist" figure that was
the earlier option of men of his class and means. He is a gentleman-in-
waiting, the heir to the title, estate, and accompanying fortune presently
held by his aging, bachelor uncle. Thus, he is "waiting for the end" of
his apprenticeship as lord of the manor and awaiting a future in which
he may continue to practice his scientific avocation. The narrator asserts: "One of the commonest symptoms of wealth today is destructive
neurosis; in [Charles's] century it was tranquil boredom" (12), without
specifying the factors that may have transformed such "tranquil boredom" into mid-twentieth-century ennui, and even "nausea," in confronting a void opening beneath the feet of those privileged by even the

barest of "wealth" to ponder the agony of choice—choice alone offering the possibility for being, or "essence," to be constructed for the moment.

Because the narrative clothes itself in Victorian culture, Charles Smithson with his apparent freedom to choose hardly seems a candidate for the role of the outsider. It is more likely to be a woman like Sarah Woodruff, who can provide for herself only by being a servant, on various levels of the term, or by marrying a man beneath her intellectually and culturally. When Sarah asks rhetorically, "Why was I not born Miss Freeman?" (141) she might have more appropriately asked, "Why was I not born Mr. Smithson?" for it is he who has the even larger gamut of choices than Ernestina, the only child of a rich father, who has little choice but to marry. Charles not only has the range of avocations preserved for males but also the option of following his uncle's initial example of not marrying anyone.

If it is the visual exchange of gazes on the Cobb that sets this narrative into motion, the important question becomes: What *plot* is this initial encounter of Sarah and Charles generating? Because the novel masquerades as a "period piece" of "Victorian" (and thus, repressed) sexuality, narrative desire seems initially channeled into the conventional erotic pursuit of knowledge to which a narratologist like Brooks might be fatally attracted. If the meeting of these two principals in the narrative was not merely accidental, it seems legitimate to ask why it was Charles on whom she fixed her gaze as an agent of some other narrative desire we might trope as a "call to adventure." That is, what are his credentials as a candidate for the fall into freedom that might be read in Sarah's apprenticeship as a New Woman? When Charles feels the sense of vertigo on the brink of his "fall," Sarah's gaze might seem a kind of "fatal attraction" like that of the Medusa. Sarah means to blackmail him, he worries, to pull him down to her own level of misery, to madden him with her embodiment of "feminine" mystery, and so on.

In his first major intrusion into the narrative, the narrator playfully attempts to create Sarah's freedom as a "character" by posing as the storytelling Author, conventionally explaining that his characters have lives of their own. "Who is Sarah? Out of what shadows does she come?" (94), he asks, only to answer his own questions at the opening of the next chapter: "I do not know. This story I am telling is all imagination. These characters I create never existed outside my own mind" (95). Granted the semblance of freedom to act beyond any plot that might attempt to contain her, or explain her motivation, she is "free." More importantly, she is "free" because she has "fallen" into the freedom of acknowledging that she is without essence or being in a world without meaning until she chooses to *make* meaning, and remake meaning again and again through her decisions to act in one way rather than another. In this way she can construct herself as the woman who chooses not to marry, for example, opting instead to explore the full range of her capacity to create meaning through her choices.

In these ways *The French Lieutenant's Woman* plays, but very seriously, with issues of choice for the characters, for the plot(s), and the ending(s). On one level it follows a traditional model of plot, implicating the desire to know in the desire to possess the object of one's sexual appetite. It offers at least two endings (if not three or even four) as a pastiche of the text of choice: the reader may "choose" a "happy ending" or a more "realistic" one, and perhaps Charles himself can choose whether to honor Sarah's declaration of independence from conventional roles and expectations that might allow her to reveal the nexus of their child, or to persist in his traditional masculinist phobias that Sarah is a Lorelei, as well as a Medusa, and thereby lose that nexus, if it ever existed. The narrative had earlier positioned Charles at the fork in the path of whether or not to marry Ernestina and enter the "prison" of his father-in-law's business: "You know your choice [the narrator tells "poor Charles"]. You stay in prison, what your time calls duty, honor, self-respect, and you are comfortably safe. Or you are free and crucified" (362). This is still a freedom *from*, not yet a freedom *for*. The latter freedom may be promised as the ending of this novel's "real" plot.

A key question in this novel's closing pages remains: Where does the alternative to the "happy ending" end? It becomes a vital question, because the very last two paragraphs of the novel can be (mis)read as a continuation of the alternative or "unhappy" ending. Once the narrative has "satisfied" one kind of reader's need for an ending with its artifice of alternative endings, it can perhaps offer another, albeit one less "satisfying," by essentially bringing the "plot" full circle with its return to the sea into whose void Sarah was gazing at the outset. The penultimate paragraph begins with a final intrusion of the narrator to tie off the more conventional sense of an ending, or even endings, offered by the "intervening god" of narrative on the way to focusing on this "life as we have . . . made it ourselves" (466). The final paragraph positions Charles, like Sarah at the outset, on an embankment, having faced the fundamental choice Camus posed: to die by one's own hand or to live with the burden of making meaning for oneself in a meaningless world. Charles sees the image of his own corpse and rejects that path, choosing instead to take up Sisyphus's assignment, now that "he has at last found

an atom of faith in himself" (467). The narrative stretches out in a poetic arabesque of statement easily missed by those for whom ending resolves itself into the choice of whether the relationship with Sarah will
end in a "happy" or "unhappy" manner. The very convolution of the
sentence mirrors the "river of life" winding toward the sea with which
the novel ends.

This ending positions Charles as an existentialist making ready to sail
off to America as the New World, to sail across the sea that the narrative has associated with the cosmic void as a kind of matrix of meaning-
making. He may not see too clearly, because his eyes are clouded by the
tears of denying death as an existentialist option; those eyes are focused,
however, in an almost dangerously melodramatic manner on "life." At
this point the narrative risks the positing of "meaning" by rejecting the
appealing "symbol" of life as an encounter with the Sphinx, in the guise
of Sarah. In preparation for the assertion of the existential condition in
the novel's very last words, the narrative denies that life is a "symbol,"
a "riddle," or whatever might "inhabit one face alone." These closing
lines instead suggest that life is "to be, however inadequately, emptily,
hopelessly into the city's iron heart, endured. And out again, upon the
unplumb'd, salt, estranging sea" (467). It is a closing gesture as risky as
Virginia Woolf's in the last line of *The Waves:* "Against you I will fling
myself, unvanquished and unyielding, O Death!" (Woolf 1931, 383).
Eschewing linearity, the narrative makes its textual return to its beginning with the powerful image of Sarah, gazing into the sea's "estranging" void.

The French Lieutenant's Woman in this way may be offering a modernist
narrative with an "open ending," masquerading as a postmodern novel
with several endings that merely *seem* to be problematizing the traditional paradigm for narrative. If that assertion sounds self-contradic-
tory, it is because of the tempting lure of structuralist binaries within
which narrative must be either modernist or postmodern. Fowles's narrative ends up being postmodern in the sense of the *mis en abîme,* or
nested narratives—that is, a modernist narrative within a postmodern
narrative that is a pastiche of the Victorian novel. Thus, *The French Lieutenant's Woman* testifies to the inevitable implication of modernism in the
postmodern, in much the same way that Fowles's stratagem of offering
alternative endings to his novel is only another way of forcing his readers to look elsewhere for the sense of an ending. His readers must paradoxically find it, not in the seemingly "existential" provision of
alternative endings but in the modernist "open ending" in which
Charles subsumes the position of Sarah on another embankment, hav-

ing experienced his own fall from the illusion of being, and gazing now, as she did earlier, into the void of the sea, bracing himself for the voyage into that nothingness from which he may fashion, and endlessly refashion, his being through the choices he makes as a sailor.

"DOUBLE" ENDING BY MISUNDERSTANDING:
ANTHONY BURGESS'S *A CLOCKWORK ORANGE*

Anthony Burgess's novella *A Clockwork Orange*—or perhaps more precisely, *Oranges*—has become a curiously problematical text, apparently through the author's misunderstanding. As Burgess writes in the introduction to the reissued American edition (1987), the English text of his novel contained twenty-one chapters, while the American text (1962) was published in a truncated version with only twenty. How this happened is a matter of interpretation. Burgess indicates that as a relatively unpublished writer he (mis)understood the publisher to be asking for the omission of the twenty-first chapter as a *condition* of its acceptance for publication.[5] Eric Swenson, his editor at Norton, claims in his own introduction to the full American text that he was merely *suggesting* the omission of the twenty-first chapter to strengthen the novel and not demanding that the chapter be removed.

Burgess's acquiescence to what he (mis)read as a demand began the weaving of a fascinating web of intertextuality. The film director and auteur Stanley Kubrick based his film adaptation on the American version of *A Clockwork Orange*, even though, as Burgess indicates, the film was made in England and even though all the translations of the novel, including those into languages such as Hebrew and Catalan, were based on the British text. As a result of Kubrick's decision to use the American edition—perhaps because the United States might represent the film's largest audience—the film, Burgess surmises, probably "seemed to his audiences outside America, [to have] ended the story somewhat prematurely" (1987, vii). More important than this premature climax, however, was the film's intense realizing of male violence. That cinematic representation of violence became notorious in the diary entries of presidential contender George Wallace's attempted assassin, Arthur Bremer, whose (mis)reading of Kubrick's film as affirming the "authenticity" of the American edition provided a pretext for his assassination attempt.[6] In the ensuing debate over the effects of violence in the media, Burgess was blamed for writing the fiction that made the Kubrick film possible and perhaps had already spawned other Arthur

Bremers ready to strike out at political leaders. Media exploitation of the Bremer diary probably contributed to the creation of Burgess's angry, anti-American novel *The Clockwork Testament,* in which a screenplay for a film based on Gerard Manley Hopkins's long poem *The Wreck of the Deutschland,* elegizing the loss of nuns in a shipwreck, is misread by the auteur director as a story about Nazi SS troopers raping nuns, leading to a spate of copycat attacks on nuns by deranged men who later admitted they had seen the film.

This web of intertextuality continued to expand in Norton's decision to publish *A Clockwork Orange* as, according to its dust jacket, "a new American edition, complete with the 'missing' last chapter with an explanatory introduction by the author." Given the author's eventual hatred of this novella, in part because it soon turned into the work for which he became famous/notorious, and given his resentment toward Kubrick's powerful (mis)reading of the text, Norton's "logical" choice of Burgess to provide this "explanatory introduction" was guaranteed to continue the misunderstanding, indeed almost as much as Swenson's apparently genuine *suggestion* for omitting the twenty-first chapter in the first place. Not only are most authors uniquely privileged, yet at the same time disabled, as readers of their own texts, but it was clearly impossible for Burgess to read *A Clockwork Orange* outside its implication in the intertextual network of all those other *Oranges* it produced. We can only wonder how an American reader, coming back to the text a quarter-century later, could be expected to (re)read this narrative without the presence of the "original" truncated text haunting with its ghostly presence the revised edition.

As Burgess explains in the introduction to the reissued American edition, the twenty-first chapter functioned as the keystone to the structure of *A Clockwork Orange.* Not only did he intend the number twenty-one to offer the hope of Alex's becoming bored with violence as he reached his majority; he also had carefully planned out an organization of three sections with seven chapters each. Burgess credits an interest in "arithmology," as he calls it. At the risk of moving down the slippery slope of numerology, we might note that it is hardly a coincidence that the numbers three and seven, with seven being a factor of three and four, are central to the structure. As Lacan archly argues, three or perhaps four may be as high as the unconscious can "count." It may be open to question whether the reader is "counting" the chapters from one to seven in each of the first two sections, so that the absence of a seventh chapter in section 3 will seem like a "hole" in the text. The original American edition, with its "missing" final chapter, may be closer to the truth of signification in its incorporation of this "hole" in the text, because this hole may be read as a "purloined letter" putting signification, and therefore narrative, into operation.

Whether the reader is "counting" to seven, the number three contributes measurably to the structure of *A Clockwork Orange*. The novella is essentially a triptych[7] of violence and victimization. In the second section, especially in the later chapters where Alex is submitted to aversive conditioning, or "Ludovico's Technique," the repetitive acts of violence in the first section are repeated within his reprogramming as a potential victim of violence. Just as Alex and his droogs robbed, beat, and raped their victims in the first section, so must Alex in the second section attend to film texts in which drug-induced nausea makes him become uncontrollably sickened by those who are violent as they rob, beat, and rape *their* victims. This conditioning may be merely an intensification of the gradual process by which the young become, if not sickened, at least bored by acts of violence and look to other outlets for their energies. The imaging of violence in this section is meant to parallel pornography, initially exciting but eventually casting a pall of tedium over desire, as the same acts are mechanically repeated and the viewer is forced to recognize the limited repertoire of acts possessing the power to excite that desire.

In a Lacanian context, much of Alex's experience of violence in this second section operates in the register of the Imaginary. The more literal entrapment of violent desire in the film images here reflects a similar operation of the Imaginary in the first section, where Alex seems compelled to be violent primarily to satisfy those desires in his fantasies. Thus, after a night of physical and sexual assault in section 1, Alex can return to his own room, put on a recording of his beloved "Ludwig van," and achieve orgasm virtually without touching himself as the music comes to its own climax. In this context, music as a mode of symbolic representation is itself a text. Eventually, the Mad Doctors become obsessed with moving Alex from the register of the Imaginary to the Symbolic order in which he must become conscious of the agency of the letter, or signification. If *A Clockwork Orange* is a text Alex is "writing" as its narrator, the narrative presupposes the completion of the action, as represented by either the English or American ending. Thus, the text posits Alex's having already moved into the register of the Symbolic in mastering representation through words, supplanting (but of course not eliminating) what had been the representation of meaning through images in the Imaginary register.

The foregrounding of the Mad Doctors toward the end of section 2 moves the narrative into a realm of complexity to which Burgess's hostility may well have blinded him. The doctors stumble on Alex's fetishism involving music when he violently responds to the (ab)use of Beethoven's Fifth Symphony to enhance the climax of violence in a Nazi propaganda film. Tellingly, Alex is especially nauseated by this perversion of Beethoven's music.[8] Dr. Brodsky muses, "So you're keen on music. I know nothing about it myself. It's a useful emotional heightener, that's all I know" (Burgess 1987, 113). When it becomes clear that Alex is sickened literally and figuratively by what the doctors are doing to the music he loves, Dr. Branom adds, "It can't be helped. Each man kills the thing he loves" (114). This section offers numerous examples of the medical staff committing acts of overt violence toward Alex. For example, the orderly and the nurse are both gratuitously cruel to him, because they are well aware that he cannot retaliate without becoming nauseated. It is the Mad Doctors, however, for whom knowledge generates a power, à la Foucault, rendering them powerless to resist abusing him. In this way the narrative "deconstructs" the conventional binary of the violent and their victims, unsettling sophisticated readers by forcing them to acknowledge that what separates the victimizer from the victim is who has the knowledge and therefore the power.[9]

This thesis is clearly borne out in section 3. Once Alex is rendered nonviolent and therefore powerless, he immediately becomes the victim of all those whom he and his droogs victimized in the first section, in a kind of "clockwork," or mechanical, repetition of their sequencing in the earlier section. Thus, just as his gang beat up the "starry veck" on his way to the library, so too Alex is beaten up by his earlier victim and his old cronies. Alone once again, Alex is beaten by Billy Boy and his droogs, now including Alex's former mate Dim, whom Alex once kept in line through violence. But of course most tellingly, Alex in the end is pushed to attempt suicide by F. Alexander and his liberal buddies, when Alex stumbles into the Alexander "Home" where he and his gang had beaten up F. Alexander and raped his wife. By this point, if not earlier, the text is performing its own variety of repetition compulsion in the seemingly endless and increasingly boring iterations of violence. The narrative appears to be trapped in its own efforts at finding a means of escape from a compulsion to repeat until such deathly impulses "master," and perhaps eliminate, unruly desires. In its own way the narrative is desperately seeking the means of ending those repetitions, of breaking through in some form of transformation in order to achieve the metaphoricity implicated in ending.

Burgess wrote the twenty-first chapter as what he hoped to be the ending of a somewhat eccentric *Bildungsroman*. Alex becomes bored with violence and begins (incredibly) to think about finding a girl to make babies with. His job at a music store has been widely read to imply, especially through the author's coaching, that Alex may be repeating the author's own early career as an aspiring composer of music. In the end, Burgess's editor may well have been right: the twenty-first chapter provides a boring ending. Burgess may have been encouraged to agree to its removal in the original American edition, not because he feared losing the opportunity to publish *A Clockwork Orange* in the United States if he didn't, I suspect, but because his unconscious spoke as a better reader of this text than Burgess "the author" has demonstrated in all the talking and writing he has done about the narrative ever since he wrote its last word.[10] The unconscious spoke clearly in asserting that the twenty-first chapter as an ending perpetuates the self-delusion that violence can be managed by separating the sheep from the goats. Such efforts to "treat" violence in the overtly violent allows our culture to ignore its more subtle and therefore perhaps more dangerous ramifications in those "civilized" adults, such as the Mad Doctors, who conspire in socially legitimated forms of violence, sanctioned by their unquestioned (ab)use of power. Thus the unconscious of the text speaks in a loud and clear voice that the twenty-first chapter is just as implicated in the endless cycle of violence as the twentieth. In this way, the externally imposed original American ending deconstructs the self-deluded British ending with its blithe, actually rather silly, assurance that all we have to do is hope the Alexes will tire of their violence and become fathers and composers of music to sublimate those energies.

In the end the masculine narrative paradigm Burgess imposed on his narrative is subverted by what one might call, with more than a bit of trepidation, a "feminine ending." The linear, transformational ending validated by the twenty-first chapter is disrupted by the ending implicit in the twentieth. It suggests that violence will continue to be a "vicious circle" until those who delude themselves into believing they number among the nonviolent finally recognize that anyone with a modicum of power has the potential to exercise it abusively in forms of violence ranging from the overt to the very subtle. These two endings, precipitated by what was misread as a "misunderstanding," represent a complex play on the traditional notion of two endings, whether it is of Dickens's *Great Expectations* after its audience protested against its first ending, or even the deceptive "two" endings of *The French Lieutenant's Woman*. Like *A Clockwork Orange*'s subtle representation of conditioning—leading many readers to query whether Alex ever has been, or could ever be, "free" of the deliberate, or happenstance, conditioning to which we may all fall prey—this "true" ending forces readers to doubt that a "masculine" ending can ever really do justice to their sense of the complexity of human experience. Does the ending that the narrative seeks to impose on Alex in the twenty-first chapter in its effort to sanitize the story and domesticate him in an almost "Victorian" fashion represent its own kind of "violence" against the middle of the narrative, over which it seeks to impose its textual power? Is there a way that narrative can escape the violence it does to the middle that may seem closer to the reader's sense of "life"? Is this kind of "way" a "feminine" ending of circling and continuance to avoid the sense that the endings sought by art are in the end the death of narrative?

Caught as all texts are in a web of textuality, *A Clockwork Orange* will continue to have "two endings" in a curiously unresolvable fashion. Burgess and Norton—perhaps after Burgess agreed to *A Clockwork Orange*'s republication *only* in its "complete" version—can posit that the "damage" of its original truncated American version has been undone. They could not, however, erase the existence of that earlier text in the memories of those who read it a generation ago, especially Stanley Kubrick, whose "misreading," or uncannily accurate *reading*, of the text will not simply vanish with this "restoration."[11] Thus, we might read the 1987 text of *A Clockwork Orange* as having its earlier version *sous rature*, to borrow Jacques Derrida's term. In this way, *A Clockwork Orange* will have an alternative ending "under erasure" in a curiously postmodern fashion, with the erasure of the erased ending persisting as a ghostly reminder that ending may determine meaning, but questions about endings may end by destabilizing meaning in narrative.

IS THERE AN ENDING IN THIS TEXT?
DAVID LODGE'S *CHANGING PLACES*

If there is a novel ready-made to problematize, perhaps even deny, the validity of ending in narrative, David Lodge's academic novel *Changing Places* seems a natural. *Changing Places* foregrounds a narrator who draws readers into the "game" of this narrative. He positions the two professors, who are "changing places," on airplanes flying toward each other "at a combined velocity of 1200 miles per hour" (1979, 7), quickly assuring readers that these two jumbo jets do not, of course, collide but pass each other, with the passengers in each airship totally oblivious of the other's proximity, like the conventional "ships in the

night." The trope of potential midair collision gets logged in here because the possibility of just such an ending for the narrative is raised in
the closing pages—a contemporary "tragedy" to resolve the plot, like
the appearance of the god of the machine in ancient Greek tragedy.
Philip Swallow is escaping from home, or at least his home school of
the University of Rummidge (bearing distinct resemblances to Lodge's
own Birmingham University) in what is rapidly becoming the "Dark
Country," or "Rust Belt," of the English Midlands. He will teach at
Euphoric State (the University of California at San Francisco) where
he looks forward to enjoying the sunshine and the orange juice he recalls from his student days and honeymoon in the early 1960s, before
the decade became the Sixties. Morris Zapp, on the other hand, is escaping from marital difficulties precipitated by the discovery by his
feminist wife, Désirée, of his indiscretion with yet another female student.

As though recognizing that the "campus novel" can become claustrophobic, the narrative snatches at the strategy of faculty exchange, with
a doubling of the "stranger in a strange land" to poke fun at the apparently different but ultimately rather similar eccentricities of academies
an ocean and a continent apart. While Morris Zapp is dealing with English inconveniences such as the absence of central heating and his
counterpart's fetish of saving empty tobacco cans, which come cascad-
ing down on him, Philip Swallow is drawn into the hippiedom of marijuana and casual sex with, it turns out, Zapp's own daughter. The
narrative constructs itself as a kind of joke whose butt is the naif. The
narrative itself appears to be posing the naive question, If professors
exchange teaching positions, do they inevitably "exchange" wives and
homes as well? Thus, along with all the obvious farcical elements of the
"campus novel" (such as Howard Ringbaum, who "wins" the game of
"Humiliation" by admitting he has never read *Hamlet*), the narrative
is raising provocative issues concerning the supplanting of traditional
notions of the individual and choice by the theorizing of a younger generation that the human "subject" is socially or culturally constructed.
That is, the narrative is foregrounding its construction of the characters
to raise larger philosophical questions of the subject's constructedness,
such as how a Swallow or Zapp can be so easily transformed into his
"other." The change seems so radical as to produce an existential vertigo in looking down into the abyss of (non)being, or at least constructedness. If a Swallow or a Zapp can seem to "become" his other by living
in the other's house and making love with the other's spouse, what hap-

pens to the conventional sense of an identity independent of external forces and circumstances?

Of the two who are "changing places," the narrative invests itself more fully in Swallow. The fifth chapter, appropriately entitled "Changing," begins with the dramatic disclosure of Désirée Zapp and Philip Swallow in bed, discussing the size of his penis. It is one thing for the narrative to nudge Philip into bed with Melanie Byrd (Zapp's daughter by a previous marriage who has taken her mother's maiden name) after an evening of wine and marijuana, but quite another thing to move Philip into Désirée's bed, without any real preparation in the plot and without any guilt on his part, as was the case in the more understandable "adultery" with Melanie. Philip's accidental involvement in student protests, ending with his arrest and Désirée's bailing him out of jail, has apparently had its effect. The deeper explanation appears to be a fundamental change in Philip—a change he himself is allowed to recognize and articulate. As Philip tells Désirée, he no longer feels "British" and cannot feel "American." He rejects Désirée's attempt to theorize his becoming "caught up in the historical process." When he begins draft after draft of a letter to his wife, Hilary, to explain his adultery, he is struck by just how radically he has changed. He fantasizes about having a clone, "some zombie replica of himself" (178), to sleepwalk through his life with his family and his job at Rummidge while he settles in with Désirée and all that "Euphoric State" connotes. Were he to return to England he would be unmasked as an "impostor," leading someone to ask, *"Will the real Philip Swallow please stand up?"*

This stream of Philip's consciousness of his own transformation continues with his decision that he has finally begun to understand American literature as an expression of American culture. His consciousness picks up on Désirée's comment that he has been drawn into the "historical process," and he notes his feeling of "expatriation." Whereas in earlier generations it was likely to be Americans following the "Gulf Stream" to escape the confinements of their own culture, now it is more likely to be Europeans drawn to America's West Coast for the very different culture of "California" (194). That is what he has been trying to write to Hilary, namely, that he has changed too much to return to a relationship of mutual possession in marriage and family. He deduces that the problem is neither hers nor his but grows out of a system of mutual expectations. In a word, their marriage has gone "stale" (196). What Philip fails to notice, and the narrative neglects to emphasize since he is its center, is that the other three in this *ménage à quatre* have been undergoing their own varieties of radical change.

The chapter whose title offers the false prospect of an ending has been well prepared for through the narrative's series of self-reflexive gestures, centering on the ongoing references to a classroom textbook, a kind of *Writing Fiction for Dummies*. This textbook surfaces in the narrative when Swallow discovers that he has been assigned English 305, Novel Writing. He asks Hilary to search for *Let's Write a Novel*, part of a series including *Let's Weave a Rug, Let's Go Fishing,* and *Let's Have Fun With Photography* (87). Actually, Zapp has already encountered it while examining his counterpart's office bookshelves, and the passages he notes are the most frequently cited passages in discussions of *Changing Places*. Because he is many times more familiar with "theory" than Swallow, Zapp reacts to this manual's simplistic dicta. The publication date—1927—as well as its companion texts in this *Let's* series position its theorizing not only well before the postmodern "era" (if indeed any such "era" ever existed) but also in a conventional context of the pragmatic "how-to" mentality, assuring its readers that anyone can write a novel or catch a fish. Most readers grab its bait as eagerly as the sophisticated Zapp, who begins with the manual's "Every novel must tell a story" by responding "'Oh, dear, yes'" and continues with "And there are three types of story, the story that ends happily, the story that ends unhappily, and the story that ends neither happily nor unhappily, or, in other words, doesn't really end at all" (87).

Perhaps because the writer of *Let's Write a Novel* seeks to instill confidence in aspiring novelists, the text maps fiction as a tripartite realm, like Caesar dividing Gaul into three parts. Tellingly, the text locates narrative's "types" in its choice of endings, suggesting the traditional perception that how a story ends is equivalent to *how* it means. Accordingly, for the writer of *Let's Write a Novel*, both a hilarious narrative whose ending is an unexpected death and a somber story whose last scene reveals the clouds parted by a shaft of brilliant sunlight are simply impossible. This manual writer, A. J. Beamish, has remarks even more apropos to *Changing Places*: "The best kind of story is the one with a happy ending [his name *is*, after all, "Beamish"]; the next best is the one with an unhappy ending, and the worst kind is the story that has no ending at all. The novice is advised to begin with the first kind of story. Indeed, unless you have Genius, you should never attempt any other kind" (88). This in-house joke, grounded in the narrative's recognition that its readers are well versed in the novels of at least the second kind and perhaps the third, energizes a tension in readers, beginning to anticipate how *Changing Places* itself is likely to end.

That "tension" becomes potentially explosive in the last pages. After readers have become more psychologically invested in these "characters," the metafictional gestures at first distancing readers by foregrounding a strong sense of the characters' constructedness give way to perceptions that these characters have been transposed into "real-life" circumstances. That is, Philip Swallow is experiencing a "midlife crisis," along with others whose numbers are legion. As it reveals his refusal to return to the constrictions of his past life, the narrative enters areas of experience in which simple laughter becomes increasingly inappropriate, because a transformation as radical as Philip's generates real power—and peril. The meaning of Lodge's title, *Changing Places*, grows beyond the sense of "faculty exchange" to suggest that if "places" such as Euphoric State are sites of genuine "changing," those who change there must confront the inevitable sadness of recognizing they cannot indeed "go home again." ("Changing places" might also denote locker rooms or cabanas in which people bare themselves in getting out of one costume and into another.) Readers' connectedness with Philip, and actually with the other three as well, sets them up for the "deconstruction" of Beamish's categories, for Lodge's farcical narrative of academic idiosyncrasies and peccadilloes includes the painful recognition that whenever we "change" outside the site of our experience with loved ones, the possibility of a journey homeward is inconceivable without the returner's feeling like an "impostor."

Because "Beamish" lumps together the unhappy ending and the absent ending as the province of the "Genius," there is the expectation that the author of *Changing Places* is about to playfully certify his "Genius" status. Because the category of narrative without an ending appears third—a kind of punch line—as the truest test of an author's talents and probably beyond the "conception" of Beamish as well as his manual's readers, the expectation is clear that the present narrative may not end but simply stop. Other citations from Beamish's manual contribute to the expectation of just such an ending. In the chapter "Corresponding," providing the exchange of letters between Hilary and Philip, as well as between Morris and Désirée, Hilary asks Philip if he still wants this "funny little book" she appears to have been looking through: "There's a whole chapter on how to write an epistolary novel, but surely nobody's done that since the eighteenth century?" (130). If this chapter shows that Beamish is wrong and the epistolary narrative is still possible, will the last chapter of *Changing Places*—readers are encouraged to wonder—attempt to do what Beamish maps out as the territory of "Genius" by emulating narrative with an "unhappy ending" or none at all? Will the ending strive to turn farce into tragedy, a notion it

may have toyed with in the near collision of the turboprops over Man-
hattan, or will it be even more transgressive by rendering more permeable the containing walls in Beamish's structuralist division of "types"
to offer an "ending" that combines all three of the manual's alternatives?

This last—and shortest—chapter in *Changing Places* may unsettle
readers by dispensing with the novel in favor of the film script as part
of a pattern of increasing self-reflexivity. To the "dialogue" of this prospective "film" the foursome appears to be planning, Morris introduces
the possibility that the four were almost "introduced in mid-air." Désirée (who also seems to have read Beamish) remarks: "'It would have
solved a lot of problems, of course. A spectacular finale to our little
drama'" (240). Morris's reply that "Perhaps God isn't angry with us
after all" (241), with its suggestions of Yahweh and the Flood story,
may be yet another metafictional gesture toward ancient tragedy with
its stock convention of the deus ex machina ending when the dramatist
could find no other means of achieving closure for his drama. And Hilary feeds the narrative's metafictionality once again with her comment
on the way that "the guys," as her fledgling feminism encourages her to
note, have taken over this "script," so that Philip and Morris "sound
like a couple of scriptwriters discussing how to wind up a play" (245).

Although Zapp fancies himself the international "star" of "theory," it
is Swallow who assumes the function of theorizing as the pages of this
chapter—and the novel, of course—are running out like the last grains
of sand in an hourglass. Given that readers of *Changing Places* are very
likely to be aware of David Lodge's ample credentials as a literary theorist, Swallow as fictional "character" seems to be not only subsuming
the narrator's role but increasingly speaking for the "author," who is
mutely observing this film scene from the shadows of the theater. Surprisingly, it is Philip and not Morris, the Austen specialist, who argues
for the "death of the novel." As Philip appears to have learned in his
frustrating efforts to teach novel writing, his students cannot escape
failure, despite his instruction, because they "are living a film, not a
novel" (250). Morris may counter with the assertion that "The paradigms of fiction are essentially the same whatever the medium. Words
or images, it makes no difference at the structural level" (250–51).
Philip has the long last word, however, with his allusion to *Northanger
Abbey,* in which Austen, or her narrator, performs her own "postmoder-
nity" through the self-reflexive gesture of addressing her readers directly with her awareness of *their* awareness that this novel they are
performing together as writer and reader is about to end, in some sense

of the term *end*. Philip brilliantly notes that a first-time film audience is unlikely to know just how close they are to the end of the film they are watching—unlike readers, who know in most cases how many pages remain. The contrast is instructive, because most film viewers have been surprised at least once by the abrupt ending, or lack of an "ending," in a film, just as few novel readers have not given in to the temptation to look ahead to estimate how many pages remain—not to "read ahead," for Brooks is on the money with his notion of "short-circuiting" desire for the end, but to "prepare" for the nearness of the end.

It cannot be stressed too strongly that Philip *dominates* the conversation; Morris recedes into the role of a "straight man," merely feeding Philip the "lines." The "stage directions" position Hilary and Désirée as audience for Philip's minilecture on the indeterminacy of ending in film, a kind of "masculine" angst about being unable to *know* ahead of time when the climax is coming. Whether it has been the raising of the specter of Peter Brooks or the marionette work of the structuralist Lodge in pulling the strings of Philip's jaws here to project his own theorizing, the gender implications just come rolling out in this episode, whose "text" is about resolving the issues of "wife-swapping," not "husband-swapping," and, more to the point, the issues arising from the "changing places" of two desiring male subjects, challenged with "how to bring it off." Désirée has earlier commented that the four ought to be concentrating on resolving the future of their desires, not doing narrative theory. Finding a means of structuring the foursome's erotic disorder through "closure" and bringing the narrative to an end, however, are inextricably bound together in this scene. And when Désirée comments, "Don't you recognize the sound of men talking?" and Hilary voices her fledgling "Women's Lib" ad-libs about "How they love those abstract words ["the structural level," "paradigms," and "historicism"]," the two women are exactly right, because this "ending" is a "masculine" discourse about getting to the end—Philip's and Morris's talk, but also David's, for Lodge is highly invested in this ending business. It is *Lodge*, after all, and *not* Swallow, who draws the reader to the closing words of *Changing Places* with his admiring "talk" about film. The novelist is willing to privilege film over the novel, generalizing that when a "director chooses, without warning, without anything being resolved, or explained, or wound up, it can just . . . end" (251), and then replicates that "ending" he is very much ending like a man.

Lodge performs a narrative cross-dressing in appearing to dispense with the "masculine" ending. He argues, at least by implication, that life does not have endings, except the Ending, by writing that "The film is going along, just as life goes along . . ." and then stopping, rather than ending or closing (251). Despite its gestures toward the "feminine," however, this fixation on ending maintains a "masculine" focus. This story in which four characters struggle to work out their relationships may go on like "life"; the story, or narrative, however, goes on with its own preoccupation with ending. The narrative poses the big question, How will this novel end? and then "ends" with the punch line of no ending, making it possible for the author to have his cake and eat it too by doing the ending in drag, masquerading as the constructor of a "feminine" ending but in the end offering beneath the surface a punch line for "English majors."

The Faked Climax and the Anticlimax in Joyce Carol Oates's Bellefleur

After having established herself a quarter-century ago as one of America's most productive and innovative writers, Joyce Carol Oates offered her readership a large challenge in the enigmatic, sprawling, multigenerational family saga, *Bellefleur.* If her readers were expecting a high-grade Harlequin Romance they were undoubtedly disappointed, perhaps even frustrated and angry, with a narrative seemingly bent on undermining the reader's effort to "get into" this novel. To its first readers *Bellefleur* may have seemed a parody of the nineteenth-century European novel. It has a huge cast of characters requiring the reader to refer repeatedly to the "Bellefleur Family Tree"—virtually to the very end of the novel. Even so, readers may be embarrassed when they are unable to recall its characters. A special problem are those who are named for Bellefleurs of earlier generations. Additionally, this narrative perversely refuses linear progression. Even readers accustomed to the difficulties of modernist novels such as William Faulkner's classic *The Sound and the Fury,* with its willful departures from "normal" time sequences, can expect to experience frustration with *Bellefleur,* as it deliberately undermines the reader's reliance on linearity in its incessant movements back and forth in time.

Bellefleur begins as though it had just encountered Robert Scholes's writing on the "orgastic" rhythm of narrative, or even more pertinently, Peter Brooks's essay "Freud's Masterplot." The opening chapter might be read as an "antibeginning." The narrative introduces the stray tomcat Mahalaleel, with the ominous suggestion that this creature will eventually have some dramatic role in the story of the family's fortunes.

Of Gideon, a major figure in the "present" generation of the Bellefleurs, it is noted that he "could not help but wish from time to time that he *had* broken the creature's neck" (Oates 1980, 17; italics in original). Much as readers might wait for an explanation of Gideon's feelings — such as the possibility this demonically powerful cat suffocates Gideon's son and heir to the Bellefleur fortunes in his cradle — the novel offers no clue to Gideon's motivation, nor even, it might be argued, *why* the narrative begins here with this arrival of Malalaleel: "For it seemed (though why it seemed so, no one knew) that everything began on that night. And, once begun, it could not be stopped" (17). In this melodramatic beginning, this text simulates the high level of eventfulness readers have been conditioned to expect in the novel, especially in a tome like *Bellefleur* with its nearly six hundred pages. But what is it that this narrative is representing? What is this "everything [that] began"? And what can explain its sense of inevitability here at the outset, or what is meant by the "why?" of "it could not be stopped"? Thus, the opening chapter offers a parody or pastiche of a beginning with its orchestration of momentousness and its insinuation that the unidentified narrator knows what is to come in this narrative, since its action has been completed. And yet the assertion that no one knew *why* it seemed as though "everything began" the evening Mahalaleel arrived may signal that this narrative is launching itself on less-charted seas than might reasonably be expected.

Chapter 2, "The Pond," should begin to clarify this initiatory "it" by setting the narrative in motion, but that expectation is not met. The viewpoint character here is not Gideon, but a young boy, Raphael Bellefleur. Immediately the narrative begins to destabilize itself by sending the reader to the "Bellefleur Family Tree" at the beginning of the novel. There the reader discovers Raphael is Gideon's nephew. This identification offers an unsatisfying sense of readerly security, however, because the narrative offers only the most ambivalent time setting for this episode.

That ambivalent gesture toward a linear time scheme occurs several pages into "The Pond," when a blank space signals the beginning a new section with the assertion: "Yet it happened, one cold October afternoon within a week of Mahalaleel's arrival at the manor, that Raphael nearly drowned in his pond" (21). Presumably as a gesture toward linearity this "within a week" is to be read as a week *following* the hellcat's arrival, yet it could just as well be read as during the week *before* Mahalaleel turned up at the front door of Bellefleur. The narrative's strategy immediately becomes further complicated with its clarification that Raphael: "Nearly *was* drowned . . ." (22; italics in original). Suddenly readers are drawn into the artifice of this narration, for the narrator is finally going to get down to the business of disclosing truth through the representation of an action already completed before the narrating began. Having offered a kind of pastiche of a Freudian "womb-wish" in the child Raphael floating serenely on "his" pond, the narrator abruptly announces the threatened violation of his rural Eden by a brutal act of attempted murder by a boy named Johnny Doan.

The narrative's next move is a classic postmodern gesture of foregrounding the process of narration itself; it toys with the reader's desires and expects the sophisticated reader to enjoy this narrational striptease. Apparently the action to follow will represent the failed attempt of this boy, Johnny Doan, to drown the innocent and vulnerable child, Raphael Bellefleur. The narrator erases any conventional construction of suspense by asserting at the outset that the boy "nearly drowned," thereby giving away the ending of this episode. As an alternative means of constructing suspense, the narrative delays—for a painfully long five pages—the actual dramatizing of the assault, while it provides "background" concerning the assailant's identity. In the context of gendered narrative, the narrator is offering a "feminine" detour into the metonyms, or details, to postpone the reader's impulsive rush toward the gratification of the desire to "know" how this scene plays itself out, the *how* of Raphael's "nearly [being] drowned" by this Johnny Doan. The reader is "treated" to the story of how the Doans entered the history of Bellefleur when the first Raphael Bellefleur, this child's great-grandfather, employed the first Doans as farm laborers to pick his hops. Next, the narrator offers a history of hop growing in the valley, followed by a rendition of Johnny's position in the Doan family, with a segue into his throwing down his pitchfork one day and setting off to "invade" Bellefleur Manor to "injure" Yolande, Vida, or even Leah Bellefleur. What follows is less a series of deliberate digressions to build suspense than a growing immersion in Johnny's fantasy of prowling the manor like a wild dog. When Johnny appears in Raphael's watery retreat and begins to cast rocks toward the boy's raft, his bizarre, "bestial" consciousness immerses the narrative, as well as Raphael's consciousness, in the power of this quasi fantasy tale of a "werewolf" more likely to lope through the fiction of Stephen King than of Joyce Carol Oates. Tellingly, the name "Raphael" is erased by Johnny's name for him, "Bellefleur," or the narrator's designation for Raphael, "the boy." After Johnny witnesses "the boy" sinking beneath the surface of Mink Pond, the mad-dog persona dissolves, and Johnny reverts to being merely a boy (28). Continuing this pattern, the next chapter, "The Bellefleur Curse," jolts the narrative back several generations, deferring the outcome of Raphael's near murder for over one hundred pages—pages filled with the stories of the older generations of Bellefleurs. When the narrative appears to remember Raphael and returns him to his violated haven the next spring in the chapter "The Nameless Child," any desire the reader might have had to know how the episode ended has all but waned. As the action is finally rendered through Raphael's dim memories of the ordeal and his recuperation, the narrative offers the irony of the middle-aged: readers get what they thought they wanted, but long after they have stopped wanting it. Surprisingly, Raphael never makes public the identity of his assailant but is satisfied the pond had helped him to survive. On the other hand, if it had been his fate to drown, the violence done him by another human being would have been of no import. Seeking revenge would be pointless (140). Raphael's decision not to call down the kind of bloody vengeance on Johnny that has implicated the Bellefleur family in vicious feuding since the massacre of the patriarch and several other Bellefleurs is certainly a testimony to his precocious "maturity." Unfortunately, his decision makes it possible for Johnny to strike again.

The puzzling scene of Raphael's near death anticipates the even more complicated disappearance of his sister Yolande as a young woman of fifteen. Some forty pages after Raphael's return to Mink Pond, the narrative focuses on Yolande setting out one morning through the "forbidden Bellefleur woods" to meet her lover, a "lover" not introduced earlier in the novel—nor *later*, as it turns out. Ominously, the narrative speaks of Yolande observing a "figure" dressed in overalls and a cap, a figure more than likely to recall Raphael's assailant (188). Menaced by this figure who must be Johnny, Yolande begins to run toward the tryst with her young lover, until the "figure" overtakes her, and she is relieved to observe, "But ah!—it wasn't a person, it was a dog. Only a dog" (189). Yolande's relief cannot erase the menace, despite the chapter's final line, in part because the dog's mouth betrays a "look of studied derision" (190). Surely this narrative must be aware that it is tormenting its readers through this strategy of breaking off on the brink of an "ending," only to leave readers unsure they will *ever* learn the outcome of this scene. If readers have not repressed the violent imagery of Johnny's attack on Raphael—clearly for Johnny a frustrating replacement for his real desire to sexually assault one of the young Bellefleur women—Yolande's relief that it is "only a dog" will certainly recuperate Raphael's sense of vulnerability in the face of Johnny's earlier attack on him. Furthermore, even if Johnny was unaware Yolande was on her way to meet a lover, the narrative has made the reader aware of the cruel irony latent in the possibility Yolande might be raped on her way to what would probably be a far less sexually intimate encounter with her lover.

This bizarre narrative even defeats the reader's impulse to "read ahead" to discover Yolande's fate, for there is no way of easily locating this episode's conclusion without moving through the remainder of the novel, whose chapter titles provide no clue to the whereabouts of the missing Yolande. And the reader's sense of Johnny Doan's continuing menace is only increased by the opening of a later chapter, "The Birthday Celebration," with the puzzling assertion: "The day Yolande ran away from home, never to return—*never* to return to Bellefleur Manor—was also the day of Germaine's first birthday" (213). If Johnny simply trotted away like a hound after frightening Yolande, the expectation persists that one day he will be more successful in venting his hostility toward the Bellefleurs through further assaults. And the narrative has certainly increased suspense by keeping open the possibility that Yolande never "ran away from home" but was murdered by Johnny, who hid her body in the vast forests surrounding the manor, just as he could easily have killed Raphael and made the death look like an accident.

With its ambiguous opening, the narrative deliberately blurs the focus of this chapter, set in motion with its assertion of Yolande's running away on Germaine's first birthday. Additionally, it is only a few paragraphs later that the narrator discloses that Yolande and her cousin Christabel have decided to have a more private celebration at Mink Creek, a feeder of the pond in which Yolande's brother Raphael was "nearly drowned" by Johnny Doan. If "the day" of this chapter is the day on which "Yolande ran away from home," the encounter with Johnny Doan at Mink Pond had to have occurred earlier, and she has returned to this menacing locale because of her delusion that it was a dog, not a potential murderer, she had encountered. When he threatens to twist off the head of a Bellefleur kitten and she attempts to placate this "beast" Johnny by feeding him chocolates, the narrative iterates the canine connection, speaking of "his mouth opening, his ugly tongue protruding like a dog's" (216). Her disclosing of her "feminine" vulnerability only excites his desire, however, and after sending Christabel home with Germaine, Johnny "makes good" on his threat to twist the kitten's neck, and then begins to tear off Yolande's clothes. When Christabel enlists the assistance of the "Bellefleur boys," Yolande rages at her brothers Garth and Albert, and their cousin Jasper, *"Oh, kill him! . . . Don't let him live!"* (219). Once again the phrase immediately following her impassioned plea—"Which is what happened" (219)—clearly gives away the ending of this episode. Beyond its description of her torn dress and her murderous injunction to eliminate her attacker, the narrative never provides any evidence Johnny did more than attempt to rape Yolande. However, as the narrative indicates after a separating blank space, the barn was soon engulfed by flames, and Johnny had been "disappeared."

The chapter continues with a lengthy and grisly account of Johnny's slaughter, a narrative whose impact is intensified by its location at the end of book 2. After setting the barn afire, the Bellefleur boys stone "the Doan boy" to prevent his escape. The canine connection recurs one last time to give Johnny's slaughter an eerie, fantasy conclusion. The boys observe a mongrel dog struggling to escape and stone it back into the fiery inferno, until "its pain-crazed cries" cease (220). Given that only the reader knows about this canine connection, the cruel killing of this "mutt" underscores the elitism and social snobbery the Bellefleurs have inherited from the patriarch, Jean-Pierre, a younger son of the duc de Bellefleur, forced out of France by the Revolution. The bloody reprisal for a Doan trespass into the "innocent" Bellefleur domain becomes only another episode in the feud that almost obliterated the family when the first Jean-Pierre's heir, Louis, and his three children were slaughtered, along with Jean-Pierre and his Indian mistress, by these "mutts" the "thoroughbred" Bellefleurs from one generation to another have held in such contempt.

Its insubstantial sense of chronology continues to trouble this narrative. The narrator seems an historian who may *know* the two-hundred-year history of the Bellefleur family yet is inept at organizing it or unwilling to "do" historiography conventionally from "beginning" to "end," perhaps because the narrative is reminding us that we delude ourselves into believing history moves in a linear fashion. There may be a "story" being told here in this disjointed fashion, but the storyteller lacks the confidence of traditional practitioners of the craft who have had less difficulty locating their beginnings as well as their endings. The first sentence—which is also the first paragraph—of *Bellefleur* offers a pastiche of that conventional strategy of dramatizing the moment of beginning by focusing on the stormy night (a year before Germaine was born) on which Mahalaleel appeared at the door of Bellefleur Manor, where he continued to live for five years (3). From the perspective of the novel's quasi ending(s), this beginning, reminiscent of Charles

Schulz's famous first sentence, "It was a dark and stormy night,"[12] slips in among its many clauses and phrases the vital identification of the time frame for the present of the novel, for if Germaine must wait two or three months for her conception—her gestation apparently *did* last ten months—and if she is in her fourth year at the explosive "ending" of the plot, then the "five years" of Mahalaleel's sojourn at Bellefleur Manor, terminated presumably by his consumption in the very flames in which most of the Bellefleurs perished, mark off the latter days of the family, sometime in the later twentieth century.

The other potential tool in establishing the time frame of the narrative is the pastiche of the family tree chart that *Bellefleur* offers between its table of contents and book 1, "Mahalaleel." Consulting it on many occasions, readers are likely to be struck by its crankiness. The tree identifies, for example, the birth and death dates for a half-dozen or more early members of the family, but it omits this vital information for all the rest. For five Bellefleurs, including the patriarch Jean-Pierre, the death year is given as 1825, creating suspense concerning the cause(s) of these deaths in the same year. (Raphael, a kind of second patriarch as Jean-Pierre's grandson because he built Bellefleur Manor, is provided a birth year, but unlike others he has no death year, suggesting he may be emulating Methusaleh.) In addition to omitting these vital statistics, the tree schematizes the family in a quirky manner through its problematical positioning of siblings, especially among family members in the present. This crucial text defies the conventional denotation of siblings in family trees (oldest to youngest in left-to-right positioning) by "beginning" with Louis, the youngest of the second generation, at the left, moving to Jedediah, and positioning Harlan, the oldest, at the right. Among Louis's children who perished with him in 1825, the conventional order is followed with oldest to the left, youngest to the right. At the bottom of the tree in the present, the conventional arrangement is followed with Leah and Gideon's older children, the twins Bromwell and Christabel to the left and Germaine to the right. The absence of birth and death years, along with the quirky arrangement of siblings, offers readers no way of discerning the relative ages of Ewan and Lily's children—a vital clue, perhaps, to this narrative's problematizing of time and linearity.

These cousins are positioned as siblings in an ambiguous fashion: Raphael Vida Yolande Garth Albert. The narrative quite scrupulously dates Raphael's discovery of Mink Pond when he was twelve (18) and his near drowning "within a week of Mahalaleel's arrival at the manor" (21), but it leaves open how much time has elapsed between that discovery and Raphael's near death. Raphael may be the youngest in the family, for certainly his sister Yolande has become an adolescent who enjoys dismissing him from the horizons of her attention. Presumably his near drowning occurs sometime before Yolande was assaulted by Johnny Doan and "ran away," perhaps because she urged her brothers Albert and Garth to exterminate the "mad dog" who had attacked her. Only the most scrupulous reader is likely to note, much less recall, that Albert is the oldest of Ewan and Lily's children. The more interesting issue is the age of Leah and Gideon's twins vis-à-vis Germaine, whose age never seems to be in doubt.

By the end of this long and disjointed narrative, it seems incredible that Germaine could be only in her fourth year, since so much seems to have changed in the family. Readers comb back through the novel for clues as to how old the twins were when Germaine was born, especially because Bromwell (like his cousin Yolande) runs away, although not to "Hollywood." The early chapter "The Pregnancy" *seems* to offer some assistance, yet it ends by merely teasing the reader who is intent on ascertaining the ages of the characters. The twins were born when Leah was nineteen (35), "but now she was twenty-six, now she was twenty-seven, soon she would be thirty . . ." (42). The last clause indicates, in part, Leah's frustration with being unable to conceive again during a period ranging back to a reasonably long time after the twins' birth, when the family began to hint it was time for Leah to continue bearing children. During that indeterminate number of years, perhaps as few as eight—"now she was twenty-seven" (42)—she struggles to conceive, until Mahalaleel's arrival in September apparently proves a good omen and she succeeds two months later (in November) in becoming pregnant with Germaine.

In a subsequent early chapter, " 'Power,' " the time is noted as April, and Leah is five months pregnant with Germaine, who will be born in August. Because she has become swollen with what seems to be twins again, Leah seldom stirs from her upstairs drawing room, where she plays gin rummy with some of the children. Eventually the precocious Bromwell reveals a notepad on which he has recorded the astounding frequency of the games his mother has won, a frequency to be explained only as her "powers" of telepathy. Tellingly, Raphael is described as the oldest child present, while Christabel is described as sucking several fingers. The much later chapter "In Motion" notes that Bromwell is somewhat younger than Raphael, and Gideon has urged Leah not to worry about their son by presciently forecasting that "he'd outlive all of them" (225). Along with Leah's perception a page earlier of "[h]er own little girl," it seems the twins are ten to twelve. Their ages are crucial, because in just a few years Bromwell will have moved out and Christabel even more incredibly will have been married off to a middle-aged man (Edgar Holleran von Schaff III "was in fact only [!] thirty-eight years old" [283]). Such a marriage with a man clearly old enough to be her father was not so unthinkable, perhaps, in the nineteenth century but would have been *bizarre* in the later twentieth century.

Yet another teasing indication of chronology, or the ages of the twins, is offered in the late chapter "Mount Ellesmere." Bromwell has been sent off to boarding school "downstate" (399). Because of its lateness in the novel and the reader's rage for linearity, it may be tempting to assume that Bromwell left Bellefleur toward the "end" of the present, that is, close to the time of Germaine's upcoming fourth birthday. After the first paragraph explaining his unhappiness away from home, the second begins with an assertion likely to pique the interest of the reader attempting to establish a chronology for the youngest Bellefleurs. At some point during his attendance at boarding school, he is "eleven and a half" (400). This age identification only teases readers, for the narrative merely *implies* that he left home at that tender age. He could have been sent away when he was younger, however unlikely that might be, since New Hazelton Academy is apparently a preparatory, or secondary, school whose students are adolescents. Then, too, he may be still writing home to complain about conditions at the school sometime *after* he arrived at the age of "eleven and a half." The information provided here that he has been away at school may explain why there have been fewer references to him, and if readers look back through the chapters of the present they may surmise he could have been sent to boarding school when Germaine was a toddler. (He had insisted on "experimenting" with Germaine until Leah feared the contact with Bromwell might not be healthful for her baby girl.)

Reading further into the chapter however, readers learn that Bromwell has made it very clear that continuing at the academy was becoming impossible. Leah is making it equally clear that he can no longer live at Bellefleur Manor (400), even though *why* is never specified. If he was "eleven and a half" when he was sent to New Hazelton Academy and he was so desperately unhappy there (he ridicules his classmates for their stupidity during classes, and one nearly drowns him in the school's swimming pool in a reprise of Cousin Raphael's near drowning by Johnny Doan), readers must find it difficult to believe he stayed longer than the two terms at the center of the narration. *However,* is it any more credible that he could have saved up $3,000 from the "allowances" sent him independently by family members and set out for the West Coast and Mount Ellesmere Institute for Advanced Study in Astronomy while still only twelve? And there is the even larger problem of Christabel: while he is at this boarding school she is not only married off to Edgar Schaff but runs off with the children's former tutor! Surely the Bellefleurs would not have married off Christabel at the tender age of twelve to a man over three times her age, and for no discernible reason.

In his provocative lecture on Shakespeare in the library chapter of Joyce's *Ulysses,* the young poet Stephen Dedalus argues that the Bard's indiscretion in impregnating Anne Hathaway, whom he then was obliged to marry, was no "mistake" at all. Stephen's explanation has encouraged many readers to surmise that he may be disclosing some of his creator's understanding of his own texts when he brilliantly asserts: "A man of genius makes no mistakes. His errors are volitional and are the portals of discovery" (Joyce 1986, 356). These problems in the chronology of *Bellefleur* may be just such "portals of discovery," or to borrow another trope, the deliberate "mistakes" woven into Persian carpets to remind the viewer that much as weavers and other artists may aspire to perfection, such an ideal must always evade their grasp. Here, however, their import is greater, for these time problems suggest that our conventional notions of linear time are the self-delusions of those who aspire to the accuracy of scientific measurement promised by those "atomic clocks," which are said to verify that time passes infinitesimally slower at the Earth's equator than it does near either of its poles.

Accordingly, time in *Bellefleur* is clearly moving — or *not moving,* as the case may be — in various fashions. To those who expect narrative to move according to the clock, *Bellefleur* offers persistent obstacles and frustrations. For example, the fairly early chapter entitled "The Whirlwind" opens with the assertion, "On that summer afternoon many years ago, several weeks before Germaine's birth" (Oates 1980, 91), suggesting that the narrative has "many years" yet to play itself out, even though the "ending(s)" will make it clear that most of the Bellefleurs have only a few years left before Gideon's flying bomb will virtually obliterate the family. The "many years" must refer to the extended vantage point of the narration, to a time at which the storytelling occurs, long after that "ending." These concerns only point up the issue of at least a double (perhaps multiple) time working in the novel's present, as readers gain the sense that "many years" have elapsed, or at least sufficient time for Leah to pursue her ambitious, if not downright obsessive, goal of restoring the immense holdings of the Bellefleurs under their patriarch Jean-Pierre the First, almost two centuries earlier, or *perhaps* that long, because it remains virtually impossible to date the novel's present, other than sometime in the later twentieth century.

The problems of determining the age(s) of the twins may be explained through this narrative's suspension of customary notions of time. Drawing on conventional wisdom concerning the discrepancies in physical, sexual, mental, and social rates of development in children who are the "same age," the twins are arguably not the same age at all! The narrative supports this claim through its incorporation of texts on time, notably in the chapter "A Still Water." Immediately before the penultimate chapter, "The Destruction of Bellefleur Manor," offers its immense faked climax, the narrative gives us a brief but seminal flash-forward into Bromwell's later life as a highly successful academic. Referring to this text in a gesture toward *mis en abîme*, the chapter opens almost mystically by asserting a "still water" beneath and beyond the time/space continuum in which we, and narrative, conventionally may be understood to function. The "still water" announced in the chapter's title is a realm outside the conventional notion of linear time. The narrative indicates that "according to the immense monograph of *A Hypothesis Concerning Anti-Matter*, by Professor Bromwell G. Bellefleur, slits in the fabric of time, 'portals' linking this dimension with a mirror-image universe composed of identical (and yet unrelated, opposed, totally distinct) beings" (544) presumably exist.

If readers expect an abstract of this crucial monograph— foregrounded by its positioning so obviously close to the novel's last pages—the text frustrates them. It remains another of those "purloined letters" whose contents never get fully cited in the texts alluding to them. What the narrative supplies instead is a future Bromwell who has achieved eminence as a philosopher-scientist of the Stephen Hawking variety, discoursing on the most arcane notions of antimatter, and, we might add, anti*time*. The "work" of Bromwell is described as a manuscript, "[e]ight hundred dense pages long" (544). This "monograph" is apparently still a work-in-progress, if it remains at the stage of "handwriting," and should readers have any doubts that Bromwell's *Hypothesis* is a mirror image of *Bellefleur*, the chapter removes such uncertainty by adding that the preface to Bromwell's magnum opus contains a passage from Heraclitus, perhaps the very same "enigmatic" passage Oates chose for *Bellefleur*: "Time is a child playing a game of draughts; the kingship is in the hands of a child."

Can readers escape the assumption that Bromwell's monograph functions as a *mis en abîme* for *Bellefleur*? If "ending" is "meaning," the narrative may well disclose its meaning here through the hardly subtle strategy of offering an alternative title for itself—"slits in the fabric of time"—because at the very time it is offering a pastiche of linear narrative *Bellefleur* is also providing those "portals" through which the responsive reader may view an "antitime," or perhaps more accurately a notion of "times" operating outside and beyond the conventional trope of time as a river. Before this chapter ends it has "given away the ending" supplied by the next chapter with its bizarre "climax" of destruction, an apocalypse from which Bromwell has wisely saved himself, as his twin, Christabel, unwittingly has saved herself, by fleeing Bellefleur and its deadly "history." Gideon's fiery apocalypse is an appropriate, even "symbolic," end of history.

Bellefleur "ends," but in the only way it can end—more than once, at the same time it essentially does not end at all. By exploding the conventional notion of "time" as linearity, *Bellefleur* sets itself the immense task of incorporating time, or times, into itself. The narrative sets itself the equally challenging task of supplying a simulacrum of the traditional "ending," while it also "gives away the ending," and encourages readers to look through the "portals" of narrative, or into its "still water," as perhaps Raphael was doing when he gazed down into the pond until it absorbed him. The narrative "ends" by providing a "masculine" ending, albeit as a kind of parody. Perhaps that is the only form it *can* take in relation to a larger and more complicated concept of time and narrative that undermines but never completely erases the traditional ending it sets out to deny. In the context of gendered endings, and therefore gendered narrative, *Bellefleur* aspires to a kind of "androgyny." Germaine, whose lifetime (ten months in utero and four years of life) presumably encompasses the present, is aptly born a hermaphrodite. Appalled by this "monster" with its penis, testicles, and doll-sized legs protruding from "her" abdomen, the new grandmother, Della, grabs a knife to confirm Germaine's sex as female by eliminating the male genitalia. Through this act of "emasculation," Della constructs a "her" from nature's "it," sputtering that she has had enough of these Bellefleur "men." This bizarre "surgery" offers yet another gesture toward *mis en abîme*, because as Bromwell will note in "examining" his baby sister in later months, the surgery leaves more than a "trace" to signify Germaine has been an Other, a representation of a diversity marked by the stigma of a futile human attempt to eliminate the double by constructing the single. A proto-"feminist" wielding her instrument of male nightmares, Della—like the feminist narratologist who would rely on a single "feminine" alternative to the "masculine" narrative and its "ending"—

demonstrates in the end that such futile attempts to (re)construct the feminine by eliminating the masculine will only confirm its existence through its permanent "trace."

If *Bellefleur* reveals time(s) as multiple, one "ending" will not do. As Perry Nodelson has perceptively argued, the "ending" represented by Gideon's deliberate act of flying his planeload of explosives into Belle-fleur Manor offers a patently "male climax" for the novel. If Julia Kris-teva is correct in sexing the concept of linear time as "male," the conventional plot *must* have its demonstrable climax or else the reader is left "frustrated." If, however, we use the "portal of discovery" by which this narrative makes it only *seem* that "many years" have passed since the arrivals of Mahalaleel and Germaine, the apparent "mistake" of marrying off Christabel at a very tender age may expose the novel's larger issues of time(s) in the novel. The ages of Germaine, Leah's "monster" child, and the twins—both Christabel, an heiress of the Gothic "child-bride," and Bromwell, her "mad scientist" brother— make their contributions to this complicating of time, and therefore the problematizing of ending(s). Even in Leah's womb, Germaine is wise beyond her uterine months, allowing her mother to be telepathic, and Bromwell seems to have skipped childhood, as often seems true of the "child prodigy," and yet he is also a case of "arrested development" physically. He is described as being "a somewhat undersized ten" (227), while his twin sister "looks like a young woman of eighteen" (284).

Because of its multiple notions of time, *Bellefleur* inevitably problema-tizes the customary sense of narrative time. Along with linear, circular, "relative" time(s), *Bellefleur* sets itself the challenge of an alternative uni-verse with its own time, that "still water" into which Raphael "actually" looks and Bromwell peers metaphorically. As Nodelson provocatively points out, *Bellefleur* "is neither conventional nor conventionally innova-tive, a novel whose innovations represent an identifiably feminine form of experimentation" (1989, 251). Perhaps Nodelson would accept the "friendly amendment" of a "feminine" form of *narrative,* one both con-ventional *and* unconventional in its notions of ending, one containing both the conventional masculine climax paradigm and its decentering, willing to tolerate that challenging state of indeterminacy in which a narrative may end and not end at the same time it undoes the notions of ending *and* not-ending.

Bellefleur seems to be undermining the masculine ending, and yet it credits that model by sending it up. Similarly, Oates's novel quite self-consciously offers a pastiche of unendingness, along with the duality of "novel time" and its conventional counterpart of "real time" clearly "running on" into some unspecified future. In that future "Professor Bromwell" may actually publish his "monograph," a text that both is and is not a mirror image of *Bellefleur*. In this way, *Bellefleur* is a narrative containing this vestigial text, as Germaine was born as a girl with the vestigial legs and genitalia of a male "twin," as though fetal development, itself a "narrative," were also uncertain how *it* wanted to finish the "it" that was Germaine-to-be. Thus, "nature" in the form of fetal development offers an alternative universe in which desire for the "end" may disclose something of the storyteller's anxiety in the face of conflicting desires: to end by specifying an ending and yet to defer that desire to end too quickly and thereby foreclose all the potential constructions of sex and gender implicit in the biology of female, hermaphroditic, and male sexuality, and in the multiplicity of a gendered subject whose orientation(s) might be conceived of as a "work-in-progress."

If virtually from the beginning of narratology's examination of ending in narrative, these quasi-"scientific" endeavors have been gendered by the subject status of the narratologist, and if it may no longer be possible, fortunately or unfortunately, to say a word about ending in narrative without a quite self-conscious reliance upon that discourse's implication in "gender," then perhaps Oates in *Bellefleur* has pointed her readers to the inevitable deconstruction of any concept of ending.

WILL THE REAL AUTHOR PLEASE STAND UP? IAN MCEWAN'S *ATONEMENT*

Ian McEwan's novel *Atonement* resembles a whodunit, or at least a psychological thriller. McEwan has a reputation for macabre, if not "perverse," tales, ranging from his first collection of short fiction, *First Love, Last Rites*, to his Booker Prize novel, *Amsterdam*. The disturbing stories in that first collection include one in which a man keeps a pickled penis in a jar and another in which a young teenager attempts to certify his "manhood" by coercing his ten-year-old sister into having sex with him. In *Amsterdam*, as we have seen, McEwan offers a macabre[13] tale of two men who promise each other a means of escaping prolonged suffering from a terminal disease, until a falling out turns the bizarre suicide pact into mutual murder.

A psychological thriller, *Atonement* organizes itself into three parts. The first takes place shortly before the Second World War, the second and the third parts early in the war, followed by what purports to be an

"epilogue," set in 1999.[14] This organization of time and narrative is critical to the working out of the plot, and, confusing as it may seem, plot is
the dominant element.[15] The first section, set in 1935 at a country
manor, arouses a nostalgia for the waning peace and innocence of what
W. H. Auden called that "dishonest decade."[16] This opening section offers an unsettling,[17] rather inchoate narrative, leaving the impression
that the story is being told by a narrator without a grip on the direction
of the plot. The effect may be unsettling because the narrative seems to
be third-person, presumably delegated to a generic narrator by the author. At the same time, this narrative simulates the clumsy narrative,
often associated with B-grade thrillers, in which readers are titillated by
the angst of a plotline that does not seem to know where it is headed.
Occasionally seeming to surprise itself as it surprises readers with its
bizarre twists and turns, the plot opens more doors to possible directions, endings, and therefore meanings than it can ever develop. Because the point of view is limited third-person, readers expect a clearer
sense of direction but are left with only an impression of impending calamity. Horror will happen here; it is less clear when and to which characters.

   In a plot apparently searching for its focus, the strongest thread is
provided by the explosive relationship beginning to develop between
Cecilia Tallis and the charlady's son, Robbie Turner, both of whom
have just finished degrees at Cambridge in—what else?!—English literature, he with a "first" and she with a barely respectable "third." Stimulated by seeing Cecilia in her wet underwear after she plunged into a
fountain on the modest Tallis country estate to retrieve shards of a broken Meissen vase, Robbie writes draft after draft of a note indicating
his romantic interest in her. When he pauses to fantasize about her before drafting a new version of his billet-doux, his unconscious speaks
his sexual desire for her, using the word *cunt*, which presumably had
settled in that unconscious while he was reading a contraband copy of
Lawrence's unexpurgated *Lady Chatterley's Lover*, a novel that would
have become available in England a half-dozen years earlier. Robbie
takes this fugitive draft of his letter with him to the dinner party at the
Tallis house, and in a "Freudian slip" of an incredible kind he gives it to
Cecilia's thirteen-year-old sister, Briony, to deliver. The narrative offers
little assistance in anticipating with any confidence what the outcome
of this "blunder" will be, especially after Briony not surprisingly reads
the message before she delivers it to its addressee. Then the narrative
exposes Robbie and Cecilia, alone in the library in an embrace appearing to Briony's innocent eyes as sexual assault. Indeed, it is only later

when the narrative returns to this scene within Robbie's memory that readers become aware of the "truth"—namely, that what the presumably not-yet pubescent Briony (mis)read as an act of rape was actually a scene of passionate lovemaking.

Much of the focus of the narrative has been on Briony, who has been preoccupied with producing her play for her family audience. The tempestuous yet innocent passion of the new lovers—Cecilia's hymen is ruptured, and Robbie seems equally virginal—is dramatized as a "story." The other story is Briony's failed playlet, *The Trials of Arabella*. It has "failed," largely because her nine-year-old twin cousins, Jackson and Pierrot, resist being impressed into acting, and Lola, their fifteen-year-old sister, finesses herself into the starring role Briony crafted for herself. These cousins are Emily Tallis's guests because her sister has run off to Paris with a man who is not her husband. Then the twins run away, necessitating a search party, or parties, as it turns out. Several parties searching in the dark may make it possible for the story of Robbie and Cecilia's earlier coitus interruptus to pick up from where it left off in the library, barring some calamity, such as the boys' being found floating in the lake.

As the first section nears its end, the "crime" hovering over the narrative is revealed. Briony reports that she has observed the rape of her cousin Lola, who, for some reason, was looking for her brothers by herself in the dark. Based on what is presumably her misreading of the library scene, Briony accuses Robbie of being the man who sexually assaulted Lola. (In this murky thriller context, readers will discover only in the next section that Robbie was not raping Cecilia.) At last the plot is set in motion, a plot whose ending will be the destruction of both Robbie and Cecilia. As further proof that Robbie is a "sex maniac"— this *is* the England that, less than a decade earlier, Lawrence had turned his back on as hopelessly beyond redemption sexually—Briony produces the fatal letter. With the relentless speed of plot in Italian opera, Robbie is led away in handcuffs.

As so often is the case in the thriller plot, the crime functions as a mask for a more genuine crime. Even though Briony's bearing of false witness appears innocent, it is a "crime," because she could not have identified Robbie in the dark. Furthermore, the narrative leaves open the possibility that it was not a rape at all, since Lola may well be hiding the identity of a lover. As in the library scene, the inexperienced Briony may have encountered another primal scene[18] in which she mistakes the physical exertions of sexual love for rape. With the emergence of two crimes—the apparent rape of Lola as well as Briony's apparently false accusation of Robbie—the narrative becomes a double-decker who-dunit. The narrative may be drawing at least some of its readers forward, however, less to find out the identity of the alleged rapist as to bear witness to the eventual completion of the coitus interruptus of those halcyon days before the eruption of the Second World War. Part 2 and much of part 3 provide evidence of the difficulties the lovers face in the final completion of that first episode of love.

Part 1 offers the framework for the novel as a mystery with the usual false leads and clues to which readers later discover they should have been paying more attention. It raises the possibility of the twins' death, only to reveal Robbie bearing them back to safety; but he is then accused of a crime for which he will serve several years' hard labor, reduced only by his willingness to enlist in the army as World War II begins. Following his release from prison, when Robbie and Cecilia are kept apart by a string of misfortunes, it seems as though some larger force is bent on keeping the lovers separated until one or the other perishes in the threatening world of war. One of the leads from the first part begins to resurface: Are the two being kept apart by yet another secret? Is the "Old Man" who has treated Robbie "like a son" the father of both lovers?

Far-fetched as it may seem, this false lead is never eliminated but only complicated by the narrative's trick ending in the very last pages of the "epilogue."[19] Failed marriage is the norm among the assemblage of the Tallis family and their guests on the fateful afternoon and evening of part 1.[20] As we have seen, the Quincey cousins are house guests because they are temporarily homeless, their passive father having decamped to Oxford after their mother ran off with another man. More importantly, the Old Man, as the Tallis children call their father, is noticeably absent from the gathering, having virtually taken up residence in London for the past two years, purportedly due to his work preparing for imminent war.[21] The migraine headaches of their mother, whom her children call "Emily," may be either the cause or the effect of the Old Man's vagrancy. And to this strained marriage might be added the failed marriage of Robbie Turner's parents, his father's having deserted his wife, Grace, many years before. Most of all, however, this segment of the narrative emphasizes again and again the fatherly concern of the Old Man for the fatherless Robbie; he risks his family's displeasure by supporting the boy's education through Cambridge and possibly even through medical school. In fact, one expectation denied by the end of part 1 is that Jack Tallis might do something to save Robbie from prison "in the final reel."

Perhaps even more telling is the strange relationship of Robbie and Cecilia, exploding into passion after many years of something closer to the affection between siblings following the virtual adoption of Robbie into the Tallis family. The relationship is first framed within the consciousness of Briony, for whom a story of "a humble woodcutter [who] saved a princess from drowning and ended by marrying her" is no stretch of the child's romantic imagination: "Robbie Turner, only son of a humble cleaning lady and of *no known father* . . . had the boldness of ambition to ask for Cecilia's hand" (McEwan 2001, 36; emphasis added). Cecilia has difficulty at first casting Robbie as a lover: "They had known each other since *they* were seven" (21; emphasis added). Since he is two years older than she, this assertion imputed to her consciousness cannot be accurate. And it may not be coincidental that Robbie seems to enter the family, perhaps openly at last, when Turner leaves.

When the narrative shifts to Robbie's consciousness, it repeats the sense of difficulty in a relationship growing out of long familiarity. "He had known her since they were children, and he had never looked at her," he thinks. Then, not unexpectedly, the narrator adds: "She was like a sister, almost invisible" (74). A half-dozen pages later the narrator describes Robbie's becoming part of the Tallis family: "His tree-climbing pal was Leon, Cecilia was the little sister who trustingly held his hand . . ." (82). At the dinner table that fateful evening, Robbie's passion for Cecilia is framed within a set of "contradictions," the first of which is "she was familiar like a sister, she was exotic like a lover" (122). Granted, these references to Cecilia might be explained as stemming from Robbie's virtual adoption by the Old Man. Even so, it is Robbie, the instigator of this passionate "affair," who constructs Cecilia as a "sister," while she is not similarly impelled to cast him as a brother.[22]

In these two key relationships of Jack Tallis/Robbie Turner and Cecilia/Robbie, the narrative offers repetitions of father-son, sister-brother relationships, exceeding the coincidental and suggesting the obsessional. As in fairy tale and myth, this narrative provides a space in which the unconscious can speak its concern that family relationships may be "too close" through the agency of compulsive repetitions—the father of the Tallis family treats Robbie "like a son," and Cecilia has been "like a sister" to Robbie—as though these repeated references were "Freudian slips." In this way, the narrative gives the impression of saying more than it intends, more than it comprehends, through its continual circling back to its concerns that the boundaries between family affection and Eros, like the fine line between sexual passion and rape, can be easily trespassed.[23]

There is also abundant extratextual evidence for this narrative's creation of the false lead of Robbie and Cecilia sharing a father. As indicated earlier, in his first collection of short fiction, *First Love, Last Rites*, McEwan unsettled his early readers with the incestuous relationship of a brother and sister. His first novel, *The Cement Garden*, returns to the subject of incest between a brother and a sister. Clearly McEwan has written on other shocking or "perverse" subjects, but incest has been prominent enough in his work to make readers who are familiar with his reputation suspicious of the relationship between Robbie and Cecilia.

In any case it is in part the false lead of potential incest between Robbie and Cecilia in this "detective story" that draws the reader forward with a desire for the end. Ironically, desire is impelling the narrative forward in anticipation of a literal climax. As it becomes apparent in part 2, it appears to be "postponed" for longer than the three years Robbie served in prison because of Briony's "crime." It is no coincidence in part 1 that the desire for the end is generated out of the earlier quiescence of the charmed life of the Tallises in their pastoral retreat to which Robbie as an "other" has been permitted entry. Robbie's crime in writing the letter in which his unconscious speaks his desire for Cecilia as well as her crime in allowing the taboo signifier to unlock her unconscious desire for one who is too close may be the logical consequences of the Old Man's crime of loving outside the bonds of marriage. The narrative reads the desire of Grace Turner, in that wedding photograph in which her husband, "Ernest,"[24] stands by her side with his arms folded, and such forbidden love may have begun during the year in which Emily was pregnant with Cecilia's brother Leon and already beyond the Old Man's desire. In a narrative with underpinnings from Greek tragedy, the House of Tallis may be living out the sins of the father, the desire of the Old Man who refused to be bound by rites and laws.

In one sense, *Atonement* is reading the narrative of desire to which it alludes in grounding Robbie's selection of the signifier *cunt* to represent his desire for Cecilia. If, as traditional narratologists such as Scholes and Brooks have theorized, narrative is generated by desire for the end in both senses of "climax," *Atonement* toys with that paradigm without mercy—indeed, sadistically. More than other novels, this narrative performs an unmistakable sadism as it encourages the desiring reader to look forward to the end of the coitus left interruptus for an incredibly and perversely long duration. The choice of the term *perversely* is scarcely an exaggeration, because the narrative has offered, through the memory of Robbie, one of the most genuinely erotic passages in mainstream writing since the appearance of Lawrence's final novel, *Lady Chatterley's Lover,* to which *Atonement* itself alludes, almost to save future scholars the effort of researching the author's background to verify his familiarity with that novel.[25] As Terry Eagleton writes, "What Briony reads as a brutal assault on her sister by her lover is in fact one of the most adroitly tender, breathtakingly exact cameos of love-making in modern fiction."[26]

At the same time, we ought to remind ourselves that coitus interruptus has traditionally been a male concern. Its Latinate name grounds the practice in ancient Roman efforts to reduce the likelihood of conception through male withdrawal before orgasm. Like the "sin of Onan" among the ancient Jews, it might be understood less as masturbation than as the "sin against fertility" through the impractical attempt to thwart conception, even within married love, by withdrawing just before ejaculation. Although in both cultures the woman's concern with avoiding conception obviously played a role, the focus appears to be the male's achieving orgasm, one way or another, ignoring the need or the desire for climax in the female. In any case, in *Atonement,* Briony's interruption of Cecilia and Robbie's lovemaking probably took place because he was delaying his orgasm to prolong the pleasure of its prelude, although we might note, at the risk of pruriency, it is hardly credible that Robbie's first sexual intercourse at twenty-two would make delaying his orgasm a likelihood. The narrative is grounded in the joking model of the Genie of Aladdin's lamp granting impulsive wishes. It is as though, in the throes of sexual passion, Robbie experiences such ecstatic pleasure that he wishes the end could be postponed forever, and his wish is granted. He will rewind the film of the "library scene" in his memory the rest of his life, and yet each time the film will stop before it ends.

And, of course, as the "library scene" is screened again and again the narrative focus is Robbie's and not Cecilia's memory of the episode, and thus his "plot" and its ending must always differ from her "plot" and its very different ending. Accordingly, the narrative centers in Robbie's unwished-for denial of orgasm for *him,* without any apparent concern for Cecilia's sexual gratification. In this way, the library scene juxtaposes traditional notions of the fulfillment of desire in the male and in the female, a "frustration" of desire in the male who is denied orgasm and a presumption of "fulfillment" in the female, whether or not orgasm occurs. As it will become increasingly apparent in this cluster and in the next, traditional notions of the differences in male and female sexual gratification may be gendering the unitary male, or masculine, paradigm with its ending-driven "plot" of desire, just as it may well be gendering alternatives to that unitary paradigm with their suggestions of more complicated endings for desire.

As Robbie Turner is being led away in handcuffs to face rape charges, in the dark ages before DNA testing could have cleared him, the narrative tantalizes its desiring readers with an array of possible endings toward which the plot could be leading them. The last page of part 1, with Grace Turner screaming "Liars! Liars!" at the Tallis family, is the exact halfway point of the novel. One scenario might feature Jack Tallis, the Old Man, rescuing Robbie in the next or final (third) reel for a future with Cecilia. Hope for Robbie's rescue is dimmed, however, by the further waning of the already absent Old Man, the phallic father unwilling perhaps to risk the exposure of his own vagrancy in fathering Robbie. Better to keep these lovers separated than explain how their beginning of a "life of crime" must be aborted before it risks the destruction of Grace Turner's reputation, the disruption of the marriage—albeit in name only—of Jack and Emily Tallis, and even the possibility of "monstrous" progeny from incestuous lovemaking. The dominance of children's fairy tales in this section opens the door to a scenario in which the narrative offers one of those standard novelistic pregnancies produced in a single sexual encounter, even though in conventionally male romantic fashion Robbie was postponing ejaculation to savor that Keatsian fetishizing of anticipatory pleasure before the fall into gratification. This horror-story scenario of a future discovery, once the initial coitus is completed, that Robbie and Cecilia are siblings hangs like a sword of Damocles over the narrative as it moves toward its climax.

At the risk of repetitiveness, it needs to be stressed once again that the apparent randomness of the plot in part 1 is crucial to the sense that it could take any number of paths, like the plots in "The Garden of Forking Paths" by Borges. Because the narrative gives a limited sense of the action's having already ended, desire for the right kind of climax is aroused in readers, especially those male readers who want to witness the completion of the scene in the library. This openness of possibilities also creates a realistic sense that life is being represented here: desire for the right ending *may* be fulfilled, and then again it may *not*. These speculations about Robbie's hidden paternity, moreover, create anxiety, because readers have been schooled in the credo that only the text exists: there is no "real" life outside it, and we cannot speculate, for example, how many children Lady Macbeth had!

The sense of a plot whose action in the "real world" has not been completed is further enhanced by part 2. Here the narrative positions Robbie as a British soldier in the mass retreat toward Dunkirk with the obvious possibility of coming home to Cecilia (or, as her brother Leon pronounces her name, "Sis-Celia"). Robbie carries her letters, imploring him to come back to her—"I love you. I'll wait for you. Come back"(190)—an eerie rewriting of her words to console Briony when she was a child awaking from a nightmare, "It's only a dream. Come back." In his spare moments Robbie is allowed to remember the course of their epistolary "love affair," recalling the novel Cee was reading on the day of their transformation. Furthermore, this "making love for years—by post" (193) is implicated even more deeply in letters, for the lovers resort to their shared background in the study of "letters" to evade the censoring psychiatrist's surveillance of Robbie, who must not betray any affection for Cecilia, to prevent even this strained "intercourse" from being brought to an end.

One sample of those letters, revealing a further implication in fiction as a form of "letters," focuses on Cecilia's amazement that Briony has followed her older sister's choice of nursing as a profession. Cecilia speculates that Briony's choice not to seek a Cambridge education but to devote herself to the relief of others' suffering offers a sign of her acknowledgment of guilt and a growing desire for atonement. In passing, Cee adds that Briony told her a story she (Briony) had submitted to the literary journal *Horizon* had been rejected by its editor, Cyril Connolly. Cecilia is reassured that "at least someone can see through her wretched fantasies" (200). Cecilia's letter, with its textualizing of her hope that Briony will indeed exonerate him, allows Robbie to bear whatever it takes to get himself back safely across the English Channel to return to the "story" of his life when it became interruptus: "The prospect was of a rebirth, a triumphant return. He would become again the man who had crossed a Surrey park at dusk in his best suit, swaggering on the promise of life. . . . The story could resume, the one that he had been planning on that evening walk. He and Cecilia would no longer be isolated. Their love would have space and a society to grow in" (213).

In such a mood of autoerotic pleasure, the narrative allows him to recall an episode when he was nineteen and Briony at nine confessed her love for him. This delayed memory of Robbie seems almost "planted" by the narrator to provide some unconscious motivation for

Briony's misreading of Robbie as the one who raped Lola after she had earlier misread Robbie as raping Cecilia in the library. Clearly, Robbie's memory constructs Briony as the innocent but cruel accuser of a man whom she "loved" but "lost" to her sister. In any case, the "joy" of an envisioned "rebirth" can soften his heart enough to remember the encounter as an explanation for her later "crime," and yet he "would never forgive her" (220). Thus, the narrative arouses a desire for the end, as it is envisioned by Robbie. The burden of part 2 will become the project of "Saving Private Turner" to bring him back to Cecilia's arms. As John Updike aptly puts it, "[I]t is the lovers that keep us turning the page; theirs is the consummation we devoutly wish," probably not unaware of the double entendre of "consummation"!

And then part 3 appears to do just that. The narrative begins to move toward atonement, in the reunion of Robbie and Cecilia, and in their wish-fulfillment reunion with the Tallis family. To the desire for the climax of sexual love is added here the desire to be "at one" again, one of the great themes, for example, of Shakespeare's dark comedies in which the lost wife or daughter is recuperated. (One recalls the stunning "awakening" of the stone statue as Hermione in *The Winter's Tale*, or the catatonic Pericles brought back to life through the discovery that his infant daughter did not perish at sea but stands before him as a young woman—Perdita, the lost one who is found.) Readers ought not to forget that both Robbie and Cecilia are "English majors" and that Briony herself is an aspiring storyteller. Indeed, looking back to part 1, it becomes apparent that Briony abandoned drama because, as a fledgling playwright, she discovered she could not control the staging of her meaning, and turned to "fiction," a more powerfully attractive "story-telling" in which she can more ruthlessly manipulate others as "characters."[27] What stronger movement toward atonement than Robbie's sharing Cecilia's flat—and more importantly, her bed—while Briony confesses her crime and seems ready to sign an affidavit to that effect? But this crucial scene in part 3 of the "family" reconciling their differences is flat, bland, and unsatisfying. Robbie and Cecilia may well have exhausted the potential for love, so long delayed after being rudely interrupted in the library. At the same time, because of the manipulations of part 1, there is a sense of anxiety in the scene: something is just not right here!

Without warning, the last page of part 3 subverts the entire narrative up to this point by ending with the following ascription of "author" and date:

BT
London, 1999

Facing the last page of part 3 with this astounding revelation is the title page of what must be the last part, an "epilogue" moving the narrative into 1999, close to the year in which *Atonement* (2001) appeared. The initials "BT" can only be those of Briony Tallis, the "she" of the last paragraph, revealing "herself" as the "author" of all that comes before.

Apparently having just learned from Cyril Connolly the deficiencies of what she had submitted as the briefer, earlier draft of this novel, the Briony of a half-century ago decided that a letter confessing her misidentification of Robbie would be insufficient to clear her conscience. Such expiation would require instead "a new draft, an *atonement*, and she was ready to begin" (330; emphasis added). She feels "ready to begin" what presumably is to be a "non-fiction novel." If the narrative to this point represents this "new draft," a fiction constructed from Briony's observations and memories, the reader suddenly begins to experience the giddy sense of vertigo in this *mise en abîme* of a narrative-within-a-narrative. What appeared to be a conventional, albeit somewhat quirky, narrative up to this point represents a modernist novel within a postmodern framework. That is, Briony is a conventional modernist artist/narrator (it might be recalled that she was criticized for writing too much like her hero, Virginia Woolf), embodying the power of the artistic imagination to transform the raw materials of life into transcendent art. The framework, however, is postmodern, because this final revelation violates the contract into which the reader entered at the outset by suppressing its own provenance as authored by one of its characters.[28]

Before examining the other implications of Briony's "authorship," it is necessary to focus on the consequences of this whodunit ending. Once again, at the heart of the detective novel/mystery/thriller, the reader/viewer on some level is racked with anxiety, because he or she is racing against time to figure out the ending before it is revealed, the timing of the narrative being masterfully controlled so that the ending is not evident too soon, lest the audience lose interest, nor comes as too much of a surprise, lest the reader/viewer feel overmastered by the narrative's too clever withholding of the truth. At first reading, the revelation at the end of part 3 is likely to astound readers and impel them toward a self-defensive gesture of surveying what led up to this revelation for the hints and clues possibly ignored. With Briony's "storytelling" supplying the "surprise ending" of part 1—the indictment of

Robbie as a rapist—the novel has established its paradigm in a *mise en abîme* construction. Briony's "art" in "framing" Robbie feeds on the sacrifice of desire—his, obviously enough, but also the reader's. Readers are likely to ask, Why didn't we *know* that? And what other knowledge has been withheld, knowledge that we may *never* know, knowledge that could provide preparation for the last segment of the narrative and yet another "ending"? Can it be that a narrative sets in motion another set of conflicting desires: a desire for art to render permanent what could not otherwise survive, juxtaposed to a desire for life with its possibility of an unendingness, leaving open those potential endings closer to the heart's desire?

In addition, the narrative's explosive revelation at the end of part 3 opens the preceding narrative to the possibilities of omissions. By foregrounding itself in a postmodern fashion as a text, the narrative posits a "real world" on which it has been based, reminding its readers of what is obvious—that fiction is always a re-presentation, a re-construction—and yet validating speculations of what Briony may not have remembered, or more crucially what she did not *know* or *understand*, given that she was a child when these events "happened." Briony, for example, may not share McEwan's interest in brother-sister incest and thus may have completely "missed" the possibility that Robbie is Cecilia's brother and hers. Like Iris, Briony may be destroying a sibling, albeit more unintentionally. We might also recall Iris's admission that whenever the writer does not erase with the left hand what he or she writes with the right hand, the intrusion of self-justification is inevitable.

In this way, the narrative as Briony's production implicates itself in one of the most interesting cruxes of modernist fiction, the "unreliable narrator," the storytelling character whose biased perspective, ignorance, or willful suppression of information forces readers frequently to read *around* the fictional discourse to a fuller understanding of what is being represented. If ever there was an "unreliable narrator," Briony has to qualify for the designation, for clearly her desire for "atonement" must turn the "truth" into a sculptor's clay to justify her crimes and her self-serving expiation. In this context, the representation of the "truth" to which the modernist is dedicated must confront the postmodern suspicion that all is ultimately textual, and "truth" may be another of Briony's "fantasies." Modernism and postmodernism in this novel represent a binary like the optical illusion of a white urn or two faces alternately in silhouette or, perversely, at the same time, as the reader longs for truth but suspects its contamination with textuality.

The last section of the novel, "London, 1999," maps the dimensions of the potential of narrative to implicate itself in something approaching sadism. This section is an epilogue in which the "author" Briony can share information about the "lives" of the characters beyond the "end" of the novel at the same time this epilogue represents the "real" ending of the novel. In narratological terms this text contributes to the sense of *Atonement* as a postmodern narrative, as the classic Möbius strip, with no clearly defined "inside" or "outside." Or, like the classic trompe l'oeil of urn and silhouetted faces in profile, this epilogue is at one and the same time "inside" and "outside" the novel. It continues the illusionism that the characters are real people by feeding the hunger to know how their lives "really" ended. Even the agency of space takes on a postmodern dimension as the surviving members of the family and their progeny gather to celebrate Briony's seventy-seventh birthday in Tallis House, now transmogrified into Tilney's Hotel. And to enhance the perverse frisson of this return, the party itself is set in the library where desire missed its "consummation"—*forever,* as it would now appear.

Like a psychological thriller the narrative has provided one surprise ending we have been reading Briony's novel—on its way to providing the "real" ending of McEwan's novel, that is, what really happened to Robbie and Cecilia after Briony visited them following her appearance at Lola and Paul Marshall's wedding in part 3. This epilogue engages readers with a variety of types of existential angst. Briony as dramatist/stage manager has come on stage from the wings to reveal herself as the crafting and crafty narrator/author. Now readers are treated to a version of *Guess Who's Coming to Dinner* with the twist that the absentees may have never had the opportunity to refuse an invitation. The narrative delays the revelation of the whereabouts of the only guests readers are likely to genuinely care about, forcing readers to be patient while the narrator offers profuse details of the Quincey family's progeny, in a strategy reminiscent of Oates's technique in *Bellefleur* and Atwood's in *The Blind Assassin.* This narrative seems deeply implicated in sadism in its telling, as Briony draws out the revelation of its ending. In passing, we learn that Jack Tallis married a second time, but no further information is offered, leaving the reader to wonder if Briony as author/narrator ever figured out the possible "secret" of Robbie's paternity.

In the end, readers confront a blank space on the page. And then the ending is revealed by Briony, a rather dotty old lady now, sentimentalizing about sailing into the sunset. In "real life" Robbie died in June 1940 of blood poisoning and Cecilia was killed in the bombing of London later that year. This information unravels the final "draft" of Briony's novel that we have been reading, more specifically, part 3. The very presence of Briony's alleged novel in the reader's hands indicates that the Marshalls at least are dead, removing the threat of legal action. Perhaps they have been joined by Briony in that "beyond," populated by much of the family. As Briony informs her readers, and McEwan's, it is only in this latest draft of the novel she struggled to write for over a half-century that the lovers survive the fates of their supposed historical antecedents. Briony is ready for her "atonement" with the lovers whom she destroyed. (And readers may be unable to resist pondering if she in fact destroyed them in order to make her art, a version of Lacan's notion that signification "murders" the signified.) Only the "bleakest realism," she argues, could be served by killing off the lovers in the novel, as she did by separating them: "How could that constitute an ending?" (350). Facing imminent death herself, she no longer has the "courage of [her] pessimism." Soon, she goes on to argue, the "real" people on whom these characters are based will all be dead and all that survives will be Briony's textualizing of their being: "[W]e will only exist in my inventions." And should any of us be that "certain kind of reader" who wants to know "But what *really* happened?" there is no answer, because the question is absurd: in the end only Art survives. Her suggestion of "As long as there is a single copy . . ." of "her" novel offers a pastiche of Shakespeare's "As long as men can breathe, or eyes can see, / So long lives this, and this gives life to thee."

This gesture of artistic fascism moves Briony's self-justification into a postmodern critique of modernism. She asks rhetorically and perhaps sophistically as well: "[H]ow can a novelist achieve atonement when, with her absolute power of deciding outcomes, she is also God?" (350). In her own self-defense Briony reminds "her" readers that her modernist hero, Virginia Woolf, killed off Mrs. Ramsay within a pair of brackets. Implicit in Briony's apologia is the notion of artistic transformation inherent in modernism, as Joyce explored it in his portrait of the young artist, intent on seeing himself either as the "priest of eternal imagination," transmuting the bread of everyday life into something holy and transcendent, or as the God who is paring his nails in the wings while his creation is being performed. Briony seems particularly attracted to a Keatsian reading of the urn as art, freeze-framing life's youthful beauty and passionate love into the perfect and eternal moment, without the other half of Keats's perception that the compensations of art offer cold comfort to the pursuing lover, cut off in the flush of life and love.

This, then, is Briony's "atonement" as an artist: I may have destroyed their lives, but I have given them a life everlasting in the deathly urn of my art. (Surely it was no coincidence that Robbie and Cecilia began to be lovers when she daringly stripped down to her underwear to retrieve the pieces of the broken Meissen vase, or urn.) "I like to think that it isn't weakness or evasion," Briony concludes, "but a final act of kindness, a stand against oblivion and despair, to let my lovers live and to unite them at the end" (351). This is her self-serving "atonement" with the lovers she destroyed, but more importantly her "atonement" with the raw material for her artistic transformation. Art in this context cannot escape the specter of a ghoulish consumption of living and loving flesh to create the fantasy-lovers she pursued as a child. There is an inescapable element of Frankenstein's creature in this artistic breathing of life into the corpses she has destroyed and dismembered in order to remake them as *her* lovers. Ironically, the McEwan who shocked his earliest readers with tales of horror has found in the monstrousness of artistic transformation—the self-deluded and self-excusing "playing God" with human lives—a horror beyond jars filled with pickled penises.

The word *perversely*, used earlier, is appropriate here as well. What turns out to be a state of the interruptus for eternity in the "real world" is compensated for by a climax perversely delayed for years until part 3 where it is related but not dramatized. Then this climax is re-presented in part 4 as a "fiction," an imagined climax, part of the writer's art atoning for the denied climax in life, rendered forever impossible by the artist's "crime." The library scene Eagleton described as "one of the most adroitly tender, breathtakingly exact cameos of love-making in modern fiction" is rendered perverse by moving it into the deathly world of Keat's "Urn" where the pursuing lover, more recently (mis)-read as a rapist,[29] is consoled by the power of art to freeze desire at the peak of its anticipated gratification in the moment before it slips over into the unsatisfying climax radically unable to realize the ideal. Keats himself better knew the price life pays to art to have its ideals frozen into the deadly permanence of transcendence.

ANOTHER QUESTION OF ENDING:
L. P. HARTLEY'S *THE GO-BETWEEN*

Ian McEwan's novel *Atonement* (2001) offers what Harold Bloom a generation ago would have called "a strong reading"[30] of L. P. Hartley's *The Go-Between* (1953). Like *Atonement*, the Hartley novel demonstrates how an epilogue can problematize the sense of an ending, although the

McEwan novel's epilogue (or final chapter) more radically unsettles the ending *Atonement*'s readers were deceived into accepting as *the* ending. Hartley's novel similarly offers a text within the text—in this case, the narrator Leo Colston's diary in which he last wrote on his thirteenth birthday a half-century earlier. Like Briony, who steps onto the stage at the end as the "author" of McEwan's novel, Leo dreamed as a child of becoming a novelist, and *The Go-Between* might be thought of as the novel he now in early old age may be ready to write. Like the final section of *Atonement*, the epilogue of Hartley's novel takes place in the present and passes itself off as a text in progress whose indeterminate ending problematizes the already vexed ending of the novel proper.

What makes the ending of the novel proper "vexed" is the total lack of preparation of the boy Leo for the earthquake of a revelation with which the novel's plot ends. As a boy about to lose his innocence, Leo, the viewpoint character as well as narrator, implicates the narrative in a complex of issues familiar to readers of *Atonement*. Once again at the center is the sensibility of a child on the brink of puberty in a culture bent on insulating children from the "facts of life." Indeed it would be virtually impossible to conceive of the plot's succeeding if Leo Colston were replaced with a boy from the present who was also about to celebrate *his* thirteenth birthday.[31] At the same time, Leo's innocence is filtered through the sensibility of the man he has become and the man to whom the responsibility for the narration has been delegated: the older Leo, who may have a vested interest in certifying his "innocence" as a boy. The prologue has the crucial function of framing the story Leo will tell about the events of fifty years before on his thirteenth birthday, events expelling him from the garden of his childhood. Or, to be more accurate, it is not so much the "events" that are important as what he *remembers* of his childhood innocence and its loss, in the way that memory is being enlisted to serve his purposes as an old man, trying to make peace with the past, to "atone" for his sins and to achieve "at-one-ment" with those against whom he sinned as well as those who sinned against him.

An apt analogy here for Leo Colston's function as the narrator/"author" of this novel is provided by Iris in *The Blind Assassin*.[32] In writing her memoirs, it might be recalled, Iris foregrounds the inevitable concern with the degree of "truth" such narratives can achieve. In one of the most memorable tropes in Atwood's novel, Iris focuses attention on the continuous line of ink flowing out onto the paper before her, asserting that the only "truth" to be achieved in these memoirs is the outcome of a writing erased by her left hand as her right hand produces it. Writing for any potential readership, even when (or especially *if*) the reader is the writer herself, can only end in the omission of any "truth" not serving the writer's purposes, or in the memoirist's falling prey to making excuses or justifying herself. If "history" is written by the victors, memoirs are written by the survivors who have the power to establish as "truth" whatever the memoirist produces as text. Similarly, even though *The Go-Between* offers no "narratee" who is listening to the story, Leo assumes an author function, making these memoirs a text within the text that is the novel itself.

This implication in textuality is offered a further dimension by the diary arousing Leo's desire to narrate. Once he has overcome his half-century-long refusal to touch this record of his days at Brandham Hall, the diary becomes his Proustian madeleine bringing back the "remembrance of things past," and particularly the memories of the boy who was traumatized by the "primal scene"[33] he was forced to witness on his thirteenth birthday. If anything, Leo is even more averse to touching this fetish-object diary, representing the events that essentially rendered him a child for life, because he now has a clearer understanding of the diary's "enervating power," as well as "its message of disappointment and defeat" (Hartley 2002, 12). The term "fetish" is appropriate here, for Leo believes that it is what the diary represents that has confined him to "this drab, flowerless room," instead of a "rainbow-hued" room in which he would not be alone (13) By focusing on the diary and the narrative it sketches, the prologue rouses its readers, like the aging Leo Colston, from a state of quiescence, generating desire for knowledge of what it was the boy saw on his fateful thirteenth birthday, a knowledge he believes has exiled him to a wasteland of loveless and uncreative death-in-life. In Ancient Mariner fashion, Leo is setting out to "tell," or write, the *story* of why he has been condemned to be an aging virgin as well as a writer manqué.

Opening the diary again, Leo enters the tomb in which a record of *the* transformative period of his life has been encrypted for fifty years. It is hardly a coincidence that the year is 1900. Ironically, the narrative is reading the ambivalent year of 1900, not as a fin de siècle, but as the beginning of a new century.[34] Or it may be more accurate to say that 1900 marked an end Leo had been misreading as a beginning. He recalls himself at twelve anticipating the fateful year as "the dawn of a Golden Age" (14). He adds: "The year 1900 had an almost mystical appeal," in part because he had been so ill that it had been for a time uncertain he would even see the new year in. " 'Nineteen hundred, nineteen hundred,' I would chant to myself in rapture" (14), he recalls. And chief among the hopes he entertained for himself was the possibility of becoming a writer.

The diary forces him, apparently for the first time in a half-century, to confront this ambition to write when he was almost thirteen. Following months of having been bullied by two older schoolmates, Leo wrote a series of curses on his tormentors in his diary and left it where they were likely to read it, as they had earlier entries. When the two are seriously injured in a fall from the school roof and Leo becomes a hero, he begins to construct himself as a "magician" whose words have the performative power to do harm to those who have harmed him—and others. "It was then that I began to cherish a dream of becoming a writer—perhaps the greatest writer of the greatest century, the twentieth" (29) Leo recalls, and that immense ambition energizes an extended argument between the twelve-year-old boy and the present man of "sixty-odd years."

Leo imagines a younger self accusing him of total failure. The younger Leo might chide him for ending up so dull, essentially as the housekeeper tending the books of others, when the younger Leo aspired to write his own. The older Leo in turn accuses his younger self of aspiring to fly too high, so that like Phaëthon he left his future self a "cindery creature" (26). Leo would also point to the twentieth century as hardly having fulfilled its promise of being "the greatest." Then the "argument" moves into its subtler phase with the older Leo chastising the younger for his failure to "call down curses" on those who harmed him, "instead of entreating me, with your dying breath[,] to think about them kindly—" to which the ghost of Leo the Younger speaks these parting words: "Try now, try now, it isn't too late" (27), urging him to curse them himself. The prologue completes its half of the framing function with the expectation that the narrative to follow will represent in some fashion the "curses" that Leo the Elder will finally "call down" on the principals in the tale of the fateful summer of 1900.

In this way the narrative establishes a conflict between the two aspects of story Tzvetan Todorov has termed *fabula* and *sjužet*, or events and their representation. The prologue sets up the expectation that the events of Leo's twenty-three days at Brandham Hall will be represented in such a manner that "curses" will be called down on Mrs. Maudsley for forcing him to witness the primal scene of Ted Burgess and Marian Maudsley making love, along with curses on the lovers for using him as their go-between and flagrantly making love where they should have known they could be seen, and even curses on Trimingham for feeding Leo's imagination on his role as "Mercury," the messenger of the gods.

And yet this *sjužet* seems powerless to resist a *fabula* certified by the narrative as a "real world" on which the older Leo still seems unable to call down curses. As the narrative framed by this prologue and the epilogue makes clear, its principals whom the older Leo might choose finally to curse—unlike the younger Leo's schoolmate-tormentors, Jenkins and Strode—were no "villains," any more than Leo was their entirely innocent victim.

Indeed, Leo reveals his younger self as far less innocent than he once chose to see himself. The younger Leo quite self-consciously feeds his ravenous imagination on the mythology of the zodiac, granting himself parity with the other figures at Brandham whom he has cast as members of that zodiac's "galaxy." He clearly enjoys Trimingham's imaginative engagement with him in the self-aggrandizing role as Mercury, just as he luxuriates in the foster-mothering of Mrs. Maudsley, a True Mother, in contrast to the Miller's Wife who is raising him, presumably with little appreciation for the magnificent splendor of his princely imagination. And Leo clearly is aroused by the erotic charge of Marian's attention, once he has cast her as Virgo in his "galaxy." Even before he has visited Brandham Hall, Leo is stimulated by the Virgin, "the one distinctively female figure in the galaxy." He claims that although he spent many "hours of dalliance" thinking of Virgo they were "innocent enough" (14). Whether it is the younger or older Leo who judges those thoughts "innocent" seems a moot point, but Leo has a vested interest in crediting his own innocence.

Leo was also strongly attracted to Lady Marian's Lover, Ted Burgess. As anyone familiar with Lawrence's last, and most notorious, novel may readily note, the figure of Ted Burgess is connected intertextually with Oliver Mellors in *Lady Chatterley's Lover*, another lover of a woman above his own class. For the younger Leo, and perhaps the older Leo as well, Ted emits a Lawrence-like aura of physical male presence. Leo is impressed by Ted's "exultation of being alone," and when he visits Ted he occasionally thinks at first that the farmer is "naked" (64). Readers of *Lady Chatterley's Lover* will note gestures here to the important early scene in which Connie Chatterley intrudes upon Mellors washing himself and exploits her advantage to gaze at him, while he too is unaware of her presence. Leo acknowledges "fear before that powerful body, which spoke to me of something I did not know" (68). Tellingly he "retreats" from that mysterious male sexuality, preferring to observe it unobserved as an ideal to which he cannot conceive of himself aspiring, for Ted alone in Leo's galaxy seems to have the ability to "give himself up to being alone with his body" (68).

Ted himself is aware of the power of his sexuality in his relationship with Marian and in his reputation, according to Trimingham, as a "lady-killer" (235). Moreover, the narrative offers an important later scene in which Ted is clearly aware of the reflection of his "physical presence" (178) in Leo's gaze. When the boy visits Ted's farm unexpectedly, he finds the farmer with no shirt on. The encounter is just as revealing of Leo as Ted, for Ted perceptively reads in Leo's face the twelve-year-old boy's uneasiness in being in the presence of a shirtless man, in part because Leo's culture licensed so little baring of the flesh. And as a farmer, of course, Ted knows about the "facts of life," and even offers to share them with Leo, who both wants to know and yet does not. Ted seems daunted by the power of sexual knowledge and the vulnerability, or "femininity," implicated in Leo's innocence and desire to *know*. Then again, Ted may be maintaining Leo's sexual ignorance to protect himself and Marian from Leo's potential suspicions of a sexual relationship, instead of the "business" Leo is led to believe the two are forced to meet secretly to conduct.

The narrative records the young Leo's efforts to maintain a position on the threshold of adult sexuality, attracted to, yet frightened by it. Ted is an attractive figure who knows about "spooning," the popular euphemism for heteroerotics; and being a devout follower of Lawrence, Ted pronounces spooning "natural," a major revelation to the boy, who has been embarrassed at least once by not understanding what "spooning" meant.[35] This "revelation" follows the more crucial disclosure that Ted and Marian are in love, all the more astonishing because Leo feels so obtuse in not having known it. It is, however, Ted's physical being that Leo finds not only attractive but spellbinding. Leo is reluctant to admit to Ted's influence: "I liked Ted Burgess in a reluctant, half-admiring, half-hating way." However, it is only possible to maintain that ambivalence when he is at Brandham Hall, some distance from Ted, for "when I was with him his mere physical presence cast a spell on me; it established an ascendancy that I could not break" (178). Ted is clearly the man Leo would like to be, and he admits that any pain Ted experiences he feels as well. Ted does, however, intrude on Leo's boyish love for Marian; thus, his ambivalence concerning Ted: "He fitted into my imaginative life, he was my companion of the greenwood, a rival, an ally, an enemy, a friend — I couldn't be sure which" (178–79).

Before examining this story's dramatic "climax" — with an eye to the novel's intertextual relationship to *Atonement* — it might be useful to pose the question: What are the saliences of this narrative? Note that virtually the entire narrative takes place at a manor in the English countryside, with its atmosphere of a self-contained, traditional world of rigid class divisions. Leo identifies himself with the farmer Ted Burgess partly because as a bank manager's son he is also at Brandham Hall on sufferance. As his schoolmate Marcus Maudsley bluntly reminds him, Leo is definitely *not* a member of the Maudsley-Trimingham class. It is also important that Leo is a boy on the brink of puberty who observes the primal scene of two lovers with whom he has become emotionally involved. Because Marian is a woman, even the otherwise incredibly naive Leo can admit that he loves her, and in his ambivalent presexual state he is very attracted to Ted as well.[36]

Having established his emotional investments in both Marian and Ted, Leo is well qualified to become a major player in the violent climax of the novel.[37] Intending to cause a separation between the lovers by deliberately misinforming Marian that the time of what would be their final tryst was six o'clock, instead of half-past six, in the hope that she would leave in impatience and Ted would believe she had abandoned him, Leo cannot foresee how the tension of the assignation, exacerbated by unseasonable heat, will push Marian toward a flagrant disregard for the risk of making love with the farmer, even though she is expected at Leo's birthday celebration. Leo's meddling is a notable blend of "innocence" and cruelty, legitimated by Trimingham's dubbing him "Mercury," one of the gods. Mrs. Maudsley's participation in the catastrophe is little short of sadism. Distraught as she may be at her daughter's delinquency, she *knowingly* coerces Leo into witnessing the scene of the lovers in flagrante delicto, because she feels authorized to act cruelly to Leo since he is her social inferior. Leo's memory of this cruelty makes him ponder: "Can it be that [Mrs. Maudsley's] spirit would like to make it right with me?" (42). That suggestion of "atonement" is a saliency worth noting at this point. Finally, were the scene from which he could not divert his gaze insufficient to traumatize him sexually, the suicide of Ted Burgess, his sexual ego ideal, would surely have sufficed.

The abrupt ending, encrypting Leo's memory of the events, demands an epilogue, not simply to match the prologue whose framing function it completes but also to provide an ending for a narrative broken off with the revelation scene and the news of Ted's suicide. This epilogue clearly has a much more crucial function than the last chapter of, say, *Tom Jones*, with its fleshing out of the details of Tom's marriage to Sophia so that readers might know the number and the sexes of their children and so forth. This epilogue, by contrast, renders problematic what passes for the novel's ending by offering Leo, the old man, some additional "facts of life." The revelation that the tenth Viscount of Trimingham was born seven months after Marian married the ninth virtually certifies that the heir to the title was the son of *Ted*—yet another "Edward." In this way the epilogue reads the novel proper, adding the painful dimension of Marian's (and perhaps even Ted's) awareness of her pregnancy in the calamitous scene of exposure. More importantly, this epilogue offers another "ending," albeit a very "open ending." This second "open ending," like Briony's revelations in the last chapter or epilogue of McEwan's novel, delegitimizes the earlier ending, urging us to ask whether epilogues and afterwords are parts of the narrative, not mere appendages. Without the epilogue, *The Go-Between* merely stops, thus denying the desire for truth in the transformative power provided by a more genuine ending.

The epilogue reveals that the "greatest century" Leo had anticipated as a boy has decimated the Maudsley-Trimingham family. Two world wars have destroyed its male members and also turned its world into a spiritual wasteland by sapping the impulse to procreate: like Marian's son, her grandson is an only child. Meeting the elderly Marian again at midcentury, Leo is pressed into service one last time as her go-between, or "postman." As Marian reads the past, she and Ted served the boy Leo as the paradigm of lovers willing to sacrifice everything for love. Like Shakespeare's Antony and Cleopatra, or Lawrence's Mellors and Connie, Ted and Marian testify to the belief in "a world well lost for love." Now it is Leo's mission to persuade Marian and Ted's grandson that the House of Trimingham need not be the House of Atreus, and that the aspirations of 1900 can be redeemed with the rehabilitation of the wasteland through the power of love.

The open ending of this narrative is troped through the gaze Leo directs toward Brandham Hall, where he has an appointment for lunch with Marian's grandson. What will Leo say? Will he listen to the ghost-boy of 1900 who has alerted him that it may not be too late to call down curses on those who buried him alive in the crypt of childhood, bereft of the potential for adult love and a career as a writer? It may be especially important that the only other survivor of the summer of 1900 is Lady Marian Trimingham, whom Leo loved and who is still a devout believer in the power of love; at the same time, as an advocate of Eros, Marian still has no conception of how her exploitation of a young boy could lock him out of even the most conventionally moderate experience of the erotic love she continues to extol. In her own way, Marian is a reincarnation of Keats's La Belle Sans Merci or Yeats's Maud Gonne, the beautiful lady with the power to energize a man's love even though in the end it might represent what Yeats in a different context termed a "murderous innocence."

At the outset of the epilogue, Leo reacts against the memory of his mother's telling him while he was recuperating that he had "nothing to be ashamed of" and "it's all over now" (300). Like Oedipus, Leo assumes greater responsibility for the tragedy than necessary ("I had betrayed them all"), especially a greater responsibility for Ted's death: "[I]t was for him I grieved. He haunted me" (301). In addition, as Leo becomes aware, "I could not injure him without injuring myself" (302). We return to the question of what Leo will tell this latest and perhaps last "Edward," Ted's grandson, and what the efficacy of that counsel will be. Will Leo accept his responsibility for the catastrophe and seek atonement with those he "betrayed," especially Ted, whose grandson is the addressee of Marian's last "love letter"? And given the trope of "the south-west prospect of the Hall, long hidden from my memory" with which the epilogue ends, will the "love letter" he bears from Marian to her grandson find its addressee, not simply the tenth Viscount of Trimingham, but also the elderly Leo, who has one last chance, perhaps, to free the young Leo from his tomb in Brandham? Whether that self-liberation will take place depends on how much compassion Leo has for the boy he was and on his willingness finally to accept citizenship in the adult world, where "evil" is too intermixed with good to be easily uprooted, like the menacing deadly nightshade, or "belladonna," he convinced himself he had succeeded in rooting out in Ted and Marian's bower of love. The epilogue cries out for "atonement," and perhaps the telling of the story by Leo as that novel he hoped as a boy to write will fulfill that desire to seek and to grant atonement to all the living and the dead.

AN ENDING OPENING TO THE FUTURE: MARGARET ATWOOD'S *THE HANDMAID'S TALE*

Margaret Atwood's narrator Offred ends *her* "Handmaid's Tale" with the ambivalent announcement that the black van associated with the menacing "Eyes" has arrived. She is escorted by her lover Nick, Commander Fred's chauffeur, who addresses her by her "real name" and informs her that it is "Mayday," the code word of the Underground.[38] This "last" chapter ends thus:

Whether this is my end or a new beginning I have no way of knowing: I have given myself over into the hands of strangers, because it can't be helped.

And I step up, into the darkness within; or else the light.

(Atwood 1985, 295)

With high expectations of what the next chapter(s) will reveal about Offred's "end or a new beginning," readers turn the page. After all, quite a few pages remain. The text subverts those expectations, however, by whisking its readers into a more distant future of 2195, suggesting *The Handmaid's Tale* "proper" has been set in 1995, a decade after the novel appeared. Like the last "parts" of novels such as *Atonement* and *The Go-Between*, this problematic text-within-the-text, entitled "Historical Notes on *The Handmaid's Tale*," calls into question once again what we mean by the term "ending" and whether "plot," as a traditional narratologist such as Brooks views it, can be the sole, or perhaps even the weightiest, component in the reader's "sense of an ending."

More than anything, this section called "Historical Notes on *The Handmaid's Tale*" problematizes the novel's apparent ending by contesting its open-endedness. As Atwood has indicated, she reads *The Handmaid's Tale* within a web of intertextuality that includes George Orwell's *Nineteen Eighty-Four*, whose "appendix" Orwell entitled "The Principles of Newspeak." Atwood (mis)reads this "appendix" as the crucial last chapter of Orwell's novel, offering hope in a farther future, when Oceania will be no more. Speaking of "The Principles of Newspeak" in the context of her "Historical Notes," Atwood claims that Orwell "did the same thing. He has a text at the end of *1984*," and she continues: "In fact, Orwell is much more optimistic than people give him credit for. . . . Most people think the book ends when Winston comes to love Big Brother. But it doesn't. It ends with a note on Newspeak, which is written in the past tense, in standard English—which means that, at the time of writing the note, Newspeak is a thing of the past" (Atwood 2006, 116).

What this indeterminate text-within-the-text stirs us to question, if we have not done so in the narrative "proper," is the provenance of this text. Were we less sophisticated readers, who merely stumbled on this text, we might question how it could have been generated at all and even dismiss as "academic" the issue of Offred's imminent death: after all, *she* is telling the story, and therefore she has to survive its telling. How did this text come into being? was the kind of a question that an

early novelist such as Daniel Defoe might have expected from his practical seventeenth-century readers, who also feared "fiction" as devil's
work, encouraging a Defoe to "justify" his tales as criminal confessions
or other varieties of "found" texts. In a sense, Atwood's novel is a pastiche of the "found" text.

If readers failed to ponder how this handmaid's tale came into being,
"Historical Notes" supplies a reconstruction of the circumstances of its
historical background. In its reliance on first-person narration, Offred's
tale, or the novel proper, represents a closed economy of subjectivity, a
consciousness trapped in "solitary confinement," with its potential for
solipsism. If the fictional editors are to be believed (and their reliability
is open to question), Offred must have stepped into the light. In that
world of light, "somewhere" in a haven from Gilead, outside its domain
or after its collapse, she dictated a series of audiotapes the editors have
transcribed and edited as this ersatz oral history. "History," with its
occasionally too easy promise of "answers," provides an unreliable explanation of this novel's ending, for this apparent "happy ending" of
Offred's deliverance becomes complicated by more questions than the
relatively obtuse scholars, Pieixoto and Wade, are perceptive enough to
raise. Although it seems a "happy ending," its implications ripple out
ever more widely into further and larger questions.

Suddenly the question arises, How could Offred have re-visioned
herself in Gilead after escaping its nightmare and having put its horrors
behind her, if in fact horrors ever are put behind us? How was Offred
able to dictate the story of her experience in Gilead in "historical present" so immediate and real that readers may find it difficult to believe
that she is not "speaking" the experience as it happens? Like Orwell's
Winston Smith, who has been hollowed out by O'Brien to be filled up
with Big Brother, Offred is a "sacred vessel" to be filled up with what
Gilead has decided she must contain, a commander's child, making her,
as she pertly tropes it, a womb on legs. Also, as Offred makes clear, she
has had no access to even primitive writing tools such as a pencil or a
pen, like Winston's leaky fountain pen, whose stains on his fingers
might be read as the stigmata of his fugitive writing. And Offred certainly has no place to hide a tape recorder, if she could lay her hands
on one in the first place, because in Gilead she has no "room of her
own," to use Virginia Woolf's phrase for the basic need of any woman
with an aspiration to "write" in any sense of the term. Because Offred
cannot lock her door, her subjectivity is always vulnerable to invasion,
a state of radical "femininity," if we read vulnerability or penetrability
gendered as "feminine."

Once readers learn in "Historical Notes" that Offred dictated the audiotapes *after* she escaped from Gilead, they are likely to return to the narrative proper with its eerie sense of an indeterminate time—and textuality. Offred offers readers a historical "present" at the same time she stresses that the narrative is a "reconstruction." Both are obviously bound up with storytelling and the sense of interminable repetition. As first-person narrative, this writing masquerades as a speaking, an oral storytelling *about* the past, as though the narrator is still *in* that past. Once the reader becomes aware of the "Historical Notes," the pastness of that past cannot be eradicated from the reader's consciousness. Furthermore, Offred acquires a historical personhood when her "tale" can be the subject of the narrative's editor, Professor James Darcy Pieixoto, who delivers the conference address, included at the end as "Historical Notes." As a scholar of literary history, Pieixoto also provides Atwood with an opportunity to poke fun at the academic world in which she got her start as a writer but from which she has distanced herself for a variety of reasons.[39]

As narrator and central consciousness, Offred performs a duplicity that readers have become accustomed to since the beginnings of the novel. Readers begin this narrative with the presumption, as Brooks reminds us, that the action has been completed, so that the re-presentation of it can commence as a variety of repetition. "Historical Notes" makes it abundantly clear that Offred already knows she will escape, but to maintain suspense she must suppress such knowledge by restricting herself to what she knew in the past. It is this sense of re-construction, of performing the recovery of the past by imaginatively reconstructing it, that complicates Offred's narrating by implying the "creative" elements of historiography, namely, writing about the past is always already immersed in textuality. This constructedness is particularly apparent in Offred's longing for the ending that she did not know in the past but now knows as a survivor of that past.

Much of Offred's narration seems to be caught in something akin to the repetition-compulsion. This narrative does have a semblance of "plot." Offred *must* conceive a child by Nick, or somebody else, because Commander Fred is sterile, a vexed issue in a patriarchal context where a leader cannot be publicly identified as sterile, for sterility would undermine his masculinity and therefore his authority. If she cannot bear a healthy child, the failure will ensure her exile to the legions of "Unwomen" and an early death from working in the contaminated waste dumps. If Nick did not exist, Offred would have had to invent him, for his narrative function is merely to impregnate her. The commander's wife may be colluding in this subterfuge to preserve her "happy home," and perhaps even Fred knows how his reputation as a "man" is being preserved by his loving wife. Nick himself may feel that he is the commander's "stud," as Oliver Mellors once told Lady Chatterley that he felt her impotent husband, Clifford, was taking class exploitation to a new limit by enlisting his gamekeeper's services to provide his master with an heir. In any case, the narrative has a plot, set in motion by Offred's desperate need to survive by conceiving a child and then by her even more desperate efforts to keep Gilead from stealing this child as it had earlier robbed her of her daughter.

The Offred she reconstructs herself as having once been, after she fled Gilead, of course had no way of knowing how this "story" would end. She is brilliantly conceived of as one deeply attracted to storytelling because its linearity offers the promise of an ending. She "says": "I would like to believe this is a story I'm telling . . . then I have control over the ending. Then there will be an ending, to the story, and real life will come after it" (39). At best it is a story she is "telling," she indicates, "because I have nothing to write with and writing is in any case forbidden" (39). She is compelled by this telling, even if this narration goes on only in her head, because a story is like a letter, and therefore there must be someone out there, even an anonymous someone, who will eventually receive her "letter," once again bending Lacan's assertion that the letter always finds its address, perhaps because the letter constructs its address or addressee. The story has such deeply rooted motives for Offred because it predicates this "you," just as it implies the prospect of an ending, preferably the "happy ending" of escape from this "nightmare of history."

This fatiguing sense of compulsion to repeat until she has somehow "earned" the ending, or release from these repetitions, becomes increasingly apparent. Offred tells us: "This is a reconstruction . . . , in my head, as I lie flat on my single bed rehearsing what I should or shouldn't have done, how I should have played it. If I ever get out of here . . ." (134). But of course she is "out of" that room in the commander's house when she is telling the story in that illusory present time, already the past now in a future awaiting her readers: "When I get out of here, if I'm ever able to set this down, in any form, even in the form of one voice to another, it will be a reconstruction then too, at yet another remove. It's impossible to say a thing exactly the way it was, because what you say can never be exact, you always leave something out . . ." (134). In many ways Offred, or "June," is Iris's sister in her concern with the impossibility of getting anything that she represents "exact" because something is inevitably left out.

As readers approach the end of Offred's narrative, they are likely to begin feeling the conventional anxiety and suspense about the ending. Once again, even though in the present of her narrating this story Offred is its "author" in her function as its narrator, she continues to reconstruct herself as a character in a story she resents being unable to control and does not know the ending of, much as she might look forward expectantly to the happy ending of her deliverance. At the brothel called "Jezebel's," she meets her pre-Gilead friend Moira, whom she had cheered on for escaping the training school for handmaids. At Jezebel's Moira has become a kind of temple prostitute. Offred says that in the story she wants to tell Moira would blow up Jezebel's when as many as fifty commanders have visited this den of iniquity. Although she envisions some apocalyptic ending for Moira she has to admit she has no idea how (or even *if*) Moira has died (Atwood 1985, 250). Ironically, it was just such a melodramatic ending that the film adaptation imposed on Atwood's novel.

In a very clear sense, Offred is preparing herself and her readers for her end. In these last pages, she foregrounds herself as narrator, as a storyteller playing with the text of her tale, even at one point (re)constructing three different versions of the first love scene with Nick, beginning the second rendition with the acknowledgment she made up that story, but the next version would represent how it actually happened (261), and the third with "It didn't happen that way either. I'm not sure how it happened; not exactly. All I can hope for is a reconstruction: the way love feels is always only approximate" (263). In "Salvaging," Offred confesses to sins against humanist values in her willingness, for example, to sacrifice Nick to save her daughter and herself, should such a sacrifice become necessary, or to participate in the mutilation of the supposed rapist, who was probably only someone the state considered its enemy and not actually a rapist. She feels compelled to continue telling "this sad and hungry and sordid, this limping and mutilated story" so that others will hear it, even though the circumstances of that hearing are completely unknown. As she stresses, it is crucial for her believe a prospective audience into existence: "Because I'm telling you this story I will your existence. I tell, therefore you are" (268). This last assertion offers a postmodern version of the Cartesian cogito: because I tell you stories you exist as a listener/reader, and I exist as the teller/writer. I write us into existence; or, existence is in the end textual.

The existential being of Offred's text is further problematized by the "Historical Notes." As Professor Pieixoto, the coeditor of the text, indicates in his conference presentation, what we have been reading as *The Handmaid's Tale* is a transcription and therefore a "translation," or a rewriting, of a spoken text rearranged and named by its editors, requiring an undisclosed amount of "guesswork" (302). The tapes were found in Maine, suggesting that Offred managed to get that far from the setting in Gilead Atwood has identified as Cambridge, Massachusetts. The editor's fixation with identifying who "Fred" was detracts from what is of most interest in these closing pages: "the ultimate fate of our narrator" (310). Pieixoto speculates about whether she managed to escape Gilead or was arrested there and suffered one of the alternative horrors of the colonies, Jezebel's, or execution (311). Shifting into comforting platitudes such as "the past is a great darkness" (311), our pompous professor ignores what are potentially the most interesting questions: Why does the narrative stop, rather than end? Did Offred have to leave for another leg of her journey to safety, or was the sanctuary of her speaking/writing violated by her pursuers, who might well have thought of her in the context of the "madwoman in the attic," if Pieixoto's guess that she ended up in an attic is a sound hypothesis? The narrative may be reading Orwell's *Nineteen Eighty-Four* with its dramatic scene of the Thought Police breaking in on Winston Smith's illusory sanctuary from Big Brother. Or, did Offred simply run out of blank tapes and could not bring herself to erase enough of the last tape to prevent this sense of an absent ending, and a sense of closure?

These questions render this narrative even more problematic as a representation of how ending might generate the substantial transformation that is supposed to provide the long middle of narrative with the sense of meaningfulness readers expect to take away from the text. By implication, the narrative is exploring many of the issues of the relationship between art and life with which numerous contemporary novels seem to be preoccupied—Atwood's own novel *The Blind Assassin* and McEwan's *Atonement* being two notable cases in point. By foregrounding the textuality of this narrative in the self-consciousness of Offred's narration and the control over her text exercised by its editors, *The Handmaid's Tale* cries out against art as a preserving yet necessarily mutilating "reconstruction" of life. By doing so, this narrative affirms how narrative as text snatches bits and pieces of life from its vast, eternal flow and lines them up in a sequence to give them a set of limits, a direction, and an ending to denote some sense of meaning. Life, however, will always exceed and transcend the reconstructions that attempt to confine and fix its being.

One focus of these issues is a perception that numerous readers have acknowledged, including Atwood herself as a reader of her own text. In the context of women's rights, and perhaps beyond to a concern that *every* human being might have the same opportunities for individual fulfilment, activists have sometimes deluded themselves into believing that once rights are established they continue in perpetuity. Atwood's narrative reminds us that what some might have (mis)read as the victory for women's rights in the 1980s could bring a backlash of culturally conservative energies to produce a "Gilead." The epilogue, "Historical Notes on *The Handmaid's Tale*," offers the not very subtle reminders that the price of preserving any group's rights really is "eternal vigilance." As many have noted, Professor Pieixoto and his coeditor Knotly Wade may have produced this narrative as a kind of historical monument to the "bad old days" of sexist oppression; "feminist" though he might proclaim himself, Pieixoto still delights in his feeble yet misogynist attempts at humor with his remarks about the "Underground Frailroad" and his silly double entendres on the handmaid's tale/tail. The female conferees may join in the laughter, now that they are "liberated," without recognizing that sexism, like all the other isms of human bias, have to be condemned again and again, not just once for all time.

This episode of lingering misogyny reminds readers that historiography is another kind of storytelling, with similar anxieties about the "inaccuracies" that are inevitable as soon as writers of any sort begin to shape life into art, or even history. We are drawn back once again to the question of Offred's "real name" and Pieixoto's apparent inability to figure out that she was probably "June," as readers of *The Handmaid's Tale* have been quick to discern. This shadowy "June," who exists beyond Offred's reconstruction of herself, and certainly beyond Pieixoto and Wade's (re)construction of her through their rewriting of her tapes, floats in a world that readers are a part of, a world in which humankind must continue to remain vigilant against threats to the rights of any member of the community, despite the appearance of the millennium's having arrived, perhaps *especially when* that arrival seems to have ushered in a utopia of "diversity" and "multiculturalism" for which the conferees are smugly congratulating themselves. How much else, readers may ponder, have these editors left out or changed in Offred's text in order to shape its meaning as a gesture toward this brave new world's congratulating itself on its triumph over bias?

That question brings us back to the issues of ending. As editors,

Pieixoto and his "silent partner," Knotly Wade,[40] have found it necessary to shape the material of the tapes into a narrative with a plot and therefore an ending. "Historical Notes" indicates they were working with a box of separate tapes they had to arrange in "order." Perhaps as a slight gesture to modernism, they devised the narrative's apparent "open ending," allowing readers to hope for the "happy ending" of Offred's deliverance from Gilead. (A cynic might suggest the decision was a ploy to provide the editors with the opportunity to profit from being hired as conference keynoters, providing the historical background to confirm this tentative "happy ending.") Obviously enough, it is yet another "open ending," because readers are left with the sole consolation of knowing that Offred escaped long enough to dictate the tapes, confirming her existence textually as a kind of message-in-a-bottle in the vaster sea of life, waiting for its addressee to recover her being. Even so, this unendingness of the narrative—its essentially having stopped a second time—posits the existence of a larger realm. It is a realm one might tentatively associate with Lacan's concept of the Real—the Real not so much in contrast to the false or the unreal, but what is outside the registers of both the Imaginary, or images, as well as the Symbolic, or textuality. Some readers may be able to situate a shadowy "June" in that larger realm of the Real, shared by the Robbie and Cecilia who escaped Briony's textual nets as well as by the elderly Leo Colston who sets out one last time for Brandham Hall to deliver the love letter of Marian to her grandson and to Leo, who is also its addressee, its message being that life need not submit itself entirely to art with its impulse to shape it into stories with their meaning-making endings. Stories can mean, even if they have no traditional "sense of an ending."

ENDING ELSEWHERE: JEAN RHYS'S *WIDE SARGASSO SEA*

Jean Rhys's renowned late novel *Wide Sargasso Sea* offers a classic example of a writer's demonstration of Roland Barthes's notion of the *déjà lu,* the "already read." Beginning with its book reviews, *Wide Sargasso Sea* has forced readers to focus on its apparent dependence on Charlotte Brontë's *Jane Eyre.* Some readers have responded aversely to this seemingly parasitic relationship with Brontë's novel, while others have defended the textual autonomy of Rhys's novel. Feminists have generally embraced *Wide Sargasso Sea* as an attempt to construct a narrative in opposition to the masculine narrative paradigm. As Ellen Friedman has provocatively argued, Rhys self-consciously rejects the male plot, or "master narrative," generating its power to dominate through the oppression of women and the suppression of the feminine.[41] If the male plot might be glossed as the efforts of patriarchy to define women and men as so fundamentally different from each other that the polarity allows for the objectification of the female in order to empower the male's subject status, a primary function of patriarchy will be to police the containment of its constructions of the feminine or masculine within the categories female and male, respectively. The interface between these two novels reminds us that traditional narrative, whether its author is male or female, has been forced to adopt a masculine plot in which ending confirms meaning. In *Jane Eyre*, Charlotte Brontë can subvert the male plot through Jane's refusal to become Rochester's mistress; she cannot, however, unravel the masculine plot that feeds her reader's appetite for an ending—namely, Jane's eventual marriage to a transformed Rochester.

Any attempt, however, to read *Wide Sargasso Sea* primarily as an expression of a female plot as a substitute for the traditional male plot runs the risk of falling into that same binary thinking Teresa de Lauretis warned against two decades ago. A more fruitful approach is offered by Caroline Rody's case for Rhys's novel as an expression of a "revisionary paradigm." In this reading Rhys provides Brontë a second chance to tell the story of Bertha Antoinetta Mason Rochester, bestowing on her repressed heroine the power to negotiate the space of both novels and to refuse to be confined finally to either. In contrast to *Jane Eyre*, in which Brontë is limited by her audience's demand for a male plot with a definite ending of Jane marrying the de-masculinized, or more "androgynous," Rochester, following the fire symbolically castrating him through the loss of his sight and the use of one hand, *Wide Sargasso Sea* provides much more than a female plot. Rhys proposes not only to provide the first Mrs. Rochester with subject status but also to subvert Brontë's enforced accession to the masculine narrative paradigm. In the process, Rhys contributes to the late twentieth-century experimentation with the possibilities of a feminine narrative paradigm. That paradigm, as we may later see, is nowhere more powerfully focused than in the provocatively complex ending(s) toward which *Wide Sargasso Sea* moves in its subversion of traditional closure.

Rhys begins with a move that might appear a mere mimicking of *Jane Eyre*. Like Brontë's novel, *Wide Sargasso Sea* begins with a viewpoint character (in this case, Antoinette) "talking about" her childhood. Rhys wants much more, however, than to produce a pastiche of *Jane Eyre*. She intends in part 1 not so much to depict the Caribbean world from which Bertha Mason was brought to its polar opposite in Yorkshire as to map the province of the feminine, inevitably quarantined by patriarchy, lest it contaminate the power and therefore the "masculinity" of the Mr. Rochesters and Richard Masons. This is the colonized world of the racial other, the class other, and the sexual other. It is more, however, since it is also the colonized world of the gendered other. The Rochesters and Masons are white, upper class, and male. As long as they can verify the racial "purity" of their brides, they appear secure in their domination of the "feminine." This "femininity" generally comprises the Others that authorize whiteness, aristocracy, and maleness. The threat to that power lies in the very looseness and disorder that make the feminine so insidious. Much as patriarchy may police what it constructs as the hard boundaries between its binary opposites, the feminine remains subversive in its unwillingness to obey artificial boundaries and its tendency to invade the male domain with its menacing otherness. It is this otherness that Rhys also allows to contaminate the male plot.

Rhys begins by dropping her readers into the Caribbean without a map. Unlike third-person narrative obliged to contextualize the action, Antoinette's first-person narrative assumes that readers share her familiarity with the islands whose names she trades in and with the characters who populate her childhood. As a young girl Antoinette has made little commitment to understanding the dominant culture of Europe — adults, men, reason, etc. — in large part because she herself has no value except as an object of trade in the marriage business. And the bottom fell out of that market for Antoinette — and her mother, whose name, Annette, may be an English version of Antoinette — when her father's death and the Emancipation Act impoverished her prospects. In this way, the earlier map positioning Antoinette and her mother within the precincts of power as marketable marriage objects has moved them into the ambiguous status of "white niggers," dispossessed by the black slaves whose liberation has now leveled the playing field for the "feminine," or powerless. It is for Antoinette and her mother as *women* that the playing field has been aversely leveled. The white, European male has lost only the most negligible power.

Antoinette's childhood, as she recollects it from adulthood, represents the femininity within which her narration is implicated. Once again, it might be appropriate to redefine "femininity" in this context as interiority, resistance to boundaries and binaries, and an embracing of the very indeterminacy that patriarchy has struggled to cordon off as exclusively female attributes. Because Antoinette functions as first-person narrator, the narrative withholds her name. The gesture seems psychologically justified by the interiority of her narrating, since the consciousness of the subject usually does not name the self in the confines of Lacan's *moi*, in contrast to the speaking, externalized *je*, related to the outside world. Antoinette represents her subjectivity by not revealing her own name until she begins to attend the convent school in Spanish Town, where she stays with her aunt Cora. It is only when she begins to be socialized through education that she identifies herself through the last names of men, as well as the contexts of time and place: "I will write my name in fire red, Antoinette Mason, née Cosway, Mount Calvary Convent, Spanish Town, Jamaica, 1839" (Rhys 1992, 53). In one sense, Antoinette has enjoyed the privilege of her own autonomous subjectivity, but now as a young female, she can no longer remain unnamed, since her whole public value is her potential marketability as a bride. That value is a mixture of assets and liabilities however: her stepfather's wealth boosts her stock, just as her mother's insanity diminishes her prospects. By revealing her name, Antoinette indicates she is nearing puberty, and soon Mr. Mason will have the challenging task of unloading this "white elephant" he has inherited through marriage. Unlike Jane Eyre's school experience, Antoinette's days as a schoolgirl pass with uneventful speed, for the convent is a "refuge" from a world of madness and marriage contracts, and it comes as something of a small shock to hear her reminding Mason that she is "over seventeen, a grown woman" (58).

Having left his mad wife in the care of servants and his stepdaughter in the care of the nuns, Mason can turn his attention elsewhere—to enhancing his wealth. It might be noted in passing that the freed slaves who burn the plantation house Coulibri are incensed by the prospects of Mason bringing in Asians, or "coolies," to work for him. Mason has little taste for Spanish Town, perhaps because of its "femininity," or evidence of laxity in the policing of boundaries fundamental to patriarchy. Old Cosway, Antoinette's father, has left behind the proof of his having sexually crossed the "color bar." This "miscegenation," or sexual crossing of racial boundaries, opens up the possibility of the "contamination" of whiteness in those who are light-skinned enough to "pass." Even the child Antoinette is made aware of this need to maintain the polarity of black and white, dramatically signified when her black friend Tia hits her in the head with a rock. But even Antoinette can contribute to the "confusion," when, for instance, she refers to her mother's second husband as "white pappy." As in the American South of a century ago, "miscegenation" was the white male's horror when it meant the menace of black men's intimacy with white women, while the intimacy of white men with black women was privately celebrated as "good for the breed." Because the first part of the narrative is seen through a little girl's eyes, the "femininity" of subverted racial polarities is understated but clearly present as a menace. The biracial Cosways present a physical threat to Antoinette and later a more serious threat to her marriage. Daniel Cosway, allegedly the Old Man's son, contributes to Antoinette's undoing by revealing family secrets to her new husband, who will eventually be so unmanned by the threat of the Caribbean world's "femininity" that he will react in a panic so severe that his only refuge, it would seem, is the cold, hard "masculinity" of Yorkshire, where he will imprison his Caribbean—and therefore "feminine"—wife.

Part 1 ends with Antoinette's recollection of a nun's consoling her after a nightmare involving her dead mother. Through Antoinette's first-person account, the narrative has moved from some undetermined point in her childhood to her young adulthood, with the "next chapter" likely to be marriage—or *not*, the "not" based on her attraction to the "refuge" of the convent, especially when she begins to surmise she may eventually replicate her mother's madness. Part 1 provides the narrative with the sense of "life" in its lack of clarity and direction. Antoinette is consigned to this female plot by a patriarchy depriving her of subject status to map her future, like the young Jean-Paul Sartre who could "write" his own obituary as the road map of his adult life. Antoinette is the mere recorder of her girlhood as a waiting for the end, as she anticipates whom the men will nominate to be her husband, a daunting task in a culture that has convinced even Antoinette that insanity can be inherited.

The opening sentences of part 2 produce a huge shock as it becomes apparent that the narrating function has been transferred to Antoinette's new husband. The author-ization of this new "I" is justified in part because it reaffirms the patriarchy within which Antoinette is imprisoned. Richard Mason, her stepfather's son, has arranged with her new husband to take Richard's "sister" off his hands by putting up a dowry large enough to attract any impoverished suitor. (The Masons are either extremely rich or unusually keen on settling the problem of how to dispose of Antoinette as the daughter of a madwoman, since 30,000 pounds would be the equivalent of several million dollars in the present.) The decision to allow the new husband to "speak" also has a more pragmatic purpose in the narrative, because it covers the absence of his name in a permanent deferral of his identity as Jane Eyre's Mr

Rochester. This shift in point of view to the new husband and then back to Antoinette provides another subversion of the masculine narrative paradigm by undermining a consistent narrative point of view. Furthermore, the confirming of this "feminine" inconsistency unravels the "logic" of first-person narrative—namely, the setting up of a framework within which readers can be drawn into the illusion of the narrative as "memoirs" or "confessions," as though spoken/written by a single narrator as a text that readers just "happen upon," like an objet trouvé. Each time one narrative "I" is displaced by another, the narrative foregrounds its textuality, in part perhaps to prepare for the "ending" when it exposes itself as a "prequel" to Brontë's masterpiece.

The segment narrated by Antoinette's new husband marks the intrusion of a male plot, with the evidence of its narrative "logic." This "male" narrator locates Antoinette and Amélie, "a little half-caste servant" "sheltering from the heavy rain under a large mango tree," and himself under another tree, supervising "two porters and a boy" who have transported "our luggage" "2,000 feet to the honeymoon house" (65). With clarity and economy, this male narrator has established the *mise en scène*, under his firm control both as narrator and as agent of patriarchy. It would not be surprising if this narrator offered a quick correction to identify the altitude as exactly 2,317 feet. This "male" narrator is intent on pointing out the stigma of Amélie's "femininity" as a "half-caste," suggesting that some white male has exercised his power to cross the color bar by siring her. That the new husband might himself desire to exercise that option is suggested by his characterizing her as a "lovely little creature but sly, spiteful, malignant perhaps, like much else in this place" (65). The "feminizing" of "this place" as a seductive menace to manhood continues in the revelation of the nearby village's name as "Massacre." In preparation for his ultimate effort to exculpate himself for the rapid wilting of the orange blossoms in his recent marriage, the narrator reveals himself as the complaisant husband, willing to honeymoon on an estate owned by his new mother-in-law on another island, adding: "I agreed. As I had agreed to everything else" (66).

The narrator's posture indicates this narrative's "psychic geography," or even "psychosexual geography." The narrator asserts that fever confined him to bed for almost three weeks of the month before his marriage—not likely to render him an especially energetic bridegroom (67). To this white male European, Antoinette's Caribbean world further connotes a seductive "femininity" as miasma, the fever of desire for the feminine with its menace of emasculation. He also focuses on Antoinette's eyes: "Long, sad, dark alien eyes. Creole of pure English descent she may be, but they are not English or European either" (67). What can these eyes be, then, except African Caribbean eyes, suggesting the allure and the menace of a femininity that has slipped loose from masculine control over the biracial?

Quickly the narrator reads into the text the letter that he wrote his father revealing the roots of his "gender trouble." If money, position, maleness, and whiteness represent the attributes of masculinity in European culture, the narrator has only his white skin to testify to his "manhood." This pained and spiteful letter constructs its writer and its addressee(s) as having become locked into the sadism/masochism at the heart of patriarchy. With title and wealth, this "Dear Father" is the alpha male who has "feminized" his younger son, relegating him to the sole function of a powerless backup heir, in case the heir apparent dies without male issue. The narrator now has thirty thousand pounds of what he calls "competence," freeing him from penury: "I will never be a disgrace to you or to my dear brother the son you love," for "I have sold my soul or you have sold it" (70). In a brilliant gesture of subversion, Rhys has "justified" this man-who-will-become-Rochester as the disposable son, recalling the scriptural question: What man, if asked for bread, would give his son a stone? In the context of the practice of dowries by which women were stigmatized as mere objects of trade between the men in their lives, this man clearly bears the stigma of femininity as one "sold" by a father for the means of establishing his "competence" as an otherwise powerless male. Later, the narrator will write another letter or perhaps redraft the earlier letter of recriminations and self-wounding to add that fever left him in his "honeymoon house" "too exhausted to appreciate it fully" (76). This "it" cannily functions in the space between the signifiers "house" and "honeymoon." "It" more specifically denotes his mother-in-law's "place" but also connotes the honeymoon and his new bride, who is the center of the island's "femininity" for him.

Recalling his "role" as Antoinette's prospective husband, the narrator emphasizes his performance—"I played the part I was expected to play"—for all the world as though he were the bartered bride, instead of the mastering husband he will ultimately become. Having finished the letter, this male narrator wonders how any of these letters will get mailed, suggesting perhaps that his father and brother are the addressees of his portion of the narrative in which he performs a feminine gesture of exposing his pain and soliciting sympathy. When he describes his sense of distance from Antoinette's relatives during the wedding, the assertions he makes are embarrassingly close to pleas for the pity of his father and brother as the addressees of his narrative. He goes out of his way to exacerbate their guilt in feminizing him by selling him off, indicating that at his wedding he could not expect the wedding guests to have any pity for him: "I who have done so well for myself?" (77) — presumably as the high-priced husband. And when there appears to be an escape hatch in Antoinette's last-minute refusal to proceed with the marriage, the narrator throws himself at her: "I did not relish going back to England in the role of rejected suitor jilted by this Creole girl" (78), presumably a fate worse than his present feminized status as a sex object, finally supplied with a "competence." These ploys for sympathy persist with an embarrassing regularity, as, for example, when the narrator comments in Byronic fashion: "I was young then. A short youth mine was" (84).

For a time, however, the "feminized" narrator surrenders to the pleasures of the tropics and the honeymoon bed. Listening to Antoinette's dreamlike recollections of waking years before to see rats in this very moonlit room, the new husband is moved to comfort her but has to struggle to overcome the aroma of flowers, which leave him feeling "giddy" (83). Obviously the modifier "giddy" is not often used by a man, especially to describe his sense of losing control. His narrative also implies sufficient concern with the way in which the earlier "fever" he contracted has rendered him less manly than he would have thought, leading him to "curse the fever or the caution that made me so blind, so feeble, so hesitating" (90). And there may be hints that he has concerns the "fever" may have reduced his sexual potency when he remarks that as his new wife became more "eager" to make love he felt "more lost and drowned afterwards" (92). The trope of drowning in the aftermath of sexual passion, of losing oneself in this "wide Sargasso Sea" over which patriarchy deludes itself into believing it exercises control seems a particularly apt representation of a "masculinity" fearing its own dissolution in the immense sea of the indeterminate realm patriarchy cannot encompass within the logic of binaries, categories, and hierarchies.

Thus, the male narrator can only struggle to escape drowning by denying any feeling for the feminine other than the sexual desire his Yorkshire upbringing has taught him to keep on a very short leash. Accordingly, any tenderness and solace he directs toward Antoinette is self-conscious performance, and she is no more than a "stranger" for whom he feels occasionally "thirsty" (93). Antoinette becomes the quintessence of the tropics and the Sargasso Sea—that Other, exciting *and* terrifying him as an alien menace. In its efforts at psychologizing Brontë's Rochester, the narrative records the man's revealing recollection of childhood. He asks himself: "How old was I when I learned to hide what I felt?" and answers that it may have been before he was five, adding that in essence he has never grown beyond that notion of self-repression of feeling (103). The tropics of desire must then inevitably give way to the jungles of savage dreads, or to a sea so immense and powerful that nothing promised by patriarchy can master its energy. Soon the forest becomes "hostile," and the frightened bridegroom himself seems on the brink of a madness the narrative will soon displace to his bride. The forest fills him with the menace of eyes watching him (104). For one who has cast himself as his family's marriage property, "feminized" by his position as younger son, the husband's construction of masculinity as a performance for the eyes of others has imploded, leaving him in a state of paranoia that threatens him with yet another stigma of femininity—madness, or the "feminine" submersion in illogic. His admission that the trees are menacing enemies points to his advancing in the race with Antoinette to perform her mother's insanity as utter isolation in a completely hostile universe. This Rochester-in-the-making begins to replicate Kurtz's sense of "the horror, the horror," a darkness at the heart of things, exacerbated by the "paradise" of tropical beauty and sensuality. Fleeing the wide Sargasso Sea of his bride's body, the bridegroom can survive only by reconstructing Antoinette as "Bertha," in the feeble attempt to separate her from her mother, who shares the same name or a similar one.

His panic in the face of the feminine implicates the Rochester figure even further in the femininity he attempts to escape. Daniel Cosway draws him into the racial indeterminacy, threatening him with the uncertainty of Daniel's grandson Sandi's "race" and perhaps even Antoinette's, raising the specter of the contaminated racial "purity" of any children they might produce. Daniel fuels that fear of contamination when he describes how his son Alexander married a very light-skinned woman, and as a result, Sandi, the grandson, is white enough to "pass." If Sandi has managed to "pass," might not Antoinette also be something other than what she appears? And when he next looks closely at his wife he notes that she resembles Amélie, to whom she may be related (127). It is instructive that after his visit to Daniel Cosway, the Rochester figure also demonstrates a fastidiousness, or preoccupation with details, conventionally associated with the feminine, when he notes that Antoinette appears slovenly, because she wears a dress so large that it slips off one shoulder. She annoys him even through her habit of holding her wrist in a certain fashion (127). The Rochester figure is becoming a "fussbudget"!

Thus, it is hardly a surprise that when "Rochester" awakens from the love potion Antoinette administered in a desperate, final attempt to recuperate his love for her he recollects dreams of live burial and feeling suffocated (137). Another index of his "femininity" is provided by the loosening of the plot so that readers are left uncertain whether he and Antoinette actually made love. He claims to remember nothing after putting out the candles surrounding his wife's bed. If they made love, it apparently was not "memorable," nor satisfying, because he ends up in Amélie's bed, well aware of the thin partition through which his wife can undoubtedly hear this lovemaking. The aftermath is an ominous confrontation between Antoinette and her husband in which she reminds him he has prostituted Amélie after condemning her father for sexual colonization of the other race and accuses her husband of vitiating her affection for her world: "I hate it now like I hate you and before I die I will show you how much I hate you" (147). When Antoinette pathetically reveals her jealousy of Amélie and asks him if he no longer loves her, he provides the denial she expects, and she tells him that he is a "stone" (148). Ironically, he accepts this condemnation as unintended counseling: if he is to recuperate his masculinity, he must flee the "green menace" of this wide sea before it drowns him. "I would give my eyes never to have seen this abominable place" (161), this Rochester-in-the-making inadvertently offers, like Oedipus unwittingly condemning the murderer of Laius to exile. If readers have not followed the clues strewn by the narrative up to this point, especially the changing of Antoinette's name to "Bertha" and her impassioned threat to make her husband pay for despoiling the country of her heart, this clue of the husband's unconsciously foreseeing his own blinding is telling. It seems an oedipal prerecognition of the need to transform himself in preparation for the marriage to Jane Eyre, as planned by Charlotte Brontë for this story.

That "ending" is suggested in the brief part 3 that both is and is not this narrative's overlapping with Brontë's. The female "I" of this part is being cared for by a "Grace Poole," Bertha Mason Rochester's warder in *Jane Eyre*. Grace's voice, as apparently recollected by Antoinette/Bertha, focuses upon the transformation of her master in the Caribbean. She claims to have known him both as a boy and as a man to be "gentle, generous, brave." The Caribbean has changed him visibly, graying his hair and filling his eyes with misery (177–78). Apparently he has joined his "mad" wife in being haunted by the tropics she now hates because he despoiled its (and her) femininity in an effort to "save himself" by retreating to the stony construction of masculinity he recalled in Yorkshire. She, if indeed "mad," has been maddened by the attempt to submit her to that very construction of masculinity. She desperately struggled to preserve her "femininity" in a patriarchy whose only defense against the incursions of the feminine into the fortress of masculinity lies in confining femininity as madness, or "hysteria," the women's disease. Her letter to Richard Mason appropriately tropes her confinement thus: "[P]lease take me away from this place where I am dying because it is so cold and dark" (183), and, we might add, *hard* with the power of patriarchy that can survive only as long as it polices the boundaries it has set up by confining the feminine within the precincts of the female so that the masculine can enjoy the security of the male.

The ending of *Wide Sargasso Sea* may not seem one, because it is a feminine ending, as perhaps the narrative has been as well. Feminists such as Sandra Gilbert and Susan Gubar would iconize Bertha Mason, this "madwoman in the attic," as Rhys's representation of female oppression under patriarchy—what Charlotte Brontë might also have wanted to do, but patriarchy would not allow her to, since it was "unspeakable." At the same time, in Antoinette/Bertha, Rhys is mapping a no-man's land and no-woman's land of gender, subverting the effort of patriarchy to confine femininity and masculinity to the realms of women and men, respectively. The female figure here is both Antoinette and Bertha, and both feminine and defeminized, in much the same way *Wide Sargasso Sea* is both an independent, large, and "feminine" narrative and one that is dependent on the defeminized narrative Brontë wrote. And *Wide Sargasso Sea*'s ending is autonomous, at the same time as it appears dependent on the ending Brontë wrote for Rochester and his first wife to transform him for his second.[42]

In a sense, gender in *Wide Sargasso Sea* is generated from the sea. We hardly need to remind ourselves that the West Indies are the products of volcanic eruptions from a sea whose coldness hardens them into the essentially fragile constructions they become, preserving themselves against the greater force of that matrix of indeterminacy of the sea that would just as well take them back, and occasionally demonstrates "her" power to do just that. Antoinette's tropical world has accommodated the interdependence of the feminine and masculine, promising the possibility of a recuperated paradise, if perhaps gender is empowered to range back and forth along a spectrum, rather than be polarized by the male into binaries of the either-or. In a sense, then, *Wide Sargasso Sea* deconstructs the male plot of *Jane Eyre* by juxtaposing to it the construction of the female plot as the Other of Brontë's novel. Just as the plot of *Wide Sargasso Sea* is neither exclusively inside or outside this narrative, so too its ending is both in this novel *and* in *Jane Eyre*.

Wide Sargasso Sea may be one of the most neglected narratives of the later twentieth century in its pioneering efforts not simply to displace the male plot by writing the female plot but also to construct one of the earliest examples of the feminine narrative paradigm. As Caroline Rody aptly reminds us, Rhys could have consoled herself with merely producing a female plot in which an empowered Antoinette/Bertha escaped the burning of Thornfield Hall to return to her homeland in the tropics. Instead Rhys chooses to leave Antoinette/Bertha in a middle ground of potential to act, but with any such action left undramatized. In a sense, what Rody seems to be pointing readers to is what Barbara Johnson identifies as central to the deconstructive turn when she writes: "Instead of a simple 'either/or' structure, deconstruction attempts to elaborate a discourse that says *neither* 'either/or,' *nor* 'both/and' nor even 'neither/nor,' while at the same time not totally abandoning these logics either. The very word *deconstruction* is meant to undermine the either/or logic of the opposition 'construction/destruction.' Deconstruction is both, it is neither, and it reveals the way in which both construction and deconstruction are themselves not what they appear to be" (Johnson 1987, 12–13; italics in original).

Thus, in contrast to parts 1 and 2, offering only ghostly suggestions of this narrative's relationship with *Jane Eyre*, part 3 allows those suggestions to achieve greater definition, like a photograph in a developing tray. Part 3 confirms that *Wide Sargasso Sea* has been "in" Brontë's narrative, just as it could *not* be in the obviously "logical" sense of these two novels being discrete entities. Similarly, the plot of *Wide Sargasso Sea* has an ending from *Jane Eyre*, though at the same time it cannot borrow that ending, because it cannot "logically" penetrate Brontë's text, any more than Rhys's "Bertha," née Antoinette, can be Eyre's Bertha Antoinetta. The ending, like the narrative as a whole, occupies a poststructural space of not the "both/and," not the "either/or," not the "neither/nor," yet also the sum of these three. That "sum" may be defined as the feminine narrative paradigm (or in the interest of further clarification/obfuscation what we might call the postmasculine narrative paradigm, on the model of the other post-ings, evident in the past half-century). This is a paradigm that subverts and explodes the male plot as well as the masculine narrative paradigm to expand the possibilities of moving beyond the masculine paradigm without attempting to eliminate it, allowing writers who are female as well as writers who are male to range the gendered spectrum of possibilities from narrative to narrative or even within the same text.

Cluster 3: Escaping the Paradigm by Ignoring It

Oᴎᴇ SALIENT FEATURE THAT SHOULD HAVE BECOME APPARENT IN THE
fiction explored in the preceding cluster is the way in which the more
self-conscious the efforts to problematize the traditional model for narrative, the more likely those efforts are to undermine their own efficacy.
John Fowles offers the classic example of the novelist who foregrounds
at least two dramatically different endings to undo the notion of a narrative with a single ending, only to confirm that *an* ending remains the
primary, perhaps sole, determinant of meaning. As earlier noted,
Fowles at the same time may well be playing a storyteller's shell game,
leaving his readers not so much doubting the power of ending as unwittingly accepting its hegemony in narrative, while the text is offering not
so much an "open ending" as a reminder that life runs on, even though
the text may provide no further words to represent it. One question
arises for the storyteller no longer satisfied with the traditional paradigm: How might it be possible to move outside the conventions of ending in narrative without resorting to a strategy of denial that legitimates
what it seeks to deny?

A beginning of an answer to that question may be found in the theorizing once again of Teresa de Lauretis, whose work also provided an
entry to the novels in the preceding section of this project. Lauretis's
interest in "Desire in Narrative" led her to the work of the Soviet semiotician Jurij Lotman, who emphasized how myths as cultural texts
were dramatically different from traditional forms of narrative. Lotman
focused on the "exclusively cyclical-temporal movement," allowing
myths to be "synchronized with the cyclical process of the seasons."
What came to be conceptualized as *story*, or *narrative*, was generated out
of the eccentric or anomalous sequence of events that departed from the
cyclical mode—a mode so common as to be unremarkable, as water
may be to fish. In the words of Lauretis, it was Lotman's conclusion
that "[b]ecause linear-temporal categories, such as beginning and end,
are not pertinent to the type of text [i.e., myth] thus generated, human
life is not seen as enclosed between birth and death, but as a recurrent,
self-repeating cycle which can be told starting at any point" (Lauretis

1984, 116–17). Narrative for Lotman becomes the effort to bring into harmony cyclical-temporal and the linear-temporal modes to construct a notion of plot as a strategy for understanding experience, "because," as Lauretis writes, "plot (narrative) mediates, integrates, and ultimately reconciles the mythical and the historical, norm and excess, the spatial and temporal orders, the individual and the collectivity" (Lauretis 1984, 120).

Accordingly, narrative becomes a cultural palimpsest, a text of the "novel" written over the mythic text that remains *sous rature*, "under erasure." In this way it might be possible to see the more effective complications of the traditional climax-oriented narrative paradigm less in self-conscious subversions of ending than in the strategy of simply ignoring the agency of a plot driving relentlessly on to a "sense of an ending." As D. A. Miller has helpfully suggested, those strategies whose intent may be to problematize the agency of ending in the traditional paradigm for narrative end up confirming the conclusion that ending is still a determinant of meaning, whether ending is multiplied, denied, or spoofed.

Miller's theorizing is also useful here in his teasing out of the implications of the relationship between what he calls the "narratable" and its other, something very much like Lotman's notion of the mythic. Miller directs attention to what makes story, or the "narratable," possible within the traditional paradigm for narrative theorized by Peter Brooks. For Miller "narratability" always operates in the context of its opposition to its other, or what might be seen as so familiar or customary as not to incite narrative. The nonnarratable is so immersed in the ordinary stuff of daily experience that it cannot arouse a potential listener's or reader's interest in what might be called the sequentiality, the "and then . . ." of narrative. Miller moves beyond these considerations, however, to offer the brilliant perception of how asymmetrical the "narratable" and its other are in narrative.

Miller makes his point by reading Brooks's favorite psychoanalytic narrative, "Freud's Masterplot." Narrative, Miller asserts, partakes of the asymmetry of Freud's story of the *"fort/∂a."* Just as Freud's *"∂a"* for the representation of the symbolic spool/mother will always pale in contrast to the anxiety/terror of the *"fort"* of its loss/disappearance, so too the consolation of the "narratable" of a plot with an ending can never adequately repay the loss of what this "narratability" distinguishes itself from. Miller seems to be working toward Julia Kristeva's critique of Lacan's analysis of the Imaginary and the Symbolic, when she asks if the irremediable loss of the Imaginary, or what she would call the "semiotic," can ever be compensated for by the accession to the register of the Symbolic. Miller writes: "In the last analysis, what discontents the traditional novel is its own condition of possibility. For the production of narrative—what we called the narratable—is possible only with a logic of insufficiency, disequilibrium, and deferral, and traditional novelists typically desire worlds of greater stability and wholeness than such a logic can intrinsically provide. Moreover, the suspense that constitutes the narratable inevitably comes to imply a suspensiveness of signification, so that what is ultimately threatened is no less than the possibility of a full or definitive meaning" (1981, 265).

Thus, Miller touches the sensitive nerve of traditional narrative: Is ending a variety of *pharmakon*, a "drug" or "medicine" that can end up being a "poison"? Ending may offer the illusion (or perhaps, more accurately, the delusion), of meaning, with this sense of constructed meaning always falling agonizingly short of what readers desire. What is more, "waiting for the end" inevitably confronts readers with a sense of Derridean *différance*, or deferral, opening the pursuit of meaning into an abyss whose bottomlessness is "the horror, the horror" of perceiving that meaning may not exist, except as a construction or fabrication. One is reminded of how in *Bellefleur* the strategies force readers to wait so long for the end, and for the meaning it promises, that when such meaning becomes apparent it seems to have emptied itself out into belatedness, or irrelevance.

Miller's provocative discussion creates a sense of belatedness here. We can only wonder if what left us with that chill at the end of *Amsterdam* or *When We Were Orphans* was the sense that this ending we longed for could no longer fully minister to a longing for "full meaning," leaving us instead with the perception that *any* ending will be contaminated with an appalling sense of insufficiency. We begin to wonder if *The White Hotel* is rehearsing its anticipation of this "last" cluster of narratives by "surprising" its readers with a mousetrap ending for Lisa at Babi Yar. As earlier noted, it is hardly a coincidence that Lisa's last role is singing Jocasta's mother/wife duet with Oedipus. Just as Oedipus's blinding recognition comes with a variety of "good news/bad news" in which fate tells him: "You solved the problem, and you're It, because you did exactly what you struggled *not* to do!" Lisa may be confronting yet another of those "trick endings" that tragedy trades in: "You struggled to flee biological motherhood, because it held some inexplicable dread, only to seek refuge in adoptive motherhood, a state that doomed/ blessed you with the horror that was waiting for you there all the time at Babi Yar." At the same time that story offers the pleasure of the narratable with Kermode's "sense of an ending," narrative can remind us that such pleasure is incredibly incommensurable with the yawning pit of insufficiency opened before us through a middle suspending—perhaps into eternity—any comforting sense of meaning inherent in achieving the end.

The novels in this final segment of the project form a cluster of narratives that may be explored together as fictions moving beyond the vexed efforts at undoing the conventional paradigm. Instead, they move toward the possibility of escaping the traditional paradigm, in part by ignoring it. Behind at least some of these narratives seems to be the concern that efforts to undo that paradigm may only support its authority, in much the same way that some might see the atheist as confirming the existence of God in attempting to deny it. The novels in this section range at one end from Doris Lessing's *The Golden Notebook* and Nawal El Saadawi's *The Fall of the Imam*, narratives following the feminine pattern of circle or cycle as an alternative to the masculine model of linearity and dramatic climax, to a narrative at the other "end" (if a cluster can have an end), such as Jeanette Winterson's *Written on the Body*, with its exciting strategy of ignoring rather than merely attempting to escape from linearity. In between are narratives such as Julian Barnes's *A History of the World in 10½ Chapters* and A. S. Byatt's *Angels & Insects*, both of which unsettle our usual sense of what constitutes the novel. Renowned for his departures from the traditional paradigm for narrative, Italo Calvino offers in *on a winter's night a traveler* a bizarre narrative, or series of nested narratives, that might be seen as a story beginning over and over again, calling into question how such a story or stories might be conceived of "ending." Manlio Argueta's *Cuzcatlán* resists the demand for an ending in somewhat the way Oates's *Bellefleur* does: by defying linearity in a family saga in which names are passed down from one generation to another.

Even more than its predecessors, this section represents a genuine "cluster" of narratives, one or more of which might conceivably be included in another cluster. In one very important sense, these clusters might be seen as overlapping rather than as discrete "categories." These explorations of narratives are meant to provoke readers to think about patterns and endings, *not* to impose an organizational chart of self-contained and mutually exclusive concepts. Frustrating as the approach may be for some readers, it is an effort toward seeking a means of organizing readings of narratives on the model of a self-deconstructing taxonomy of narrative strategies for ending.

THE GREAT CIRCLE: DORIS LESSING'S *THE GOLDEN NOTEBOOK*

As the novelist and theorist Malcolm Bradbury has suggested, *The Golden Notebook* is one of the two late twentieth-century novels—John Fowles's *The French Lieutenant's Woman* being the other—with which contemporary British narrative begins. It is scarcely a coincidence that these two novels demonstrate their postmodern tendencies by problematizing the traditional notion of plot and consequently the reliance of traditional narrative on the sense of an ending. The second cluster of this book began with a discussion of *The French Lieutenant's Woman* in large part because the Fowles novel is clearly bent on undoing the traditional masculine paradigm for narrative by making use of multiple endings. *The* ending is arguably Charles Smithson's replication of Sarah Woodruff's position of existential confrontation of the void, the narrative having circled back to position Charles at the sea's edge, ready to begin making the choices that will construct whatever meaning is possible in a state of incessant becoming, with its illusory moments of being. The discussion to follow will explore Doris Lessing's anticipation of that sense of becoming in the Fowles novel, as well as her attraction to the image of the circle to counter the traditional masculine "plot" of narrative.

The Golden Notebook (1962) joins *The French Lieutenant's Woman* (1969) in yet another hallmark of postmodern fiction: its self-reflexivity.[1] Just as the narrator in the Fowles novel startles readers by stepping forward to announce the narrative's problematizing of its ending(s), and even introduces an "Author" who impersonates John Fowles before the novel ends, *The Golden Notebook* foregrounds authorship and indeed creates, as we shall see, an even more vertiginous *mise en abîme* effect as the novel's "author" and viewpoint character, Anna Wulf, drafts a novel in which the novelist Ella is struggling with the draft of her own novel, in which a novelist is writing a novel, and so forth. This *mise en abîme* effect, of course, ultimately opens outward, as readers become aware that even though Doris Lessing may *not* have suffered from Anna Wulf's "writer's block," much of Anna's African experience is Lessing's, and readers may struggle with the impulse to wonder how much else Anna shares with Lessing. Indeed, when Lessing got around to writing her memoirs in the 1990s, she indicated that she could not write anything as accurate about her own experience as a young woman in Africa as the "fiction" she had created for Anna. Because *The Golden Notebook* is so well known, having arrived at the status of contemporary "classic," its story will not require the detailed analysis of more recent novels such as Ian McEwan's *Amsterdam*. And because so many have written about *The Golden Notebook*, it should be possible to focus more extensively upon the novel's effort to escape the traditional masculine paradigm.

At the same time, some review of salient features may be helpful. It will be recalled that *The Golden Notebook* foregrounds its textuality by working through a number of apparently discrete texts. First there is the conventional narrative, the "frame(d) novel,"[2] providing the "notebooks" with a framework. This narrative, a sort of novel-within-the-novel with its own title, *Free Women*, begins with the bland, rather blasé statement "The two women were alone in the London flat" and calls attention to itself with the distancing, almost alienation-effect device of the blurb: "Anna meets her friend Molly in the summer of 1957 after a separation," for all the world like the titles lofted above the stage during the production of a Bertolt Brecht play such as *Mother Courage.* Set over against this *Free Women* narrative moving toward stage play with its emphasis on sophisticated dialogue are the notebooks themselves. These texts exist as notebooks because, as she will tell Molly's son (and Anna's spiritual offspring) Tommy, every time she sits down to write her second novel she is overcome by "disgust" and "futility" (Lessing 1962, 40). Much of the novel's textual tension results from the strain between *Free Women*, a novel presumably beyond Anna's capabilities at present, and the notebooks. The latter must remain separate texts, she argues, because the only way she can organize the chaos of her experience is by writing about it in watertight compartments, color-coded by apparent subject matter. Initially at least, the Black Notebook contains her African experience and the consequences of her writing about it in her novel *Frontiers of War;* the Red Notebook contains her experiences as a member of the British Communist Party; the Yellow Notebook contains her failed efforts at writing fiction, in particular the Ella novel; and the Blue Notebook contains her perceptions about current events, becoming a scrapbook of newspaper clippings, supporting her justification for not writing another novel. To Anna, narrative has become a suspect, illegitimate mode of response to the immense horrors of the world at midcentury.

Those horrors delegitimate any novel Anna might write, particularly the novel of which she offers a specimen, *Free Women*. This specimen novel is earnest, serious, sensitive to the complexity of the issues raised by midcentury experience, especially the struggle of women to break out of the traditional mold of the long-suffering "wifey," earlier represented by Molly's ex-husband Richard's next wife, Marion. Just as the first segment of *Free Women* shows strain in its leading figures, who are "cracking up," so too the conventional form of narrative struggling to represent their spiritual/psychological disintegration also betrays its own movement toward textual "breakdown." In the end, the notebooks become less and less viable as alternatives to the frame narrative of *Free Women*, seeping from one disparate compartment to another. The notebooks do not "end"; instead, Anna stops them with her heavy lines of demarcation to note their failure or breakdown. So, too, the conventional narrative of the two women alone in the London flat must inevitably become Anna and Nelson (or Saul, or any of the other men who make their brief entrances), locked into a madness they can no longer escape, a madness that may in the end be the cure for the larger and deeper madness that is contemporary experience.

Many of these issues become gendered through what the narrative says, as well as the way it works. Molly's son, Tommy, tells his father, Richard, that he rejects the masculine option Richard represents in favor of the feminine in his mother and her friend, because "they're not just one thing" and have the potential for change that, by implication, he fails to see in his father (36). If Richard is the typical male in his investment in oneness for the sake of stability and power, Molly and Anna put their hold on oneness and stability at risk by striving for diversity and complexity, even if it moves them into vulnerable—that is, powerless and therefore "feminine"—positions. If Richard's success rides upon the illusion of mastery that ignores complexity because it looks like chaos, Anna represents the artist presently undone by that chaos. She quotes a painter who argues that "the world is so chaotic art is irrelevant" (42), denying the modernism of a Virginia Woolf or a W. B. Yeats with its faith in the power of art to stand against that tide of chaos. Against the conventional narrative of *Free Women* that eventually has *its* own "breakdown," *The Golden Notebook* sets up the notebooks as a gesture toward accommodating chaos by sectioning it off in disparate texts, suggesting that conventional masculine narrative must acknowledge its feminine other. Ultimately, however, as we shall see, *The Golden Notebook* transgenders both of these conventionally masculine and feminine constructs to posit a larger, more powerful, perhaps more "feminine" alternative (or alternatives) to the limitations of both constructs.[3]

As a postmodern novel, *The Golden Notebook* is very much about writing novels and the generation of its own textuality. Anna in a sense rejects the very "novel" in which she is a character, if we consider *Free Women* a novel per se and the notebooks a series of texts outside the novel proper. To Anna the novelist, *Free Women* is very much the type of contemporary novel she disdains. This kind of novel, she writes in her Black Notebook, belongs to the field of journalism: it merely provides experience readers may be unaware of. A few pages later in the same notebook, Anna will criticize herself for falling prey to a nostalgia for World War II; she does not, however, acknowledge a more subtle nostalgia, a literary nostalgia for the modernist novel.[4] She feels she cannot write a novel "powered with an intellectual or moral passion strong enough to create order, to create a new way of looking at life" (61). Ironically, of course, this is the very "kind of novel" Lessing is writing in *The Golden Notebook*, albeit not with the same faith that her literary "mother," Virginia Woolf, had crafting her masterpiece *To the Lighthouse* as a monument to the power of art to compel life to "stand still" and transform itself into a testimony to the possibility of order.[5]

The Black Notebook may well be the most productive, and provocative, text for those readers who share Anna's fascination with the relationship between art and life. This relationship has been an ongoing concern in the present book, especially in the explorations of McEwan's *Atonement* and Atwood's *The Blind Assassin*, since those two narratives also have viewpoint characters who are authors. Narratives such as McEwan's *Amsterdam* and perhaps even Ishiguro's *When We Were Orphans*, written on the model of masculine narrative, are arguably almost exclusively art closing off the life from which this art was made. With narratives such as *The Golden Notebook* positing a life from which the art of the novel is being transformed, the questions of ending must inevitably complicate themselves with issues of how the tape of life continues in the movie theater after spectators have left, confident in their belief, or self-delusion, that the narration has come to an end.

For these purposes, Anna Wulf creates a narrative, *Frontiers of War*, accessible to Lessing's readers only through Anna's comments about it and the synopses she archly constructs to lure or tease prospective filmmakers with its possibilities for film adaptation. (After all, a carefully managed contract for film rights could ensure enough financial independence to make it unnecessary to rush her second novel.) Anna's memories of Africa, recorded in the Black Notebook as the life from which the art of her novel was generated, are a deeper layer of the art that masquerades as life. At the same time, the Mashopi scenes have a undeniable power to provide us the deep satisfaction of a fragment, with no discernible beginning or ending, a fragmentary middle of life that "goes on" outside the bounds of what Anna writes about these "characters." One example is her variety of "epilogue" for Jimmy Mc-Grath, who helped to precipitate disaster when he hugged and kissed

Paul Blackenhurst on the dance floor and then made a pass at Mrs. Boothby's African cook, with whose wife another member of the group had been having an affair. Unlike the upper-class Paul, who saw himself as only playing at being a "homosexual," as he played at being a "communist," to outrage his elders, Jimmy was genuinely same-sex in his orientation. As in an epilogue, this latter news that he has married and fathered a child confirms that a Jimmy exists somewhere in a life very different from the circle of airmen waiting for their postings to one or another theater of war. Jimmy may have no more than a walk-on role in *Frontiers of War*, but in life he was a major player in the tragedy of Mashopi. Readers may recall the nasty episode in which Mrs. Boothby sends the group out to shoot pigeons for a pie, and Paul sadistically exploits Jimmy's love to turn him into a bird dog.

At the center of the Mashopi memoirs is Anna's brief and bittersweet "affair" with Paul Blackenhurst, the model for her aviator-hero in *Frontiers of War*. In Anna's novel, the complications of life get simplified as well as further complicated in its transformation into art. Anna superimposes the affair of the wife of Mrs. Boothby's cook and the middle-aged George—who fathers a son with her but is hopelessly trapped in family responsibilities—onto her own brief relationship with Paul to produce a narrative of the "colour bar." Anna exposes her weaving together of these two story lines as justification for their transformation in the doomed biracial affair by informing her readers that she is envious/jealous of the cook's wife going to spend the night in George's caravan. George, she adds with relish, is constructed as the kind of "man who really, very much needed women" (124). Thus, George's deeply masculine need for the young black woman is combined with Paul's virginal love of Anna, whom he "compliments" by confessing his innocence (149). Using the *donnée* of the fragmentary notebook, Lessing allows Anna as novelist to record this key episode in her life—"key," because giving herself to Paul after the disaster at Mashopi was quintessentially the madness of war—by maintaining the semblance here of life with its tendencies merely to stop without any of the closure readers expect in an ending. The text seems to delegitimate "analysis" of Paul's death as either suicide or accident. The event belies the oversimplification of the traditional paradigm for narrative in which a death as dramatic as Paul Blackenhurst's ought to convey some powerful meaning through a "sense of an ending," and yet Anna as both lover and novelist hasn't a clue about the circumstances of his death, even though some days earlier—during their lovemaking, as it turns out—she had already decided to write *Frontiers of War*.

Much of the power of *The Golden Notebook* grows out of the dynamic between the "novel" *Free Women* and the notebooks it frames. *Free Women* is at one and the same time both the novel Anna may feel compelled to write and the novel she rejects because of its being gendered masculine in its illusion of mastery, its faith that the disorderliness of life can be readily transformed into meaning through art. The text licenses Anna to read its title, *Free Women*, ironically: "'Men. Women. Bound. Free. Good. Bad. Yes. No. Capitalism. Socialism. Sex. Love . . .'" (44), she famously asserts in reaction against the easy optimism that women, and perhaps even men, can be free. Even earlier she had savored the painful irony of the term "Free women" because it is their relationships with men that determine how women are defined (4). Sex differences, as we shall see, have major implications for gender differences and for the gendering of models for narrative in this novel.

Almost halfway through *The Golden Notebook*, Anna recounts an incident in her affair with Michael. This "incident" begins the day that will spell the "end of the affair" with her married lover of several years as well as her departure from the Communist Party. If readers are looking for a traditional "ending," this has to be about as major a pair of events as they are likely to encounter. Anna awakens to Michael cuddling up to her back with an obvious erection. He wants to make love, even though, or *because* he knows, that she must listen for the signs her daughter, Janet, is awake. Anna has prepared readers for this incident both by including Michael's much earlier mocking question about the end of "our great love affair" (330) and by her thinking: "[A]ll I care about is that Michael should turn in the dark and put his face against my breasts" (299). Also, Anna recalls a session with Mother Sugar— her analyst, Mrs. Marks—who reminded her that she suffers from the housewife's disease, or Freud's Hausfrau's complex, of preoccupation with details from which men are freed by women. Furthermore, Anna is aware that Michael's desire is "political" in the context of sexual politics: because he is performing "impersonally," she is unable to respond (333). Michael even mocks her after his climax by asking if she is going to "desert" him for Janet, and Anna is allowed to be honest enough to admit that she would be just as self-absorbed if she were a man and were lucky enough to have women to take care of the details in her life (334).

After Anna gets Janet off to school, Michael, who has enjoyed the luxury of two extra hours of postcoital rest in bed, goes on to mock her for being "so efficient and practical in the morning" (337). Anna senses that today is the day Michael will leave her. She has begun to menstruate and must change her stockings: "Michael notices this sort of detail" (340). This is one "detail" he can be counted on to notice, presumably only because menstruation is likely to mess up his lovemaking. Because Anna sees herself "on the practical treadmill" of concern for the "things I have to do today," she resents "this business of being conscious of everything" (340). As Woman, Anna has been "feminized" by a patriarchy not only forcing her to be tasked with details but also making her envious of "men's time." When her daughter Janet's desire to attend a boarding school frees her to return to her youth, Anna recuperates a sense of the "women's time" Virginia Woolf imputes to Mrs. Ramsay, released for a few moments from the responsibility of mothering. Anna writes in her diary that being a mother means never losing consciousness of clocks with their reminders of what needs to be done. Janet's birth eliminated the Anna who had been relatively free of responsibility associated with the clock and details; that Anna "died," but now perhaps the earlier Anna has a chance to be reborn. She notices (as Mrs. Ramsay does in the first segment of *To the Lighthouse*) that her mode of "telling time" is changing, so that the "quality of light means it must be evening, instead of: in exactly an hour I must put on the vegetables" (548). Paradoxically, the responsibility for details and paying attention to the clock feminize Anna through the imposition of male order on another, older notion of time, outside linearity.

Anna's perceptions foreground a major cause of her malaise as a novelist—her being overwhelmed with the details of life forced on her by a powerful patriarchy that will not allow her to unmoor her gender from her sex identification as a female. She has been disabled as a writer because her experience in the "man's world" has swamped her with the details that make her world chaotic. Those details insist that she follow the male pattern of denying complexity, because of its associations with chaos, and resort to the (over)simplification of "narrative" such as *Free Women* or *Frontiers of War*. This second novel would also be "male" in its obedience to the masculine paradigm for narrative, not only in its linearity but also in its utter dependence on transformation, another transforming of the author's experience into the text, but more importantly in its reliance on a major climax to give readers the perhaps illusory sense of meaning. In psychoanalytic terms this transformation marking the climax or ending of the analysis is the "transference," or reconstruction of the past in a moment of understanding. As Freud reminded his followers, however, the analysis is interminable, and those moments of transference are way stations on an endless journey, or perhaps a journey simply interrupted by death.

At the end of this long narrative, covering almost forty pages in the Blue Notebook, Michael telephones very late to tell her he will be unable to join her for the dinner she has prepared. This call makes real his rhetorical question two days earlier, concerning the end of their "'great love affair'" (330). Now she must cope with the "awful black whirling chaos"(367), waiting to invade her being. Readers may return to the section of the Yellow Notebook appearing just before the diary entries that signal the movement into what amounts to a complete short narrative Anna might entitle, "The End of the Affair." In Anna's draft of the novel she is trying to write, Paul has just walked out on Ella, raising interesting questions of timing in *The Golden Notebook*. There is, of course, no date for the writing of the Ella passage; readers may have the uncanny feeling, however, that life is imitating art here, that Anna's effort to write and therefore to understand the experience of Michael's leaving *her* has been shaped by the "earlier" passage of Paul's having left Ella. The text has, of course, made it obvious that Anna is aware of the parallels between these two "stories"; for example, she notes that she has given the name of her lover, Michael, to Ella's son. Most tellingly, however, Anna adds in brackets, following this "end of the affair" narrative, that the "whole of the above was scored through—cancelled out and scribbled underneath: No, it didn't come off. A failure as usual" (367–68). It is as though she has been attempting to avert whatever in her psyche has been refusing to allow her to write narrative by writing this ersatz diary entry, but she got caught by whatever censoring agency she had been licensing to defeat her, and from her viewpoint the effort at narrative failed. She replaces the "flowing and untidy" (368) narrative she canceled out with a brief and breezy, conventional diary entry. This "more neat and orderly" (368) entry gives a synopsis of the day's events, but leaves out the emotional details of what it felt like to shake herself loose from the Party on the same day Michael deserted her. Clearly, the narrative she canceled out has too many of those very details that continue to swamp her, like a dark tide she must build dikes against, lest she drown. In a Lacanian sense, these details are the metonyms of desire that she may struggle futilely to "contain," but must fail to in the end. Indeed, to make matters worse, she *knows* those dikes of containment will fail and she will be pulled under by the tide, for the alternative is the sterile masculine illusion of mastery in Richard, Michael, and virtually all the men in this novel.

Most importantly for Anna, it will be impossible to write, much less *be*, until she submits herself to that tide of desire's metonyms. This process of consigning herself to the tide she has attempted to hold back is more accurately troped as "cracking up." Early in the first of the five *Free Women* passages, Anna thinks that "everything's cracking up" (3). Initially this "cracking up" may be (mis)read as negative, as mere destruction. As the narrative moves forward, however, it becomes more apparent that "cracking up" shares the ambivalence of the apocalyptic within which destruction must make way for creation. Eventually, Anna will recall that Mother Sugar has been leading her toward "the creative aspects of destruction" (545), and much of the last third of *The Golden Notebook* will be implicated in the wide range of meanings of Freud's *Schadenfreude*, "joy in destruction," or as Anna will translate the term "joy-in-spite." Increasingly it is difficult not to think in terms of W. B. Yeats's "All things fall, and are built again, / And those who build them are gay."

With this annunciation, readers may begin looking for "signs" of the apocalypse to come. Tellingly, the notebooks offer the first clear signs that *anticipate* rather than *follow* or even coincide with the cracking up in the *Free Women* frame narrative. Thus, in the Yellow Notebook Ella thinks about the potential course of the novel with which she is struggling, as Anna is in hers, so that both novels being drafted have two people cracking up together, but with the hope that each will gain a greater strength from the descent into chaos (467). Similarly, in the Yellow Notebook when Anna is generating a long list of narrative germs of short stories Ella might write, one involves an English woman and an American man who "secretly read each other's diaries" (538). These germs occur well before the entry of any avatar of The American or the painful episode of Saul and Anna writing spiteful items in their diaries because each knows the other is reading his or her entries. What is fascinating here, of course, is that the narrative Anna strives to construct through Ella's creative groping to move her novel forward is the very narrative toward which Anna as a "character" is headed in the remainder of the *Free Women* and the notebooks of *The Golden Notebook*.

Along with the breakdown of the notebooks' separateness and their failures for Anna—made clear by her terminating (not *ending*) them with those emphatic lines—the "cracking up" of the narrative is evident in the increasingly important role of Mother Sugar. As an analyst, Mrs. Marks is, after all, the person to whom analysands go when they "break down." Not only does Mrs. Marks establish the principle of *Schadenfreude* so central to the form as well as the content of the last third of *The Golden Notebook;* she also grounds the legitimacy of cultural and psychic primitivism providing a basis for this novel's radical departures from the masculine paradigm for narrative. In a passage too long to cite in its entirety, Anna is attracted to psychoanalysis with its focus on "intellectual primitivism," based in childhood and the early stages of culture we know through folklore and myth (468). This passage seems to credit an older way of knowing, a preconscious cognition, even a prehistorical context within which time and stories are circular rather than linear. Several pages after the passage just cited, Anna announces her desire to delimit the "old and cyclic, the recurring history, the myth" (472–73) in herself. Anna seems to be positing a structure for narrative that has been displaced by history, with its inevitable implication in linearity.

Anna's thinking is illuminated by the Soviet semiotician Jurij Lotman's theorizing about the concepts of time and narrative that are much older than our usual sense of either concept. As Teresa de Lauretis generalizes, it is possible to find in Lotman's insights the origins of plot in what she calls a "text-generating mechanism . . . coextensive with the origin of culture itself." She continues: "This central mechanism engenders myths, or texts subject to an exclusively cyclical-temporal movement and synchronized with the cyclical process of the seasons, the hours of the day, the astral calendar. Because linear-temporal categories, such as beginning and end, are not pertinent to the type of text thus generated, human life itself is not seen as enclosed between birth and death, but as a recurrent, self-repeating cycle which can be told starting from any point" (Lauretis 1984, 116–17).

This "central, cyclical textual mechanism," Lauretis writes, establishing the "laws" of the recurrent and permanent, is juxtaposed to "another text-generating mechanism" concerned with departures from the cyclical text. "And it is the latter which, organized according to a linear, temporal succession of events, generated oral tales about incidents, calamities, crimes, chance occurrences—in short, anything contravening, or in excess of, the mythically established order of things" (167). It is scarcely coincidence, Lotman reminds us, that our term for an extended narrative is "novel," a "piece of news" (1979, 117), a representation of the different, in contrast to the same or the recurrent in sacral or mythic texts. Modern narrative, then, is the product of a reciprocal interchange between the cyclic or recurrent, on the one hand, and the linear or temporal, on the other.

Lotman goes on to talk about fictional characters in a manner that is highly useful in reading *The Golden Notebook.* He explains that the interchange between "myth" and "story" results in the proliferation of pairs of characters in narrative.[6] In "story," the "one single or cyclical text-image" of earlier, mythic narrative may be displaced by duos such as twins, father and son, or a woman and man. Fictional characters, ac-

cording to Lotman, may be divided into the "mobile," almost exclusively male figures, who cross the "frontier," and those who are
immobile, the female figures, representing space. The hero is male, despite the sex of the text image, because the obstacle, or space, is female,
the womb. The gendering here is critical: the hero, or mythic subject,
is male, the active principle of culture as difference, while the female
represents the principle of that which cannot be transformed, is not sus-
ceptible to life or death, because "she" is "plot-space," or "matrix."

The Golden Notebook begins aptly with "The two women were alone in
the London flat" (Lessing 1962, 3) and ends with "The two women
kissed and separated" (666),[7] perhaps as an expression of Lotman's duo
in narrative. Ultimately this duo gives way to another: Anna's relation-
ship(s) with The American who crosses her threshold, psychically, as
well as physically and sexually. Whether his name is James Schafter,
Nelson, or Saul Green matters little, because he is important only as
The Man, or the male principle of difference, mobility, the potential for
transformation. This merging of several figures into The American produces a sense of the déjà vu, or more accurately the *déjà lu*, as readers
are jolted by the impression of having "already read" a passage; for example, Anna writes in her diary that Saul said, "Come'n, baby, let's
fuck, I like your style" (572), and earlier Nelson had said, "Com'n, let's
fuck, baby, I like your style" (492). As The Woman, Anna is "merely"
the text space, the single and ongoing. These elements coalesce with the
"breakdown" of the narrative at the end as psychoanalysis and narratology overlap—a reminder that psychoanalysis has always been deeply
implicated in mythology, narrative, and the notion that the only way to
go forward is by going back.

The "mythic" method in the late chapters is focused on the ambivalent Russian vase figure. If Anna's writer's block stems from a refusal
to write yet another "men's novel" because she is overwhelmed with the
feminizing details imposed on her by the "men's world," it is no surprise
that the vase figure is sexually ambivalent, as is the psyche itself. Increasingly the dancing figure reveals itself as both The Man (Nelson-
Saul) and The Woman (Anna, perhaps also Molly?) locked in a love-
hate relationship, enjoying the joy-in-spite in sadomasochistic dealing
or feeling the pain of being hurt by or hurting the lover. And this relationship is implicated in textuality, as each diarist reconstructs the narrative of his or her day to hurt the other. Anna feels no shame in reading
Saul's diary, but is "full of triumphant ugly joy because I've caught him
out," especially when she has felt deeply wounded by his asserting he
did not enjoy sex with her (573). In a dream Anna recognizes herself as

the "malicious male-female dwarf figure, the principle of joy-in-destruction," with Saul as her "counterpart . . ., and we were dancing . . . together in spiteful malice" (594).

Anna's awareness that she and Saul are really twin halves of the vase
figure involved in joy-in-destruction becomes critical to her role as the
viewpoint character and to the impact of her "author" function. Anna
seems to be moving toward curing herself by obliterating the domination of the male principle with its emphasis on difference and linearity,
as well as its fixation on the reader's anticipation of the ending. The
effort is not to obliterate the male principle but to diminish its hegemony because it has feminized her as the one whose "place" is the
"house" to which it has consigned her to labor at the details of a sched-
ule freeing men to "work," as patriarchy defines work. The effort to
recuperate a sense of balance through the destruction of that domination and through the recovery of diversity as well as the ability to see
complexity as something other than "chaos" has tremendous import for
the narrative and for its own effort to break out of the traditional paradigm.

In yet another gesture toward the "mythic method," the narrative
tropes Anna's consciousness as a spectator at the screening of a film,
made from her experience. The trope's origins are in the Black Notebook, where she records her involvement in failed efforts to adapt *Frontiers of War* to the screen. The filmmakers failed because no one dared
to tackle the violation of the "colour bar," central to the novel, but not
central to the life from which it was transformed, that is, Anna's brief
"affair" with Paul Blackenhurst. The narrative repeats the many encounters in which Anna toys with the desire of filmmakers and televi-
sion producers for her text, especially the Americans, whose interest
she can quickly shut down by appearing to casually slip into the conversation something such as, "But of course you know I'm a member of the
Communist Party." In a dream Anna watches a film of the Mashopi
episode, leaving her with the impression the director has deliberately
"changed the story." Eventually, however, she has to acknowledge that
the film is a record of what was there, while it is her own memory that
"changed the story." At this point she closes out the Black Notebook
with comments such as "total sterility" and "It's all gone" (524–25).
When Saul appears on the scene and they become involved in their
"cycle of bullying and tenderness" (581), Anna tells Saul that *he* is the
film projectionist, presumably screening her past in her dreams.

The key trope, however, is not film but the Golden Notebook, especially as Anna shuts down the four notebooks. Any confusion readers

feel in this interpenetration of narratives is salutary. It offers a means of incorporating "breakdown," or "cracking up," as the arbitrary logic of categories and compartments gives way to the indeterminacy of life. The novel's very title obviously has established the expectation that eventually the Golden Notebook will appear, as though Henry Fielding had deferred the appearance of Tom Jones until the last chapters of his novel. Although Anna has established her disdain for "narrative" because of its inevitable implication in "nostalgia" and therefore in falsity, and although she may not be aware that she is doing it, the notebook in which she has been writing has emerged as a narrative whose author and central character she has unwittingly become. The film-projection trope justifies Anna's sense of experience running on without her control; for example, she registers surprise in hearing herself tell Saul she will now write in only one notebook—the Blue Notebook, earlier threatening to become a scrapbook of newspaper clippings. Eventually this "scrapbook" gets externalized in the actual clippings she has pinned up all over her walls, stripped away by "Milt" in the fifth and last section of *Free Women*.

Shortly after Anna informs Saul of her decision to write in just one notebook and even acknowledges for the first time that she has a "writer's block," the Golden Notebook puts in its long-awaited appearance. When she shows Saul the notebook she bought, with its "heavy cover, of dull gold" (605), he immediately attempts to appropriate it, and she almost gives it to him. As the representative of the masculine principle[8] in Anna, as well as in the narrative, Saul lays claim to it by scribbling his name in it. Now a kind of narrative shell game begins, with Anna and Saul as authors assigning each other an opening sentence, as though each were the teacher of a writer's workshop in fiction, challenging aspiring writers through this exercise to "make something" of these assigned sentences by turning them into a narrative. The sentence Saul assigns Anna is the opening sentence of the first chapter of *Free Women* and therefore *The Golden Notebook:* "The two women were alone in the London flat" (639, 3). He glosses this opening sentence by adding that the "two women," "Molly" and "Anna," are, in fact, two aspects of Anna. Readers may begin to experience some sense of vertigo here, as the narrative moves toward *mise en abîme*, with the recognition that Anna may be not only the author of the notebooks but also the "author" of the frame narrative, *Free Women*.[9]

The appearance of a textual shell game grows with Anna's recording (we are still in the Blue Notebook) that she reciprocated by assigning Saul the first sentence of *his* novel. (It is no coincidence that the sentence does not appear.) When he again asks Anna to give him the Golden Notebook she relinquishes it,[10] and following this interchange she notes that the rest of what is in the Golden Notebook represents Saul's novel. With that preparation, readers turn to the last section of *Free Women*, with the expectation that this will comprise Saul's novel, or the last chapter of it, even though it has been written in the notebook in which Anna had been supposedly assigned *her* first sentence. Having been trained by the narrative to accept *Free Women* as somehow the real life of Anna, readers may be unpleasantly surprised to follow the course of her life, as though it had not been transformed into art. Anna's life is written as devastatingly banal: after Janet decides to go to boarding school (as earlier indicated in the Blue Notebook) and Molly plans to marry, Anna announces her intention of getting a job and her decision not to write anymore. The last sentence, "The two women kissed and separated" (666), is incredibly insufficient as an "ending," seeming a mere narrative "book end" to the opening sentence. If Anna will never write again, what has been the purpose of this very long novel?

In a crucial sense, this ersatz "ending" in the last sentence of *The Golden Notebook* enjoins readers to launch themselves on the arc of the great circle back to the beginning sentence, "The two women were alone in the London flat." In its apparent ending, the novel is showing forth its beginning, with its intricate and complicated interpellation of layered and counterpart narratives.[11] It is instructive that *The Golden Notebook* has moved itself as narrative, as well as Anna as its author/ viewpoint character, into a state of "breakdown." This breakdown is both a revelation of the complexity and diversity of Anna as author and character as well as of the narrative whose subject and author she functions as. *The Golden Notebook* offers two narratives, one representing the masculine narrative paradigm, the other representing a feminine alternative, the two together representing a wholly new paradigm that is gendered, transgendered, and extragendered.

"Anna" as "Saul" produced *Free Women*. She is in *Free Women*, and yet also outside it. As an expression of traditional realist prose, *Free Women* is of course the kind of narrative Lessing herself has excelled at. Indeed, her writing from her own first novel *The Grass Is Singing* and the Martha Quest novels represents that very achievement, a production of which in some senses *Free Women* might be read as a pastiche. That "masculine" narrative attributed to "Saul" has a clear beginning, middle, and end: Anna has a writer's block; Anna struggles to deny it and retreats into her notebooks, before her "breakdown"; Anna accepts the impossibility of writing again and takes a job. It is as though Anna has incorporated the masculine dismissal of Virginia Woolf's Charles Tansley, whose "Women can't write, women can't paint" tracks through Lily Briscoe's consciousness like a cruel indictment of her self-delusion that she might do what only men can do. "Anna" decides against writing another novel because apparently she would have to write a *Free Women* that must end by reducing the complexity of experience to the conventional plot of beginning, middle, and end "theorized" by Aristotle, who is in one sense the "father" of literary criticism.

Instead, Anna is impelled to write a counternarrative, or a narrative outside the traditional paradigm. The notebooks are one expression of this "other" paradigm for narrative, as they resist but find themselves drawn into conventional storytelling. Obviously the notebooks have no real beginnings or endings. They merely *stop* when Anna recognizes she cannot compartmentalize her experience, the effort to obey that "logic" of compartments as a means of resisting "chaos" being only a matter of rushing like Oedipus toward what she deceives herself into believing she is fleeing. Her "breakdown" forces her to acknowledge that she cannot continue to be gendered "feminine" or "masculine," that these compartments, like virtually all categories, are hopelessly prone to "leakage," and that she *is* both "Molly" and "Anna" as well as both "Anna" and "Saul." Similarly, narrative cannot be contained by categories such as "masculine" or "feminine" but must be either "both" or "neither" as well as neither "both" nor "neither."

Readers also need to pay more attention to Anna's assertion she will write in only one notebook, and they should then reevaluate the usual assumption that the notebook she chooses will be the golden one. It is imperative that we remetaphorize this notebook with the gold-colored covers to explore how the novel focuses on the transformation of that object Anna buys into an equivalent for her writing and, by extension, the novel bearing the title *The Golden Notebook*. She has been writing the Golden Notebook in the last segment of the Blue Notebook in which the conventional boundaries between life and art, between memoir and fiction, have dissolved. Accordingly, Anna can relinquish the *literal* Golden Notebook to Saul, for clearly the "one notebook" in which she has already been writing is the *metaphorical* Golden Notebook. In the end "Saul" fails to understand that the Golden Notebook is a trope for Anna's writing, as it embraces *Free Women* as well as the notebooks, especially the latter part of the Blue Notebook, thus pointing the way to a narrative both "masculine" and "feminine." It is the element outside *Free Women*, but at the same time embracing that framework, that it is legitimate to call "feminine" in its subversion of "masculine" linearity and longing for the end. It may be in that sense, finally, that *The Golden Notebook* cannot actually end but must circle back to the beginning again—to begin again—with the frame novel Anna as Saul will write, only to subvert, along with the four notebooks, denying the validity of such narrative while they incorporate it. In this way *The Golden Notebook* both "ends" and does not end in a brilliant strategy of constructing a narrative that makes a gesture toward the traditional paradigm it is denying in order to posit narrative without any clear-cut beginning, middle, and end.[12] In writing a novel that both is and is not supporting the masculine paradigm for narrative, Lessing offers the most useful entry to a variety of postmodern narrative that refuses to offer only the traditional paradigm or only its alternative, choosing instead to do both alternatively and perhaps even at the same time.

Recurrent Circles: Nawal El Saadawi's *The Fall of the Imam*

The movement from Doris Lessing's *The Golden Notebook* to Nawal El Sadaawi's *The Fall of the Imam* entails what might seem an abrupt shift from a novel of almost 700 pages by a famous British writer to a novel of barely one-third its length by an Egyptian writer who is, sad to say, relatively unknown in the West.[13] Saadawi was trained as a physician and later became a psychiatrist, accomplishments that speak to her intelligence and determination in the Arab world, with its very long tradition of oppressing women. As she writes in her memoirs, Egypt may be one of the more moderate Arab nations, but it continues such things as the barbaric practice of cliterodectomy. In the 1970s, Saadawi became Egypt's director of public health under Anwar Sadat, a hero of the West when he and Menachem Begin negotiated the first Arab-Israeli peace agreement and shared the Nobel Peace Prize for their efforts. Touted as an Arab "democracy," Sadat's (like Mubarak's today) Egypt was hardly a free state, as witnessed by the fact that in 1981 Saadawi and hundreds of other potentially "subversive" intellectuals were imprisoned by Sadat. Her "crime" was addressing issues of Arab women's rights and speaking frankly about sexuality, especially in her book *Women and Sex* (1972). Her writings continue to be banned in Egypt, and she has spent her recent years outside her native land.

In her preface to *The Fall of the Imam*, Saadawi provides some fascinating background for the novel. She explains how the text draws on her experience in the Middle East over a period of ten years before the novel appeared in 1987, and how it includes her many conversations with the victims of Arab culture, such as the Irani who speaks of her "little girl" being raped by her jailers or the Sudanese woman who took the author on a tour of the "Association for People with Amputated Hands," where Saadawi saw the victims of the severe Muslim law known as the "Shariat." After confronting the horrors of what men do to men, or more to the point what men do to women and children, she constructed a narrative, reminiscent of "magic realism," in which a girl called Bint Allah, or the Daughter of God, is stoned to death for fornication, but also for crimes against the state and against God, the two having become synonymous in her culture. The decision to employ elements of fantasy or magic realism entailed a significant risk in Saadawi's efforts to bear witness to atrocities against women. In this regard she works in a context similar to the modus operandi of other fantasists who have chosen to deal with the "unspeakable." Art Spiegelman in *Maus* (1986) and Jane Yolen in *The Devil's Arithmetic* (1988) are two other examples of writers who have attempted to represent the Holocaust using fantasy, whereas others, such as Elie Wiesel, condemn all efforts at representation as a desecration of the suffering by Holocaust victims. According to Wiesel, the experience defies imagination and therefore resists the ultimate oversimplification and aesthetic transformation that art must inevitably lend such horrors.

Despite the apparent differences in the backgrounds of the authors, Saadawi's *The Fall of the Imam* demonstrates important parallels to not only the women's issues of *The Golden Notebook* but also to the radical departures from the traditional paradigm for narrative in Lessing's novel, especially the later sections of the Blue Notebook. Like that section of *The Golden Notebook*, *The Fall of the Imam* seeks an "other" model for narrative in its radical subversion of the masculine paradigm. That subversion is most evident in Saadawi's use of a shifting point of view and her evasion of the firm boundaries between fictional "characters" that are usually expected by readers. However it is Saadawi's almost obsessive attraction to repetition, with its sense of a narrative continually circling back to a crucial event, that marks her most radical subversion of the linear, or masculine, plot and underlines her kinship with Lessing's narrative practices in *The Golden Notebook*.

The crucial event to which *The Fall of the Imam* keeps circling back occurs on "the night of the Big Feast." It is on this night that the central consciousness, Bint Allah, is presumably killed. The repeated narrating of this event becomes like the recurrent nightmares of those World War I veterans whose haunting dreams impelled Freud to theorize the death instinct in *Beyond the Pleasure Principle*. Like a recurrent nightmare, the killing of Bint Allah follows a pattern of theme and variation: the theme of flight, capture, and death repeats itself endlessly with the variations of death by stabbing, shooting, or stoning. The killers are alternately the legal arm of the Imam, enforcing the "Shariat," a kind of Egyptian Gestapo, or they are simply a mob of thugs. Because of the recurrent nightmare analogue, *The Fall of the Imam* offers a narrative that appears to "end" but ends over and over again to underscore Saadawi's recognition that the oppression goes on and on, as the death of a particular victim recurs as the death of the next, and the next after that. The only hope for release of this narrative from its repetition compulsion lies in the possibility of somehow breaking out of this culture's obsessive impulse to oppress the most vulnerable of its members.

Bint Allah's verbal exchange with her persecutors is endlessly repeated with variations. In its first occurrence she asks them: "Why do you always let the criminal go free and punish the victim? I am young. My mother died a virgin and so will I" (Saadawi 1988, 1).When they reply that she is the daughter of an adulterous mother who was put to death by stoning, she responds that she is Bint Allah, or the daughter of Allah. When her persecutors persist, saying that her mother has gone to hell, Bint Allah enrages them by claiming her father is none other than the Imam. Described as a "religious leader and ruler, representative of God on earth" (1), the Imam is supposed to be beyond reproach. The scream of her persecutors, "May your tongue be cut out of your head" (1), is immediately actualized in the very next paragraph with the apparent carrying out of their sentence: "They cut out her tongue first. Later came the rest" (1). Readers may wonder what to do with this "her" that has suddenly appeared in what began as first-person narrative. How can a first-person narrator "tell" her story if her tongue has been cut out at the very beginning? Is the "her" referred to here Bint Allah or her mother? If the latter, how would the narrator know what happened, having been an infant when her mother was executed? Or, as we increasingly come to expect, is the object of brutality *any* woman whose body is the site of persecution?

Repeatedly the narrative unsettles the reader's expectation of a comfortable story to settle into—well, about as "comfortable" as a narrative of threatened brutality can be. By its third paragraph the narrative has taken the immense risk of shifting point of view to return to the "eve of the Big Feast" in order to provide background for Bint Allah's being freed, along with many other political prisoners and criminals, so that the Imam can forgive them their sins and crimes on the day of the Big Feast. She is no longer the narrator but now the object of the narration:

"She had almost given [her persecutors] the slip when something struck her in the back." This allows for a repetition—"Why do you let the criminal go free, and kill the victim?" (2)—actually preceding in time what it follows in the narrative. In this sense, Bint Allah becomes a representation of the split subject: both a speaking subject as well as the object of the discourse of others.

In this way, Sadaawi offers a narrative in which segments of consciousness are arranged along a continuum between author and reader with a center in which a third-person narrator is sharing the responsibility of telling the story with a first-person narrator/viewpoint character. Moving toward the center of the continuum, there is another "Saadawi," or a consciousness/voice, presumably for this text alone. Often this voice merges with Bint Allah's consciousness, and readers are offered the sense of this "character" Bint Allah as a vehicle for mediating between author and reader, with less sense that the two are mutually exclusive. This narrative strategy—similar to Virginia Woolf's method in *Mrs. Dalloway* (1925)—erases the sharp boundaries readers normally encounter in a text, boundaries on which the traditional reader has depended to posit the logical categories grounding an illusion of mastery. The narrative is deconstructing the conventional binary of first-person narrative and third-person narrative to produce a site in which the "either/or" of first-person or third-person narrative has been supplanted by the "both/and" of alternating points of view.

Bint Allah is alternately the "Daughter of God" as well as the child of the Imam, or perhaps of some other earthly father less "holy"—or *more* holy—than the Imam, who is supposed to be the "representative of God on earth." As narrator, Bint Allah repeats what Saadawi herself has written in the preface to *The Fall of the Imam*, a text outside yet inside this novel: children are able to see the face of God in their dreams, and the face they see is the face of their fathers. Like her mother, Bint Allah claims to be both a virgin and a mother. Also like her mother, Bint Allah has borne a child who is the child of both God and the Imam, as she herself is. Bint Allah is her mother's only child, yet she speaks of a sister and a brother, an issue more easily resolved when it is revealed that they are her foster siblings. These apparent contradictions persist in Bint Allah's stories of the two faces of God: one is like her mother's, while the other resembles the face of Baba, who punished her and may have raped her in the orphanage. As in so many other matters, the role of Baba in Bint Allah's life leaves readers with the impression of indeterminacy—did he or did he not rape her?—an indeterminacy resembling less art with its much clearer lines of demarcation around the truth than life with its permeable boundaries.

Following this first chapter, establishing the paradigm for the rest of the novel, the narrative continues to deconstruct conventional assumptions. (Barely a few years into the new century and millennium how antiquated that term *deconstruct* is already beginning to sound!) The identity of the recurring "she" is seldom certain, as the narrative allows her outline to encompass more than a single figure as well as more than a fictional character. As we have seen, the narrative is bent on allowing this "she" to embrace all the women who continue to suffer oppression because of their sex. Any certainty readers may cling to is provided by the appearance on the scene of Bint Allah's dog, Marzouk. Any mention of Marzouk ensures that the "she" is specifically Bint Allah, for she believes that this dog took a chunk out of the seat of the Imam's pants when he was leaving her mother, who had just conceived Bint Allah. The narrative's gesture resembles the stock image of popular art forms such as the comic strip or animated cartoon, in which ferocious dogs are forever biting the pursued villain in the last part of him to leave the scene. As such, the gesture is another calculated risk with the potential to undermine the seriousness of the narrative's effort at foregrounding the persecution of women. Once again an excellent analogy is Art Spiegelman's risky business of representing the Jewish victims of the Holocaust as "mice," the prey of Nazi "cats," in a sense de-metaphorizing the Nazi trope of "vermin" to denote those they sought to exterminate. When, in one of the recurrent scenes of Bint Allah's murder, readers encounter the assertion that "the bullet struck her in the back" (4), after they had been led to believe she was stoned to death, the narrative indicates that her corpse is literally petrified, like a gravestone by which her faithful dog waits for her return (5). The narrative flirts with sentimentality by drawing upon the popular notion of dogs pining away at the graves of their masters or mistresses.

Once the narrative has lulled readers into a false sense of security that they are confronting a recognizably coherent narrative strategy of shifting between the first-person and third-person point of view, the text unexpectedly undermines its readers' expectation yet another time. In the seventh chapter, entitled "Chief of Security," the narrative positions Bint Allah as the object of the gaze; surprisingly, however, the gazing subjects are not only the chief of security but also the Imam. In addition, the dark glasses of the chief of security take on a magical power, allowing him to see through the Imam's disguise as he sneaks out of a house of prostitution (24). The text decenters reader expecta-

tions by beginning the fourth paragraph of this chapter, with the assertion, "I was standing in the first row" (25). When this "I" soon refers
to "my dark glasses," the reader is forced to recognize that the narrative
has shifted, even if very briefly, to the Imam's chief of security, who will
of course ultimately fulfill his responsibility for the Imam's "security"
by murdering Bint Allah.

The pattern replicates itself in the next chapter, entitled "Allah is on
the Side of the Imam." When this chapter begins with the assertion, "I
heard the sound of gunshots ringing in my ears" (31), the logical assumption is that Bint Allah is the "I" who hears these gunshots. The
narrative, however, had done the unthinkable: it has authorized the
Imam himself to speak, the Imam who is the very embodiment of evil
and who may in fact be dead, if those gunshots have found their mark.
With this licensing of the Imam's voice, the narrative allows entries into
his consciousness, another risky gesture that might backfire by human-
izing evil as readers follow him back in memory to his childhood and
confront the universality of the author's own assertion in her preface
that in their dreams children see the face of Allah wearing the mask of
their father's face.

The narrative seems quite willing to humanize evil by allowing the
Imam to recall Allah's appearance in his boyhood dreams. Just where
the delineating boundaries of Allah end and those of the Imam's father
begin may be open to question, for this Allah jabs the boy who will be
Imam with a sword and enjoins him to take up arms against those who
would disobey the Imam's commands in the future; in other words, he
is an "Allah" who seems painfully more reminiscent of the Imam's brutal and self-engaged father, than he does of God. This analysis is supported by the boy's awakening to the presence of his father, who has
just sold all the family's possessions so that he, the father, can journey
to Mecca to wash away his sins. The Imam's mother is left with no
money to feed the family and certainly no money to make her own journey to Mecca, for as the title of a short story by Saadawi would have it,
"She Has No Place in Paradise" anyway. The future Imam proves to
be his father's son by promising to return when he has made his fortune.
Like many other self-made men, however, the Imam never seems to find
the time to make sentimental journeys, especially back to the squalor
that spawned him and would offer painful memories of his humble beginnings. At the risk of eliciting sympathy for the Imam, like those stories of how kind Hitler was to dogs, the narrative's strategy reminds us
that evil wears a human face, a familiar or even *familial* face.

In keeping with the indeterminacy of the text, the "fall" or death of the Imam is rendered problematic by his own strategy of protecting himself with doubles. To thwart assassination attempts he has fitted his bodyguards with rubber masks that are replicas of his face. Thus, the narrative withholds clear evidence that it was indeed the Imam who was shot, especially after allowing access to the consciousness of one of the bodyguards who wears the mask. The narrative even offers an extended example of one bodyguard's role-playing a sentimental journey home to visit his mother whom he has not seen in twenty years, a journey that could easily be misidentified as the Imam's, so strong is the stand-in's enactment of his master's role. Like Bint Allah's dying, the fall of the Imam—or his decoy—plays itself out over and over again, so that an impression of eternal repetition establishes the inescapable conclusion that evil defies any easy eradication. Evil persists regardless of the mask it wears to face an unending succession of victims, the Bint Allahs of Saadawi's world, as well as the reader's. At the same time, the plot does seem to have an ending, promised in its title.

In the concluding chapters, the narrative presents a fantasy of family reunion. Bint Allah's mother, Gawaher, becomes the all-encompassing Woman as Prostitute/Victim of patriarchy. In the penultimate chapter Gawaher performs a dance allowing all the men who have come to her House of Joy, from the Imam down to his "lowest henchmen," to merge into the single figure of the Man. If "clothes make the man," or at least can distinguish one from another publicly, all distinctions dissolve in the House of Joy, once the visitors have removed "their turbans and their pants" (173). The closing paragraphs rise in a rhapsodic dance of words and images as Gawaher, the Whore Mother in the eyes of The Man, obliterates the distinctions by which logic deceives us into believing we know the world. Gawaher is described singing and dancing, impervious to the knife wounds inflicted on her. She continues to dance in a realm beyond the Party of God or the Party of Satan, "and she was not a man or a woman, and she was not a human being or a devil, but she was all these things at once and even if part of her happened to fall off, the whole was always there to continue the dance" (173). In her dying embrace of all humanity in the dance of art, Gawaher brings together woman and man, good and evil, in a world where logical distinctions and linear time are the tricks reason plays on those who hunger for the illusion of mastery. In such a context the traditional notions of beginning, middle, and end—but especially of endings that perform the transformation of life's "mire and blood" into the meaning readers go to art to find—dissolve into an older, deeper notion of time and being as a series of endless repetitions in the great circle of life.

Is There a Novel in This Text:
Julian Barnes's *A History of the World in 10½ Chapters*

If the publication of *Flaubert's Parrot* left any doubt about his aim to undermine the traditional narrative paradigm, Julian Barnes eliminated it in *A History of the World in 10½ Chapters*. Like Fowles in *The French Lieutenant's Woman*, Barnes employs the self-reflexivity of the postmodern novel to unsettle his reader's expectations of what the novel is and does. His title announces that this narrative is to be a "history," lulling the unwary reader into the comfort of its purported similarity to all those titles of traditional, especially eighteenth-century, novels beginning, "A History of . . ." By its end, however, the title draws the sophisticated reader's attention to its joking attempt to "slip one over on" its less sophisticated audience with its problematic promise of a "half-chapter." A chapter may be shorter by half than the others in a narrative, but chapters are obviously not loaves of bread to be offered in halves or sixteenths. Even more than its title, however, *A History of the World in 10½ Chapters* undermines the conventions of narrative by offering a "history" flagrantly defying the need for *the* essence of historiography—chronology.[14]

Indeed, rather than offering a chronological "history," Barnes's *Chapters* appears to be providing a pastiche of the composite novel. Although the efforts to establish the genre of composite novel postdate the composition of *A History of the World in 10½ Chapters*, this narrative offers just such a collection of related, shorter narratives. At least on first reading, each "chapter" bears very little resemblance to the examples of this recently theorized genre of the composite novel, such as James Joyce's *Dubliners* or Sherwood Anderson's *Winesburg, Ohio*, with their unity of setting and similarities of characters and situations. In *A History of the World in 10½ Chapters* the first chapter offers a raucously funny retelling of what "really" happened on Noah's ark—a seemingly appropriate starting point for a "history of the world," or at least from a Western vantage point. Chapter 2 moves into the present with a very contemporary seizure of a Mediterranean cruise ship by terrorists, bent on executing passengers two by two every hour until their fellow terrorists are released from prison, an "incident" reminiscent of the *Achille Lauro* episode that occurred about the time Barnes was writing this novel. Immediately the reader is disoriented by a "history" beginning several thousands of years ago and moving in its next chapter to what has not yet come to seem "history" at all, but "current events." At this juncture first-time readers are likely to feel the narrative is being constructed by P. T. Barnum, encouraging them to become increasingly wary readers and to laugh when they find they have exited the exhibit through a door marked "To the Egress."

Not surprisingly, chapter 1 establishes patterns for the reading of subsequent chapters. This first chapter, as will become more apparent, introduces key issues in the novel; even more, however, it stages the narrative's ongoing effort to laugh, rather than to cry. The chapter is narrated by one of the creatures Noah attempted to exclude from the promise of survival on the Ark. The withholding of the narrator's identity sets up the narrative as a joke for which the punch line will be the revelation of that identity. Playing again with the expectations of a "literate" reader, the narrative raises questions of whether this is an "unreliable narrator," since the narrator may well be reconstructing the biblical Flood story as a "revenge plot" to get back at God's Chosen for attempting to doom the narrator's species to extinction.

This rendition of the Flood story certainly pays little respect to those humans who have been set aside to repopulate a postdiluvian world. As the narrator reminds us, the Flood episode in biblical history was no "Mediterranean cruise," and no attempt will be made to tint the lens through which the sleaziness of Noah and his family's behavior will be viewed. Much as it might upset the reader to be told so, Noah was no "nice man" but a "monster" (Barnes 1990, 12). In fact, Noah turned the Ark quite literally into a "shambles" (7). The plural "arks" is actually more accurate, since Noah's family and the animals could not have conceivably fit on a single ship. As the narrator indicates, the biblical story of Noah makes no reference to the incompetent leadership that led to the extinction of species and the loss of family members as well. The narrative plays here on the traditional notion that Noah's three sons were the progenitors of the three "races," so that the demise of a fourth son, Varadi, the "youngest and strongest of Noah's sons," robbed the human gene pool of a valuable legacy. Varadi, we learn, was the cheerful, less tyrannical member of the family who "fraternized" with the animals, causing the resentment of his brothers, who may well have done him in, along with one-fifth of the animals that were supposed to be "saved."

The narrative begins to move toward irreverence as it offers a comic, but also grim, view of the Ark as a floating sty and slaughterhouse. Just as man had his Fall, so did the animals with the implementation of Noah's "animal policy." This second "Fall" was quite a different fall from innocence: "Noah—or Noah's God—had decreed that there were two classes of beast: the clean and the unclean" (10), and the Ark was to be stocked with many more of the former than the latter, turning the Ark into a "floating cafeteria" (14). The irreverence—"Clean and unclean came alike to them on the Ark; lunch first, then piety, that was the rule" (14)—becomes blasphemy, as the narrative makes clear that Noah was indeed made in "God's image," for Noah's God had chosen his family as the only (relatively) "clean" beings to be saved, while the thousands of perhaps only slightly more "unclean" were to be washed to perdition in the Flood. If readers have wondered why "history" begins with this "Fall" of the beasts, rather than the Fall in the Garden, the narrative is insinuating that this was the Fall of Noah's God, who was seduced by the binary of the clean and the unclean to eradicate the disappointing results of a laboratory experiment and start over again. Tellingly, however, this is where "history" begins, for this specious dichotomy of the saved and the damned, the clean and the unclean, will become a powerful narrative following its own desire for the end, as it implicates itself in a repetition compulsion of the generations betrayed by Noah into believing that salvation, or at least survival, is possible for some, if only the "others" can be eliminated. The term "animal policy" used by Noah's God reverberates with echoes of the "racial policy" of the Third Reich, whose "unclean" would be condemned not to the Flood, but to "the fire next time."

Such a reading of the first chapter must of course be a rereading, because once a narrative has been read, its middle and ending make it impossible to read its beginning against the "innocence" of the first time. When readers move into the second chapter and its more modern Ark, or Ship of Fools, they confront a retelling of the Noah story for our time—at what has seemed to some the "end of history." The middle to which subsequent chapters can be expected to return will offer variations on these themes and issues, but with the elimination of a specious "hope" of an escape *within history* from the master narrative set in motion by "Noah—or Noah's God—" in causing the Fall of the animals into the clean and the unclean. The revelation at the end of chapter 1 that the narrator is a woodworm addresses the moral inversion of a cosmos within which even such a lowly species can perceive the injustice built into a world, where some are allowed to delude themselves into believing they deserve to survive while thousands, and more recently millions, may have to be destroyed to make the survival of a few possible.

On the cruise ship the terrorists and their captives act out the legacy of Noah and his sons. Because the terrorists pursue a political goal of

WAITING FOR THE END

enhancing the well-being of their people, they must reeducate their prisoners, who initially refuse to assume the political responsibility inherent
in their national identities. Once again the narrative moves into the
messy world, where those whose power locates itself at the end of a gun
barrel can nominate themselves for status as "the clean" and coerce the
unclean into accepting a hierarchy of uncleanness whereby the cleanest
of the unclean are those who rise to the surface of the cesspool. The
hostages wait in the hope that time will save them if they allow their
captors systematically to "come for" those who are farther down the
scale of uncleanness. Like the readers of this grim narrative, the captives assuage their guilt with reminders of the powerful instinct to survive, read into the narrative through the tour director's story of the
sadistic testing of the so-called maternal instinct in the laboratory,
where a female chimpanzee and her baby were shut into a chamber
whose floor was gradually heated until the mother resorted to standing
upon her child to protect herself from the unbearable heat. (Once
again, the echoes of atrocities in the Nazi laboratories cannot be ignored.) Eventually the tour director will attempt to save his latest girlfriend by encouraging her to pass as Irish and as his wife. In the end
she refuses the shabby possibility of surviving at the expense of others.
In her refusal she provides some small hope: in a world quite willing to
accede to injustice just so long as it assures survival, there may be one
Last Just Man—or in this case, one Last Just Woman.

Moving into the "middle" of this novel, readers are enlisted as "detectives." They seek not so much "whodunit," or even how this narrative—if it can be legitimately identified as a single, coherent
narrative—will "end" by construing some meaningful event to provide
the kind of revelation or transformation on which the traditional narrative paradigm depends. Instead, readers are enlisted in the search for
how these shorter narratives are bound together, and how the narrative
can pull off the impossible. That is, if narrative may be read as a variety
of "history," or a series of events structured through cause and effect,
and if history appears to be trapped in a "desire for the end," or death,
how can a narrative as slender as this—a narrative bent on telling jokes
about the Flood, for instance—demonstrate the possibility that humans
can free themselves from history's "repetition compulsion" without
obliterating the future for humanity? Can a narrative be imagined that
offers hope for escape from a deathly repetition, an antihistory within
history? Will such an ending offering a new beginning be found in the
last chapter? What will be in the half-chapter? Why $10\frac{1}{2}$ and not $12\frac{1}{2}$
or $2\frac{1}{2}$? Where will this "half-chapter" occur? Following chapter 10 or

between two of the "full" chapters? How much "working through," as in psychoanalysis, must there be before the ending seems to be coming at the "proper time"? And finally, if the first two chapters have already violated the chronology of "history," does the order in which subsequent chapters appear in this novel's middle have any legitimacy, or could they be shuffled and redealt? Perhaps even before that "final" question, can we legitimately speak of a "middle" without presupposing an "ending" and a "beginning," thereby begging the question of examining the "ending" of this presumed narrative?

The "chapters" draw readers forward, then, through what appears to be the narrative's compulsive repeating of "history." Each generation seems unaware of the truism that those who refuse to learn the lessons of history are doomed to bear the consequences of repeating it. Along the spectrum from a solemn, occasionally agonizing seriousness, at one end, to shades of carnival reaction against the lunacy of "justice" in this world, and the world beyond, at the other end of the spectrum, the chapters work through the permutations of how the desire to survive will lead to endless rewriting of the division of humanity into the clean and the unclean. The third chapter, "The Wars of Religion," offers the harmless but painful lunacy of the medieval system of justice, in which endless hours of time in the short lives of the best minds of the age were spent disputing the issue of whether the woodworm responsible for weakening the bishop's throne, causing him to fall over, ought to be excommunicated. Far less "harmless" is the more rational-seeming lunacy of Amanda Fergusson, in "The Mountain," who sets off in the nineteenth century to Mt. Ararat, where she hopes to collect the water of its pure snow in order to save the soul of her dead and unbelieving father. Maddened by delusions of her own purity, she watches with grim satisfaction the destruction of a mountain village and its monastery in an avalanche. She chooses to read these events as a revelation of Divine Wrath on the descendants of Noah who have allowed themselves to be seduced by the fruit of the vine in the uncleanness of self-degradation. This chapter offers a potentially revisionist reading of the Flood when it indicates that Miss Logan, Amanda Fergusson's companion, notes how the earthquake may have wiped out the people but seems to have left untouched the grape vines that according to Miss Fergusson were supposed to be the "very source of their temptation and punishment" (167).

Toward the other end of the spectrum are two chapters between the two just noted, both of which are much more somber in tone. Chapter 4, "The Survivor," seems the hallucination of a troubled young Australian woman, who sets off in a small boat with her two cats, Linda and Paul—two by two, again—following an apparent nuclear war, repeating the themes of survival and vessels at sea. Chapter 5, "Shipwreck," has two parts. The first comprises the narrative of the famous wreck of the French ship *Medusa*, and the longer second part offers an *explication de texte*. The brilliant *explication* does not focus on a literary text, however, but a painting—Theodore Géricault's *The Raft of the Medusa*. Thus, in addition to the narrative in the first part, based on the contemporary account of Savigny and Corréard, two of the *Medusa*'s survivors, this chapter includes a discussion of the painting, together with a full-color reproduction, ostensibly to demonstrate how paintings can tell stories, but in actuality to explore how art deals with catastrophe—in a clear sense the subject of this novel as a whole.

The story offered in both the print and graphic texts is another grim expression of the Noah story, the urtext compulsively repeated by *A History of the World in 10½ Chapters*. The sinking of the *Medusa* need not have led to such great loss of lives, for it was sailing along the African coast with four other ships. A raft to bear some of the *Medusa*'s crew was constructed to be towed by another ship in this small flotilla. Without warning or explanation, however, the raft was abandoned; it was left to float with little protection from the tropical sun and with no compass or charts, and even had no means to steer or propel its movement. Although the survivors were on the raft for "only" fifteen days, supplies soon ran out, and some resorted to cannibalism to survive. Most importantly, the survivors decided that to forestall the death of all on the raft the sick had to be cast overboard, repeating history's recurrent theme of separating the unclean from the clean (121). Yet another incident confirms this survival journey as a rehearsal of the Flood story: a white butterfly appears, reminiscent of the dove appearing to Noah (121). Since these survivors have baked in the fiery tropical sun on the raft, *this* Flood story with its own messenger of redemption provides disturbing echoes of James Baldwin's allusion to the old spiritual's warning: Jehovah's covenant with the survivors never to send another flood led some to expect "the fire next time." If "history" began with the Flood story, the modern age may have been haunted by the notion of apocalypse, or the "end of history," in the fiery ovens built by the Third Reich's mad engineers. Water and fire symbolism, with the promise of the rainbow in the delicate balance of mist and light, may not be such a stretch in the context of this band of those who are apparently unclean, abandoned by the petrifying *Medusa* and recovered by the hundred-eyed *Argus*.

The second part of the chapter, focusing on the Géricault painting, offers an inquiry into contemporary reading practices. This *explication* explores the painting in the context of the painter's life, as well as both cultural and political history, by examining what the painting as narrative chose *not* to represent, working on the principle that the elimination of potential aspects of a story tells us a great deal about the narrative as it finally takes shape—if you will, its "plot." This foregrounding of the "decisions," conscious or otherwise, made by the "artist" unmistakably suggests that Barnes the writer is inviting his readers into his own workroom. The painter *almost* painted the mutiny aboard the raft, but may have discarded that episode of the narrative because he was perceptive: "You can tell more by showing less" (128). The elimination of scenes of cannibalism draws in the Flood story, as the narrator reminds us that the absence of a major painting of Noah's Ark in the Western history of art has to raise provocative questions about why painters chose to avoid the subject. "Barnes" seems to expose his own views by repeating the blasphemous suggestions of the woodworm in the first chapter. He ponders the virtual absence of pictorial representations of the Ark, speculating the reason may lie in artists across the centuries agreeing that the story of the Flood just may not "show God in the best possible light" (128). Later, almost as an afterthought, the narrator remembers that the Ark appears in a Sistine Chapel painting. Michelangelo reduces the Ark's significance, however, by moving it to the background, quite literally *foregrounding* those who have been consigned to the Flood: "The emphasis is on the lost, the abandoned, the discarded sinners, God's detritus" (138), those souls abandoned by God and therefore "the unclean."

This "reading" of Géricault's painting offers further discussion of reading practices. When the narrator directs attention to the painting Géricault actually produced, he begins with a subversive gesture: "Let us reimagine our eye into ignorance" (130). At the risk of exaggerating this advice, it might be taken as an extremely useful reading strategy. It reminds us as readers that the "informed eye" passes over what the "ignorant eye" may insist on attending to. Readers of Ishiguro's *The Remains of the Day*, for example, may ignore the important questions concerning the bizarre provenance of this narrative. As a kind of P. T. Barnum, Ishiguro may have so fully persuaded readers that the narrative is a journal Stevens composes day by day that he can stretch their "gullibility" by asking them to "believe" Stevens is actually "writing" a chapter in the Rose Hotel tearoom as he awaits Mrs. Benn's appearance; and if readers will "swallow" that, he will next ask them to believe it possible for Stevens to "write" the climactic chapter on the boardwalk in the waning light of "the remains of the day." Occasionally one wonders if the "informed eye" of the sophisticated reader may not depend to a potentially embarrassing degree on the "ignorant eye" of the first-time reader who may "see" in, say, *To the Lighthouse* what the "informed eye" of his or her instructor may be too sophisticated to see. As the Barnes narrator is quick to add, however, this is of course not meant as a prescription for remaining an "ignorant eye." Indeed, as the acknowledgments clearly indicate, Barnes is happy to credit the "informed eyes" of art historians who allow his narrator such sparkling insights into this masterpiece of romantic painting. It is those eyes that brought to his attention the Father and Son motif in the painting, a remnant of an earlier sketch in which Géricault experimented with the representation of cannibalism, thereby adding an echo of Dante's *Inferno* with its grisly tale of Count Ugolino, whose confinement in a tower without food forced him to eat the bodies of his own sons who had been imprisoned with him.

The *mise en abîme* effect of these nested narratives—Barnes reading Géricault reading Savigny and Corréard reading their memories of the nightmare—allows this novel to make its widest gestures toward issues of what art is good for and the relationships between the historical and the textual. Indeed, part 2 of Barnes's chapter begins with considerations of how catastrophe may be transformed into art and speculates that art may be "what catastrophe is *for*" (125). The narrator goes on to confirm the value of "aesthetics," in a gesture some students of literature might envy, since students of art history never seem to find it necessary to direct effusive attention to kitsch simply because tenth-rate "art" has some alleged cultural significance. In fact, the narrator voices a viewpoint modernists such as W. B. Yeats would have applauded: namely, that it is what the painting represents that survives.

That modernist viewpoint gives way in the end to the Yeats of "Lapis Lazuli," who was forced in 1938 by the coming apocalypse of world war again to adjust his faith in the permanence of art. The chapter's last paragraph begins with the assertion that the suffering of those on the *Medusa*'s raft has been "transformed," perhaps even "justified by art" in the form of an image on a museum wall, apparently "fixed, final, always there" (139). Not quite, the narrator reminds us; "The masterpiece, once completed, does not stop: it continues in motion, downhill" (139). Earlier, in examining the sense that *The Raft of the Medusa* was "fated" to depict this scene of either ecstatic hope or supreme delusion, the narrator comments on the viewer's (mis)apprehension that this ending was inevitable. In stressing the double logic of "narrative," or experience in time, the narrator seems to be making a gesture toward conventional narrative, in which the ending exists before the first words of the narrative are read: "[The painter] saw only at the very end what we take for granted at the beginning. For us the conclusion was inevitable; not for him" (134–35). The narrator concludes: "The painter isn't carried fluently downstream towards the sunlit pool of that finished image, but is trying to hold a course in an open sea of contrary tides" (135). This passage, more than anything else in the novel, voices the fiction writer's frustration with the linearity of narrative, trapping its readers into simplistic assumptions that narrative with its impulse toward ending can offer the safe harbor of artifice, as preferable to that "open sea of contrary tides," perhaps closer to our sense of what genuine narrative might be. The appearance of the sea image here certainly underscores the dominance of the sea voyage as a structuring principle in Barnes's *Chapters*. It may also be a self-reflexive representation of this novel itself and its efforts to tell an extended story with sufficient provision for the desire of narrative to complete its repetition compulsion before it leaves its readers with a satisfying sense that it is now time to end.

The powerful evocation of the mighty themes of art and catastrophe, especially as the chapter ends with the recognition that art itself confronts the threat of its own destruction through catastrophe, makes this "Shipwreck" chapter difficult to push off from to begin the next "voyage." If narrative conventionally allows itself to become entrapped in the linearity of the "voyage," *A History of the World in 10½ Chapters* offers the notion of periplum: rather than interconnected dots on a map of, say, the Mediterranean, this novel offers us a view of the coast seen over the ship's bow as the ship nears land. If *A History of the World in 10½ Chapters* is a sea voyage, it is as circuitous as the meandering voyage home of Odysseus, raising questions of how eager Homer's hero was to return to his Penelope, that is, how much he was looking forward to the ending. Readers move from chapter to chapter as though each were an island in the same sea, but not necessarily "before" or "after" each other and not necessarily moving toward some anticipated "ending" at which it may be more clearly revealed what it all has been leading "up" to. And yet this "novel" is not suspending sequentiality entirely, for the medieval trial of the woodworm in chapter 3 would be tediously pointless were it not for the punch line of the first chapter, revealing that its narrator is a woodworm. Similarly, in the opening pages of chapter 6, "The Mountain," the traveling show of "Monsieur Jerricault's Great Picture" might seem puzzling without the preceding chapter, "Shipwreck." And chapter 9, "Project Ararat," arguably the "last" chapter of this "novel," would lose some of its significance without the earlier chapter, "The Mountain." Readers must know that the bones misidenti-fied by Spike Tiggler as Noah's are probably Amanda Fergusson's.

At the same time the narrative is crediting its residual sequentiality, it is also problematizing its dependence on the reader's perception of a larger structure of meaning in which an individual chapter plays a clearly discernible role. An example is the chapter "Upstream!" told through the postcards, letters, and telegrams of a film actor on a shoot in the Amazon; the outgoing mail to his significant other becomes in-creasingly desperate as the addressee refuses to reply, apparently hav-ing discovered that the correspondent has been "two-timing" her again. Furthermore, the novel problematizes the slippery definition of "chap-ter" in "Upstream!" and its immediate predecessor, chapter 7, "Three Simple Stories," to prepare for the unnumbered "half-chapter," "Paren-thesis."

"Three Simple Stories" combines three narratives, none of which is as "simple" as the title pretends. All together they offer a model for the novel as a whole: What is the justification for combining these stories? Like the chapter "Shipwreck" that they follow, the three stories share the question: "How do you turn catastrophe into art?" The middle story seems simple: a late nineteenth-century Jonah named Bartley was sup-posedly swallowed by a sperm whale near the Falkland Islands and re-covered from the captured whale in whose belly the man allegedly spent about a full day. Such "survival" beyond a few minutes would have been miraculous, the narrator suggests, and yet Bartley's story was ac-cepted as history, like the myth of Jonah, who encountered the rough justice of Noah's God.

The first of the three stories of survival focuses on Lawrence Beesley, a notorious survivor of the *Titanic* catastrophe. Beesley gained fame with his book *The Loss of the Titanic* in which he described his harrowing experience of being rescued. In his book Beesley makes no mention of his having donned a woman's clothing to find a place in a lifeboat re-served for women and children. Of course, many steerage-class women *and* children never made their way up to the deck on which the lifeboats were being launched, some with many empty spaces. Those in steerage were among "the unclean" in the *Titanic*'s rigid caste system. Decades after the catastrophe, when the film *A Night to Remember* was being shot, Beesley's attempt to pass himself off as an extra on the set by faking a pass was foiled by the director, who recognized him and forced him off the replica of the *Titanic*, allowing the cynical narrator to cite Marx's rendition of Hegel's observation that "history repeats itself, the first time as tragedy, the second time as farce" (175). Clearly, this story rehearses the Noah story of chapter 1, for here again it is "the clean" who are offered "redemption" through the sacrificing of "the unclean" for whom there is insufficient room in the lifeboat, or "Ark."

The irony of this first story as "farce" finds its counterpart in the tragic irony of the third, the calamity of another modern "Ark," the cruise ship *St. Louis*, sailing from Hamburg, Germany, on May 13, 1939, with 937 passengers. Most were Jews attempting to escape the coming deluge of the Holocaust being prepared by the Third Reich, which had already identified them as "the unclean," or *Untermenschen*. These passengers became the visible "tip of the iceberg" of the Nazi Final Solution; they were to be eradicated as a first step toward a future "race" of the superclean, so to speak, the *Übermenschen*, whose *Lebensraum* these and other "vermin" were presently occupying. When the *St. Louis* docked in Havana, Cuba, bureaucratic problems arose. The agreement through which the 937 passengers were allowed to depart from the Third Reich, as it geared up for its *Blitzkrieg* in helpless Poland, required that 250 were to make the return voyage on another ship. As the narrator poses the questions, "But how would you choose the 250 who were to be allowed off the Ark? Who would separate the clean from the unclean? Was it to be done by casting lots?" (184). The *St. Louis* became international news, and the leading German newspaper promised that the 250 who would return would have accommodations awaiting them at Dachau and Buchenwald. Visas were refused to the Jews by various nations, including the United States, where unemployment and xenophobia made even the Roosevelt administration unwilling to risk rescuing them. Eventually almost half were admitted by Great Britain; the majority, however, were "rescued" by nations such as France and the Netherlands, where they had the same chances as the resident Jews after those countries were overrun by the Nazis. The chapter ends: "Estimates of how many survived vary" (188).

"Upstream!" is the novel's most inane chapter, and it is positioned between this ironically understated assertion of "history" and the interlude, "Parenthesis." In its own way this "half-chapter," "Parenthesis" announces the "end of history," for if history is the long saga of the injustice inherent in the survival of the few at the expense of the many, the only possible ending to such a sequence of repeated narratives is an opting out of history through the power of love. History can be brought to an end only after humanity recognizes that, until the survival of all is guaranteed, those with power will continue to find the means of identifying themselves as "the clean" who deserve survival enough to justify the eradication of "the unclean." At the risk of being accused of pursuing the illusion of the ahistorical, this "Parenthesis" directs attention to a skeptical investigation of love in a world that seems to have flooded the discourse of love.

Our culture has been content, according to "Julian Barnes," this half-chapter's constructed narrator, to allow nature to teach us how to love. Nature, however, is no reliable "automatic pilot," "Barnes" points out in a context where the naive are encouraged to believe in love as the "promised land, an ark on which two might escape the Flood" (229).[15] Love is no guarantee of happiness; and it is probably unnecessary, since sexual desire could be fulfilled much more easily without it. "Perhaps love is essential because it's unnecessary" (Barnes 1990, 234), the implication being that within history one can *survive* without love, but one may not be able to *live* without love because survival is obviously not synonymous with living. Then, in a gesture toward rationalizing the structure of this novel and preparing its readers for its subverting of their expectations of what the ending of this, or any other, narrative might be, the narrator focuses on the provenance of this chapter's "halfness."

"Barnes" grounds "Parenthesis" in the fugitive space bracketed off from the repetition compulsion called history, endlessly chronicling the survival of the clean at the expense of the unclean. It may be a surprise to find love included in a history of the world: "It's an excrescence, a monstrosity, some tardy addition to the agenda" (234). Love is the half-house designated, for example, as 2041½ Yonge Street, a house "Barnes" claims to have visited, presumably in Toronto. This fragile half-house exists outside the logic that tells us "history" is reality and "love" is "impossible." "Barnes" makes huge efforts to avoid being dismissed as a self-deluded sentimentalist, acknowledging the power of history to seduce us into the illusion of experience's linearity and the insufficiency of love, and yet love may be necessary in the end: "We must believe in it, or we're lost. . . . And when love fails, we should blame the history of the world" (244).

In both its content and its form, this "half-chapter" called "Parenthesis" represents the ending of *A History of the World in 10½ Chapters*. The organization of the chapters seems to contradict this assertion: obviously enough, "Parenthesis" is followed by chapters 9 and 10. However "10½" turns out to be something closer to "8½ + 2" chapters, that is, numerically the ½ *follows* the 10 in arithmetic representation. "Parenthesis" may seem to denote what is "outside" history, and yet it is "inside" history, bent on subverting history through its promise of redemption from a history of injustice and suffering. This bracketed "half-chapter" is followed by chapter 9, offering "more of the same," as a reminder that "history," as it is being defined here, continues.

In the end, the "ending" is a parody of endings. It recalls the "Author" of *The French Lieutenant's Woman* cautioning against the impulse to equate lastness with ending. The narrator of chapter 10 awakens from the dream of death into the dream of a hereafter. The chapter has to be narrated in the first person by a new arrival, suggesting that there may be no author-ity behind the narrative to establish an absolute truth. The closest the chapter comes to that authority is the "old-timer" Brigitta, who provides the narrator with whatever he wants and who seems well enough acclimated to the hereafter to understand its options. "Heaven" is the farcical wish fulfillment of the hedonist, a dream come true of literally perfecting one's performance in golf, sex, and so on. After a few centuries of getting whatever he always thought he wanted, the dreamer, in the end, wants the end, a quiescence reminiscent of Freud's notion of the end, or aim, of the death wish. The dreamer's pursuit of his wishes becomes a farcical rendition of the repetition compulsion, perhaps, evacuating the force of desire in its conventional denotation on the way to finding peace in the end as the total absence of desire in the "real" death beyond desire in narrative. In its radical, or perverse, fashion, "The Dream" may be providing an ending closer to what actually underlies desire in narrative than its farcical façade would suggest.

CAN TWO NOVELLAS MAKE A NOVEL?
A. S. BYATT'S *ANGELS & INSECTS*

On the model of Barnes's *A History of the World in 10½ Chapters*, whose chapters are joined thematically, we turn to A. S. Byatt's *Angels & Insects* (1992) and yet another variety of composite novel. Although the composite novel usually comprises a half-dozen or more pieces of short fiction, *Angels & Insects* might be legitimately examined under that rubric, because its framework demonstrates a clear intent to have these two novellas read together as a single text, a kind of literary diptych.[16] Each novella, or section, bears a title different from its representation in the title of the whole work, and in inverse order. "Morpho Eugenia," the first of the two, is the *Insects*, while "The Conjugial Angel," the second, is the *Angels*. A cynical reader might immediately dismiss this line of inquiry, pointing out that Byatt and her publisher may have been motivated simply by marketing concerns: a single novella would be difficult to market, and two novellas published together as *Morpho Eugenia & The Conjugial Angel* would pose an even greater challenge to market—except perhaps to entomologists and religionists. Additionally, the author, or her editor, wisely decided to position "Morpho Eugenia" first in the text, since it is undoubtedly the more attractive of the two, even to readers who are not entomologists. Clearly, Byatt's efforts in these novellas deserve credit for their daring in attempting to draw in readers who have no predisposition to read about either spiritualism or bugs. Once again, the cynic might point to "Byatt" as a very marketable commodity in the literary marketplace, especially after the best-seller-dom of her critically acclaimed Booker Prize-winning academic detective-story, *Possession*. It was no mean feat, however, to have the *Times Literary Supplement* pronounce *Angels & Insects* her "best work to date." With this *TLS* cachet, *Angels & Insects* may one day be judged Byatt's most important (composite) novel.

The opening of "Morpho Eugenia" clearly reveals a plot incited by a desire for the end, or a climax of the narrative's erotic desire. Working within the subgenre of the stately-home novel, "Morpho Eugenia" introduces William Adamson to Bredely Hall, as though he were a spermatozoon bringing to life the static and basically feminine sanctum of Bredely. The year is 1859, and it is not to be lost on the reader that this is the annus mirabilis of Darwin's *Origin of Species*. Like Darwin—as well as Alfred Wallace or Walter Bates, who might have "scooped" Darwin by publishing first on evolutionary theory—Adamson is an entomologist, just back from collecting specimens in the Amazon territory, most of which he lost in a shipwreck on his return to England. (Like the survivors of the *Medusa*, William was a castaway for exactly fifteen days.) Of the few specimens Adamson managed to save, the crown jewel is the Morpho Eugenia. This specimen of a prize butterfly offers him an entrée to Bredely, since Alabaster has an interest in "bug collections," and given Adamson's combination of poverty and expertise, his host is delighted to support his guest as an archivist of Alabaster's specimens and a tutor to the youngest Alabasters.

William Adamson has other attractions for Alabaster, who represents the conjunction of several cultural currents in mid-nineteenth-century England. As a younger son, Alabaster followed the tradition of entering the church and inherited the title and estate only a dozen years before the novel begins. At that time his older brother died without an heir, freeing Alabaster from a clerical assignment in the Fens. His interest in science stems from the avocation of the naturalist, popularized by William Wordsworth and the romantics, who directed the attention of the leisured class to nature. Alabaster is intent on writing a book reconciling the new science with traditional Christian belief, and stimulated by the possibility of persuading his guest to stay on in the role of scientist as loyal opposition to Alabaster's enlightened religious viewpoint, Alabaster is especially enthusiastic about playing host. William has come to science out of a relevant family background: he has a devoutly Methodist father who did very well for himself as a butcher. William left the house of his father, or was expelled, because he was revolted by his father's God, who bears strong resemblance to the God of Barnes's Noah. And Alabaster has a daughter not so coincidentally named Eugenia, with whom William (too) quickly falls in love (he *has* been in the jungle for a long time), persuading himself he cannot live without her, even though, as he will eventually remind her, "you have a fortune, and I cannot support a wife, or even myself" (Byatt 1993, 64).

With its roots in Victorian fiction, this opening indicates that William Adamson's situation bears an obvious resemblance to Charles Smithson's. The plot appears to be moving toward a resolution of the question central to romantic comedy: Will the means be found to bridge the gap between his penury and her prosperity so that the man can get the girl and the money, or at least enough to support a family as well as his return to the Amazon? Because this novella is part of a longer text, readers are unlikely to have much help in managing their expectations, unless they thumb through the later pages to determine how long the novella runs. A reasonable estimate of length is crucial, because the "already read" of other Victorian novels might impel readers to expect that this resolution will provide the ending of the novella and thus will be deferred for a substantial time. Readers may find themselves turning into literary detectives focusing on the hints and clues that might suggest the narrative is working toward a comic resolution of the conflict.

That effort brings mixed results. Alabaster appears "taken" with William, as a kind of intellectual heir, given that his sons by an earlier marriage, Lionel and Edgar, share no interest in his intellectual pursuits. Additionally, Alabaster, as a younger son shunted at first into the clergy, has known penury in his function as a spare heir, awaiting the possibility of acceding to position and fortune, and thus he may be sympathetic to William's present straits. And Eugenia is a woman with a past; she was betrothed to a man who had committed suicide "because he didn't want to marry me" (63). The assertion takes us back to William's detective work while speaking of Eugenia with her father. When Alabaster follows his guest's admiring statement, "She is very beautiful" with his own "hope she will also be very happy," the narrative says: "He did not sound, William thought, listening for every nuance of meaning, *entirely* convinced that this would be the case" (17; italics in original). William's detective work seems the conventional "good news/ bad news" of encouragement: Eugenia appears more accessible than might normally be expected but is also less attractive for some yet to be revealed reason.

When, some sixty pages into the text, William proposes marriage and Eugenia accepts his proposal to speak to her father, Adamson and the reader seem equally prepared for the distinct possibility that Alabaster will be outraged by his guest's effrontery in wooing his daughter, while enjoying the comforts of Bredely Hall's bower of bliss. "The patriarch would brandish the protecting sword," William thinks, and sets down Eugenia's "total confidence" in her father's acceptance of his prospective son-in-law to her "innocent trustfulness" (65). William's desire for Eugenia is now excited to its peak, reminiscent of Keats's Grecian lover: "I shall die if I cannot have her, his blood cried on its one note" (65). However, as Alabaster seems to agree to the proposal, William's "blood" rapidly gives way to his intelligence. He notes that Alabaster never mentions William's "prospects." He does not speak of any allowance so that William will have money of his own but insists on his guest essentially staying on as a married servant: "He was to pay, [William] saw, with his thoughts" (66), as a variety of intellectual hustler.

Readers are likely to share William's sense of deflation. The gratification of a desire for the end has come too quickly for him and for those readers who expected the resolution of obstacles to erotic union to provide the climax of the narrative. Clearly, desire has been short-circuited, as though the impatient reader had read ahead to the ending and now feels the cloying dissatisfaction of premature gratification. Or the narrative may be putting readers on notice that their earlier sense of unease was justified: something is not quite right here, or, what they *thought* was the "plot" may well not be; some other plot is at work here, and readers have been led astray by William's impatience to come to the end of the marriage plot. Once desire is gratified in the erotically sumptuous wedding night scene—Eugenia is surprisingly uninhibited in her sexuality—the narrative focuses on the new husband's actual function in the household.

Indeed, the narrative foregrounds reader expectations that this marriage has served as the traditional ending of romantic comedy. Of William as a newlywed, the narrator asks rhetorically: "And so he lived happily ever after? Between the end of the fairy story with its bridal triumph, between the end of the novel, with its hard-won moral vision, and the brief glimpse of death and due succession, lies a placid and peaceful pseudo-eternity of harmony, of increasing affection and budding, and crowing babes, of ripe orchards and heavy-headed cornfields, gathered in on hot nights" (80). Almost immediately Eugenia informs him she is pregnant, and having fulfilled his function in this hive of fertility, William is dismissed until his services are again required. His services apparently were regularly required, since he produces five children in three years, all of them Alabasters rather than Adamsons. William is left to his own devices. Clearly this is not the expected ending. Earlier put off by his position as Harald Alabaster's intellectual lackey, now he feels like the family's stud, lacking any other purpose in a hothouse of suffocated intellect.

The intellectual exploration of William's function is shaped by his profession as an entomologist and by the growing role played by Matty Crompton, who increasingly functions as a liberator of the man who has been willing to enslave his intellect to the luxury offered by a rich wife, rather like Sarah Woodruff before Charles has a chance to sell himself. If William's duties restrict him to Bredely, Matty encourages him to adapt his scientific investigations to the "nearer to hand"—for example, the ant colony he might observe—with an eye to writing a book directed to a prospective audience of hundreds of thousands of "amateurs" of science. To make a long story short, William is freed by Matty intellectually and perhaps erotically, too, through their undercover work together and the distinct possibility that it is she who encourages the servants to summon him to Eugenia's bedroom, where he discovers his wife and her brother Edgar in flagrante delicto. In the "climax" for which this narrative has all the time been preparing us, William has a classic moment of recognition in which the scales fall from his eyes, and he learns that Eugenia and her half-brother have been lovers before and obviously during her marriage. To transform William further, this scene of anagnorisis makes it clear that Edgar probably fathered Eugenia's children. It is in part a tragically ironic revelation, since William had felt guilt in leaving behind in the Amazon children he might have sired, just as he felt guilty in "smutching" the allegedly virginal Eugenia on their wedding night, when the narrative is opening up the distinct possibility of his sterility. Any possibility of "tragedy" is quickly dispelled, however, by the relief William feels in this "ending," for he can now escape Bredely Hall with Matty and without any guilt in abandoning "his" children.

That this recognition scene exposes the incest of a brother and sister has uncanny parallels in the nineteenth-century novel. One recalls in particular Charles Dickens's *Great Expectations*, where Pip discovers that his erotic choice, Estella, is the daughter of Magwitch, who has been Pip's spiritual father. Peter Brooks is especially helpful here in theorizing incest as a short-circuiting of erotic desire, in line with the short-circuiting of narrative desire when the climax of plot is premature. What Brooks says of Estella could just as well describe Eugenia: "[s]he, like so many Romantic maidens, is marked by the interdict, as well as the seduction, of incest, which, as the perfect androgynous coupling, is precisely the short-circuit of desire" (Brooks 1984, 128). Presumably Byatt has not read Brooks, and as a result, her intuiting of the connection between incest and a narrative that reaches its end too quickly offers those with an interest in narratology a variety of anagnorisis of their own. The compression of the plot's "middle" in the over-hasty removal of obstacles to the gratification of William's (and the reader's) desire for the end has been a short-circuiting of narrative desire metaphorized by the incestuous bed William enters on his wedding night. This premature "ending" was indeed a symptom of finding gratification too easily, too "near to hand."

"Morpho Eugenia" ends aboard the "strong little ship *Calypso*" with William and Matty heading to the Amazon. "They breathe salt air, and hope, and their blood swims with the excitement of the future" (Byatt 1993, 182). It is an open ending *and* the opening of another story yet to happen but already stimulated by the desire for its own end. The *Calypso* is captained by Arturo Papagay, for whom this is his maiden voyage as a skipper. The threesome at the ship's rail examine a monarch butterfly brought to them by a crew member for Matty (now "Matilda") to render symbolic as a paradoxically fragile yet strong flier. Surely, the narrative is not ignoring the overdetermined linking of Psyche, the lover of Eros who lent her name to both the soul and the butterfly, as the basis here of the spirit's aspiration to escape the obstacles holding it back from an eternal future of transformations.

When readers turn to "The Conjugial Angel," the other novella, or second section of the "novel" *Angels & Insects*, they are like detectives searching for clues to its connection with "Morpho Eugenia." A false "clue" is offered in the opening paragraphs in the figure of Lilias Papagay. Several pages later, readers discover that Lilias is the widow of the same Captain Papagay who was conveying William and Matilda to their futures in the Amazon basin. To dispel fears fostered by this news, the narrator assures us that Captain Papagay and the *Calypso* went down in the Antarctic, not between England and the Amazon. In any case, Papagay's loss appears to sever any connection of this segment of the novel, tenuous as it may have been, with its mate, "Morpho Eugenia." Even so, readers, especially those who have just finished the Barnes novel, are drawn into the latter half of this narrative by the desire for an end at which some meaningful connection between the two segments of the novel might be established. That desire remains ungratified, for "The Conjugial Angel" moves into the smarmy, claustrophobic world of spiritualism, focused on the séance as the desperately pathetic reaching toward the Beyond for a connection with the spirits of the departed.

As other readers have noted, the spiritualism of "The Conjugial Angel" has an analogue in Byatt's *Possession*, where the present-day Maud Bailey also has an interest in such late nineteenth-century fakery. This long—and, for those with diminishing patience, *tedious*—narrative of the cluster of women whose lives center on this cult of table-rapping seems without a discernible plot. Lacking a plot to energize desire for a knowledge of the ending, the narrative leaves readers likely to long for the end, merely to escape the clammy world of spiritualism, a counterpart to the stuffy nursery atmosphere of the breeding taking place at Bredely Hall. If readers harbor any desire to know, that desire might be concentrated in knowing just exactly where the narrator stands vis-à-vis spiritualism. Surely, the narrative will explode in an ending that demolishes the sanctimony and foolery of sentimental belief in the possibility of communicating with the dead! At one of its ends, however, the narrative provides the exact contrary: the angel of Arthur Hallam awaiting the "widow" he left behind as his betrothed. This "angel" is a variety of heavenly monster, because of the belief that the souls of two lovers comprise a single angel. Hallam's angel is left as a spiritual construction manqué also because the narrative makes clear that it was less Tennyson's sister Emily who was Hallam's beloved than Tennyson himself in a culture without a strategy for constructing angels from the souls of two *men*.

And finally, having offered this surprise ending apparently confirming the validity of spiritualism through the appearance of this "Conjugial Angel," the narrative even provides a pastiche of the more conventional surprise ending. Walking home from the séance, Lilias Papagay encounters her lost husband, not as an angel, conjugial or conjugal, but very much "in the flesh," the very flesh she has missed so intensely that she almost married someone such as Mr. Hawke, who hardly promised much in that area. This pastiche of the Victorian novel's predilection for surprise endings may push readers toward a rethinking of the connections between these two novellas. It may be reminding readers that if endings fail to bring plots to satisfying conclusions, it just could be because readers are looking in the wrong place for the plot.

BEGINNING AGAIN—AND AGAIN:
ITALO CALVINO'S *IF ON A WINTER'S NIGHT A TRAVELER*

If on a winter's night a traveler seriously challenges the traditional paradigm for narrative. As readers have become aware, Calvino writes out of a fascination with the reading process and the ways in which that process impacts the author's consciousness in writing narrative. The author produces a text to which readers can be expected to respond with conventional reading strategies, even though those strategies continue to be frustrated by a narrative refusing to play by the rules of the reading game. Readers attempt to engage in "reading for the plot," but discover again and again that rather than not having a recognizable plot, *If on a winter's night a traveler* has too many. Calvino's strategy draws his readers into a plot, only to become aware that just as the "plot" gets underway and reaches a dramatic moment, it abruptly stops. What appears initially to be a gesture toward the suspenseful "cliff-hanger" ending of a chapter, practiced by fiction writers for centuries, is in fact the "ending" of that tentative "novel," to be supplanted by the next in a series of ten beginnings. Gradually readers recognize the increasingly dominant position of the narrator, whose pursuit of the Second Reader, Ludmilla, subsumes the plot of this narrative of aborted narratives. Along the way readers may ponder their willingness to begin again, and yet again, with a growing awareness that each subsequent "novel" will stop abruptly at its first dramatic turn. The question arises, then, Why do readers begin narratives they can be reasonably certain will stop, not end? Granted there may be an "overplot" involving the narrator and Ludmilla; the possibility remains, however, that Calvino is positing a "pleasure of the text" itself, transcending the traditional notion of a plot whose ending offers a transformation of meaning.

Chapter 1 begins with its narrator preparing to read what is announced as "Italo Calvino's new novel, *If on a winter's night a traveler*" (Calvino 1981, 3), foregrounding the text as text, a hallmark of postmodernism.[17] After several pages aimed at putting readers at ease, the novel apparently begins with the prosaic assertion, "The novel begins in a railway station . . ." (Calvino 1981, 10), and yet it has already begun some pages earlier. Itself entitled "If on a winter's night a traveler," this section is actually part of a chapter, or a section, numbered one. The narrator depends on the *déjà lu* to cultivate reader expectations: surely, pages of descriptive material *must* give way eventually to some plot to indicate what is of import here. He foregrounds the reading process again and again, cautioning readers, for example, that they must be par-adoxically "oblivious" and "alert" (18): they must allow the details to wash over them, yet be ready to pay careful attention, following the model of the narrator, who can in a moment be on the alert for a salient detail.

What adds to the difficulty of this narrative is its rather Kafkaesque sense of indeterminacy. The narrative seems to be "in process"; that is, whatever mysterious action its slender plot may be based on appears not to have completed itself, and thus the narrator resembles an author composing a narrative without any clear idea of where it is going or how it will end. As in so much postmodern fiction that invites its readers in, as though the artist is playing open house with the writing site, this narrative leaves us with a distinct sense of a story-in-the-making, not a repetition of an action already completed. Furthermore, the narrator performs the function of a hapless actor shoved onto the stage with very little awareness of what he is supposed to be doing. Early on he inti-mates that he may be part of some intrigue, for he has been ordered by "the organization" to appear at this railway station, where he will seem to exchange his suitcase "accidentally" for another's, when this stranger gives the password. While he waits for this exchange, he becomes en-gaged in a local scene of betting on whether a Dr. Marne or Police Chief Gorin will arrive first for a drink. The scene is further dramatized by a beautiful woman, presumably the doctor's ex-wife, who may prom-ise the beginning of a "plot." It comes to an abrupt end, however, with the chief himself giving the narrator the password and ordering him out of town in three minutes. The end of this first section indicates the narrator's being "erased" from the chief's view by the express train that makes an unscheduled stop for him, and readers are moved into the next section with frustrated expectations of ever learning anything sub-stantial concerning what the "plot" of this first section was all about.

Section 2 announces a confusion that is not "really" in *If on a winter's night a traveler.* Readers may be nonplussed when the narrator steps for-ward in the opening sentences to acknowledge their alleged confusion: they are supposed to become aware that they are beginning the first section again, a textual disaster produced by the bindery's error of in-cluding another copy of the novel's first sixteen pages, rather than the next sixteen pages. What's more, as the narrator discovers when he returns to lodge a complaint at the bookshop where he bought this novel, section 1 that he just "finished" as its narrator and central character was *not* part of *If on a winter's night a traveler* by "Calvino" after all, but a Polish novel entitled *Outside the town of Malbork* by Tazio Bazakbal (28), even though readers may return to section 1 and read the Calvino title at the top of each page. The narrative begins its further descent into this textual maze with the narrator's purchase of a copy of the Bazakbal novel. It is scarcely a surprise that the novel he purchases is not a continuation of the "plot" interrupted by the narrator's being swept away on the express train. It is not a Polish novel at all, but a "Cimmerian novel," as the narrator discovers in his encounter with Ludmilla, who schedules a meeting with the narrator in the office of a Professor Uzzi-Tuzii, a specialist in Cimmerian studies. Professor Uzzi-Tuzii says the novel whose beginning the narrator has just read, thinking it was Tazio Bazakbal's *Outside the town of Malbrok*, was actually *Leaning from the steep slope*, a novel by the Cimmerian poet Ukko Ahti (53). When the professor actually produces a copy and begins to read aloud from it, readers are likely to take heart that the "plot" of this story is finally underway. Unfortunately, those expectations are groundless, as Uzzi-Tuzii snaps *Leaning* shut and announces that having written these words Ahti fell prey to depression and committed suicide.

Professor Uzzi-Tuzii then lectures on the Ahti narrative as the quintessence of all texts, because it remains unfinished. "All books continue to the beyond," he argues, as "steps of the threshold" into the "wordless language of the dead" (71). The professor must deal with readers, however, and in particular Ludmilla, who refuses to buy into that "beyond," desiring instead to read only the text itself. Furthermore, Ludmilla has a sister, Lotaria, an other reader, who startles this group of readers by announcing that the novel in question is not unfinished and not even Cimmerian, but Cimbrian. Its title, she adds, is now *Without fear of wind or vertigo* (73). This "plot" thickens with the Professor's angry retort that the text is a "forgery . . . disseminated by the Cimbrian nationalists during the anti-Cimmerian propaganda campaign at the end of the First World War!" (73). Lotaria produces her own expert, Professor Galligani, a specialist in Cimbrian literature who has offered to conduct a seminar on the novel *Without fear of wind or vertigo*. One convolution threatens to give way to another!

In the midst of these continuing steps down into the maze, or perhaps the maelstrom, of textuality, the narrative foregrounds an ongoing discourse on the conflicting desires of the reader(s). The closing lines of chapter 4, across the page from *Without fear of wind or vertigo*, record the exchanged glances of the central readers, the narrator and Ludmilla. These glances acknowledge their recognition that this novel energizes a desire strong enough to keep them reading (76). The appearance of continual "stopping" ought to indicate that the plot lies elsewhere, not in the beginnings of the ersatz novels but in the growing relationship between the central readers. Ludmilla does become the spokesperson for a viewpoint that begins to sound very reminiscent of the narrative in which she has a central role. She wants to read a novel grounded only in the "desire to narrate, to pile stories upon stories . . ." (92). Surely nothing could be further from the traditional paradigm for narrative with its insistence on "reading for the plot," whose ending provides the central index of "meaning." In contrast, the narrator is disappointed when Ludmilla refuses "on principle" to join him in his pursuit of the solution of this puzzle of textuality by accompanying him to the publisher. Ludmilla cautions the narrator, as well as the readers of *If on a winter's night a traveler*, that a "boundary line" exists for the reader, who must resist the temptation to slip over it into the professional world of books (93). Crossing that "boundary line" entails immersion in the text, and no longer forcing the narrative into submitting itself to the reader's desire that it "mean." When the narrator pursues the "answer" in the office of the publisher, Cavedagna, and comes to the end of the photocopied pages he has been supplied, he sees the wisdom of Ludmilla's viewpoint. Now he too worries that he may have lost the notion of the text as "finished and definitive," allowing for neither additions nor deletions (115).

Cavedagna, the publisher, provides the narrator with the next step down into the maze by supplying the name of Ermes Marana, who has been translating these beginnings of novels as projects he never completes. Marana becomes a surrogate for "Calvino," offering Cavedagna "an option on the new and eagerly awaited novel *In a network of lines that enlace* by the famous Irish writer Silas Flannery" (117). Even more importantly, Marana offers readers a rationale for the text they are reading as *If on a winter's night a traveler*. Marana, it would appear, became enmeshed in a plot of intrigue in a sultanate in the Persian Gulf. The sultana has had written into her marriage contract that she must never lack material to read, and she has ordered that she must never be interrupted while reading; furthermore, she is the leader of a potential palace coup, thwarted by Marana. In doing so, Marana ensures that the sultana is never allowed to stop reading, on the model of Scheherazade's strategy of keeping her head by keeping her Bluebeard husband always wanting more—stories, that is. Marana shares his stratagem with the sultan: once he has moved the narrative to the point of being a cliff-hanger he will stop and begin to translate a second novel, having linked the new with the old in a manner such as "a character in the first novel opens a book and starts reading" (125). Thus, Marana proposes a "trap-novel designed by the treacherous translator with beginnings of novels that remain suspended . . ." (125), a work eerily reminiscent of the "trap-novel" the readers of *If on a winter's night a traveler* should already have discovered they themselves have become ensnared in.

Interestingly enough, even though the text foregrounds itself as a "trap-novel," the narrative continues its strategy of trapping readers ever more deeply. It is as though its warning paradoxically disarms readers to draw them in further. As mentioned, the next beginning— and readers cannot escape fatigue, as in listening to a joke carried more than one step too far—*In a network of lines that enlace*, is allegedly the text of Silas Flannery's novel, shared in photocopies by the publisher Cavedagna. The narrator's commentary following this excerpt foregrounds once again the issues of narration with which *If on a winter's night a traveler* has been engaged. As it becomes impossible to determine when a story begins, it becomes equally impossible to establish when it ends. The narrator blurs the structuralist's lines between *fabula* and *sjužet* to credit an ongoing "action" from which "story" must always carve its artificial slice. "Action" is privileged over "story" in a line of thinking Peter Brooks would support: "Everything has already begun before, the first line of the first page of every novel refers to something that has already happened outside the book . . ." (Calvino 1981, 153). Any story becomes a piece broken off from the "plot" of human experience outside the story, life always taking precedence over art. This is the human continuum, before and outside of narration, that writers are obliged to respect, recognizing that just as beginnings are arbitrary, so too are endings. How does any ending escape the illusion that the continuum can be forced to submit to the reader's rage for "meaning," for that moment of transformation through which desire for "death"/ending/meaning may be gratified?

At this point the narrative accelerates its eroticizing of narration as it tropes lovemaking as a reading of the other's body. The narrator ponders: "A direction can be recognized in [reading the body of love], a route to an end, since it tends toward a climax, and with this end in view it arranges rhythmic phases, metrical scansions, recurrence of motives. But is the climax really the end?" (156). The narrator continues: "If one wanted to depict the whole thing graphically, every episode, with its climax, would require a three-dimensional model, perhaps four-dimensional, or, rather, no model: every experience is unrepeatable. What makes lovemaking and reading resemble each other most is that within both of them times and spaces open, different from measurable time and space" (156). Here Calvino is foregrounding an impulse implicit in narrative such as *Atonement* with its internal resistances to the artifices of plot and ending, opting instead to preserve the immense time and space beyond story because that "beyond" offers an infinitude of possibilities that a single ending, to borrow Stephen Dedalus's trope for contraception, can only "impossibilize."

Inevitably, the narrative foregrounds its awareness that even though the continuum of life has no beginning, middle, and end, narration must. It emphasizes such awareness with the title of its last *named* segment—"What story down there awaits its end?" The "down there" is instructive for readers who have a sense perhaps that having been drawn down into the narrative's maze, or maelstrom, it must have an "end" of some sort. This final "beginning" gives way to section 11 with its direct address once again to the reader of *If on a winter's night a traveler.* The narrator tropes the experience of reading as sea voyage, asking rhetorically what better port the reader can find than a library (253). This chapter offers over a half-dozen expressions of what might be termed the philosophy of reading. The discourse ranges from the notion that texts read their readers and texts are to be reread as measures of how much their readers perceive they have changed, on the one hand, to the notion that each book is a part of "the book" representing the reader's compendium of reading experience up to that point. The seventh reader is the most pertinent to our discussion.

The seventh reader claims that "it is the end that counts . . ., but the true end, final, concealed in the darkness, the goal to which the book wants to carry you" (256). It is this seventh and last reader whose viewpoint is privileged by his "having the last word." The seventh reader breaks in to question whether all stories must have a beginning and end. He reminds us that traditionally narrative has ended with either marriage or death: "The ultimate meaning to which all stories refer has two faces: the continuity of life, the inevitability of death" (259). Confronted with this stark option, the narrator opts for life as the ending for himself and Ludmilla. And yet the choice of life provides no ending: the brief last section revealing the narrator as Reader and Ludmilla as Reader together in bed reading themselves to sleep credits the continuity of life. Like Molly and Leopold Bloom, the narrator and Ludmilla are headed toward the dark voyage of sleep. However, the novel's last line is a kind of "punch line," for *If on a winter's night a traveler* cannot "end" until the narrator "finishes" *"If on a winter's night a traveler* by Italo Calvino" (260). And yet he never *does*, because the novel ends with his assertion, "Just a moment, I've almost finished . . ." (260). Thus, Calvino offers a narrative waiting into eternity for its narrator to "finish," perhaps stretching art to become life with all its unendingness.

Troubling Linearity: Manlio Argueta's *Cuzcatlán*

Manlio Argueta's Salvadoran novel *Cuzcatlán: Where the Southern Sea Beats* (1987) offers the possibility for an alternative to the "masculine" linearity usually associated with the traditional paradigm for narrative. While other narratives may trouble the traditional paradigm for literary or intellectual purposes, *Cuzcatlán's* search for an alternative may be politically motivated. If one function of linearity in narrative has been to offer readers the (false) security of a logic of events following each other in a time sequence, *Cuzcatlán* undermines that logic with its alternative logic of continuity and a sense of the uneventfulness of life.[18] One is reminded of Jurij Lotman's writing on "primitive" peoples in an era before history and before narrative; for such peoples time was a continuum into which event or story intruded as a kind of violation of stability and sameness. The focus of *Cuzcatlán* is a single day in the "present" of 1981. The narrative begins with "I / Microbus to San Salvador *January 9, 1981*" and ends with its "bookend," "XV / Microbus to San Salvador *January 9, 1981*," returning to this "day" throughout the narrative with a sense of incessant, almost obsessive recurrence. The other chapters, however, range backward over the experience of the Martinez family in the half-century preceding this "day" of January 9, 1981. "Logic" is further undermined by the decision to conceal the story's organization by omitting a table of contents to prepare readers for repeated jumps backward and forward through the generations of the Martinezes.

The effect of this darting around in time is to merge the generations of the family. Although chapters may be headed with titles such as "BEATRIZ, EUSEBIO *1956*," the strategy of rejecting linearity may cause confusion for those readers who are used to thinking in terms of generations receding into the past, that is, parents, grandparents, great-grandparents, and so on. Thus, readers encounter "the family" in an ongoing process of finding a *compañero/compañera*, and this process of repetition encourages readers to see "the family" as perhaps the only real protagonist for the narrative, as it represents incessant renewal

through merging and repeating. Some readers may even find it necessary to sketch out a family tree as a reference to remember which generation Emiliano, say, or Eusebio lived in. The pattern is further
complicated by the decision of Lucia, the protagonist, to adopt her
grandmother's name, Beatriz or Ticha, as her alias in her subversive
activities with her *compañero*. Assuming her grandmother's identity not
only represents her bonding with a respected family elder but reminds
us that the Martinez family is a family in which "individuals" survive
only *through* the family. Indeed, the cultural context emphasizes that in
the Martinez family the Western notion of the individual is only beginning to write itself as a construction through those who break away
from the family—preeminently Lucia, who has gained some measure of
personhood.

The departures of this narrative from the traditional narrative paradigm are immediately apparent. In the opening sentence, when Lucia,
the protagonist, announces that she has taken the alias of her grandmother, "Ticha," she establishes the pattern for the narrative, especially
its orality, with the repetitiveness suggestive occasionally of litany. She
keeps circling back, for example, to assertions about the priority of surviving, such as "We must also survive" (Argueta 1987, 4). Similarly, in
this first representation of the most eventful day in her life, Ticha "gives
away the ending" by announcing again and again the death of her *compañero*. She expresses some variant of an assertion such as "Once they
killed my *compañero*, things changed" (7).

Eventually these two mighty themes combine to lift the "peasant"
Ticha to tragic status. With the loss of her *compa* (short for *compañero*),
her own survival and also her children's depend on her giving up her
sons into her parents' care. The needs of her larger "family"—the class
of *compesinos/compesinas* she works for—demand the sacrifice of her loving presence in her children's daily lives. In addition, her activities, although necessary for the progress of her people, clearly put the lives of
her children at risk. That sense of sacrifice and risk is further enhanced
by the carefully selected details of her *compañero*'s death, such as in her
statement about the "last time we traveled together on this same microbus" (9). Subjected to the close scrutiny of the government forces that
have stopped the microbus in hopes of drawing the insurgents into an
ambush, Ticha's *compañero* "surreptitiously" slips her hand around his
waist so that she can feel the gun under his shirt. The gesture speaks
his desire to save her by making her aware that he will probably have
to use the gun to keep from being taken captive and facing the possibility of betraying her and other insurgents while being tortured. Her as-

sertion, "My *compa* and I were sitting together without saying a word. Like total strangers" (11), represents the survival mode that his desire to save her generates in this powerful scene, as she must sit like a statue, resisting the impulse to say, "I love you," or even "Good-bye." The chapter ends with Ticha's memories of happy times in the past when, even though her *compañero* was away on a mission for as long as six months, she knew that he would be back. His sudden disappearance from her life tests her strength, and she becomes aware that without their two sons she could never have survived his loss. Ticha's quiet strength seems the stuff that tragedy is made of.

When the next chapter, "II / BEATRIZ, EUSEBIO *1936*," jolts us back without warning almost a half-century, the immediate question becomes, Why do the selected episodes of the family's past begin here, rather than at some other juncture in its history? One obvious answer is that these two characters of the chapter title, Beatriz and Eusebio, are Lucia's grandparents, and the narrative is propelling itself back to a time when the family's culture and the larger peasant culture it participated in were dominant, as they may no longer be with El Salvador's "troubles," represented in microcosm by the death of Lucia's *compa* and her own very untraditional activities as a political subversive. The grandfather, Eusebio, as we will later learn, is the one who came from outside the community to win the love of Beatriz, the only child of Emiliano and his Catalina, who died shortly after Beatriz was born. Beatriz, Ticha's grandmother, we are told, had known Eusebio many years before she accepted him at fifteen as her *compañero*. The reader senses that this encounter is foundational for the culture, and it could scarcely be more appropriate that the terms *compañero*s and *compañera*s are consistently used, rather than "husbands" and "wives," in large part because the Christianity imposed on their ancestors four centuries before represents an overlay to their indigenous culture in which a woman and a man are "companions" for life, surviving through their progeny, rather than two souls married for eternity.

This pattern of very young women finding *compañero*s and beginning to bear children is, of course, central to the theme of survival. Lucia speaks strongly for large families to provide extra hands for the family's work activities, even though those same children represent extra mouths to feed. They all eat a subsistence diet of cornmeal tortillas and salt, with the occasional treat of a few beans in the tortilla. Many children are born, because relatively few survive chronic dysentery and malnutrition in their first five years. The biggest job each generation must do is help ensure another generation to replace itself, life being short and grim, and old men like Lucia's great-grandfather Emiliano being rarities. Furthermore, even though this second chapter begins with a contemporary slant on the traditional custom of killing a rooster to celebrate the birth of a son, but never a daughter's birth, it becomes clear that the "feminine" is central here to the survival of the family and the culture.

In addition, the culture functions on "women's time," to borrow Julia Kristeva's term for telling time not by the clock or the notion of linear time generally. Among the Martinez family and their neighbors, time is "natural." Even in this second, "founding" chapter, we read: "You measure weeks by counting mornings and evenings. To calculate months you count moons. And you count years from the start of the rainy season. Six months of rain, six months of sun. Invariably May is the first month of rain. The peasant year begins in May" (16). Time becomes "political" as this paragraph continues with the reminder of the imposition of Western "men's time." Ticha's people had a calendar, but the European calendar erased it. This political struggle between the time introduced by the Spanish masters and the time that native peoples "told" several millennia before the arrival of their masters finds dramatic expression in the death of the young woman who misread the time by observing the quality of light and stayed out of doors a few fatal minutes after the curfew imposed by the masters.

One impulse of this narrative, then, is to undermine linearity and "modern" notions of time in order to supplant them with a structure of the same or an organization of circularity to stress continuity and stability, before and outside "men's time" and the masculine narrative paradigm. The chapter in which Lucia's uncles Pedro and Manuel are captured by the government forces and dragooned into becoming soldiers ends with the native creation myth that sustains this people. The myth lies outside the Christianity imposed by the conquistadors, and it sustained Lucia's ancestors before this "New World" was "discovered" by Europe. In the myth the first people are described thus:

> They went naked and barefoot. Like savage angels. They endured hunger and thirst. They survived for thousands of years, because they had hearts and understanding. They could not disappear from the face of the earth. We are here.
>
> We are corn and water. The species will not perish. That is how it is told from generation to generation. (73)

Clearly, this is the faith that moves Lucia's people, and its notion of time and continuity underlines the unconventional manner in which the story of that people is getting itself told by Manlio Argueta.

Thus, instead of a linear "family chronicle" narrative, Argueta offers a structure of recurrence and circularity. Incidents from one generation recur in subsequent generations, whether they be catastrophic torrential downpours from which the family members seek shelter or the driving of pigs to market many miles away or those ordinary but major generative encounters of finding one's *compa*. The sense of the same is enhanced by the frequent occurrence of monologue demanding that readers pay careful attention to the identification of the speaker, lest they find themselves in a long passage whose speaker could be from any of the several generations of the family. For example, in the third chapter, entitled "III / EMILIANO *1950*," centering on the memories of the very old family patriarch, point of view occasionally becomes uncertain. There are passages prefaced with announcements such as "Sometimes Emiliano's interior voice is exuberant like an erupting volcano:" (40), whose helpful colon points to a memory passage expressed as though he were telling a story to a younger family member. There are also interspersed passages, all or partly italicized, that are difficult to place in the context of Emiliano's reminiscences. And once again there is the deliberate merging of Lucia's voice with the voice of the grandmother whose name she has assumed.

This undermining of separate points of views becomes more evident in "IX / JUANA, TOÑA, LUCÍA *1960*." Although the chapter begins with an indefinite "we," it moves to a more definite "I" that has to be Jacinto describing the birth of the fourth child but the first to survive — Toña. It is clearly Jacinto who speaks of going to town to celebrate the birth with some friends, adding that he has no problem with his daughter's not looking like him, as long as she resembles Juana, his *compañera* (135). The narrator, who may be Jacinto providing a little cultural background, adds that daughters are supposed to look like fathers and sons like their mothers. Abruptly, however, the narrator stops being Jacinto and becomes the object of the narration. In this continually shifting of point of view from first-person to third-person at will, reminiscent of *The Fall of the Imam*, the narrative seems determined to escape the watertight compartments of conventional narrative point of view. Another segment of this chapter begins with what is presumably Jacinto's point of view, only to reveal that the viewpoint is third-person. What follows is a long passage announced by the phrase "Juana, the mother, thinks:" and yet it is represented as dialogue. The next segment begins as though it were Jacinto's or Juana's viewpoint but identifies itself as third-person and announces its movement into Lucia's viewpoint with the phrase "Or dreaming:" but what follows is not enclosed in quotation marks, even though it is written in a very conversational idiom.

Once this "feminine" pattern has established itself by subverting linearity and the logic of mutual exclusivity, the novel allows the incessant entry of a more conventional, "masculine" plot with the indications that Lucia's *compañero* is dead. That death may suggest the opening of a detective novel, and later chapters such as "XI / MICROBUS TO SAN SALVADOR *January 9, 1981*" will provide the details and explanations to fulfill the reader's desire for closure. One late chapter typifies the circling back to the key episode. It begins with Ticha's repetition of her *compa*'s furtive movement of her hand to the gun beneath his shirt and her indication of surprise that he is carrying a weapon (179). The revelation of surprise that he is armed is probably more important than yet another statement of what the reader already knows, that is, his effort to bring the gun to her attention. The "surprise" adds a new dimension to the drama of the scene, even though once again readers already know this episode's outcome, or at least *think* they do. Lucia has only a few moments to react: as she indicates, he is extremely aware of how close death is and how few seconds they have to look fleetingly at each other. She has the special burden of memorizing his face, since she is well aware that chances are she will never see him alive again, perhaps never even see his body (179).

This strategy of circling back throughout the novel to this central episode in Lucia's life pays off by reminding us of how we learn through repetition, a going back over the past time and again, and each time recalling yet another salient detail. Twice more the narrative will circle around to January 9, 1981. The first of these two differs from its predecessors, because after touching the wound again of her *compañero*'s loss — "It seems hard to believe you can go back to hoping and dreaming after losing what you most cherish" (231) — the chapter focuses on the family's sorrow at the recent loss of the patriarch Emiliano. This return to January 9, 1981, has been precipitated by the identification of "Corporal Martinez" as the villain of the plot. As the family-history chapters spurt ahead to 1980 and the growing brutality with which the government suppresses the insurgents, this "corporal" discloses his identity by speaking of "my great-grandfather Macario" (211) to the "old man" he is harassing, who reveals that he is Emiliano Martinez. When the corporal identifies himself as Pedro Martinez, his grandfather curses him and attempts to assault him before he (the grandfather) is gunned down.

The second of the two remaining episodes from the more conventional narrative — "XV / MICROBUS TO SAN SALVADOR *January*

9, 1981"—focuses on the trial of Corporal Martinez who has been captured by the insurgents. Lucia sits on the "jury" that astounds the court
by finding him "not guilty," allowing him to evade execution. Lucia's
strategy of using her grandmother's name as her alias takes on an extraordinary power in reducing Pedro to a boy's sorrow and remorse in
facing his "mother" after having killed her father. The narrative's construction of Pedro here as a variety of Oedipus, who, we might recall,
gouged out his eyes because he could not face an afterlife in which
he must look into the eyes of not only the mother he bedded but the
father he slew. Suddenly, even though it might appear that the "masculine" plot—and what could be more "masculine" than the Oedipus
story?—has taken over *Cuzcatlán,* a "feminine" pattern overpowers that
plot. It is not so much the traditionally "feminine" context here of compassion and forgiveness pushing Pedro into the position of a need for
atonement as it is the supremacy of the traditional culture that survives
in the peasants and preeminently in the Martinezes, even though it
might seem in abeyance because Lucia has "abandoned" her children
to minister to the needs of all the children who deserve a better life than
a grim legacy of poverty, oppression, and extermination. In one sense,
as Shoshana Felman has so brilliantly argued, the real story of Oedipus
is not the revelation scene with its self-inflicted blinding but the end of
the Colonus segment, with Oedipus becoming aware of his potential for
being mythologized in the form of a story (a possibility too, perhaps, for
Pedro Martinez). Argueta forestalls the traditional sense of an ending
demanded by the "masculine" paradigm for narrative, an ending potentially more satisfying to those who have been recently programmed to
relish the drama of a revenger's tragedy. *Cuzcatlán* has no ending, because such an ending would give the lie to the larger, older paradigm
within which the novel has invested its energies. It is that paradigm of
continuity and the circle of life to which Lucia has engaged herself, living for her children and the next generation. In choosing life Lucia may
have had to sacrifice the attractive gesture of going down in flames with
her *compañero* by embracing him in his last moments of life, like Juliet
joining her Romeo in the operatic gesture of dying for love. Unlike Juliet, Lucia has two children to live for.

The End Is in the Beginning:
Jeanette Winterson's *Written on the Body*

Although Jeanette Winterson patently manipulates the open question of whether this novel's narrator is a man or a woman,[19] *Written on*

the Body never seriously leaves in doubt the outcome of whatever "plot" this narrative may have. Its opening sentence reads: "Why is the measure of love loss?" The narrator sets out to dispel any illusions that her/his love affair with Louise will have a "happy ending." In matters of love the traditional paradigm for narrative with its orientation to the anticipation of ending must radically undo itself. Just as it may be impossible in the end to establish the sexual identity of the narrator, so too love as an emotion, a complex of desires, a construct of inner and outer experience, must always defy the constraints of conventional narrative.[20] Or perhaps, to choose a more appropriate trope, love will spill over the walls of the compartment represented by the traditional model for narrative, or seep through its porous walls with a fluidity, or liquidity, traditionally gendered "feminine." In the end the unisex[21] lover/narrator of *Written on the Body* seems intent on providing readers with instructions on how to read the body as the text of desire in a manner that may be light years distant from the masculine narrative paradigm. If that paradigm takes as its essential focus the whodunit, *Written on the Body*, by contrast, asserts another paradigm in which Desire must inevitably be the loving and beloved murderer of contentment. Traditional notions of beginning and ending pall in the face of this narrative's rehearsal of the eternal constants of a love that is already lost, that may be measurable only through its loss, as the power of bombs may be measured by the craters they leave behind as presence-marking absences.

Borrowing Jerry Flieger's joke structure for narrative, *Written on the Body* offers a very old "plot," but with a twist. Its plot might be construed as follows: Boy/Girl—or we might add "Girl/Boy," to resist the privileging that sequentiality generates—meets and falls in love with Girl, who is married; Girl/Boy "loses" Girl to Husband/Rival, who *claims* he can extend her life as she battles cancer.[22] The verb "loses" demands scare quotes because this simple plot is complicated by the Boy/Girl's "sacrifice" of Girl (Louise) to Love. The narrative quite self-consciously tailors this old plot of the myth of romantic love to a context in which the unidentified sex of the narrator opens the narrative to a universal plot of love—same-sex or different-sex love—undermining that "anticipation of retrospection" offered by the climax of plot within the traditional, or "masculine," paradigm for narrative. At the center of *Written on the Body* is the pained perception that because there may be no way to measure love other than through "loss," plots that attempt to attract readers with the promise of some revelation to generate "meaning" are a kind of "boy's play," autoerotic, if not homoerotic.[23]

Not only is the narrative employing an old plot and "giving away the ending" to boot, it also moves more like a lyric poem than like conventional fiction.[24] It chooses to make meaning through imagery more than through character-analysis or action. Because all the language of love has been exhausted, the narrative conveys a sense of fatigue, bordering on the decadent, in its willingness to resort to cliché, or stale metaphor.[25] The narrator asserts: "I am desperately looking the other way so that love won't see me. I want the diluted version, the sloppy language, the insignificant gestures. The saggy armchair of clichés" (Winterson 1993, 10). In this experienced world of love, only the naive could believe in endings such as, "And they all lived happily ever after" (10). Fewer than a dozen pages into the novel, when Louise makes the surprise announcement that she plans to leave her husband, the narrator indicates she has been handed the "wrong script," with its outworn language of anger and tears that would have been in its own place more familiar and comfortable. At another juncture the narrator discovers how easily she has allowed herself to become trapped "in the slop-bucket of romance" (21). As readers come to see, these clichés prepare them for the poetry of his/her experience of the "real thing" with Louise.

This "affair" evokes a language of love spilling over into the lyric. The narrator's strategy suggests the postmodern in at least two ways: first, it expresses a willingness to embrace even cliché to represent love, and second, it argues the impossibility of finding new ways of expressing love while demonstrating its possibility.[26] The narrator says: "In the heat of her hands I thought, This is the campfire that mocks the sun. . . . The world will come and go in the tide of a day but here is her hand with my future in its palm" (51). This lyricism is evident in numerous passages, and it becomes difficult not to cite them endlessly, despite their length. In one such passage the narrator's love of Louise is troped as a house without end, whose "stairs in their twisting shape took us higher . . . into an attic in a tower where birds beat against the windows. . . . The light, channeled by the thin air, heated the panes of glass too hot to open" (51). In its own way this lyrical aspiration to find a new language of love undermines conventional plot and its orientation to ending.

The "unisex" character of the narrator undermines the logic of plot even more by confronting readers with a radical departure from traditional reading strategies sexed by the identification of the narrator as fitting into compartments of either different-sex or same-sex constructs. *Written on the Body* makes great efforts to provide its narrator with gender characteristics traditionally associated with both sexes. Initially, readers might sex the narrator as male because "he" frequently refers to girlfriends and at one point even lists them (69). Louise expresses her concern that she may be only another "scalp" on the narrator's "pole" (53). Eventually, however, the narrator speaks at least twice of having had boyfriends as well.[27] Readers may identify the narrator as "bisexual" in sexual orientation, but obviously at birth s/he had the sexual organs of one sex or the other. Just when the detective-reader, intent on identifying the narrator's sex, has concluded that *probably* the narrator is female, the narrator says to Louise, "I want to roll on to you and push myself into you" (110). The impulse to "penetrate" Louise is not sex-specific, however, since not only penises but also fingers, tongues, and dildos can penetrate.

The narrator's indeterminate identity appears to be a matter of that vexed term "gender" more than a question of the narrator's "sex," a term almost as vexed. S/he has characteristics conventionally gendered "feminine," such as blushing, admittedly a reaction of both women and men, although of men less frequently. The narrator also has a number of characteristics conventionally gendered "masculine," such as reading *Playboy*, but just as gay men have read *Playgirl* for years, presumably lesbians read *Playboy*. The narrator buys him/herself a "large bunch of flowers," an unlikely gesture for a man, concludes "I was nothing, a weak piece of shit," and then goes on to consider: "Self-respect. They're supposed to teach you that in the Army. Perhaps I should enlist" (46), an unlikely possibility for a woman, but perhaps not an impossibility. The narrator recalls a "tiff" with a lover named Judith that resulted in being locked out in the snow and cold, "wearing only my Mickey Mouse one-piece" (75), seemingly not male attire. Then the narrator remarks: "With Jacqueline I settled into a parody of the sporting colonel, the tweedy cove with a line-up of trophies and a dozen reminiscences about each" (77). With Louise, the narrator asserts in the same paragraph: "I had Mercutio's swagger" (81) and "I quivered like a schoolgirl" (82). It is difficult not to agree with Leigh Gilmore that the narrator is a woman masquerading as a man, although Gilmore perhaps inescapably blurs the distinction between "sex" and "gender."

The problem of the narrator's sexual identity is further complicated by the author's. Despite the notion of the death of the author in the theorizing of Roland Barthes and Michel Foucault, *this* author, Jeanette Winterson, is very much alive and biologically female. And just as male authors have been faulted over the decades for their failures to "do" female characters, so too Winterson has her difficulties encouraging men to believe that the narrator is male. Granted, she ascribes a large number of apparently male characteristics to her narrator. And yet they seem forced, or contrived. In the narrator's final encounter with Louise's husband, Elgin, the narrator reminds him that as a doctor he should be able to "guess the size of someone's heart by the size of their fist" and uses both of her/his "fists, locked together in unholy prayer" (172), to hit Elgin under the chin, a *most* unorthodox manner for a man to punch out another man. Similarly, the narrator offers the following passage that undermines her male identity by acknowledging as one of "life's mysteries" that s/he "went to pee behind a bush" all alone in the night (186). Such "modesty" would be incomprehensible to most men, night or day—especially in the "middle of nowhere"!

The narrator may have tipped her hand even earlier, however. In a passage concerning a Dutch lover named Inge who is an "anarcha-feminist," or terrorist of sorts, the narrator describes their collaboration in bombing a urinal because Inge considers it a "symbol of patriarchy." The narrator's job is to "warn the row of guys that they were in danger of having their balls blown off . . ." (22). Typically the narrator would find "five of them, cocks in hand." For the narrator this communal urination raises the question: "Why *do* men like doing everything together?" Male readers might quickly respond, "because the urinal is there," just as women continue to queue up for their turn in a stall without complaint, though some might ponder why "anarcha-feminists" have not planted bombs in women's rooms until the architects, presumably male, provided enough stalls so that women would not have to stand in line, say, during intermissions at the theater. In any case, this gesture of political protest encourages the narrator to ask further questions, such as: Why would any man who has been threatened with "castration followed by certain death" not quickly "wipe his dick" and flee? Instead they "just flicked the drops" and went on talking (22–23). This passage moves our discussion even further into the difficult area of toileting practices, one on which relatively little has been written, since most men have been acculturated *not* to pay any attention to what other men are doing in the facilities. In addition, American readers long ago discovered the differences in British English and American English, so that an American male might be surprised by the verb "flicked," but let it pass as British usage. An American male would most likely replace this verb with "shook off," since "flicked" in American English denotes removing "as with the fingernail," according to the *New World Dictionary*. Consulting the *Oxford English Dictionary* might encourage the American reader *not* to assume that "flicking" the penis after urination is a British idiom, for the *OED* indicates a similar denotation of removing with the end of the finger(s). That said (and once again, few men would be likely to pass themselves off as authorities in the matter), it seems *highly* unlikely that "a normal man" would "wipe his dick." Most male readers might well ask Winterson's narrator: Wipe it on *what?*

This apparent detour from the larger issues of sexual identity and gender characteristics into the more mundane matters of toileting is more relevant than it might at first seem, for it such an investigation of the narrator's "sex" is arguably central to *Written on the Body*.[28] Furthermore, it might be argued that the narrator is a "woman" masquerading occasionally as a "man," and for very good reason.[29] That "reason" represents the reader's ready acceptance of the experience of love as universal, whether the two people involved are of the same or of different sexes. Beyond that, it might be argued that once "gender" as a social construction has been unmoored from biological differences and from sexual orientation, the "feminine" might be conceptualized as a larger category than the "masculine." Such an analysis is implicit in Teresa de Lauretis's reluctance to follow other female narratologists into the structuralist trap of accepting a single model for "feminine" narrative in opposition to the masculine narrative paradigm, as theorized by narratologists such as Scholes and Brooks. This brilliant strategy of Lauretis in pluralizing the search for an alternative to the traditional paradigm, with its implication in male sexuality, clearly deconstructs the simplistic structuralist notion of a unitary masculine model for narrative, *or*, perhaps even more importantly, a single *feminine* narrative paradigm. Furthermore, even though Lauretis does not go the next step, we might propose the notion of a feminine paradigm as not only exploring alternatives to that restrictive masculine model but also incorporating that model in line with Barbara Johnson's complex view in describing the troublesome term "deconstruction": "Instead of a simple 'either/or' structure, deconstruction attempts to elaborate a discourse that says *neither* 'either/or,' *nor* 'both/and' nor even 'neither/nor,' while at the same time not totally abandoning these logics either. Deconstruction is both, it is neither, and it reveals the way in which both construction and deconstruction are themselves not what they appear to be" (Johnson 1987, 12–13). As *Written on the Body* deconstructs gender, it also deconstructs our notion of models for narrative as they might be construed as oppositional and mutually exclusive.

It now becomes possible to begin thinking in terms of a paradigm that at one and the same time both denies and supports traditional emphasis on "plot" with its orientation to the sense of an ending as a mode of meaning-making. *Written on the Body* offers its readers a "plot" at the same time it undoes the conventional notion of plot by beginning with its ending. As the final pages of this novel make clear, its ending really is in its beginning, for the completed action announced in its first words suggests that love is over, and this narrative will attempt to measure that love through its loss. In the end Louise "returns," probably as a fantasy to mock the reader's unwillingness to surrender that irresistible readerly impulse for a "happy ending." In this way, an "ending" is supplied, even if only as an expression of the narrator's subjectivity. This ersatz ending, however, may be a key to the larger strategies of this narrative.

In an essay in *Art Objects*, Winterson writes: "I realised that . . . plot was meaningless to me. . . . I had to accept that my love-affair was with language, and only incidentally with narrative" (1996, 155). The author's stress here that her "love-affair was with language" opens this text to a potentially more radical undoing of narrative, appropriate to the effort of its apparently "feminine" paradigm to incorporate the "masculine." Winterson seems to cue her readers that anyone who has experienced love knows that not only is its plot embarrassingly the same, but that its plot can end only in loss—in one form or another. The narrator's foregrounding of this text's textuality reminds its readers that *Written on the Body* may be much less about the experience of falling in love and losing the beloved than it is about the *process* of telling that story.[30]

This seems a fruitful approach, because by foregrounding its own textuality this narrative repeatedly calls into question the existence of any "real world" outside itself. As others have noted, the narrator ends up frustratingly insubstantial, not only in the matter of his or her sexual identity but in his or her very being. I say "being" because even the narrator senses this text may be the representation of a solipsistic world enclosed by her/his body. Reading backward from the strange "ending" in which Louise "returns" to express even the narrator's irresistible desire to recuperate the beloved, all the while mocking the reader's desire for a happy ending, we begin to pay more attention to the bookishness of this book. Early on, for example, the narrator says that Louise wanted to be a character in a novel, and in the final paragraphs the narrator questions whether s/he invented Louise, because she seemed like a character in a novel (1993, 189). Similarly, the narrator's employer, Gail Right accuses her/him of "want[ing] to live in a novel" (160). As the ending indicates, the "you" in the opening pages may be "Louise" in some sense of the term "Louise." Although the narrator is a "translator," not a writer, this narrative works on the contemporary notion that translating is inevitably a (re)writing, and thus the narrative is taking readers into itself, into the process by which textuality is generated.

The narrator in *Written on the Body* may remind readers of Briony as the narrator and "writer" of *Atonement*. Although Winterson's narrator claims to have left Louise in the "gentleman's agreement" with Elgin when he promised to extend his wife's life only if the triangle became a duo, readers have every right to be suspicious of the narrator's motives as being too contaminated with textuality to accept at face value. The narrator makes inescapably clear that experience has taught her/him that love has a shelf life of about six months before passionate desire moderates into something that in a heterosexist context might be termed "married love," certainly not without desire and passion but also *with* a great deal to get in the way of love. Once again, the narrator is *not* a writer at the same time s/he *is* in part because Winterson can virtually guarantee that her readers will take the narrator for a thinly disguised Jeanette Winterson.

It is, finally, the writerly aspect of the narrator that moves this text into the territory of modernism, with its essential concern with transformation/sacrifice. This is not to deny the postmodern structure of *Written on the Body*, but only to remind ourselves that modernism is the center of postmodernism, the center that at one and the same time it denies and employs to define itself. The narrator is the modernist obsessed with sacrifice as a means of "proving" one's love—"I love you enough to promise never to see you again, if that will save your life"—at the same time that she is the modernist knowing that life cannot escape paying the price of loss and death (as Briony argues, they are inevitable, anyway) as admission to the realm of art. Love cannot last, except in art.[31] As we have seen, Keats taught its lessons to Yeats, the great poet of modernism, who also savored the exorbitant price life pays. Winterson, who saw herself as the heir of Virginia Woolf,[32] also savors the price, as perhaps her narrator does not. Like Woolf, her "spiritual mother," Winterson is trying to tell a story that ends by undoing itself through its clear demonstration that to be genuinely "realistic," narrative must avoid "plot" with its inevitable orientation to "ending," seeking ending instead in the power of transformation that turns life into art.[33]

Written on the Body cannot "end," in part because it has not actually "begun." It may make gestures toward "plot," but it refuses to invest in it, raising questions of whether this text is indeed a novel, and not the "meditation" it aspires to be. The lover cannot "begin" the narrative of an "affair," a "love story," because love is already implicated in its measurement through loss. Thus, *Written on the Body* at one and the same time both is and is not a narrative. As narrative it draws its readers into the representing of love, the simulation of a "love story." In its radical foregrounding of its own text, *Written on the Body* may be the quintessential postmodern novel, offering a "virtual" love story, as perhaps *any* love story is virtual. Like the Persian Gulf War for Jean Baudrillard, it becomes conceivable that the narrator's "affair" with Louise "did not take place." It was not simply the author's but also the narrator's construction of the ideal of love; a friend of the narrator calls the affair with Louise "the perfect romance" (187), a simulation of a "real" affair. As an "artist" the narrator knows the price of perfection: its price is life itself.

∾

    In the end, this exploration of ending finds itself back at its beginning with Winterson's homage to Virginia Woolf, who shared Winterson's aspiration to move outside the conventional paradigm for narrative. This circling back offers a reminder of the advice given to innocents who find themselves lost in the wilderness: circle back until you find where you were going forward. This exploration has been just that, an attempt to look at the conventional paradigm for narrative, as Woolf herself did in *Mrs. Dalloway,* to find a larger and more complex paradigm with the power to resist the temptation merely to reject the male plot and to replace it with a "female plot" that completely excludes the elements of that traditional male model. Woolf's plot includes the Septimus Warren Smith gesture of a male plot with its climax in the more than "little death" of Smith's flinging away his body *within* the larger and more complex "plot" of Clarissa Dalloway's day that *seems* oriented to the "ending" of her party's success or failure, but such an "ending" pales before the most important existential issue for Clarissa: Can I still read the testimony of my worth in the eyes of a Peter Walsh, whose excitement as I enter a room validates my existence? In one sense the circle is the ideal figure for narrative: it appears one-dimensional but is also two-dimensional, because it inscribes a space it implicitly encloses; additionally, it appears linear like the "male plot" but reminds us that lines go in two directions, not one. This exploration itself has difficulty finding its "ending," for traditionally such a study has been impelled, if not *com*pelled, to end with "conclusions."
    The difficulty, if not outright impossibility, of appending a conclusion, or "ending," to this long exploration of nearly two dozen novels

ought to be implicit in the effort throughout to work outside the conventional notion of an extended study of fiction divided into parts and chapters. The "logic" of the conventional approach certifies the validity of the traditional, structuralist paradigm for narrative, going all the way back to Aristotle and his seemingly benign and obvious division of plot into beginning, middle, and end. Like Freud and other structuralists, Aristotle was something of a "conquistador," not a metaphor that many women have traditionally employed to trope their own aspirations. Unlike the logic of divisions and compartments, the figure of clusters has been appealing as a means of complicating the traditional, "masculine" notion of plot with its ending in an unmistakable "money shot." Because the "logic" of clusters undermines the finality of an item's placement, coming to the end of a project such as this one generates its frustrations for the reader. The latter might be sympathetic to the student who asks in the final seconds of a long class, All this discussion has been very interesting, but what do *you* think this poem means? There is also in the end a frustration for the leader of that discussion: Time has run out, and there is no opportunity to hear arguments against the placement of a novel—say, *The White Hotel*—in the first section, rather than the second or third. One almost wants to append an e-mail address with an invitation to continue the discussion.

Acknowledgments

I WOULD LIKE TO THANK THE FOLLOWING COPYRIGHT HOLDERS FOR granting permission to quote material from their work to support my readings of the nearly two dozen novels discussed at length in this monograph. The effort to acquire permissions consumed my attention and much of my energy for a half-year of my life. If any holders of copyright were overlooked, apologies are extended here for omissions.

Manlio Argueta, *Cuzcatlán.* Reprinted by permission of Caryn Burtt of Random House, USA.

Margaret Atwood, *The Blind Assassin.* Reprinted by permission of Carol Christiansen for Random House, USA. *The Handmaid's Tale.* Copyright © 1985 by O. W. Toad, Ltd. Reprinted by permission of Houghton Mifflin Company. *The Handmaid's Tale,* published by Jonathan Cape. Reprinted by permission of Gabrielle White of The Random House Group Ltd.

Julian Barnes, *The History of the World in 10½ Chapters.* Reprinted by permission of Bette Graber of Random House, USA, and Carol Macarthur of the Peters, Fraser and Dunlop Group Ltd. on behalf of Julian Barnes.

Anthony Burgess, *A Clockwork Orange.* Reprinted by permission of Elizabeth Clementson of W. W. Norton and Leslie Gardner for Artellus Ltd. on behalf of the Estate of Anthony Burgess.

A. S. Byatt, *Angels & Insects.* Reprinted by permission of Sterling Lord Literistic, Inc. Copyright © by Antonia Byatt. And by permission of Caryn Burtt of Random House, USA.

Italo Calvino, *If on a winter's night a traveler.* Reprinted by permission of Monika Brunner of Harcourt. Copyright © 1981 by Italo Calvino, permission by The Wylie Agency.

John Fowles, *The French Lieutenant's Woman.* Reprinted by permission of Sharon Weiss of Little, Brown and Company and Gabrielle White of The Random House Group Ltd.

L. P. Hartley, *The Go-Between.* Copyright © 1953 by L. P. Hartley.

Copyright © Douglas Brook-Douglas, 1997. Reprinted by permission of Sara Kramer of New York Review of Books Classics and Penguin Group (UK).

Kazuo Ishiguro, *When We Were Orphans*. Copyright © 2000 by Kazuo Ishiguro. Reprinted by permission of Faber and Faber, Random House USA, and Knopf Canada.

Doris Lessing, *The Golden Notebook*. Copyright © 1962, and renewed 1990, by Doris Lessing. Reprinted by permission of Simon & Schuster Adult Publishing Group and kind permission of Jonathan Clowes Ltd. London, on behalf of Doris Lessing.

David Lodge, *Changing Places*. Reproduced with permission of Florence Eichin of Penguin USA and Curtis Brown Group Ltd. London on behalf of David Lodge. Copyright © David Lodge 1975.

Colum McCann, *This Side of Brightness*. Copyright © 1998 by Colum McCann. Reprinted by permission of The Wylie Agency and Weidenfeld & Nicholson.

Ian McEwan, *Amsterdam*. Reprinted by permission of Carol Christiansen of Random House, USA. *Atonement*. Reprinted by permission of Carol Christiansen of Random House, USA.

Steven Millhauser, *Edwin Mullhouse*. Reprinted by permission of International Creative Management. Copyright © 1972 by Steven Millhauser.

Joyce Carol Oates, *Bellefleur*. Copyright © 1980 Joyce Carol Oates, Inc. Used by permission of Dutton, a division of Penguin Group (USA) Inc. Reprinted by permission of John Hawkins & Associates, Inc.

Jean Rhys, *Wide Sargasso Sea*. Copyright © 1966 by Jean Rhys. Extracts are reproduced by permission of Sheil Land Associates Ltd. on behalf of Jean Rhys Ltd.

Salman Rushdie, *Midnight's Children*. Reprinted by permission of the author and the Wylie Agency.

Nawal El Saadawi, *The Fall of the Imam*. Reprinted by permission of the author. Many thanks for Dr. Saadawi's warm support for the project.

Graham Swift, *Waterland*. Reprinted by permission of Louise Lamont of A. P. Watt Ltd. on behalf of Graham Swift.

D. M. Thomas, *The White Hotel*. Copyright © 1981 by D. M. Thomas. Used by permission of Viking Penguin, a division of Penguin Group (USA) Inc. Reprinted by permission of Michele Bird as representative of J. M. Dent, a division of The Orion Publishing Group.

Jeanette Winterson, *Written on the Body*. Copyright © 1993 by Jeanette

Winterson. Reprinted by permission of International Creative Management, Inc.

Virginia Woolf, *Mrs. Dalloway.* My thanks to Monika Brunner at Harcourt and to Lisa Dowdeswell for the Society of Authors (England), as representative of the Estate of Virginia Woolf.

Notes

Notes to the Introduction

1. I am indebted to Marianne Hirsch in *The Mother-Daughter Plot* for this term.

2. Note the notion of a "feminine" versus "masculine" time in this passage: "[B]ut here the other clock, the clock which always struck two minutes after Big Ben, came shuffling in with its lap full of odds and ends, which it dumped as if Big Ben were all very well with his majesty laying down the law, so solemn, so just, but [St. Margaret's Church] must remember all sorts of little things besides" (Woolf 1953, 193).

3. As it is widely known, Woolf originally planned for Clarissa to commit suicide at the end of this novel. Septimus functions, then, as a kind of "deodand," a human gift to God, or forfeiture to remedy human injustice. I am grateful to Anthony Hecht's note for his poem "Deodand" in *Venetian Vespers*.

4. The term "existential" is appropriate here, because for the great existentialist Albert Camus this was indeed the question: Is there a justification not to commit suicide?

5. Freud faced the demolition of his central thesis that dreams serve as outlets for the repressed libido. His problem was how to explain the persistent nightmares of veterans for whom the unconscious was clearly screening scenes of excruciatingly painful horrors, rather than dreams of earthly delights.

6. I am struck by the coincidence of Doris Lessing, one of the mothers of modern feminism, indicating her shock one day in noting that when she entered a room the eyes of men no longer turned in her direction, a revelation to her that men took less interest in her intelligence and conversation than in her physical attractiveness. Suddenly she had become old.

7. It must be emphasized that Clarissa's value here is probably not Woolf's, since (at the risk of intruding the life of the author on this text) Woolf was extremely self-conscious about others looking at her, whether on the street, where she felt strangers might be laughing at her, or whether she was shopping for clothing, an ordeal that would draw attention to her body.

Notes to Cluster 1

1. The use here of what the British call "scare quotes" is not gratuitous but an effort at acknowledging psychoanalysis less as a system of scientific principles and more as a collection of texts.

2. Ironically, Lacan gets much less prominence in the extended book form of "Freud's Masterplot," perhaps because Freud offered a better fit for Brooks's essentially structuralist thinking in *Reading for the Plot*.

3. See Lacan 1988.

4. It is impossible not to recall here the climactic scene of *The Miracle Worker* in which Helen Keller experiences the elation of finally connecting sign language with first "water" and then with virtually everything else in her limited environment in a kind of ecstatic *jouissance* of access to representation in the Symbolic register.

5. I follow Lacan's lead in reserving for an endnote the term *jeux d'occultation* and his further explanation of how the toy becomes associated with the disappearance and reappearance of the mother. He says it is "evidence of the child's beginning to master his environment actively through speech, for the active repetition seemed clearly to replace the passivity of the situation where the child's mother was alternately present and absent" (1977, 104).

6. As Anthony Wilden and others have suggested, Lacan must have anticipated these two terms, "Imaginary" and "Symbolic," confusing his readers, for the former is not connected with the fantastic so much as with images, just as the latter is not to be confused with symbol in literary or psychoanalytic terms but is more "simply" a means of signifying representation. Misreading the two terms as what they mean conventionally is a kind of "allegory" of our implication in "the illusion of mastery."

7. The connections here with the psychoanalytic session are not coincidental, and in his later work, *Psychoanalysis and Storytelling*, Brooks makes quite a point of the ending of narrative being like "transference," or the analysand's recounting a past whose recounting establishes the pastness of the past so that the analysand can move forward without continuing to repeat the past compulsively—that is, without being trapped within that past. Brooks writes: "The compulsion to repeat gives patients a sense of being fatefully subject to a 'perpetual recurrence of the same thing'; it can indeed suggest pursuit by a demonic power" (1994, 99).

8. This passage is crucial in "answering" Julia Kristeva as well as Deleuze and Guattari, who would privilege the Imaginary register because they conclude Lacan privileged the Symbolic. It is clear that Lacan understood the price the subject pays for entry into the Symbolic.

9. Some readers have lamented that the Booker Prize came a novel too early, since *Atonement*, his next novel, seemed eminently more worthy of recognition. This ironic circumstance helps to explain why many readers undervalue McEwan's accomplishments in *Amsterdam*. Beryl Bainbridge, who had been short-listed even more times than McEwan, was the sympathetic favorite, and the bookmakers' choice, to win the Booker for her novel *Master Georgie*. In addition, McEwan's success cannot have been sweetened by the announcement of Douglas Hurd, the Booker committee's head, that the committee considered none on that year's short list a "masterpiece." Ironically, like the novel's Julian Garmony, Douglas Hurd had been foreign secretary.

10. Dana Chetrinescu (2001) makes a point—perhaps too large a point—of illness in this novel.

11. Walter Benjamin, qtd by Brooks (1984, 22).

12. See Genette 1980, 10–11.

13. The reviewer David Wiegand writes: "With 'Amsterdam,' [McEwan] has created a new subgenre in novel writing: the morality farce" ("Deceit in the Name of Duty: Humorous Novel Satirizes Millennial Moral Decay," *San Francisco Chronicle*, December 13, 1998).

14. It might be noted that book reviewers have not been "sympathetic" to either Vernon or Clive. As I later point out, the narrative is a variety of "joke" or "mousetrap,"

through its focalization and entries luring readers into the consciousness of Vernon and especially Clive. When the trap springs and readers discover that they have been "tricked" into empathizing with morally reprehensible behavior, I suspect they suppress any memory of having found either character "sympathetic." Peter Ho Davies writes in his *Chicago Tribune* review: "Overall [McEwan] strikes a wonderful balance between our engagement with the characters and our creeping distaste for them" ("From Victors to Victims: A Political Fable of Millennial Revenge in Britain," December 13, 1998).

15. Paul Elie, reviewing the book for the *Village Voice*, ("Going Dutch," December 22, 1998), writes that "Clive seems to embody the serious artist. . . . McEwan keeps the reader guessing about Clive—genius, or fake?—until the end." Then Elie misreads the disaster of this "Millennial Symphony" as casting doubt on the worth of Clive's work up to this point—a conclusion that does not follow logically. Peter Ho Davies seems closer to the truth when he writes: "We need to see Clive as both arrogant and capable of attaining great art" ("From Victors to Victims," *Chicago Tribune*, December 13, 1998). Davies goes on to say that "McEwan's work on his oratorio, 'And Now We Die,' seems to have given him a real insight into the swelling, symphonic inner life of a composer." Could the title of McEwan's own foray into the composition of music offer a more telling analogue for his own preoccupation with the end in *Amsterdam?* Perhaps as a writer himself, Davies is aware that creating requires an oversized ego to bring projects to completion.

16. In the next novel, *Atonement*, McEwan structures a whole narrative on the basis of a literal episode of coitus interruptus, reflecting how, it might be argued, the novel's plot is itself a case of narratological coitus interruptus.

17. Few writers, across the gamut of the term, can escape feeling some pained empathy for a Clive who deludes himself into believing he has created a great work, only to discover on reading it sometime later that the composition is far less than a "masterpiece."

18. The fifth edition of the *Norton Anthology of English Literature* offers this informational footnote for the ending of *The Rime of the Ancient Mariner*: "Coleridge said in 1830, answering the objection of the poet Mrs. Barbauld that the poem 'lacked a moral': 'I told her that in my own judgement the poem had too much, and that the only, or chief fault, if I might say so, was the obtrusion of the moral sentiment so openly on the reader as a principle or cause of action in a work of pure imagination'" (Abrams 1986, 352). The "moral" at issue here might be glossed as the "meaning" the poet found a too obtrusive consequence of the narrative's ending.

19. See the Jean Stein interview in Faulkner 1956.

20. One recalls, for example, the scene in which Stephen Dedalus awakens from a wet dream to compose a villanelle and perhaps masturbates to recover the erotic energy that first stimulated his creative impulses.

21. In a related context, Terry Eagleton in his review of *Atonement* in the *Lancet* (London) speaks of "the brutal monomania of the imagination" ("A Beautiful and Elusive Tale," December 22, 2001).

22. Readers who have dismissed *Amsterdam* may well have oversimplified the author's response to the novel when they speak of it as "thin and irritatingly clever-clever" ("Saying Sorry" *Economist*, Sept. 22, 2001) or "a lightweight farce that throws a wrench into the oleaginous contentment of two successful middle-aged men" (Daphne Merkin, "The End of Innocence" *Los Angeles Times*, March 10, 2002). In an interview with *News-*

week McEwan notes that despite Briony's destruction of her sister and Robbie Turner's lives he is still sympathetic toward her: "I can't help loving her because I spent so much time making her" ("Luminous Novel from Dark Master" 139, no. 11, Feb. 22, 2002). One hardly needs to add that, like Briony, Clive Linley is an artist.

23. It is more than a bit ironic that George, whom the narrative cast as the complaisant husband of an adulterous wife, becomes the major "plotter," or force generating the plot of this narrative.

24. That Vernon repeats the phrase "It's a spoiler" as he is dying from the lethal injection may suggest that in some corner of his unconscious an awareness persists that he has been hoisted by his own petard.

25. Brian Finney (2002b) also identifies *When We Were Orphans* as a detective novel but has little interest in the implications of that identification.

26. One recalls Joyce's brilliant perception of the child listening for clues concerning adult experience in the first *Dubliners* story, "The Sisters."

27. One wants to call this novel's viewpoint character "Banks," but "Christopher" continues to be irresistible, because obviously he remains a child into middle age.

28. Finney reads Christopher as a "representative of colonialism": "In the course of the novel Ishiguro forces the reader to recognize that the representatives of colonialism, while attempting to foist onto the colonized the stigma of eternal childishness, are in fact themselves childlike, having evaded maturation by projecting the unacceptable within themselves onto the subjects of their colonial discourse" (2002b).

29. Finney (2002b) sees the meeting of Christopher with his senile mother as much more positive than the text supports.

30. Speaking recently with the writer Jim Shepard, Millhauser revealed some interesting background: "When I wrote *Edwin Mullhouse*, I made use of a number of models, such as Leon Edel's five-volume biography of Henry James, Nabokov's *Pale Fire* and Mann's *Doctor Faustus*. But to say that any of those books somehow engendered my own would be, I think, false. My book came from something deeper, more personal, more intimate, more ungraspable, more obscure than other people's books, though at the same time it was pleased to make use of those books in order to become itself, in order to give birth to itself. Books as midwives—maybe that's what I mean" (Shepard 2003, 78).

31. In a provocative article John Boyd argues perhaps a bit too ingeniously that the death of Edwin "may be interpreted in several ways," beginning with the "literal" in which a "planned suicide . . . becomes instead his murder by Jeffrey" (1988, 44). Douglas Fowler in his article appears to have "missed" Boyd's article; among other things, he asserts that Edwin, "now abandoned by his 'immortal masterpiece' after he has completed *Cartoons*, kills himself on his eleventh birthday rather than face a life of postpartum anticlimax" (1996), a fascinating possibility were it not for Edwin's murdering him. Finally, Alejandro Herrero-Olaizola in an article acknowledges Boyd's article but speaks of "Mullhouse's mysterious death" by "suicide" (2002). All this despite Timothy Adams's unequivocal statement in the first substantial article on *Edwin Mullhouse*: "When Jacques Barzun remarked that 'Every biography is something like a detective story,' he could hardly have imagined the grisly ending of *Edwin Mullhouse*, in which the biographer murders his subject for artistic effect and a smooth ending" (1982, 213).

32. In her review of *The Blind Assassin*, Barbara Mujica writes: "[T]he blind force of evil lurks everywhere in Atwood's novel; we are all potential blind assassins. But the most heartless assassin is time. Atwood is obsessed with time" (2001, 61). Karen Stein

notes that Atwood told an interviewer, Mel Gussow, that Iris was the blind assassin (2003, 149).

33. In her review of the novel, Roberta Rubenstein asserts: "Atwood is a fiendishly clever manipulator of the reader's knowledge" (1994, 234).

34. Marta Dvorak (2002) and Karen Stein (2003) also comment on the *mise en abîme* effects of the narrative.

35. One hears a tropological echo here of Grace's sewing, or quilting, in the earlier novel.

36. Atwood seems to be working here in the context of feminist theorizing about women writing through the body, grounded in the work of Julia Kristeva, Luce Irigaray, and Hélène Cixous.

37. In her interviews Atwood strongly asserts that this is Iris speaking for herself as a writer and that her view is not necessarily a view Atwood herself shares.

38. The notion of the "unreliable narrator," usually associated with the Wayne Booth of *The Rhetoric of Fiction*, is a cornerstone of modernism. If we follow Brian McHale's useful point of the epistemological dominant in modernism, the reader is forced to acknowledge the difficulty of knowing the truth and has to seek it in the modernist text often by reading around the unreliable narrator's rendition of the narrative.

39. Marta Dvorak (2002) argues, perhaps too ingeniously, for the presence here of the Three Fates in Iris's spinning a line.

40. It may be appropriate that Iris envisions her writing as moving "crabwise," since the forward motion of narrative is also a backward motion toward the end of the action (Laura's suicide) that occurred before Iris's narrating began. At the same time, there is a problematic element in the "present" segments of this novel: in the context of narrating, the "present" is a variety of "journal" written in segments with no definite outcome, other than presumably Iris's death. The question is, How will Atwood manage the representation of Iris's demise, given that readers expect a first-person narrator to be alive at the end of the narrative?

41. In "Nineteen Hundred and Nineteen" (Yeats 1983, 208). In his later poetry Yeats was preoccupied with the making of art as memorials and eventually with the fragility of those memorials—in "Lapis Lazuli" they are as short-lived as mayflies, and, in "The Circus Animals' Desertion" they are as "stilted" as old stage props, compared to the "foul rag and bone shop of the heart" that generates them.

42. One recalls Ibsen's Hedda Gabler maliciously burning Lövborg's manuscript in which he claims to have envisioned how Western civilization could save itself from disaster.

43. In "Sailing to Byzantium" (Yeats 1983, 193). Indeed, Atwood seems to have had Yeats in mind in crafting her old author Iris, for Yeats, it might be recalled, was still writing into the very last days before his death at seventy-three.

44. Karen Stein discusses Gothic elements in *The Blind Assassin*, especially "hiding/revealing, and speech/silence" (2003, 138). As Stein notes, Atwood has long been fascinated with this genre. Her early novel *Lady Oracle* is a spoof in which the narrator is an author of "Costume Gothics," and parts of the latter, *Stalked by Love*, are interspersed in *Lady Oracle*. See also Atwood's comments on the genre in her interviews in *Conversations with Margaret Atwood*.

45. Atwood has had a real fascination with the cruelty of women. In *Cat's Eye*, for example, female cruelty runs the gamut from the sadistic child Cordelia to the evil Mrs. Smeath, who knows Elaine is being tortured by her young friends but feels she deserves it.

46. As Robert Healy indicates, the historical "blowout" occurred in 1905. The *New York Times* title for the story, printed on March 28, 1905, capitalizes on the drama: "Worker Shot Skyward From Under River Bed" (Healy 2000, 107).

47. Healy seems more willing to accept Nathan Walker's death as accidental, the result of his impulsive gesture of reaching down to retrieve the fetishistic tea cozy. The context suggests that the patriarch of the Walker family may be reaching out to embrace the comfort of death and the possibility of joining not only his wife, Eleanor, but also her father, Con O'Leary. At the very least, his death seems a tragic event, resulting from an act of hubris, in the context of being "so high up [spiritually] I believe I'm looking down at up" (254).

48. Healy offers an extensive and extremely useful examination of the crane, literally and symbolically in Western and Eastern cultures, emphasizing the symbol's import to Nathan Walker's need to recover balance in coping with the racism and personal losses in his life. If these notes seem a dialogue with John Healy, it is because at this point (July 2006) the MLA bibliography lists his article as the only entry for McCann's novel.

49. Ashutosh Banerjee makes this claim (24).

50. Banerjee writes: "At a first reading *Midnight's Children* is calculated to give the reader the impression of a vast ambitious amorphous work in which some of the author's intentions and devices are at cross-purposes" (1990, 24).

51. The difficulties of constructing an ending for the narrative are adumbrated in Heffernan 2000, in which Heffernan grounds her discussion in Frank Kermode's classic study *The Sense of an Ending* and employs the term "postapocalypse" for the birth of India as a nation, an end to history.

52. Banerjee asserts: "The dominant mood of the novel seems to oscillate between the apocalyptic and the expansive" (1990, 24).

53. Neil ten Kortenaar (2002) (mis)identifies the ending as "nightmare," while it might be more accurate to speak of a metaphoric transformation like W. B. Yeats's notion of "a terrible beauty is born."

54. Of the score or so novels examined here, *Waterland*, like Doris Lessing's *The Golden Notebook*, is certainly among the most widely discussed. Many (Brewer and Tillyard 1985; Janik 1989; Landow 1990; Cooper 1996; Decoste 2002) focus on the theme of history and historiography, while several others are particularly relevant to the present discussion of ending. These include Higdon 1991; Irish 1998; and Wells 2003. Leon Higdon's article is especially valuable, because he addresses most fully the issue of ending(s). As his title clearly indicates, he argues for a "double closure" in the novel, because of its two story lines, both of which he views as endings significantly more optimistically than the text would perhaps support.

55. As Robert Irish writes, "The first motivation for Crick [to become a "historian" chronicling his family's past] is curiosity, variously referred to as 'detective spirit,' the need to explain, and 'Whywhywhy' (*Waterland* 93)" (Irish 1998, 919).

56. Lynn Wells asserts that the "disjointed narrative revolves around a series of interrelated, fundamentally Oedipal traumas" (2003, 69).

57. Robert Irish (1998) makes explicit what most readers are unlikely to miss in Dick's name. Apropos of Dick's name, I concur with John Schad's suspicion that the narrative works on the "Tom, Dick, or Harry" phrase. Tom's father is a "Henry," but Mary's widowed father is a "Harold," tempting the ingenious reader with the long-shot possibility that "History" has repeated itself with father-daughter incest, and Mary is

intent on aborting the fetus because it may be her father's child. The novel provides a modicum of "evidence" for such detective work in Mary's impulsive decision to abort the fetus without giving a thought to doing more than informing Tom of her intention. Also, from Tom's rendition of their adolescent lovemaking—enhanced by memory, of course, as well as the pleasure of sharing the experience with his adolescent students—he and Mary were engaged in presumably unprotected sex for a long time before the pregnancy. Mary's apparent sterility following the abortion could well cover Tom's from the beginning, and as first-person narrator Tom cannot tell us what he himself does not know.

58. The *OED* indicates the origin of "stigma" and its plural "stigmata" as the Greek word *stigma*, literally a "prick."

59. Lynn Wells also points out the relevance of Freud's *Beyond the Pleasure Principle* to *Waterland* (2003, 69–71).

60. Leon Higdon reads the earlier "ending" of Dick's suicide more optimistically, even slightly mystically. He takes Dick as "the very embodiment of the water-person and all the uncivilised irrationality water has come to symbolise in the novel" (1991, 92). Also, Higdon reads Price as Tom's "son" to whom "he has passed his sense of history's value and the necessity of defending civilisation," keeping alive in Price "the idea of a saviour of the world" (92).

61. Robert Newman writes: "The Prologue [of *The White Hotel*] invites us to read the text as psychoanalytic detectives . . ." (1989, 194).

62. Garry Leonard cannot resist reading O'Madden Burke's umbrella at the end of Joyce's story "A Mother" as a "phallic symbol" (1993, 271).

63. Freud mourned the loss of Sophie, his "Sunday child," but less than "Heinele," the toddler in the *fort/da* game who survived his mother by only three years. Following the death of his grandson Freud wrote of how Heinele represented "all my children and other grandchildren, and since then, since Heinele's death, I no longer care for my grandchildren, but also take no pleasure in life" (qtd. by Gay 1988, 422). Gay might be faulted for ignoring that Freud, as a German-speaking Jew, was calling Sophie his "Friday's child," since Freud's "Sabbath" would not occur on Sunday. Consulting the perpetual calendar reveals that the day of Sophie's birth—April 12, 1893—was neither a Sunday nor a Friday but a Wednesday.

64. Robert Newman aptly notes, "The novel functions as palimpsest where we read backward as we move forward" (1989, 195). He also reminds us of Freud's essay "Note on a Mystic Writing Pad," in which Freud tropes the psyche as a "Magic Slate." Experience writes on the conscious what survives as ghostly remnants in the unconscious, or waxen slate beneath, once the plastic sheet is lifted, giving the illusion of erasure (Newman 1989, 207).

65. David Cowart writes: "But at the same time that he exploits the formal convenience of Freudian procedure, the author of *The White Hotel* subverts the positivistic (not to mention male-centered) assumptions of Freudian theory. Undermining these assumptions, Thomas undermines the vaunted empiricism of science itself and thereby makes possible an exciting new aesthetic" (1986, 216–17). Similarly, Robert Newman writes that "Lisa's clairvoyance becomes the epistemological vector of the text that counters rational analysis" (1989, 194).

66. An apocryphal story indicates that when Freud visited the United States in 1909 he wondered to a colleague whether the Americans knew they were letting in the "plague."

67. In her essay "The Frame of Reference: Poe, Lacan, Derrida," Barbara Johnson reads the Queen's letter in Poe's story in the context of gender as positionality: the letter "feminizes (castrates) each of its successive holders" (1980, 123).

68. Higdon argues that the "climax" inheres in the Hebrew citation from the Song of Songs Lisa screams at the guard to "prove" her "Jewishness": "Mayim rabbi[m] lo yukhelu lekhabbot et—ha—ahavah u—neharot lo yishtefuha!" or "Set me a signet on your heart, / As a signet on your arm. / For love is as strong as Death / Passion fierce as Hell, / Its darts are darts of fire, / Its flames . . . / Mighty waters cannot quench Love, / No torrents can sweep it away" (Higdon 1991, 329). Higdon sees as one of several functions of the citation the impulse "to mark that epiphanous moment when Lisa experiences crucial insight about human love and acts on this insight" (331). Without a knowledge of Hebrew or some linguistic detective work, the citation lies outside the perception of the vast majority of readers; therefore, it seems questionable that Thomas would ground the climax of his narrative on this passage.

69. Mary Robertson notes that "many readers are annoyed that Thomas did not end there [with Lisa's rape and apparent death]. What could possibly be left to say after such a stark reconstruction of just one of our century's many horrible facts?" (1984, 463). Ellen Siegelman points out that one of several interpretations of "The Camp" is "the prophecy of Palestine become Israel, sanctuary for the remnant of the Holocaust" (1987, 75). This chapter also reminds Siegelman of the clinically dead reporting the experience of a "crossing over, a reunion with the beloved dead" (75).

70. Ellen Siegelman terms "The Camp" a "timeless, placeless reverie that serves as an epilogue to this extraordinary work" (1987, 69).

71. Robert Lougy perceptively writes: "Providing us with a closure that does not close, *The White Hotel* seems to offer us 'a fiction of the end,' while also calling attention to the indeterminacy of its narrative structure and to the equally conditional status of any fictional closure" (1991, 103). And Lars Ole Sauerberg notes that the narrative would have had "a kind of tragic unity" if Thomas had ended the book with Babi Yar.

72. Wallhead 1999 is especially helpful in focusing attention on this "epiphany."

NOTES TO CLUSTER 2

1. It is to be recalled that Charles Smithson *is* a member of the aristocracy, as the French *de* would indicate.

2. In Booth (1961).

3. Katherine Tarbox (1988) discusses the presence of existentialist thought in this novel.

4. See the provocative discussion in Doherty (1987) of metaphor in the Fowles novel.

5. In his interviews and memoirs Burgess tells the story of being informed by a doctor that he had only a year to live. As a result, he was understandably desperate to add to the small legacy he would leave his semi-invalid wife, and write several novels during that year of waiting for the end.

6. Bremer's diary indicates he had nothing against Wallace, but in fact also stalked other presidential campaigners such as Richard Nixon.

7. In verifying the spelling of the word, I was delighted to discover in my *New World*

Dictionary that the first meaning of *triptych* is "an ancient writing tablet of three leaves hinged together" (1522).

8. Speaking with an interviewer about evil, Burgess said that evil is tantamount to farting during a performance of Beethoven's Ninth Symphony.

9. The deconstruction of violence recalls Beckett's novel *Comment c'est* (1961), translated as *How It Is* (1964), in which two figures crawl through the mud until the second overtakes the first, removes a can opener from his sack, scores the back of the first figure with it. He continues until he is overtaken by his victim, only to have the very same act of violence perpetrated against him. The two figures presumably continue to reverse their roles into eternity.

10. Another major segment of the intertextuality in which *A Clockwork Orange* exists is the cluster of Burgess interviews in which he talks about the novel and his perception of its genesis in the near-fatal attack on his pregnant wife, a volunteer nurse, by four American G. I. deserters in London during the blackouts through which she had to find her way home. She was not raped, but in the attempt of her assailants to wrest her wedding ring from her finger she miscarried and began a long siege of bleeding and depression, leading to alcoholism and sexual dysfunction. Burgess indicates that it was her poor health that impelled him to write a handful of novel manuscripts in the bizarre year of the inaccurate "death sentence" of his doctors.

11. An interestingly inverted analogy to Kubrick's film is D. H. Lawrence's misreading of Herman Melville's *Moby-Dick* in his *Studies in Classic American Literature.* Lawrence read the Melville novel in its English edition of the novel, which for some unexplained reason left out the last chapter, in which readers discover that Ishmael alone survived the sinking of the *Pequod*—a circumstance of which Lawrence seems never to have been aware.

12. Like many beginning writers, Charles Schulz's Snoopy unconsciously "borrows" from another writer. In Snoopy's case, the "fledgling" writer "lifts" his famous opening from Edward Bulwer-Lytton's 1840 novel *Paul Clifford.*

13. According to Margaret Boerner ("A Bad End," *Weekly Standard*, April 29, 2002), the British tabloids have dubbed him "Ian Macabre."

14. It is difficult not to conclude that McEwan is deliberately setting the "epilogue" in 1999, not only because that year is close to the publication date of *Atonement*—2001—but also because in the popular imagining of the fin de siècle and the end of the millennium, 1999 would be the last year before a new century and millennium. As I point out in my section on *Amsterdam*, one of the two "friends," Clive Linley, is composing a work, dubbed a "Millennial Symphony" by the media.

15. In a review of *Atonement*, Tom Shone writes: "[O]ne of the great things about McEwan is how much faith he has in the urgings of plot. His books have a 45-degree tilt, leaning forward, through a fog of mounting unease, toward claret-dark revelation." ("White Lies: Ian McEwan's Novel Chronicles the Disintegration of an English Family, Idyllic Life," *New York Times Book Review*, March 10, 2002).

16. In his poem "September 1, 1939."

17. As I discovered in the reviews of *Atonement*, I was not alone in being attracted to the modifier "unsettling" for his latest novel, for several reviewers have used it as well, and McEwan himself used the term in an interview with David Wiegand in the *San Francisco Chronicle* ("Deceit in the Name of Duty: Humorous Novel Satirizes Millennial Moral Decay," December 13, 1998).

18. Anita Brookner in the *Spectator* ("A Morbid Procedure," September 15, 2001)

and Merritt Moseley in *The World & I* ("A Dangerous Imagination," (August 2002) also use the term "primal scene."

19. This term "epilogue" deserves the scare quotes, because this "epilogue" is not an "afterword" to a novel whose plot has ended; it is the "real" ending to the narrative, undermining the false ending in section 3.

20. It comes as no surprise that John Updike, himself the writer of numerous novels of failed marriage, should conclude it is probably not war work alone that is keeping Jack Tallis away from home.

21. Updike speaks of "Jack Tallis, the powerful absentee Old Man, an offstage deus ex machina [who] never descends" (2002, 80).

22. In part 2 Robbie recalls the brief time between his release from prison and his embarkation for France, expressing his concern that Cecilia could revert to being a "sister" (McEwan 2001, 193), rather than his lover.

23. It may not be too far afield to note the violation of sanctions against sexual relations with family members in *The Blind Assassin* as well, for Griffen is, after all, having sex with his *sister*-in-law. And at the risk of being too suspicious of brother-sister relationships, it might be noted that Griffen and his sister seem to function very much like parents to Iris.

24. The spilling of gay usage into mainstream discourse tempts the reader to wonder if the connotation of "gay" in the term "earnest"—evident in Oscar Wilde's title *The Importance of Being Earnest*—may not offer another cause of the failed Turner marriage.

25. In a similar gesture McEwan told David Wiegand: "In fact, one of the books I read at 12 that in some way formed the seed for 'Atonement' was [L. P. Hartley's novel] *The Go-Between*" ("Deceit in the Name of Duty," *San Francisco Chronicle*, December 13, 1998). As we shall see, in Hartley's novel a young boy loses his innocence while serving as a messenger for a young lady and her socially inferior lover.

26. See Eagleton's review, "A Beautiful and Elusive Tale," *Lancet*, December 22, 2001.

27. The text is implicated in this ambivalence of storytelling as art and as lies, just as Joyce cannot have been unaware of the ambivalence of Stephen Dedalus's aspiration to "*forge* in the smithy of the imagination the conscience of the race" (emphasis added).

28. It comes as no surprise that reviewers have been irritated by the ending of *Atonement*. In her review Margaret Boerner writes: "Was there ever a great novel that concluded by saying, in essence, 'I was only kidding—it was just a dream'? Someone needs to sit Ian McEwan down and make him read Frank Kermode's *The Sense of an Ending*" ("A Bad End," *Weekly Standard*, April 29, 2002).

29. Geraldine Friedman (1989) writes of the lover's "rape" of a "maiden loath" on Keats's urn.

30. Although this discussion of ending in narrative lacks room to deal fully with Bloom's rather oedipal notion of how a poet "reads," or rewrites, an earlier poet's texts to make them *his* (and the masculine pronoun is appropriate, since Bloom ignores female authors), it should be noted that Bloom's views of "influence" have given way to the French thinking about "intertextuality" theorized by Julia Kristeva and Roland Barthes. At the risk of oversimplifying their differing and complex theorizing, it might be generalized that both posit a notion of the text operating in a web of intertextuality, embracing not only early texts but also, by implication, texts not yet written.

31. A Leo Colston of a century ago might at age thirteen still be some years from sexual maturation since, as we have been reminded, the onset of puberty has continued

to advance. A literary example of delayed puberty is W. B. Yeats, who indicates in his memoirs that he was sexually undeveloped until his sixteenth year.

32. Referencing Atwood's *The Blind Assassin* is more appropriate than it would seem, for in the context of the discussion of *Atonement*, John Updike has joined me in seeing "a striking happenstance resemblance" of McEwan's novel to Atwood's.

33. Mentioning Freud's term "primal scene" is almost guaranteed to involve one in a mare's nest of psychoanalytic terminology. However, several reviewers, including Anita Brookner and Merritt Moseley, have used it in the looser, popular manner to describe the library scene of McEwan's *Atonement*. As Naomi Morgenstern aptly reminds us, "The primal scene . . . is an impossible scene (an unseen scene) because it is only witnessed as a repetition" (2003, 68).

34. Purists might quibble that 1901 is actually the first year of the twentieth century; in the popular consciousness, however, centuries—and millennia, as we have recently noted—begin with years ending in zero, not one.

35. It should be noted here that Lawrence might have agreed that sexuality was "natural," but he had serious reservations about "spooning" as a perverse teasing of the body. He makes clear in his posthumous novel *Mr Noon* (1984) that "spooning" is perversion of erotic experience.

36. It would be an overreading to make claims of some homosexual relationship between Leo and Ted, despite the "classical" case of the overmothered son of an absent father.

37. Mrs. Maudsley's dragging Leo off to witness the consequences of his "go-betweening" provides a postmodern pastiche of the celebrated Joycean epiphany, or "showing forth." Additionally, the destructive power of the climax seems a kind of *Götterdämmerung*, a "twilight of the gods," appropriate to Leo's elevation to the function of Mercury.

38. Various readers have speculated that Offred's "real name" is "June," since in the list—"Alma. Janine. Dolores. Moira. June" (Atwood 1985, 4)—ending chapter 1, a kind of prologue, "June" is the only name not recurring in the novel. "Mayday," Offred recalls her husband Luke telling her, is an Englishing of the French *m'aidez*, or "help me."

39. Professor Pieixoto offers an ironical representation of the traditional literary historian, perhaps even the "New Historicist" by becoming so focused on the impossible task of identifying a historical antecedent for Fred, the Handmaid's commander, that he ignores the audience's larger and more relevant questions, such as What happened to Offred, or "June," if that was her name? Many readers have noted Pieixoto's misogyny, but even those who have figured out Offred may have been originally named June fail to emphasize that Pieixoto probably did *not* succeed as a textual detective, because he was less interested in her than in her commander.

40. Perhaps I am being too cynical in speculating that the academic world has not changed, even though the date for the epilogue is 2195; however, I suspect that Knotly Wade is a traditional "Anglo" whose collaboration with Pieixoto may be a partnership of tradition and the contemporary in which Pieixoto did much of the work and Wade shared half the billing on the book jacket.

41. Ellen Friedman's essay "Breaking the Master Narrative: Jean Rhys's *Wide Sargasso Sea*" continues to be one of the most provocative readings of this novel—a novel she calls an "aggressive" (1989, 117) revision of *Jane Eyre*.

42. As Caroline Rody brilliantly notes: "Forever resisting the self-sacrificial closure

of her plot in *Jane Eyre*, forever forestalling the closure of Rhys's narrative, Antoinette/
Bertha in her last lines advances in furious opposition to her pre-scripted fate, leaving
her potential act, and her, to our memories of literary history" (1993, 302).

Notes to Cluster 3

1. Suzette Henke opens her essay "Doris Lessing's *Golden Notebook:* A Paradox of
Postmodern Play" with the assertion: "Doris Lessing is a fascinating figure, perched, as
she is on the cusp of postmodernism and impossible to categorize as either traditionally
modernist or postmodern *avant la lettre*" (1994, 159). Once past the possible infelicity
of locating Lessing as "perched . . . on the cusp of postmodernism," Henke offers a
useful discussion of Lessing's novel in a poststructuralist context, noting Lessing's "producing a deformed, formless, or deconstructed text" (171) and "placing the entire frame
story under erasure" (177).

2. Henke (1994) deserves the credit for this cleverly ambivalent modifier
"frame(d)."

3. Influenced perhaps by Lacan's trope of the fragmented body, or *le corps morcelé*,
Henke writes: "Instead of giving us a unified body of textual fragments, the book offers
a disturbingly fractured simulacrum of feminine writing—a burnt-out case of the illusory quest for feminist freedom in the social context of patriarchal hegemony" (1994,
160). Even more to the point, Henke writes: "Lessing's move in the direction of postmodernism articulates a feminine/feminist response to the contemporary crisis of male
master narratives" (162).

4. See Roberta Rubenstein's sensitive discussion of nostalgia in Rubenstein (1994).

5. The artistic kinship of Doris Lessing and Virginia Woolf has been extensively
examined in Saxton and Tobin (1994).

6. Claire Sprague (1982) analyzes the doubling of characters at great length in her
helpful essay.

7. Sprague offers an extremely useful discussion of the "doubletalk" of these beginning and finishing sentences of *Free Women*, writing: "Beautifully clear and uncompli-
cated, these ordinary sentences turn out to be simple only in their syntax. In every other
way they are deceptive and complicated" (1982, 182). Sprague herself performs some
"doubletalk" of her own when she writes: "The opening line is not Doris Lessing's line.
It is Saul Green's who gives it to Anna who gives it to the reader" (182).

8. Sprague is also concerned with the gendering of narrative; however, she seems
tied into a 1970s interest in writing itself as masculine and in androgyny rather than a
more contemporary notion of bisexuality. She writes: "Is Anna (Lessing?) perceiving
writing as a male-dominated activity, saying if writing is male I will therefore become
male? The naming pattern suggests another postulate. Anna, we may say, begins life as
an androgynous figure. If so, she does not become androgynous because of her interac-
tion with Saul. She was born an androgyne" (1982, 187).

9. As Henke writes, "With Saul's sentence: 'The two women were alone in the London flat,' we recognize the opening of *The Golden Notebook* and realize, for the first time,
that 'Free Women' is not an objective account of Anna's life in 1957. It constitutes,
instead, the conventional novel into which Lessing's protagonist incorporates the multi-
dimensional perceptions earlier recorded in separate notebooks" (1994, 165). Later,
Henke tropes the situation of Anna as implied narrator in both *Free Women* and the

notebooks as a "house of mirrors endlessly reflecting mimetic distortions of an ever-elusive ur-experience that is to be found nowhere in literature" (173).

10. Lessing's sleight of hand in this shell game seems to have confused Magali Cormier Michael, who speaks of Anna's "writing in only one notebook, the golden notebook" (1996, 50), while the novel indicates that Anna has given that notebook to Saul to write *his* novel.

11. In her essay "Multipersonal and Dialogic Modes in *Mrs. Dalloway* and *The Golden Notebook*" Claire Sprague allows her fascination with Bakhtin to move her into a very conventional (and, one might add, "masculinist") reading of Lessing's novel, speaking of its "double ending" (1994, 12) and the novel as two books with "two endings" (13). Even though she closes with the assertion that *The Golden Notebook* joins Woolf's novel to "celebrate process over closure," Sprague underestimates Lessing's radical subversion of Woolf's modernism. By choosing Woolf's clearly postmodern novel *Between the Acts* as the Woolf text to examine comparatively with *The Golden Notebook*, Magali Cormier Michael (1996) seems more accurate in appraising the Lessing novel as "postmodernist."

12. Despite her helpful discussion of the doubles in *The Golden Notebook*, Claire Sprague may be a little too quick to read its plot traditionally when she writes: "The final collision of Anna and Saul is climactic. Their separation ends the inner novel as the deceptive separation of Anna and Molly ends the outer Free Women novel" (1982, 183). Magali Cormier Michael would concur with my assessment of *The Golden Notebook:* "The novel as a whole is also circular; it has no set beginning or ending" (Michael 1996, 47).

13. In the blurb for the paperback Minerva translation of *The Fall of the Imam*, Lessing commented: "This novel is unlike any other I have read, more like a poem or a lamenting ballad, with something hypnotic about it, with its rhythmic, keening language, returning again and again to the same incident, a woman killed in the name of religion by the men who have used her. This is a wonderful book and I hope a great many people will read it."

14. Brian Finney (2003) brings in Frank Kermode's concerns but does not mention Kermode's notion of the "tick tock" of chronology.

15. Finney may be taking the trope a bit too far when he examines the connections the narrator "Barnes" makes between love as an ark and the horrors of Noah's Ark detailed in the first of these "chapters": "Love, the only possible resistance to the lies of history, is itself cannibalistic [?] and highly unpredictable" (Finney 2003).

16. Heidi Hansson (1999) also uses the term "diptych." Her approach, like that of Susan Poznar (2004), is typical of the tendency of critics to think of these two narratives as novellas, or discrete texts.

17. Nella Cotrupi speaks of *If on a winter's night a traveler* as "Calvino's most self-consciously self-reflexive novel" (1991, 280).

18. Argueta has indicated that when he turned from poetry to fiction, he found a number of writers who were sympathetic to his interests in narrative; among them were Mario Vargas Llosa, Carlos Fuentes, "and especially Julio Cortazar who, I felt, had a style that approached my own in the sense of its rhythm and its poetry. I was a great admirer of *Rayeula* [*Hopscotch*], more than [of] any other novel in Spanish" (qtd. in Bencastro 2001, 49).

19. See the helpful overview in Rubinson (2001) of the reviewers' responses to the "gimmick" or "trick" of the narrator's sexual identification.

20. As Brian Finney aptly notes of Winterson in *Written on the Body*, "Her subject is less love than the problems associated with describing it in narrative or textual form" (2000, 23).

21. Brian Finney's term "ungendered narrator" (2000) is less than satisfactory. Gregory Rubinson (2001) speaks of an "androgynous reading," and yet the complexities of gender, as well as Judith Butler's notion of sex as socially constructed, like gender, cannot obscure the fact that the narrator probably has either a vagina or a penis.

22. Leigh Gilmore (1997) writes of the "awkward and rather implausible blackmail" of Elgin's offer to treat Louise's leukemia only if the narrator leaves his wife.

23. See the fascinating study of the erotic exchange between male novelist and male reading in Hardin (2000). The eroticizing of the relationship of the novelist and reader is also evident in a more conventional form in Brooks (1991).

24. Brian Finney generalizes that "each of her books has become more meditative and less narrative, a trend of which she is fully conscious" (2000, 24).

25. As Finney aptly points out in his discussion of *Written on the Body*, "This novel is less about desire than it is about the language of desire, and less about the phenomenon of love than about the problem of its fictional representation" (2000, 23).

26. These postmodern strategies are reminiscent of the persona's tactics in W. B. Yeats's poem "The Circus Animals' Desertion."

27. Ute Kauer asserts that "the boyfriend-stories are just another form of disguise for the (female) narrator" (1991, 49).

28. Rubinson would vigorously disagree: "The fact is, there is no information about the narrator's body that can lead us to determine whether the narrator is male, female, transsexual, intersexed, or XXY. And that is exactly the point: it implies that such information is or should be irrelevant" (2001).

29. Once again Kauer asserts: "The point of view is clearly a female one. . . . In spite of all the masks, the narrator cannot suppress a feeling of solidarity with some of the women protagonists" (1991, 50).

30. Finney also makes this point in the introduction to Finney (2002a).

31. I would contest Kauer's assertion that "The narrator does not propagate a romantic notion of love . . ." (1991, 50), when the novel stresses such great willingness to sacrifice the continuation of the narrator's affair with Louise, in part to preserve its power and intensity.

32. See Haines-Wright and Kyle (1996).

33. Finney writes that "The conclusion . . . celebrates the transformative effects of art itself" (2002a, 30). Haines-Wright and Kyle, however, assert: "Like Woolf [in *Orlando*] Winterson [in *Written on the Body*] defers closure" (1996, 181), in the end troping the novel's readers as "open fields" toward which the ending is "let loose."

References

Abrams, M. H., ed. 1986. *The Norton Anthology of English Literature*. Vol. 2. 5th ed. New York: Norton.

Adams, Timothy Dow. 1982. "The Mock-Biography of Edwin Mullhouse." *Biography: An Interdisciplinary Quarterly* 5, no. 3:205–14.

Argueta, Manlio. 1987. *Cuzcatlán: Where the Southern Sea Beats*. Trans. Clark Hansen. New York: Random House.

Atwood, Margaret. 1976. *Lady Oracle*. New York: Simon & Schuster.

———. 1985. *The Handmaid's Tale*. Boston: Houghton Mifflin.

———. 1989. *Cat's Eye*. New York: Doubleday.

———. 1996. *Alias Grace*. New York: Doubleday.

———. 2000. *The Blind Assassin*. New York: Doubleday.

———. 2006. *Waltzing Again: New and Selected Conversations with Margaret Atwood*. Ed. Earl G. Ingersoll. Princeton, NJ: Ontario Review Press.

Auden, W. H. 1945. *The Collected Poetry of W. H. Auden*. New York: Random House.

Banerjee, Ashutosh. 1990. "Narrative Technique in *Midnight's Children*." *Commonwealth Review* 1, no. 2:23–32.

Barnes, Julian. 1990. *A History of the World in 10½ Chapters*. New York: Random House.

Barthes, Roland. 1975. *The Pleasure of the Text*. Trans. Richard Miller. New York: Hill and Wang.

———. 1974. *S/Z: An Essay*. Trans. Richard Miller. New York: Farrar, Straus, and Giroux.

Baudrillard, Jean. 1995. *The Gulf War Did Not Take Place*. Bloomington: Indiana University Press.

Beckett, Samuel. 1964. *How It Is*. New York: Grove Press. Translation of *Comment c'est*, 1961.

Bencastro, Mario. 2001. "El Salvador's Poet of Recovery." *Americas* 53, no. 2:48–52.

Boone, Joseph A. 1987. *Tradition Counter Tradition: Love and the Form of Fiction*. Chicago: University of Chicago Press.

Booth, Alison, ed. 1993. *Famous Last Words: Changes in Gender and Narrative Closure*. Charlottesville: University Press of Virginia.

Booth, Wayne. 1961. *The Rhetoric of Fiction*. Chicago: University of Chicago Press.

Borges, Jorge. 1964. "The Garden of the Forking Paths." In *Labyrinths: Selected Stories and Other Writings*. New York: New Directions.

Boyd, John. 1988. "The Double Vision of *Edwin Mullhouse*." *Biography: An Interdisciplinary Quarterly* 11, no. 1:35–46.

Bradbury, Malcolm. 1993. *The Modern British Novel.* London: Secker & Warburg.

Brewer, John, and Stella Tillyard. 1985. "History and Telling Stories: Graham Swift's *Waterland.*" *History Today* 35, no. 1:49–51.

Brontë, Charlotte. 1943. *Jane Eyre.* New York: Random House.

Brooks, Peter. 1977. "Freud's Masterplot: Questions of Narrative." *Yale French Studies* 55–56:280–300.

———. 1984. *Reading for the Plot: Design and Intention in Narrative.* New York: Knopf.

———. 1994. *Psychoanalysis and Storytelling.* Cambridge, MA: Blackwell.

———. 1999. *World Elsewhere.* New York: Simon & Schuster.

Bulwer-Lytton, Edward. 1830. *Paul Clifford.* London: H. Collburn and R. Bentley.

Burgess, Anthony. 1974. "*Playboy* Interview: Anthony Burgess." By C. Robert Jennings. *Playboy,* September: 68–86.

———. 1987. *A Clockwork Orange.* New York: Norton.

Butler, Judith. 1993. *Gender Trouble.* New York: Routledge.

Butler, Marilyn. 1992. "*Angels & Insects.*" *Times Literary Supplement,* October 16, 22.

Byatt, A. S. 1990. *Possession.* New York: Random House.

———. 1993. *Angels & Insects.* New York: Random House.

Calvino, Italo. 1981. *If on a winter's night a traveler.* Trans. William Weaver. New York: Harcourt, Brace.

Camus, Albert. 1955. *The Myth of Sisyphus, and Other Essays.* New York: Knopf.

Chetrinescu, Dana. 2001. "Rethinking Spatiality: The Degraded Body in Ian McEwan's *Amsterdam.*" *British and American Studies/Revista de Studii Britanice si Americane* 7, no. 2:157–65.

Cixous, Hélène. 1980. "The Laugh of the Medusa." Trans. Keith Cohen and Paula Cohen. In *New French Feminisms,* ed. Elaine Marks and Isabelle de Courtivron, 245–64. Amherst: University of Massachusetts.

Cooper, Pamela. 1996. "Imperial Topographies: The Spaces of History in *Waterland.*" *Modern Fiction Studies* 42, no. 2:371–96.

Cotrupi, C. Nella. 1991. "Hypermetafiction: Italo Calvino's *If on a winter's night a traveler.*" *Style* 25, no. 2:280–90.

Cowart, David. 1986. "Being and Seeming: *The White Hotel.*" *Novel: A Forum on Fiction* 19, no. 3:216–31.

Decoste, Damon Marcel. 2002. "Question and Apocalypse: The Endlessness of *Historia* in Graham Swift's *Waterland.*" *Contemporary Literature* 63, no. 2:377–99.

Deleuze, Gilles, and Félix Guattari. 1977. *Anti-Oedipus: Capitalism and Schizophrenia.* Trans. Robert Hurley, Mark Seem, and Helen R. Lane. New York: Viking.

Derrida, Jacques. 1988. "The Purveyor of Truth." In *The Purloined Poe: Lacan, Derrida, and Psychoanalytic Reading,* ed. John P. Muller and William J. Richardson, 173–212. Baltimore: Johns Hopkins University Press.

———. 1998. "Différance." In *Literary Theory: An Anthology,* ed. Julie Rivkin and Michael Ryan, 383–407. Malden, MA: Blackwell.

Dickens, Charles. 1942. *Great Expectations.* New York: Dodd, Mead.

Doherty, Gerald. 1987. "The Secret Plot of Metaphor: Rhetorical Design in John Fowles's *The French Lieutenant's Woman.*" *Paragraph* 9, no. 3:49–68.

Doyle, Arthur Conan. 1965. *The Adventure of the Speckled Band and Other Stories of Sherlock Holmes*. New York: New American Library.

DuPlessis, Rachel Blau. 1985. "Seismic Orgasm: Sexual Intercourse and Narrative Meaning in Mina Loy." In *Writing beyond the Ending: Narrative Strategies in Twentieth-Century Women Writers*. Bloomington: Indiana University Press.

Dvorak, Marta. 2002. "The Right Hand Writing and the Left Hand Erasing in Margaret Atwood's *The Blind Assassin*." *Commonwealth Essays and Studies* 25, no. 1:59–68.

Faulkner, William. 1951. *Absalom, Absalom!* New York: Modern Library.

———. 1956. William Faulkner. Interview by Jean Stein. *Paris Review* 3, no. 12:28–52.

Felber, Lynette. 1996. *Gender and Genre in Novels Without End*. Gainesville: University of Florida Press.

Fielding, Henry. 1950. *The History of Tom Jones: A Foundling*. New York: Modern Library.

Finney, Brian. 2002a. "Bonded by Language: Jeanette Winterson's *Written on the Body*." *Women and Language* 25, no. 2 (Fall):23–31.

———. 2002b. "Figuring the Real: Ishiguro's *When We Were Orphans*." *Jouvert: A Journal of Postcolonial Studies* 7, no. 1: electronic journal, 32 paragraphs.

———. 2003. "A Worm's Eye View of History: Julian Barnes's *A History of the World in 10½ Chapters*." *Papers on Language and Literature* 39, no. 1:49–70.

Flieger, Jerry Aline. 1983. "The Purloined Punchline: Joke as Textual Paradigm." In *Lacan and Narration: The Psychoanalytic Difference in Narrative Theory*. Ed. Robert Con Davis. Baltimore: Johns Hopkins University Press.

———. 1991. *The Purloined Punch Line: Freud's Comic Theory and the Postmodern Text*. Baltimore: Johns Hopkins University Press.

Flieger, Jerry Aline. 1991. *The Purloined Punch Line: Freud's Comic Theory and the Postmodern Text*. Baltimore: Johns Hopkins University Press.

Foucault, Michel. 2003. *The Essential Foucault: Selections from Essential Works of Foucault, 1954–1984*. Ed. Paul Rabinow and Nikolas Rose. New York: New Press.

Fowler, Douglas. 1996. "Steven Millhauser, Miniaturist." *Critique* 37, no. 2:139–49.

Fowles, John. 1969. *The French Lieutenant's Woman*. Boston: Little, Brown.

Freud, Sigmund. 1961. *Beyond the Pleasure Principle*. In *The Standard Edition of the Complete Works of Sigmund Freud*, 18:1–64. New York: Norton.

Friedman, Ellen G. 1989. "Breaking the Master Narrative: Jean Rhys's *Wide Sargasso Sea*." In *Breaking the Sequence: Women's Experimental Fiction*, ed. Ellen G. Friedman and Miriam Fuchs, 117–28. Princeton, NJ: Princeton University Press.

Friedman, Geraldine. 1993. "The Erotics of Interpretation in Keats's 'Ode on a Grecian Urn': Pursuing the Feminine." *Studies in Romanticism* 32, no. 2:225–43.

Gay, Peter. 1988. *Freud: A Life for Our Times*. New York: Norton.

Genette, Gérard. 1980. *Narrative Discourse: An Essay in Method*. Trans. Jane E. Lewin. Ithaca, NY: Cornell University Press.

Gerhart, Mary. 1992. *Genre Choice, Gender Questions*. Norman: University of Oklahoma Press.

Gilbert, Sandra, and Susan Gubar. 1979. *The Madwoman in the Attic: The Woman Writer and Nineteenth-Century Literary Imagination*. New Haven, CT: Yale University Press.

Gilmore, Leigh. 1997. "An Anatomy of Absence: *Written on the Body, The Lesbian Body,* and Autobiography without Names." In *The Gay '90s: Disciplinary and Interdisciplinary Formations in Queer Studies,* ed. Thomas Foster, Carol Siegel, and Ellen E. Berry, 224–51. New York: New York University Press.

Grice, Helena, and Tim Woods, eds. 1991. *"I'm Telling You Stories": Jeanette Winterson and the Politics of Reading.* Amsterdam: Rodopi.

Haines-Wright, Lisa, and Raci Lynn Kyle. 1996. "Fluid Sexuality in Virginia Woolf." In *Virginia Woolf: Texts and Contexts; Selected Papers from the Fifth Annual Conference on Virginia Woolf,* ed. Beth Rigel Daugherty and Eileen Barrett, 177–88. New York: Pace University Press.

Hansson, Heidi. 1999. "The Double Voice of Metaphor: A. S. Byatt's 'Morpho Eugenia.'" *Twentieth Century Literature* 45, no. 4:452–66.

Hardin, Michael. 2000. *Playing the Reader: The Homoerotics of Self-Reflexive Fiction.* New York: Peter Lang.

Hartley, L. P. 2002. *The Go-Between.* New York: New York Review Books.

Healy, Robert F. 2000. "Dancing Cranes and Frozen Birds: The Fleeting Resurrections of Colum McCann." *New Hibernia Review* 4, no. 3:107–18.

Hecht, Anthony. 1979. *Venetian Vespers: Poems.* New York: Atheneum.

Heffernan, Teresa. 2000. "Apocalyptic Narratives: The Nation in Salman Rushdie's *Midnight's Children.*" *Twentieth Century Literature: A Scholarly and Critical Journal* 46, no. 4:470–91.

Henke, Suzette. 1994. "Doris Lessing's *Golden Notebook:* A Paradox of Postmodern Play." In *Rereading Modernism: New Directions in Feminist Criticism,* ed. Lisa Rado, 159–87. New York: Garland.

Herrero-Olaizola, Alejandro. 2002. "Writing Lives, Writing Lies: The Pursuit of Apocryphal Biographies." *Mosaic* 35, no. 3:73–89.

Higdon, David Leon. 1991. "Double Closures in Postmodern British Fiction: The Example of Graham Swift." *Critical Survey* 3, no. 1:88–95.

Hirsch, Marianne. 1989. *The Mother-Daughter Plot: Narrative, Psychoanalysis, Feminism.* Bloomington: Indiana University Press.

Hopkins, Gerard Manley. 1971. *The Wreck of the Deutschland.* Boston: D. Godine.

Ibsen, Henrik. 1989. *"Hedda Gabler" and "A Doll's House."* Trans. Christopher Hampton. Boston: Faber and Faber.

Ingersoll, Earl G. 2001. "Nawal El Saadawi and the Possibility of a Feminine Writing." *International Fiction Review* 28, nos. 1 and 2:23–31.

———. 2003. "Waiting for the End: Closure in Margaret Atwood's *The Blind Assassin.*" *Studies in the Novel* 35, no. 4:543–58.

———. 2004. "Intertextuality in L. P. Hartley's *The Go-Between* and Ian McEwan's *Atonement.*" *Forum for Modern Language Studies* 40, no. 3:241–58.

———. 2005. "City of Endings: Ian McEwan's *Amsterdam.*" *Midwest Quarterly* 46, no. 2:123–38.

Irigaray, Luce. 1985. *This Sex Which Is Not One.* Ithaca, NY: Cornell University Press.

Irish, Robert K. 1998. "'Let Me Tell You': About Desire and Narrativity in Graham Swift's *Waterland.*" *Modern Fiction Studies* 44, no. 4:917–34.

Ishiguro, Kazuo. 1989. *The Remains of the Day.* New York: Knopf.

———. 2000. *When We Were Orphans*. New York: Knopf.

Janik, Ivan Del. 1989. "History and the 'Here and Now': The Novels of Graham Swift." *Twentieth Century Literature*, 35, no. 1 (spring): 74–88.

Johnson, Barbara. 1980. "The Frame of Reference: Poe, Lacan, Derrida." In *The Critical Difference: Essays in the Contemporary Rhetoric of Reading*, 110–46. Baltimore: Johns Hopkins University Press.

———. 1987. "Nothing Fails Like Success." In *A World of Difference*, 11–16. Baltimore: Johns Hopkins University Press.

Joyce, James. 1956. *A Portrait of the Artist as a Young Man*. New York: Viking.

———. 1968. *Dubliners*. New York: Viking.

———. 1986. *Ulysses*. Ed. Hans Walter Gabler. New York: Random House.

Kauer, Ute. 1991. "Narration and Gender: The Role of the First-Person Narrator in *Written on the Body*." In Grice and Woods 1991, 41–51.

Kermode, Frank. 1967. *The Sense of an Ending: Studies in the Theory of Fiction*. New York: Oxford University Press.

Kristeva, Julia. 1984. *The Revolution in Poetic Language*. Trans. Margaret Waller. Ithaca, NY: Cornell University Press.

———. 1986. "Women's Time." In *The Kristeva Reader*, ed. Toril Moi, 187–213. New York: Columbia University Press.

Lacan, Jacques. 1968. *Speech and Language in Psychoanalysis*. Trans. Anthony Wilden. Baltimore: Johns Hopkins University Press.

———. 1977. *Écrits: A Selection*. Trans. Alan Sheridan. New York: Norton.

———. 1978. *The Four Fundamental Concepts of Psycho-Analysis*. Trans. Alan Sheridan. Ed. Jacques-Alain Miller. New York: Norton.

———. 1988. "Seminar on 'The Purloined Letter.'" Trans. Jeffrey Mehlman. In *The Purloined Poe: Lacan, Derrida, and Psychoanalytic Reading*, ed. John P. Muller and William J. Richardson, 28–54. Baltimore: Johns Hopkins University Press.

Landow, George P. "History, His Story, and Stories in Graham Swift's *Waterland*." *Form: Studies in the Literary Imagination* 23, no. 2:197–211.

Lauretis, Teresa de. 1984. *Alice Doesn't: Feminism, Semiotics, Cinema*. Bloomington: Indiana University Press.

Lawrence, D. H. 1984. *Mr. Noon*. Ed. Lindeth Vasey. New York: Cambridge University Press.

———. 1987. *Women in Love*. Ed. David Farmer, Lindeth Vasey, and John Worthen. New York: Cambridge University Press.

———. 1989. *The Rainbow*. Ed. Mark Kinkead-Weekes. New York: Cambridge University Press.

———. 1993. *Lady Chatterley's Lover*. Ed. Michael Squires. New York: Cambridge University Press.

———. 2003. *Studies in Classic American Literature*. Ed. Ezra Greenspan, Lindeth Vasey, and John Worthen. New York: Cambridge University Press.

Leonard, Garry M. 1993. *Reading "Dubliners" Again: A Lacanian Perspective*. Syracuse, NY: Syracuse University Press.

Lessing, Doris. 1962. *The Golden Notebook*. New York: Simon & Schuster.

————. 1994. *Doris Lessing: Conversations*. Ed. Earl G. Ingersoll. Princeton, NJ: Ontario Review Press.

Lodge, David. 1979. *Changing Places: A Tale of Two Campuses*. New York: Penguin.

Lotman, Jurij M. 1979. "The Origin of Plot in the Light of Typology." Trans. Julian Graffy. *Poetics Today* 1, nos. 1 and 2:161–84.

Lougy, Robert. 1991. "The Wolf-Man, Freud, and D. M. Thomas: Intertextuality, Interpretation, and Narration in *The White Hotel*." *Modern Language Studies* 21, no. 3:91–106.

Martin, Wallace. 1986. *Recent Theories of Narrative*. Ithaca, NY: Cornell University Press.

McCann, Colum. 1998. *This Side of Brightness*. New York: Henry Holt.

McEwan, Ian. 1975. *First Love, Last Rites*. New York: Random House.

————. 1978. *The Cement Garden*. New York: Simon & Schuster.

————. 1998. *Amsterdam*. New York: Random House.

————. 2001. *Atonement*. New York: Random House.

McHale, Brian. 1986. "Change of Dominant from Modernist to Postmodernist Writing." In *Approaching Postmodernism*, ed. Douwe Fokkema and Johannes Bertens, 53–79. Amsterdam: Benjamins.

Metz, Christian. 1982. *The Imaginary Signifier: Psychoanalysis and the Cinema*. Trans. Celia Britton, Annwyl Williams, Ben Brewster, and Alfred Gussetti. Bloomington: Indiana University Press.

Mezei, Kathy, ed. 1996. *Ambiguous Discourse: Feminist Narratology and British Women Writers*. Chapel Hill: University of North Carolina Press.

Michael, Magali Cormier. 1996. *Feminism and the Postmodern Impulse: Post World War II Fiction*. Albany: State University of New York Press.

Miller, D. A. 1981. *Narrative and Its Discontents: Problems of Closure in the Traditional Novel*. Princeton, NJ: Princeton University Press.

Millhauser, Steven. 1972. *Edwin Mullhouse: The Life and Death of an American Writer 1943–1954 by Jeffrey Cartwright*. New York: Random House.

Morgenstern, Naomi. 2003. "The Primal Scene in the Public Domain: E. L. Doctorow's *The Book of Daniel*." *Studies in the Novel* 35, no. 1: 68–88.

Mujica, Barbara. 2001. "*The Blind Assassin*." *Americas* 53 (January): 61.

Mulvey, Laura. 1975. "Visual Pleasure and Narrative Cinema." *Screen* 16, no. 3:8–18.

————. 1989. *Visual and Other Pleasures*. Bloomington: Indiana University Press.

Newman, Robert D. "D. M. Thomas's *The White Hotel*: Mirrors, Triangles, and Sublime Repression." *Modern Fiction Studies* 35, no. 2:193–209.

Nodelson, Perry. 1989. "The Sense of Unending: Joyce Carol Oates's *Bellefleur* as an Experiment in Feminine Storytelling." In *Breaking the Sequence: Women's Experimental Fiction*. Ed. Ellen G. Friedman and Miriam Fuchs. Princeton, NJ: Princeton University Press.

Oates, Joyce Carol. 1980. *Bellefleur*. New York: Dutton.

Orwell, George. 1949. *Nineteen Eighty-Four*. New York: Harcourt, Brace.

Poznar, Susan. 2004. "Tradition and 'Experiment' in Byatt's 'The Conjugial Angel.'" *Critique* 45, no. 2:173–89.

Rhys, Jean. 1992. *Wide Sargasso Sea*. New York: Norton.

Robertson, Mary F. 1984. "Hystery, Herstory, History: 'Imagining the Real' in Thomas's *The White Hotel*." *Contemporary Literature* 25, no. 4:452–77.

Rody, Caroline. 1993. "Burning Down the House: The Revisionary Paradigm of Jean Rhys's *Wide Sargasso Sea*." In *Famous Last Words: Changes in Gender and Narrative Closure*, ed. Alison Booth, 300–325. Charlottesville: University Press of Virginia.

Rubenstein, Roberta. 1994. "Fixing the Past: Yearning and Nostalgia in Woolf and Lessing." In Saxton and Tobin 1994, 15–38.

Rubinson, Gregory J. 2001. "Body Languages: Scientific and Aesthetic Discourses in Jeanette Winterson's *Written on the Body*." *Critique* 42, no. 2:218–32.

Rushdie, Salman. 1981. *Midnight's Children*. New York: Knopf.

Saadawi, Nawal El. 1988. *The Fall of the Imam*. Trans. Sherif Hetata. London: Minerva.

Sauerberg, Lars Ole. 1989. "When the Soul Takes Wing: D. M. Thomas's *The White Hotel*." *Critique* 31, no. 1:3–10.

Saxton, Ruth, and Jean Tobin, eds. 1994. *Woolf and Lessing*. New York: St. Martin's Press.

Schad, John. 1992. "The End of the End of History: Graham Swift's *Waterland*." *Modern Fiction Studies* 38, no. 4:911–25.

Scholes, Robert. 1967. *The Fabulators*. New York: Oxford University Press.

Sedgwick, Eve Kosofsky. 1990. *The Epistemology of the Closet*. Berkeley and Los Angeles: University of California Press.

Siegelman, Ellen. 1987. "*The White Hotel:* Visions and Revisions of the Psyche." *Literature and Psychology* 33, no. 1:69–76.

Shepard, Jim. 2003. "Steven Millhauser." *Bomb* 83 (Spring): 76–80.

Sophocles. 1977. *The Oedipus Cycle*. Trans. Dudley Fitts and Robert Fitzgerald. New York: Harcourt, Brace.

Sprague, Claire. 1982. "Doubletalk and Doubles Talk in *The Golden Notebook*." *Papers on Language and Literature* 18, no. 2:181–97.

———. 1994. "Multipersonal and Dialogic Modes in *Mrs. Dalloway* and *The Golden Notebook*." In Saxton and Tobin, 3–14.

Stein, Karen. 2003. "A Left-Handed Story: *The Blind Assassin*." In *Margaret Atwood's Textual Assassinations: Recent Poetry and Fiction*, ed. Sharon Rose Wilson, 135–53. Columbus: Ohio State University Press.

Swift, Graham. 1983. *Waterland*. London: Heinemann.

Tarbox, Katherine. 1988. *The Art of John Fowles*. Athens: University of Georgia Press.

ten Kortenaar, Neil. 2002. "Salman Rushdie's Magic Realism and the Return of Inescapable Romance." *University of Toronto Quarterly: A Canadian Journal of the Humanities* 71, no. 3:765–85.

Thomas, D. M. 1993. *The White Hotel*. New York: Penguin.

Updike, John. 2000. "Flesh on Flesh: A Semi-Austenesque Novel from Ian McEwan." *New Yorker*, March 4, 80–83.

Wallhead, Celia. 1999. "Eros and Thanatos in the Epiphany in D. M. Thomas's *The White Hotel*." In *Moments of Moment: Aspects of the Literary Epiphany*, ed. Wim Tigges, 421–33. Amsterdam: Rodopi.

Wells, Lynn. 2003. "The Whole Story: Graham Swift's *Waterland*." In *Allegories of Telling: Self-Referential Narrative in Contemporary British Fiction*, 67–102. Amsterdam: Rodopi.

Winnett, Susan. 1990. "Coming Unstrung: Women, Men, Narrative, and the Principles of Pleasure." *PMLA* 105, no. 3:505–18.

Winterson, Jeanette. 1993. *Written on the Body*. New York: Knopf.

———. 1996. *Art Objects: Essays on Ecstasy and Effrontery*. New York: Random House.

Woolf, Virginia. 1931. *The Waves*. New York: Harcourt, Brace.

———. 1953. *Mrs. Dalloway*. New York: Harcourt, Brace.

Worthen, John. 1991. *D. H. Lawrence: The Early Years*. New York: Cambridge University Press.

Yaeger, Patricia. 1988. *Honey-Mad Women: Emancipatory Strategies in Women's Writing*. New York: Columbia University Press.

Yeats, William Butler. 1983. *The Poems of W. B. Yeats*. Ed. Richard J. Finneran. New York: Macmillan.

Index

PR888.C587 I54 2007

Ingersoll, Earl G.,

Waiting for the end :
 gender and ending in the
    c2007.

MAY 0 6 2008   STORAGE

0 1341 1068522 6

2008 04 21

MAY 0 6 2008